Ford Explorer & Mazda Navajo Automotive Repair Manual

by Alan Ahlstrand and John H Haynes
Member of the Guild of Motoring Writers

Models covered:
All Ford Explorer and Mazda Navajo models
1991 through 1995

(8Z9 - 36024)
(2021)

ABCDE
FG

Haynes Publishing Group
Sparkford Nr Yeovil
Somerset BA22 7JJ England

Haynes North America, Inc
861 Lawrence Drive
Newbury Park
California 91320 USA

Acknowledgements

We are grateful to the Ford Motor Company for assistance with technical information, certain illustrations and vehicle photos.

© **Haynes North America, Inc. 1992, 1995**

With permission from J.H. Haynes & Co. Ltd.

A book in the Haynes Automotive Repair Manual Series

Printed in the U.S.A.

ISBN 1 56392 168 5

Library of Congress Catalog Card Number 95-79397

While every attempt is made to ensure that the information in this manual is correct, no liability can be accepted by the authors or publishers for loss, damage or injury caused by any errors in, or omissions from, the information given.

Contents

About this manual 0-5
Introduction to the Ford Explorer and Mazda Navajo 0-5
Vehicle identification numbers 0-6
Buying parts 0-7
Maintenance techniques, tools and working facilities 0-7
Booster battery (jump) starting 0-14
Jacking and towing 0-14
Automotive chemicals and lubricants 0-15
Safety first! 0-16
Conversion factors 0-17
Troubleshooting 0-18

Chapter 1
Tune-up and routine maintenance 1-1 **1**

Chapter 2 Part A
4.0L V6 engine 2A-1 **2A**

Chapter 2 Part B
General engine overhaul procedures 2B-1 **2B**

Chapter 3
Cooling, heating and air conditioning systems 3-1 **3**

Chapter 4
Fuel and exhaust systems 4-1 **4**

Chapter 5
Engine electrical systems 5-1 **5**

Chapter 6
Emissions control systems 6-1 **6**

Chapter 7 Part A
Manual transmission 7A-1 **7A**

Chapter 7 Part B
Automatic transmission 7B-1 **7B**

Chapter 7 Part C
Transfer case 7C-1 **7C**

Chapter 8
Clutch and drivetrain 8-1 **8**

Chapter 9
Brakes 9-1 **9**

Chapter 10
Suspension and steering systems 10-1 **10**

Chapter 11
Body 11-1 **11**

Chapter 12
Chassis electrical system 12-1 **12**

Wiring diagrams 12-22

Index IND-1 **IND**

1991 Mazda Navajo

1991 Ford Explorer

About this manual

Its purpose

The purpose of this manual is to help you get the best value from your vehicle. It can do so in several ways. It can help you decide what work must be done, even if you choose to have it done by a dealer service department or a repair shop; it provides information and procedures for routine maintenance and servicing; and it offers diagnostic and repair procedures to follow when trouble occurs.

We hope you use the manual to tackle the work yourself. For many simpler jobs, doing it yourself may be quicker than arranging an appointment to get the vehicle into a shop and making the trips to leave it and pick it up. More importantly, a lot of money can be saved by avoiding the expense the shop must pass on to you to cover its labor and overhead costs. An added benefit is the sense of satisfaction and accomplishment that you feel after doing the job yourself.

Using the manual

The manual is divided into Chapters. Each Chapter is divided into numbered Sections, which are headed in bold type between horizontal lines. Each Section consists of consecutively numbered paragraphs.

At the beginning of each numbered Section you will be referred to any illustrations which apply to the procedures in that Section. The reference numbers used in illustration captions pinpoint the pertinent Section and the Step within that Section. That is, illustration 3.2 means the illustration refers to Section 3 and Step (or paragraph) 2 within that Section.

Procedures, once described in the text, are not normally repeated. When it's necessary to refer to another Chapter, the reference will be given as Chapter and Section number. Cross references given without use of the word "Chapter" apply to Sections and/or paragraphs in the same Chapter. For example, "see Section 8" means in the same Chapter.

References to the left or right side of the vehicle assume you are sitting in the driver's seat, facing forward.

Even though we have prepared this manual with extreme care, neither the publisher nor the author can accept responsibility for any errors in, or omissions from, the information given.

NOTE

A **Note** provides information necessary to properly complete a procedure or information which will make the procedure easier to understand.

CAUTION

A **Caution** provides a special procedure or special steps which must be taken while completing the procedure where the Caution is found. Not heeding a Caution can result in damage to the assembly being worked on.

WARNING

A **Warning** provides a special procedure or special steps which must be taken while completing the procedure where the Warning is found. Not heeding a Warning can result in personal injury.

Introduction to the Ford Explorer and Mazda Navajo

The models covered by this manual are available in a variety of trim options.

All models use the 4.0L V6 engine.

Chassis layout is conventional, with the engine mounted at the front and the power being transmitted through either a manual or automatic transmission to a driveshaft and solid rear axle on 2WD models. On 4WD models a transfer case transmits power to the front axle by way of a driveshaft. Transmissions used are a five-speed overdrive manual and four-speed overdrive automatic.

1994 and earlier vehicles use twin I-beam front suspension with coil springs and radius arms. 1995 and later models use upper and lower control arms and torsion bars. All models use semi-elliptical leaf springs at the rear.

All models are equipped with power assisted front disc and rear drum brakes. 1994 and earlier models are equipped with a rear wheel anti-lock brake system, while 1995 and later models are equipped with a four wheel anti-lock brake system.

Vehicle identification numbers

Vehicle identification numbers

Modifications are a continuing and unpublicized process in vehicle manufacturing. Since spare parts manuals and lists are compiled on a numerical basis, the individual vehicle numbers are necessary to correctly identify the component required.

Vehicle Identification Number (VIN)

This very important identification number is located on a plate attached to the left side dashboard just inside the windshield (see illustration). The VIN also appears on the Vehicle Certificate of Title and Registration. It contains information such as where and when the vehicle was manufactured, engine type, the model year and the body style.

Vehicle Certification Label

The Vehicle Certification label (VC label, also referred to as the Truck Safety Compliance Certification label) is attached to the front of the left (driver's side) door pillar (see illustration). The upper half of the label contains the name of the manufacturer, the month and year of production, the Gross Vehicle Weight Rating (GVWR), the Gross Axle Weight Rating (GAWR) and the certification statement.

The VC label also contains the VIN number, which is used for warranty identification of the vehicle, and provides such information as manufacturer, type of restraint system, body type, engine, transmission, model year and vehicle serial number.

Engine numbers

Labels containing the engine code, calibration and serial numbers, as well as plant name, can be found on the valve cover, as well as stamped on the engine itself (see illustration).

Manual transmission numbers

The manual transmission identification number and serial numbers can be found on a tag on the left or right side of the transmission main case (see illustration).

Automatic transmission numbers

Tags with the automatic transmission serial number, build date and other information are attached with a bolt, usually at the extension housing (see illustration).

Vehicle Emissions Control Information (VECI) label

This label is found under the hood (see Chapter 6).

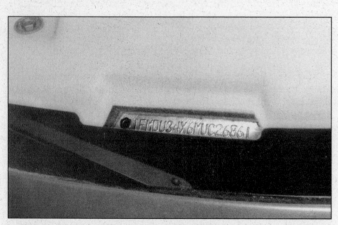

The Vehicle Identification Number (VIN) is visible through the driver's side of the windshield

The Vehicle Certification label, also known as the Truck Safety Compliance Certification label is located on the left front door pillar

An engine identification label can usually be found on the valve cover

A – FORD MOTOR COMPANY PART NUMBER
B – SERIAL NUMBER
C – BAR CODE (INVENTORY PURPOSES)

The manual transmission identification label is mounted on the side of the transmission case

TRANSMISSION MODEL   LINE SHIFT CODE

87GT-MAA

07   G   17
YEAR MONTH DAY

BUILD DAY CODE

The automatic transmission identification label is attached with a bolt, usually to the extension housing

Buying parts

Replacement parts are available from many sources, which generally fall into one of two categories - authorized dealer parts departments and independent retail auto parts stores. Our advice concerning these parts is as follows:

Retail auto parts stores: Good auto parts stores will stock frequently needed components which wear out relatively fast, such as clutch components, exhaust systems, brake parts, tune-up parts, etc. These stores often supply new or reconditioned parts on an exchange basis, which can save a considerable amount of money. Discount auto parts stores are often very good places to buy materials and parts needed for general vehicle maintenance such as oil, grease, filters, spark plugs, belts, touch-up paint, bulbs, etc. They also usually sell tools and general accessories, have convenient hours, charge lower prices and can often be found not far from home.

Authorized dealer parts department: This is the best source for parts which are unique to the vehicle and not generally available elsewhere (such as major engine parts, transmission parts, trim pieces, etc.).

Warranty information: If the vehicle is still covered under warranty, be sure that any replacement parts purchased - regardless of the source - do not invalidate the warranty!

To be sure of obtaining the correct parts, have engine and chassis numbers available and, if possible, take the old parts along for positive identification.

Maintenance techniques, tools and working facilities

Maintenance techniques

There are a number of techniques involved in maintenance and repair that will be referred to throughout this manual. Application of these techniques will enable the home mechanic to be more efficient, better organized and capable of performing the various tasks properly, which will ensure that the repair job is thorough and complete.

Fasteners

Fasteners are nuts, bolts, studs and screws used to hold two or more parts together. There are a few things to keep in mind when working with fasteners. Almost all of them use a locking device of some type, either a lockwasher, locknut, locking tab or thread adhesive. All threaded fasteners should be clean and straight, with undamaged threads and undamaged corners on the hex head where the wrench fits. Develop the habit of replacing all damaged nuts and bolts with new ones. Special locknuts with nylon or fiber inserts can only be used once. If they are removed, they lose their locking ability and must be replaced with new ones.

Rusted nuts and bolts should be treated with a penetrating fluid to ease removal and prevent breakage. Some mechanics use turpentine in a spout-type oil can, which works quite well. After applying the rust penetrant, let it work for a few minutes before trying to loosen the nut or bolt. Badly rusted fasteners may have to be chiseled or sawed off or removed with a special nut breaker, available at tool stores.

If a bolt or stud breaks off in an assembly, it can be drilled and removed with a special tool commonly available for this purpose. Most automotive machine shops can perform this task, as well as other repair procedures, such as the repair of threaded holes that have been stripped out.

Flat washers and lockwashers, when removed from an assembly, should always be replaced exactly as removed. Replace any damaged washers with new ones. Never use a lockwasher on any soft metal surface (such as aluminum), thin sheet metal or plastic.

Fastener sizes

For a number of reasons, automobile manufacturers are making wider and wider use of metric fasteners. Therefore, it is important to be able to tell the difference between standard (sometimes called U.S. or SAE) and metric hardware, since they cannot be interchanged.

All bolts, whether standard or metric, are sized according to diameter, thread pitch and length. For example, a standard 1/2 - 13 x 1 bolt is 1/2 inch in diameter, has 13 threads per inch and is 1 inch long. An M12 - 1.75 x 25 metric bolt is 12 mm in diameter, has a thread pitch of 1.75 mm (the distance between threads) and is 25 mm long. The two bolts are nearly identical, and easily confused, but they are not interchangeable.

In addition to the differences in diameter, thread pitch and length, metric and standard bolts can also be distinguished by examining the bolt heads. To begin with, the distance across the flats on a standard bolt head is measured in inches, while the same dimension on a metric bolt is sized in millimeters (the same is true for nuts). As a result, a standard wrench should not be used on a metric bolt and a metric wrench should not be used on a standard bolt. Also, most standard bolts have slashes radiating out from the center of the head to denote the grade or strength of the bolt, which is an indication of the amount of torque that can be applied to it. The greater the number of slashes, the greater the strength of the bolt. Grades 0 through 5 are commonly used on automobiles. Metric bolts have a property class (grade) number, rather than a slash, molded into their heads to indicate bolt strength. In this case, the higher the number, the stronger the bolt. Property class numbers 8.8, 9.8 and 10.9 are commonly used on automobiles.

Strength markings can also be used to distinguish standard hex nuts from metric hex nuts. Many standard nuts have dots stamped into one side, while metric nuts are marked with a number. The greater the number of dots, or the higher the number, the greater the strength of the nut.

Metric studs are also marked on their ends according to property class (grade). Larger studs are numbered (the same as metric bolts), while smaller studs carry a geometric code to denote grade.

Grade 1 or 2   Grade 5   Grade 8

Bolt strength markings (top - standard/SAE/USS; bottom - metric)

Grade	Identification
Hex Nut Grade 5	3 Dots
Hex Nut Grade 8	6 Dots

Standard hex nut strength markings

Class	Identification
Hex Nut Property Class 9	Arabic 9
Hex Nut Property Class 10	Arabic 10

Metric hex nut strength markings

CLASS 10.9   CLASS 9.8   CLASS 8.8

Metric stud strength markings

It should be noted that many fasteners, especially Grades 0 through 2, have no distinguishing marks on them. When such is the case, the only way to determine whether it is standard or metric is to measure the thread pitch or compare it to a known fastener of the same size.

Standard fasteners are often referred to as SAE, as opposed to metric. However, it should be noted that SAE technically refers to a non-metric fine thread fastener only. Coarse thread non-metric fasteners are referred to as USS sizes.

Since fasteners of the same size (both standard and metric) may have different strength ratings, be sure to reinstall any bolts, studs or nuts removed from your vehicle in their original locations. Also, when replacing a fastener with a new one, make sure that the new one has a strength rating equal to or greater than the original.

Tightening sequences and procedures

Most threaded fasteners should be tightened to a specific torque value (torque is the twisting force applied to a threaded component such as a nut or bolt). Overtightening the fastener can weaken it and cause it to break, while undertightening can cause it to eventually come loose. Bolts, screws and studs, depending on the material they are made of and their thread diameters, have specific torque values, many of which are noted in the Specifications at the beginning of each Chapter. Be sure to follow the torque recommendations closely. For fasteners not assigned a specific torque, a general torque value chart is presented here as a guide. These torque values are for dry (unlubricated) fasteners threaded into steel or cast iron (not aluminum). As was previously mentioned, the size and grade of a fastener determine the amount of torque that can safely be applied to it. The

Metric thread sizes	Ft-lbs	Nm
M-6	6 to 9	9 to 12
M-8	14 to 21	19 to 28
M-10	28 to 40	38 to 54
M-12	50 to 71	68 to 96
M-14	80 to 140	109 to 154

Pipe thread sizes		
1/8	5 to 8	7 to 10
1/4	12 to 18	17 to 24
3/8	22 to 33	30 to 44
1/2	25 to 35	34 to 47

U.S. thread sizes		
1/4 - 20	6 to 9	9 to 12
5/16 - 18	12 to 18	17 to 24
5/16 - 24	14 to 20	19 to 27
3/8 - 16	22 to 32	30 to 43
3/8 - 24	27 to 38	37 to 51
7/16 - 14	40 to 55	55 to 74
7/16 - 20	40 to 60	55 to 81
1/2 - 13	55 to 80	75 to 108

Standard (SAE and USS) bolt dimensions/grade marks

- G Grade marks (bolt strength)
- L Length (in inches)
- T Thread pitch (number of threads per inch)
- D Nominal diameter (in inches)

Metric bolt dimensions/grade marks

- P Property class (bolt strength)
- L Length (in millimeters)
- T Thread pitch (distance between threads in millimeters)
- D Diameter

figures listed here are approximate for Grade 2 and Grade 3 fasteners. Higher grades can tolerate higher torque values.

Fasteners laid out in a pattern, such as cylinder head bolts, oil pan bolts, differential cover bolts, etc., must be loosened or tightened in sequence to avoid warping the component. This sequence will normally be shown in the appropriate Chapter. If a specific pattern is not given, the following procedures can be used to prevent warping.

Initially, the bolts or nuts should be assembled finger-tight only. Next, they should be tightened one full turn each, in a criss-cross or diagonal pattern. After each one has been tightened one full turn, return to the first one and tighten them all one-half turn, following the same pattern. Finally, tighten each of them one-quarter turn at a time until each fastener has been tightened to the proper torque. To loosen and remove the fasteners, the procedure would be reversed.

Component disassembly

Component disassembly should be done with care and purpose to help ensure that the parts go back together properly. Always keep track of the sequence in which parts are removed. Make note of special characteristics or marks on parts that can be installed more than one way, such as a grooved thrust washer on a shaft. It is a good idea to lay the disassembled parts out on a clean surface in the order that they were removed. It may also be helpful to make sketches or take instant photos of components before removal.

When removing fasteners from a component, keep track of their locations. Sometimes threading a bolt back in a part, or putting the washers and nut back on a stud, can prevent mix-ups later. If nuts and bolts cannot be returned to their original locations, they should be kept in a compartmented box or a series of small boxes. A cupcake or muffin tin is ideal for this purpose, since each cavity can hold the bolts and nuts from a particular area (i.e. oil pan bolts, valve cover bolts, engine mount bolts, etc.). A pan of this type is especially helpful when working on assemblies with very small parts, such as the carburetor, alternator, valve train or interior dash and trim pieces. The cavities can be marked with paint or tape to identify the contents.

Whenever wiring looms, harnesses or connectors are separated, it is a good idea to identify the two halves with numbered pieces of masking tape so they can be easily reconnected.

Gasket sealing surfaces

Throughout any vehicle, gaskets are used to seal the mating surfaces between two parts and keep lubricants, fluids, vacuum or pressure contained in an assembly.

Many times these gaskets are coated with a liquid or paste-type gasket sealing compound before assembly. Age, heat and pressure can sometimes cause the two parts to stick together so tightly that they are very difficult to separate. Often, the assembly can be loosened by striking it with a soft-face hammer near the mating surfaces. A regular hammer can be used if a block of wood is placed between the hammer and the part. Do not hammer on cast parts or parts that could be easily damaged. With any particularly stubborn part, always recheck to make sure that every fastener has been removed.

Avoid using a screwdriver or bar to pry apart an assembly, as they can easily mar the gasket sealing surfaces of the parts, which must remain smooth. If prying is absolutely necessary, use an old broom handle, but keep in mind that extra clean up will be necessary if the wood splinters.

After the parts are separated, the old gasket must be carefully scraped off and the gasket surfaces cleaned. Stubborn gasket material can be soaked with rust penetrant or treated with a special chemical to soften it so it can be easily scraped off. A scraper can be fashioned from a piece of copper tubing by flattening and sharpening one end. Copper is recommended because it is usually softer than the surfaces to be scraped, which reduces the chance of gouging the part. Some gaskets can be removed with a wire brush, but regardless of the method used, the mating surfaces must be left clean and smooth. If for some reason the gasket surface is gouged, then a gasket sealer thick enough to fill scratches will have to be used during reassembly of the components. For most applications, a non-drying (or semi-drying) gasket sealer should be used.

Hose removal tips

Warning: *If the vehicle is equipped with air conditioning, do not disconnect any of the A/C hoses without first having the system depressurized by a dealer service department or a service station.*

Hose removal precautions closely parallel gasket removal precautions. Avoid scratching or gouging the surface that the hose mates against or the connection may leak. This is especially true for radiator hoses. Because of various chemical reactions, the rubber in hoses can bond itself to the metal spigot that the hose fits over. To remove a hose, first loosen the hose clamps that secure it to the spigot. Then, with slip-joint pliers, grab the hose at the clamp and rotate it around the spigot. Work it back and forth until it is completely free, then pull it off. Silicone or other lubricants will ease removal if they can be applied between the hose and the outside of the spigot. Apply the same lubricant to the inside of the hose and the outside of the spigot to simplify installation.

As a last resort (and if the hose is to be replaced with a new one anyway), the rubber can be slit with a knife and the hose peeled from the spigot. If this must be done, be careful that the metal connection is not damaged.

If a hose clamp is broken or damaged, do not reuse it. Wire-type clamps usually weaken with age, so it is a good idea to replace them with screw-type clamps whenever a hose is removed.

Tools

A selection of good tools is a basic requirement for anyone who plans to maintain and repair his or her own vehicle. For the owner who has few tools, the initial investment might seem high, but when compared to the spiraling costs of professional auto maintenance and repair, it is a wise one.

Micrometer set

Dial indicator set

Dial caliper

Hand-operated vacuum pump

Timing light

Compression gauge with spark plug
hole adapter

Damper/steering wheel puller

General purpose puller

Hydraulic lifter removal tool

Valve spring compressor

Valve spring compressor

Ridge reamer

Piston ring groove cleaning tool

Ring removal/installation tool

Ring compressor

Cylinder hone

Brake hold-down spring tool

Brake cylinder hone

Clutch plate alignment tool

Tap and die set

To help the owner decide which tools are needed to perform the tasks detailed in this manual, the following tool lists are offered: *Maintenance and minor repair, Repair/overhaul* and *Special*.

The newcomer to practical mechanics should start off with the *maintenance and minor repair* tool kit, which is adequate for the simpler jobs performed on a vehicle. Then, as confidence and experience grow, the owner can tackle more difficult tasks, buying additional tools as they are needed. Eventually the basic kit will be expanded into the *repair and overhaul* tool set. Over a period of time, the experienced do-it-yourselfer will assemble a tool set complete enough for most repair and overhaul procedures and will add tools from the special category when it is felt that the expense is justified by the frequency of use.

Maintenance and minor repair tool kit

The tools in this list should be considered the minimum required for performance of routine maintenance, servicing and minor repair work. We recommend the purchase of combination wrenches (box-end and open-end combined in one wrench). While more expensive than open end wrenches, they offer the advantages of both types of wrench.

Combination wrench set (1/4-inch to 1 inch or 6 mm to 19 mm)
Adjustable wrench, 8 inch
Spark plug wrench with rubber insert
Spark plug gap adjusting tool
Feeler gauge set
Brake bleeder wrench
Standard screwdriver (5/16-inch x 6 inch)
Phillips screwdriver (No. 2 x 6 inch)
Combination pliers - 6 inch
Hacksaw and assortment of blades
Tire pressure gauge
Grease gun

Oil can
Fine emery cloth
Wire brush
Battery post and cable cleaning tool
Oil filter wrench
Funnel (medium size)
Safety goggles
Jackstands (2)
Drain pan

Note*: If basic tune-ups are going to be part of routine maintenance, it will be necessary to purchase a good quality stroboscopic timing light and combination tachometer/dwell meter. Although they are included in the list of special tools, it is mentioned here because they are absolutely necessary for tuning most vehicles properly.*

Repair and overhaul tool set

These tools are essential for anyone who plans to perform major repairs and are in addition to those in the maintenance and minor repair tool kit. Included is a comprehensive set of sockets which, though expensive, are invaluable because of their versatility, especially when various extensions and drives are available. We recommend the 1/2-inch drive over the 3/8-inch drive. Although the larger drive is bulky and more expensive, it has the capacity of accepting a very wide range of large sockets. Ideally, however, the mechanic should have a 3/8-inch drive set and a 1/2-inch drive set.

Socket set(s)
Reversible ratchet
Extension - 10 inch
Universal joint
Torque wrench (same size drive as sockets)
Ball peen hammer - 8 ounce
Soft-face hammer (plastic/rubber)
Standard screwdriver (1/4-inch x 6 inch)

Standard screwdriver (stubby - 5/16-inch)
Phillips screwdriver (No. 3 x 8 inch)
Phillips screwdriver (stubby - No. 2)
Pliers - vise grip
Pliers - lineman's
Pliers - needle nose
Pliers - snap-ring (internal and external)
Cold chisel - 1/2-inch
Scribe
Scraper (made from flattened copper tubing)
Centerpunch
Pin punches (1/16, 1/8, 3/16-inch)
Steel rule/straightedge - 12 inch
Allen wrench set (1/8 to 3/8-inch or 4 mm to 10 mm)
A selection of files
Wire brush (large)
Jackstands (second set)
Jack (scissor or hydraulic type)

Note: *Another tool which is often useful is an electric drill with a chuck capacity of 3/8-inch and a set of good quality drill bits.*

Special tools

The tools in this list include those which are not used regularly, are expensive to buy, or which need to be used in accordance with their manufacturer's instructions. Unless these tools will be used frequently, it is not very economical to purchase many of them. A consideration would be to split the cost and use between yourself and a friend or friends. In addition, most of these tools can be obtained from a tool rental shop on a temporary basis.

This list primarily contains only those tools and instruments widely available to the public, and not those special tools produced by the vehicle manufacturer for distribution to dealer service departments. Occasionally, references to the manufacturer's special tools are included in the text of this manual. Generally, an alternative method of doing the job without the special tool is offered. However, sometimes there is no alternative to their use. Where this is the case, and the tool cannot be purchased or borrowed, the work should be turned over to the dealer service department or an automotive repair shop.

Valve spring compressor
Piston ring groove cleaning tool
Piston ring compressor
Piston ring installation tool
Cylinder compression gauge
Cylinder ridge reamer
Cylinder surfacing hone
Cylinder bore gauge
Micrometers and/or dial calipers
Hydraulic lifter removal tool
Balljoint separator
Universal-type puller
Impact screwdriver
Dial indicator set
Stroboscopic timing light (inductive pick-up)
Hand operated vacuum/pressure pump
Tachometer/dwell meter
Universal electrical multimeter
Cable hoist
Brake spring removal and installation tools
Floor jack

Buying tools

For the do-it-yourselfer who is just starting to get involved in vehicle maintenance and repair, there are a number of options available when purchasing tools. If maintenance and minor repair is the extent of the work to be done, the purchase of individual tools is satisfactory. If, on the other hand, extensive work is planned, it would be a

good idea to purchase a modest tool set from one of the large retail chain stores. A set can usually be bought at a substantial savings over the individual tool prices, and they often come with a tool box. As additional tools are needed, add-on sets, individual tools and a larger tool box can be purchased to expand the tool selection. Building a tool set gradually allows the cost of the tools to be spread over a longer period of time and gives the mechanic the freedom to choose only those tools that will actually be used.

Tool stores will often be the only source of some of the special tools that are needed, but regardless of where tools are bought, try to avoid cheap ones, especially when buying screwdrivers and sockets, because they won't last very long. The expense involved in replacing cheap tools will eventually be greater than the initial cost of quality tools.

Care and maintenance of tools

Good tools are expensive, so it makes sense to treat them with respect. Keep them clean and in usable condition and store them properly when not in use. Always wipe off any dirt, grease or metal chips before putting them away. Never leave tools lying around in the work area. Upon completion of a job, always check closely under the hood for tools that may have been left there so they won't get lost during a test drive.

Some tools, such as screwdrivers, pliers, wrenches and sockets, can be hung on a panel mounted on the garage or workshop wall, while others should be kept in a tool box or tray. Measuring instruments, gauges, meters, etc. must be carefully stored where they cannot be damaged by weather or impact from other tools.

When tools are used with care and stored properly, they will last a very long time. Even with the best of care, though, tools will wear out if used frequently. When a tool is damaged or worn out, replace it. Subsequent jobs will be safer and more enjoyable if you do.

Working facilities

Not to be overlooked when discussing tools is the workshop. If anything more than routine maintenance is to be carried out, some sort of suitable work area is essential.

It is understood, and appreciated, that many home mechanics do not have a good workshop or garage available, and end up removing an engine or doing major repairs outside. It is recommended, however, that the overhaul or repair be completed under the cover of a roof.

A clean, flat workbench or table of comfortable working height is an absolute necessity. The workbench should be equipped with a vise that has a jaw opening of at least four inches.

As mentioned previously, some clean, dry storage space is also required for tools, as well as the lubricants, fluids, cleaning solvents, etc. which soon become necessary.

Sometimes waste oil and fluids, drained from the engine or cooling system during normal maintenance or repairs, present a disposal problem. To avoid pouring them on the ground or into a sewage system, pour the used fluids into large containers, seal them with caps and take them to an authorized disposal site or recycling center. Plastic jugs, such as old antifreeze containers, are ideal for this purpose.

Always keep a supply of old newspapers and clean rags available. Old towels are excellent for mopping up spills. Many mechanics use rolls of paper towels for most work because they are readily available and disposable. To help keep the area under the vehicle clean, a large cardboard box can be cut open and flattened to protect the garage or shop floor.

Whenever working over a painted surface, such as when leaning over a fender to service something under the hood, always cover it with an old blanket or bedspread to protect the finish. Vinyl covered pads, made especially for this purpose, are available at auto parts stores.

Booster battery (jump) starting

Observe these precautions when using a booster battery to start a vehicle

a) *Before connecting the booster battery. make sure the ignition switch is in the Off position.*
b) *Turn off the lights, heater and other electrical loads.*
c) *Your eyes should be shielded. Safety goggles are a good idea.*
d) *Make sure the booster battery is the same voltage as the dead one in the vehicle.*
e) *The two vehicles MUST NOT TOUCH each other!*
f) *Make sure the transmission is in Neutral (manual) or Park (automatic).*
g) *If the booster battery is not a maintenance-free type, remove the vent caps and lay a cloth over the vent holes.*

Connect the red jumper cable to the positive (+) terminals of each battery.

Connect one end of the black jumper cable to the negative (-) terminal of the booster battery. The other end of this cable should be connected to a good ground on the vehicle to be started, such as a bolt or bracket on the engine block **(see illustration)**. Make sure the cable will not come into contact with the tan, drivebelts or other moving parts of the engine.

Start the engine using the booster battery, then, with the engine running at idle speed, disconnect the jumper cables in the reverse order of connection.

Make the booster battery cable connections in the numerical order shown (note that the negative cable of the booster battery is NOT attached to the negative terminal of the dead battery)

Jacking and towing

Jacking

Warning: *On vehicles equipped with a limited slip differential, do not run the engine with the vehicle on a jack.*

When lifting the vehicle with either the supplied jack or a floor jack, block the wheel that is diagonally opposite the one being lifted to prevent the vehicle from moving. **Warning:** *If equipped with an under-chassis mounted spare tire, remove the tire or tire carrier from the rack before the vehicle is raised in order to a void sudden weight release from the chassis.*

When using the vehicle jack, the manufacturer recommends positioning the jack under the axles, shock absorber or jacking bracket, as close to the wheel to be removed as possible.

When raising the vehicle for service, always place jackstands under the frame rails. NEVER work under the vehicle when it is supported only by a jack!

Towing

When the vehicle is towed with the rear wheels raised, the steering wheel must be clamped in the straight ahead position with a special device designed for use during towing. **Warning:** *Don't use the steering lock to keep the front wheels pointed straight ahead. It's not strong enough for this purpose.*

Equipment specifically designed for towing should be used. It should be attached to the frame members of the vehicle, not the bumpers or brackets.

Safety is a major consideration when towing and all applicable state and local laws must be obeyed. A safety chain system must be used at all times. Remember that power steering and power brakes will not work with the engine off.

Front axle jacking point

Rear axle jacking point

Automotive chemicals and lubricants

A number of automotive chemicals and lubricants are available for use during vehicle maintenance and repair. They include a wide variety of products ranging from cleaning solvents and degreasers to lubricants and protective sprays for rubber, plastic and vinyl.

Cleaners

Carburetor cleaner and choke cleaner is a strong solvent for gum, varnish and carbon. Most carburetor cleaners leave a dry-type lubricant film which will not harden or gum up. Because of this film it is not recommended for use on electrical components.

Brake system cleaner is used to remove grease and brake fluid from the brake system, where clean surfaces are absolutely necessary. It leaves no residue and often eliminates brake squeal caused by contaminants.

Electrical cleaner removes oxidation, corrosion and carbon deposits from electrical contacts, restoring full current flow. It can also be used to clean spark plugs, carburetor jets, voltage regulators and other parts where an oil-free surface is desired.

Demoisturants remove water and moisture from electrical components such as alternators, voltage regulators, electrical con-nectors and fuse blocks. They are non-conductive, non-corrosive and non-flammable.

Degreasers are heavy-duty solvents used to remove grease from the outside of the engine and from chassis components. They can be sprayed or brushed on and, depending on the type, are rinsed off either with water or solvent.

Lubricants

Motor oil is the lubricant formulated for use in engines. It normally contains a wide variety of additives to prevent corrosion and reduce foaming and wear. Motor oil comes in various weights (viscosity ratings) from 5 to 80. The recommended weight of the oil depends on the season, temperature and the demands on the engine. Light oil is used in cold climates and under light load conditions. Heavy oil is used in hot climates and where high loads are encountered. Multi-viscosity oils are designed to have characteristics of both light and heavy oils and are available in a number of weights from 5W-20 to 20W-50.

Gear oil is designed to be used in differentials, manual transmissions and other areas where high-temperature lubrication is required.

Chassis and wheel bearing grease is a heavy grease used where increased loads and friction are encountered, such as for wheel bearings, balljoints, tie-rod ends and universal joints.

High-temperature wheel bearing grease is designed to withstand the extreme temperatures encountered by wheel bearings in disc brake equipped vehicles. It usually contains molybdenum disulfide (moly), which is a dry-type lubricant.

White grease is a heavy grease for metal-to-metal applications where water is a problem. White grease stays soft under both low and high temperatures (usually from -100 to +190-degrees F), and will not wash off or dilute in the presence of water.

Assembly lube is a special extreme pressure lubricant, usually containing moly, used to lubricate high-load parts (such as main and rod bearings and cam lobes) for initial start-up of a new engine. The assembly lube lubricates the parts without being squeezed out or washed away until the engine oiling system begins to function.

Silicone lubricants are used to protect rubber, plastic, vinyl and nylon parts.

Graphite lubricants are used where oils cannot be used due to contamination problems, such as in locks. The dry graphite will lubricate metal parts while remaining uncontaminated by dirt, water, oil or acids. It is electrically conductive and will not foul electrical contacts in locks such as the ignition switch.

Moly penetrants loosen and lubricate frozen, rusted and corroded fasteners and prevent future rusting or freezing.

Heat-sink grease is a special electrically non-conductive grease that is used for mounting electronic ignition modules where it is essential that heat is transferred away from the module.

Sealants

RTV sealant is one of the most widely used gasket compounds. Made from silicone, RTV is air curing, it seals, bonds, waterproofs, fills surface irregularities, remains flexible, doesn't shrink, is relatively easy to remove, and is used as a supplementary sealer with almost all low and medium temperature gaskets.

Anaerobic sealant is much like RTV in that it can be used either to seal gaskets or to form gaskets by itself. It remains flexible, is solvent resistant and fills surface imperfections. The difference between an anaerobic sealant and an RTV-type sealant is in the curing. RTV cures when exposed to air, while an anaerobic sealant cures only in the absence of air. This means that an anaerobic sealant cures only after the assembly of parts, sealing them together.

Thread and pipe sealant is used for sealing hydraulic and pneumatic fittings and vacuum lines. It is usually made from a Teflon compound, and comes in a spray, a paint-on liquid and as a wrap-around tape.

Chemicals

Anti-seize compound prevents seizing, galling, cold welding, rust and corrosion in fasteners. High-temperature ant-seize, usually made with copper and graphite lubricants, is used for exhaust system and exhaust manifold bolts.

Anaerobic locking compounds are used to keep fasteners from vibrating or working loose and cure only after installation, in the absence of air. Medium strength locking compound is used for small nuts, bolts and screws that may be removed later. High-strength locking compound is for large nuts, bolts and studs which aren't removed on a regular basis.

Oil additives range from viscosity index improvers to chemical treatments that claim to reduce internal engine friction. It should be noted that most oil manufacturers caution against using additives with their oils.

Gas additives perform several functions, depending on their chemical makeup. They usually contain solvents that help dissolve gum and varnish that build up on carburetor, fuel injection and intake parts. They also serve to break down carbon deposits that form on the inside surfaces of the combustion chambers. Some additives contain upper cylinder lubricants for valves and piston rings, and others contain chemicals to remove condensation from the gas tank.

Miscellaneous

Brake fluid is specially formulated hydraulic fluid that can withstand the heat and pressure encountered in brake systems. Care must be taken so this fluid does not come in contact with painted surfaces or plastics. An opened container should always be resealed to prevent contamination by water or dirt.

Weatherstrip adhesive is used to bond weatherstripping around doors, windows and trunk lids. It is sometimes used to attach trim pieces.

Undercoating is a petroleum-based, tar-like substance that is designed to protect metal surfaces on the underside of the vehicle from corrosion. It also acts as a sound-deadening agent by insulating the bottom of the vehicle.

Waxes and polishes are used to help protect painted and plated surfaces from the weather. Different types of paint may require the use of different types of wax and polish. Some polishes utilize a chemical or abrasive cleaner to help remove the top layer of oxidized (dull) paint on older vehicles. In recent years many non-wax polishes that contain a wide variety of chemicals such as polymers and silicones have been introduced. These non-wax polishes are usually easier to apply and last longer than conventional waxes and polishes.

Safety first!

Regardless of how enthusiastic you may be about getting on with the job at hand, take the time to ensure that your safety is not jeopardized. A moment's lack of attention can result in an accident, as can failure to observe certain simple safety precautions. The possibility of an accident will always exist, and the following points should not be considered a comprehensive list of all dangers. Rather, they are intended to make you aware of the risks and to encourage a safety conscious approach to all work you carry out on your vehicle.

Essential DOs and DON'Ts

DON'T rely on a jack when working under the vehicle. Always use approved jackstands to support the weight of the vehicle and place them under the recommended lift or support points.

DON'T attempt to loosen extremely tight fasteners (i.e. wheel lug nuts) while the vehicle is on a jack - it may fall.

DON'T start the engine without first making sure that the transmission is in Neutral (or Park where applicable) and the parking brake is set.

DON'T remove the radiator cap from a hot cooling system - let it cool or cover it with a cloth and release the pressure gradually.

DON'T attempt to drain the engine oil until you are sure it has cooled to the point that it will not burn you.

DON'T touch any part of the engine or exhaust system until it has cooled sufficiently to avoid burns.

DON'T siphon toxic liquids such as gasoline, antifreeze and brake fluid by mouth, or allow them to remain on your skin.

DON'T inhale brake lining dust - it is potentially hazardous (see *Asbestos* below).

DON'T allow spilled oil or grease to remain on the floor - wipe it up before someone slips on it.

DON'T use loose fitting wrenches or other tools which may slip and cause injury.

DON'T push on wrenches when loosening or tightening nuts or bolts. Always try to pull the wrench toward you. If the situation calls for pushing the wrench away, push with an open hand to avoid scraped knuckles if the wrench should slip.

DON'T attempt to lift a heavy component alone - get someone to help you.

DON'T rush or take unsafe shortcuts to finish a job.

DON'T allow children or animals in or around the vehicle while you are working on it.

DO wear eye protection when using power tools such as a drill, sander, bench grinder, etc. and when working under a vehicle.

DO keep loose clothing and long hair well out of the way of moving parts.

DO make sure that any hoist used has a safe working load rating adequate for the job.

DO get someone to check on you periodically when working alone on a vehicle.

DO carry out work in a logical sequence and make sure that everything is correctly assembled and tightened.

DO keep chemicals and fluids tightly capped and out of the reach of children and pets.

DO remember that your vehicle's safety affects that of yourself and others. If in doubt on any point, get professional advice.

Asbestos

Certain friction, insulating, sealing, and other products - such as brake linings, brake bands, clutch linings, torque converters, gaskets, etc. - contain asbestos. Extreme care must be taken to avoid inhalation of dust from such products, since it is hazardous to health. If in doubt, assume that they *do* contain asbestos.

Fire

Remember at all times that gasoline is highly flammable. Never smoke or have any kind of open flame around when working on a vehicle. But the risk does not end there. A spark caused by an electrical short circuit, by two metal surfaces contacting each other, or even by static electricity built up in your body under certain conditions, can ignite gasoline vapors, which in a confined space are highly explosive. Do not, under any circumstances, use gasoline for cleaning parts. Use an approved safety solvent.

Always disconnect the battery ground (-) cable at the battery before working on any part of the fuel system or electrical system. Never risk spilling fuel on a hot engine or exhaust component. It is strongly recommended that a fire extinguisher suitable for use on fuel and electrical fires be kept handy in the garage or workshop at all times. Never try to extinguish a fuel or electrical fire with water.

Fumes

Certain fumes are highly toxic and can quickly cause unconsciousness and even death if inhaled to any extent. Gasoline vapor falls into this category, as do the vapors from some cleaning solvents. Any draining or pouring of such volatile fluids should be done in a well ventilated area.

When using cleaning fluids and solvents, read the instructions on the container carefully. Never use materials from unmarked containers.

Never run the engine in an enclosed space, such as a garage. Exhaust fumes contain carbon monoxide, which is extremely poisonous. If you need to run the engine, always do so in the open air, or at least have the rear of the vehicle outside the work area.

If you are fortunate enough to have the use of an inspection pit, never drain or pour gasoline and never run the engine while the vehicle is over the pit. The fumes, being heavier than air, will concentrate in the pit with possibly lethal results.

The battery

Never create a spark or allow a bare light bulb near a battery. They normally give off a certain amount of hydrogen gas, which is highly explosive.

Always disconnect the battery ground (-) cable *at the battery* before working on the fuel or electrical systems.

If possible, loosen the filler caps or cover when charging the battery from an external source (this does not apply to sealed or maintenance-free batteries). Do not charge at an excessive rate or the battery may burst.

Take care when adding water to a non maintenance-free battery and when carrying a battery. The electrolyte, even when diluted, is very corrosive and should not be allowed to contact clothing or skin.

Always wear eye protection when cleaning the battery to prevent the caustic deposits from entering your eyes.

Household current

When using an electric power tool, inspection light, etc., which operates on household current, always make sure that the tool is correctly connected to its plug and that, where necessary, it is properly grounded. Do not use such items in damp conditions and, again, do not create a spark or apply excessive heat in the vicinity of fuel or fuel vapor.

Secondary ignition system voltage

A severe electric shock can result from touching certain parts of the ignition system (such as the spark plug wires) when the engine is running or being cranked, particularly if components are damp or the insulation is defective. In the case of an electronic ignition system, the secondary system voltage is much higher and could prove fatal.

Conversion factors

Length (distance)

Inches (in)	X 25.4	= Millimetres (mm)	X 0.0394	= Inches (in)
Feet (ft)	X 0.305	= Metres (m)	X 3.281	= Feet (ft)
Miles	X 1.609	= Kilometres (km)	X 0.621	= Miles

Volume (capacity)

Cubic inches (cu in; in^3)	X 16.387	= Cubic centimetres (cc; cm^3)	X 0.061	= Cubic inches (cu in; in^3)
Imperial pints (Imp pt)	X 0.568	= Litres (l)	X 1.76	= Imperial pints (Imp pt)
Imperial quarts (Imp qt)	X 1.137	= Litres (l)	X 0.88	= Imperial quarts (Imp qt)
Imperial quarts (Imp qt)	X 1.201	= US quarts (US qt)	X 0.833	= Imperial quarts (Imp qt)
US quarts (US qt)	X 0.946	= Litres (l)	X 1.057	= US quarts (US qt)
Imperial gallons (Imp gal)	X 4.546	= Litres (l)	X 0.22	= Imperial gallons (Imp gal)
Imperial gallons (Imp gal)	X 1.201	= US gallons (US gal)	X 0.833	= Imperial gallons (Imp gal)
US gallons (US gal)	X 3.785	= Litres (l)	X 0.264	= US gallons (US gal)

Mass (weight)

Ounces (oz)	X 28.35	= Grams (g)	X 0.035	Ounces (oz)
Pounds (lb)	X 0.454	= Kilograms (kg)	X 2.205	= Pounds (lb)

Force

Ounces-force (ozf; oz)	X 0.278	= Newtons (N)	X 3.6	= Ounces-force (ozf; oz)
Pounds-force (lbf; lb)	X 4.448	= Newtons (N)	X 0.225	= Pounds-force (lbf; lb)
Newtons (N)	X 0.1	= Kilograms-force (kgf; kg)	X 9.81	= Newtons (N)

Pressure

Pounds-force per square inch (psi; lbf/in^2; lb/in^2)	X 0.070	= Kilograms-force per square centimetre (kgf/cm^2; kg/cm^2)	X 14.223	= Pounds-force per square inch (psi; lbf/in^2; lb/in^2)
Pounds-force per square inch (psi; lbf/in^2; lb/in^2)	X 0.068	= Atmospheres (atm)	X 14.696	= Pounds-force per square inch (psi; lbf/in^2; lb/in^2)
Pounds-force per square inch (psi; lbf/in^2; lb/in^2)	X 0.069	= Bars	X 14.5	= Pounds-force per square inch (psi; lbf/in^2; lb/in^2)
Pounds-force per square inch (psi; lbf/in^2; lb/in^2)	X 6.895	= Kilopascals (kPa)	X 0.145	= Pounds-force per square inch (psi; lbf/in^2; lb/in^2)
Kilopascals (kPa)	X 0.01	= Kilograms-force per square centimetre (kgf/cm^2; kg/cm^2)	X 98.1	= Kilopascals (kPa)

Torque (moment of force)

Pounds-force inches (lbf in; lb in)	X 1.152	= Kilograms-force centimetre (kgf cm; kg cm)	X 0.868	= Pounds-force inches (lbf in; lb in)
Pounds-force inches (lbf in; lb in)	X 0.113	= Newton metres (Nm)	X 8.85	= Pounds-force inches (lbf in; lb in)
Pounds-force inches (lbf in; lb in)	X 0.083	= Pounds-force feet (lbf ft; lb ft)	X 12	= Pounds-force inches (lbf in; lb in)
Pounds-force feet (lbf ft; lb ft)	X 0.138	= Kilograms-force metres (kgf m; kg m)	X 7.233	= Pounds-force feet (lbf ft; lb ft)
Pounds-force feet (lbf ft; lb ft)	X 1.356	= Newton metres (Nm)	X 0.738	= Pounds-force feet (lbf ft; lb ft)
Newton metres (Nm)	X 0.102	= Kilograms-force metres (kgf m; kg m)	X 9.804	= Newton metres (Nm)

Power

Horsepower (hp)	X 745.7	= Watts (W)	X 0.0013	= Horsepower (hp)

Velocity (speed)

Miles per hour (miles/hr; mph)	X 1.609	= Kilometres per hour (km/hr; kph)	X 0.621	= Miles per hour (miles/hr; mph)

Fuel consumption*

Miles per gallon, Imperial (mpg)	X 0.354	= Kilometres per litre (km/l)	X 2.825	= Miles per gallon, Imperial (mpg)
Miles per gallon, US (mpg)	X 0.425	= Kilometres per litre (km/l)	X 2.352	= Miles per gallon, US (mpg)

Temperature

Degrees Fahrenheit = (°C x 1.8) + 32

Degrees Celsius (Degrees Centigrade; °C) = (°F - 32) x 0.56

*It is common practice to convert from miles per gallon (mpg) to litres/100 kilometres (l/100km), where mpg (Imperial) x l/100 km = 282 and mpg (US) x l/100 km = 235

Troubleshooting

Contents

Symptom	Section
Engine backfires	13
Engine diesels (continues to run) after switching off	15
Engine hard to start when cold	4
Engine hard to start when hot	5
Engine lacks power	12
Engine lopes while idling or idles erratically	8
Engine misses at idle speed	9
Engine misses throughout driving speed range	10
Engine rotates but will not start	2
Engine stalls	11
Engine starts but stops immediately	7
Engine will not rotate when attempting to start	1
Pinging or knocking engine sounds during acceleration or uphill	14
Starter motor noisy or excessively rough in engagement	6
Starter motor operates without rotating engine	3

Engine electrical system

Battery will not hold a charge	16
Ignition light fails to come on when key is turned on	18
Ignition light fails to go out	17

Fuel system

Symptom	Section
Excessive fuel consumption	19
Fuel leakage and/or fuel odor	20

Cooling system

Symptom	Section
Coolant loss	25
External coolant leakage	23
Internal coolant leakage	24
Overcooling	22
Overheating	21
Poor coolant circulation	26

Clutch

Symptom	Section
Clutch pedal stays on floor when disengaged	32
Clutch slips (engine speed increases with no increase in vehicle speed)	28
Fails to release (pedal pressed to the floor - shift lever does not move freely in and out of Reverse)	27
Grabbing (chattering) as clutch is engaged	29
Squeal or rumble with clutch fully disengaged (pedal depressed)	31
Squeal or rumble with clutch fully engaged (pedal released)	30

Manual transmission

Symptom	Section
Difficulty in engaging gears	37
Noisy in all gear	34
Noisy in Neutral with engine running	33
Noisy in one particular gear	35
Oil leakage	38
Slips out of high gear	36

Automatic transmission

Symptom	Section
Fluid leakage	42
General shift mechanism problems	39
Transmission slips, shifts rough, is noisy or has no drive in forward or reverse gears	41
Transmission will not downshift with accelerator pedal pressed to the floor	40

Transfer case

Symptom	Section
Lubricant leaks from the vent or output shaft seals	46
Noisy or jumps out of four-wheel drive Low range	45
Transfer case is difficult to shift into the desired range	43
Transfer case noisy in all gears	44

Driveshaft

Symptom	Section
Knock or clunk when the transmission is under initial load (just after transmission is put into gear)	48
Metallic grinding sound consistent with vehicle speed	49
Oil leak at front of driveshaft	47
Vibration	50

Axles

Symptom	Section
Noise	51
Oil leakage	53
Vibration	52

Brakes

Symptom	Section
Brake pedal feels spongy when depressed	57
Brake pedal pulsates during brake application	60
Excessive brake pedal travel	56
Excessive effort required to stop vehicle	58
Noise (high-pitched squeal with the brakes applied)	55
Pedal travels to the floor with little resistance	59
Vehicle pulls to one side during braking	54

Suspension and steering systems

Symptom	Section
Excessive pitching and/or rolling around corners or during braking	63
Excessive play in steering	65
Excessive tire wear (not specific to one area)	67
Excessive tire wear on inside edge	69
Excessive tire wear on outside edge	68
Excessively stiff steering	64
Lack of power assistance	66
Shimmy, shake or vibration	62
Tire tread worn in one place	70
Vehicle pulls to one side	61

This section provides an easy reference guide to the more common problems which may occur during the operation of your vehicle. These problems and possible causes are grouped under various components or systems; i.e. Engine, Cooling System, etc., and also refer to the Chapter and/or Section which deals with the problem.

Remember that successful troubleshooting is not a mysterious black art practiced only by professional mechanics. It's simply the result of a bit of knowledge combined with an intelligent, systematic approach to the problem. Always work by a process of elimination, starting with the simplest solution and working through to the most complex - and never overlook the obvious. Anyone can forget to fill the gas tank or leave the lights on overnight, so don't assume that you are above such oversights.

Finally, always get clear in your mind why a problem has occurred and take steps to ensure that it doesn't happen again. If the electrical system fails because of a poor connection, check all other connections in the system to make sure that they don't fail as well. If a particular fuse continues to blow, find out why - don't just go on replacing fuses. Remember, failure of a small component can often be indicative of potential failure or incorrect functioning of a more important component or system.

Engine

1 Engine will not rotate when attempting to start

1   Battery terminal connections loose or corroded. Check the cable terminals at the battery. Tighten the cable or remove corrosion as necessary.
2   Battery discharged or faulty. If the cable connections are clean and tight on the battery posts, turn the key to the On position and switch on the headlights and/or windshield wipers. If they fail to function, the battery is discharged.
3   Automatic transmission not completely engaged in Park or Neutral or clutch pedal not completely depressed.
4   Broken, loose or disconnected wiring in the starting circuit. Inspect all wiring and connectors at the battery, starter solenoid and ignition switch.
5   Starter motor pinion jammed in flywheel ring gear. If manual transmission, place transmission in gear and rock the vehicle to manually turn the engine. Remove starter and inspect pinion and flywheel at earliest convenience (Chapter 5).
6   Starter solenoid faulty (Chapter 5).
7   Starter motor faulty (Chapter 5).
8   Ignition switch faulty (Chapter 12).

2 Engine rotates but will not start

1   Fuel tank empty.
2   Fault in the fuel injection system (Chapter 4).
3   Battery discharged (engine rotates slowly). Check the operation of electrical components as described in the previous Section.
4   Battery terminal connections loose or corroded (see previous Section).
5   Fuel pump faulty (Chapter 4).
6   Excessive moisture on, or damage to, ignition components (see Chapter 5).
7   Worn, faulty or incorrectly gapped spark plugs (Chapter 1).
8   Broken, loose or disconnected wiring in the starting circuit (see previous Section).
9   Broken, loose or disconnected wires at the ignition coil pack or faulty coil pack (Chapter 5).

3 Starter motor operates without rotating engine

1   Starter pinion sticking. Remove the starter (Chapter 5) and inspect.
2   Starter pinion or flywheel teeth worn or broken. Remove the flywheel/driveplate access cover and inspect.

4 Engine hard to start when cold

1   Battery discharged or low. Check as described in Section 1.
2   Fault in the fuel or electrical systems (Chapters 4 and 5).

5 Engine hard to start when hot

1   Air filter clogged (Chapter 1).
2   Fault in the fuel or electrical systems (Chapters 4 and 5).
3   Fuel not reaching the injectors (see Chapter 4).

6 Starter motor noisy or excessively rough in engagement

1   Pinion or flywheel gear teeth worn or broken. Remove the cover at the rear of the engine (if equipped) and inspect.
2   Starter motor mounting bolts loose or missing.

7 Engine starts but stops immediately

1   Loose or faulty electrical connections at distributor, coil or alternator.
2   Fault in the fuel or electrical systems (Chapters 4 and 5).
3   Vacuum leak at the gasket surfaces of the intake manifold or throttle body. Make sure all mounting bolts/nuts are tightened securely and all vacuum hoses connected to the manifold are positioned properly and in good condition.

8 Engine lopes while idling or idles erratically

1   Vacuum leakage. Check the mounting bolts/nuts at the throttle body and intake manifold for tightness. Make sure all vacuum hoses are connected and in good condition. Use a stethoscope or a length of fuel hose held against your ear to listen for vacuum leaks while the engine is running. A hissing sound will be heard. A soapy water solution will also detect leaks.
2   Fault in the fuel or electrical systems (Chapters 4 and 5).
3   Plugged PCV valve (see Chapters 1 and 6).
4   Air filter clogged (Chapter 1).
5   Fuel pump not delivering sufficient fuel to the fuel injectors (see Chapter 4).
6   Leaking head gasket. Perform a compression check (Chapter 2).
7   Camshaft lobes worn (Chapter 2).

9 Engine misses at idle speed

1   Spark plugs worn, fouled or not gapped properly (Chapter 1).
2   Fault in the fuel or electrical systems (Chapters 4 and 5).
3   Faulty spark plug wires (Chapter 1).
4   Vacuum leaks at intake or hose connections. Check as described in Section 8.
5   Uneven or low cylinder compression. Check compression as described in Chapter 1.

10 Engine misses throughout driving speed range

1   Fuel filter clogged and/or impurities in the fuel system (Chapter 1).
2   Faulty or incorrectly gapped spark plugs (Chapter 1).
3   Fault in the fuel or electrical systems (Chapters 4 and 5).
4   Defective spark plug wires (Chapter 1).
5   Faulty emissions system components (Chapter 6).
6   Low or uneven cylinder compression pressures. Remove the spark plugs and test the compression with a gauge (Chapter 2).
7   Weak or faulty ignition system (Chapter 5).
8   Vacuum leaks at the throttle body, intake manifold or vacuum hoses (see Section 8).

11 Engine stalls

1   Idle speed incorrect. Refer to the VECI label.
2   Fuel filter clogged and/or water and impurities in the fuel system (Chapter 1).
3   Fault in the fuel system or sensors (Chapters 4 and 6).
4   Faulty emissions system components (Chapter 6).
5   Faulty or incorrectly gapped spark plugs (Chapter 1). Also check the spark plug wires (Chapter 1).
6   Vacuum leak at the throttle body, intake manifold or vacuum hoses. Check as described in Section 8.

12 Engine lacks power

1   Fault in the fuel or electrical systems (Chapters 4 and 5).
2   Faulty or incorrectly gapped spark plugs (Chapter 1).
3   Faulty coil (Chapter 5).
4   Brakes binding (Chapter 1).
5   Automatic transmission fluid level incorrect (Chapter 1).
6   Clutch slipping (Chapter 8).
7   Fuel filter clogged and/or impurities in the fuel system (Chapter 1).
8   Emissions control system not functioning properly (Chapter 6).
9   Use of substandard fuel. Fill the tank with the proper octane fuel.
10   Low or uneven cylinder compression pressures. Test with a compression tester, which will detect leaking valves and/or a blown head gasket (Chapter 2).

13 Engine backfires

1   Emissions system not functioning properly (Chapter 6).
2   Fault in the fuel or electrical systems (Chapters 4 and 5).
3   Faulty secondary ignition system (cracked spark plug insulator or faulty plug wires) (Chapters 1 and 5).
4   Fuel injection system in need of adjustment or worn excessively (Chapter 4).
5   Vacuum leak at the throttle body, intake manifold or vacuum hoses. Check as described in Section 8.
6   Valves sticking (Chapter 2).
7   Crossed plug wires (Chapter 1).

14 Pinging or knocking engine sounds during acceleration or uphill

1   Incorrect grade of fuel. Fill the tank with fuel of the proper octane rating.
2   Fault in the fuel or electrical systems (Chapters 4 and 5).
3   Improper spark plugs. Check the plug type against the VECI label located in the engine compartment. Also check the plugs and wires for damage (Chapter 1).
4   Faulty emissions system (Chapter 6).
5   Vacuum leak. Check as described in Section 9.

15 Engine diesels (continues to run) after switching off

1   Idle speed too high. Refer to Chapter 1.
2   Fault in the fuel or electrical systems (Chapters 4 and 5).
3   Excessive engine operating temperature. Probable causes of this are a low coolant level (see Chapter 1), malfunctioning thermostat, clogged radiator or faulty water pump (see Chapter 3).

Engine electrical system

16 Battery will not hold a charge

1   Alternator drivebelt defective or not adjusted properly (Chapter 1).
2   Electrolyte level low or battery discharged (Chapter 1).
3   Battery terminals loose or corroded (Chapter 1).
4   Alternator not charging properly (Chapter 5).
5   Loose, broken or faulty wiring in the charging circuit (Chapter 5).
6   Short in the vehicle wiring causing a continuous drain on the battery (refer to Chapter 12 and the Wiring Diagrams).
7   Battery defective internally.

17 Ignition light fails to go out

1   Fault in the alternator or charging circuit (Chapter 5).
2   Alternator drivebelt defective or not properly adjusted (Chapter 1).

18 Ignition light fails to come on when key is turned on

1   Instrument cluster warning light bulb defective (Chapter 12).
2   Alternator faulty (Chapter 5).
3   Fault in the instrument cluster printed circuit, dashboard wiring or bulb holder (Chapter 12).

Fuel system

19 Excessive fuel consumption

1   Dirty or clogged air filter element (Chapter 1).
2   Emissions system not functioning properly (Chapter 6).
3   Fault in the fuel or electrical systems (Chapters 4 and 5).
4   Fuel injection system internal parts excessively worn or damaged (Chapter 4).
5   Low tire pressure or incorrect tire size (Chapter 1).

20 Fuel leakage and/or fuel odor

1   Leak in a fuel feed or vent line (Chapter 4).
2   Tank overfilled. Fill only to automatic shut-off.
3   Evaporative emissions system canister clogged (Chapter 6).
4   Vapor leaks from system lines (Chapter 4).
5   Fuel injection system internal parts excessively worn or out of adjustment (Chapter 4).

Cooling system

21 Overheating

1   Insufficient coolant in the system (Chapter 1).
2   Water pump drivebelt defective or not adjusted properly (Chapter 1).
3   Radiator core blocked or radiator grille dirty and restricted (see Chapter 3).
4   Thermostat faulty (Chapter 3).
5   Fan blades broken or cracked (Chapter 3).
6   Radiator cap not maintaining proper pressure. Have the cap pressure tested by gas station or repair shop.

22 Overcooling

1   Thermostat faulty (Chapter 3).
2   Inaccurate temperature gauge (Chapter 12).

23 External coolant leakage

1   Deteriorated or damaged hoses or loose clamps. Replace hoses and/or tighten the clamps at the hose connections (Chapter 1).
2   Water pump seals defective. If this is the case, water will drip from the weep hole in the water pump body (Chapter 3).
3   Leakage from the radiator core or side tank(s). This will require the

radiator to be professionally repaired (see Chapter 3 for removal procedures).

4   Engine drain plug leaking (Chapter 1) or water jacket core plugs leaking (see Chapter 2).

24   Internal coolant leakage

Note: *Internal coolant leaks can usually be detected by examining the oil. Check the dipstick and inside of the valve cover for water deposits and an oil consistency like that of a milkshake.*

1   Leaking cylinder head gasket. Have the cooling system pressure tested.

2   Cracked cylinder bore or cylinder head. Dismantle the engine and inspect (Chapter 2).

25   Coolant loss

1   Too much coolant in the system (Chapter 1).
2   Coolant boiling away due to overheating (see Section 15).
3   External or internal leakage (see Sections 23 and 24).
4   Faulty radiator cap. Have the cap pressure tested.

26   Poor coolant circulation

1   Inoperative water pump. A quick test is to pinch the top radiator hose closed with your hand while the engine is idling, then let it loose. You should feel the surge of coolant if the pump is working properly (see Chapter 1).

2   Restriction in the cooling system. Drain, flush and refill the system (Chapter 1). If necessary, remove the radiator (Chapter 3) and have it reverse flushed.

3   Water pump drivebelt defective or not adjusted properly (Chapter 1).

4   Thermostat sticking (Chapter 3).

Clutch

27   Fails to release (pedal pressed to the floor - shift lever does not move freely in and out of Reverse)

1   Leak in the clutch hydraulic system. Check the master cylinder, slave cylinder and lines (Chapter 8).

2   Clutch plate warped or damaged (Chapter 8).

28   Clutch slips (engine speed increases with no increase in vehicle speed)

1   Clutch plate oil soaked or lining worn. Remove clutch (Chapter 8) and inspect.

2   Clutch plate not seated. It may take 30 or 40 normal starts for a new one to seat.

3   Pressure plate worn (Chapter 8).

29   Grabbing (chattering) as clutch is engaged

1   Oil on clutch plate lining. Remove (Chapter 8) and inspect. Correct any leakage source.

2   Worn or loose engine or transmission mounts. These units move slightly when the clutch is released. Inspect the mounts and bolts (Chapter 2).

3   Worn splines on clutch plate hub. Remove the clutch components (Chapter 8) and inspect.

4   Warped pressure plate or flywheel. Remove the clutch components and inspect.

30   Squeal or rumble with clutch fully engaged (pedal released)

1   Release bearing binding on transmission bearing retainer. Remove clutch components (Chapter 8) and check bearing. Remove any burrs or nicks; clean and relubricate bearing retainer before installing.

31   Squeal or rumble with clutch fully disengaged (pedal depressed)

1   Worn, defective or broken release bearing (Chapter 8).
2   Worn or broken pressure plate springs (or diaphragm fingers) (Chapter 8).

32   Clutch pedal stays on floor when disengaged

1   Linkage or release bearing binding. Inspect the linkage or remove the clutch components as necessary.

2   Make sure proper pedal stop (bumper) is installed.

Manual transmission

Note: *All the following references are in Chapter 7, unless noted.*

33   Noisy in Neutral with engine running

1   Input shaft bearing worn.
2   Damaged main drive gear bearing.
3   Worn countershaft bearings.
4   Worn or damaged countershaft endplay shims.

34   Noisy in all gears

1   Any of the above causes, and/or:
2   Insufficient lubricant (see the checking procedures in Chapter 1).

35   Noisy in one particular gear

1   Worn, damaged or chipped gear teeth for that particular gear.
2   Worn or damaged synchronizer for that particular gear.

36   Slips out of high gear

1   Transmission loose on clutch housing.
2   Dirt between the transmission case and engine or misalignment of the transmission (Chapter 7).

37   Difficulty in engaging gears

1   Clutch not releasing completely (see clutch adjustment in Chapter 1).

2   Loose, damaged or out-of-adjustment shift linkage. Make a thorough inspection, replacing parts as necessary (Chapter 7).

38   Oil leakage

1   Excessive amount of lubricant in the transmission (see Chapter 1 for correct checking procedures). Drain lubricant as required.
2   Driveaxle oil seal or speedometer oil seal in need of replacement (Chapter 7).

Automatic transmission

Note: *Due to the complexity of the automatic transmission, it's difficult for the home mechanic to properly diagnose and service this component. For problems other than the following, the vehicle should be taken to a dealer service department or a transmission shop.*

39   General shift mechanism problems

1   Chapter 7 deals with checking and adjusting the shift linkage on automatic transmissions. Common problems which may be attributed to poorly adjusted linkage are:
   a) *Engine starting in gears other than Park or Neutral.*
   b) *Indicator on shifter pointing to a gear other than the one actually being selected.*
   c) *Vehicle moves when in Park.*
2   Refer to Chapter 7 to adjust the linkage.

40   Transmission will not downshift with accelerator pedal pressed to the floor

Kickdown cable misadjusted.

41   Transmission slips, shifts rough, is noisy or has no drive in forward or reverse gears

1   There are many probable causes for the above problems, but the home mechanic should be concerned with only one possibility - fluid level.
2   Before taking the vehicle to a repair shop, check the level and condition of the fluid as described in Chapter 1. Correct fluid level as necessary or change the fluid and filter if needed. If the problem persists, have a professional diagnose the probable cause.
3   If the transmission shifts late and the shifts are harsh, suspect a faulty vacuum diaphragm (Chapter 7).

42   Fluid leakage

1   Automatic transmission fluid is a deep red color. Fluid leaks should not be confused with engine oil, which can easily be blown by air flow to the transmission.
2   To pinpoint a leak, first remove all built-up dirt and grime from around the transmission. Degreasing agents and/or steam cleaning will achieve this. With the underside clean, drive the vehicle at low speeds so air flow will not blow the leak far from its source. Raise the vehicle and determine where the leak is coming from. Common areas of leakage are:
   a) *Pan: Tighten the mounting bolts and/or replace the pan gasket as necessary (see Chapter 7).*
   b) *Filler pipe: Replace the rubber seal where the pipe enters the transmission case.*
   c) *Transmission oil lines: Tighten the connectors where the lines enter the transmission case and/or replace the lines.*
   d) *Vent pipe: Transmission overfilled and/or water in fluid (see checking procedures, Chapter 1).*
   e) *Speedometer connector: Replace the O-ring where the speedometer cable enters the transmission case (Chapter 7).*

Transfer case

43   Transfer case is difficult to shift into the desired range

1   Speed may be too great to permit engagement. Stop the vehicle and shift into the desired range.
2   Shift linkage loose, bent or binding. Check the linkage for damage or wear and replace or lubricate as necessary (Chapter 7).
3   If the vehicle has been driven on a paved surface for some time, the driveline torque can make shifting difficult. Stop and shift into two-wheel drive on paved or hard surfaces.
4   Insufficient or incorrect grade of lubricant. Drain and refill the transfer case with the specified lubricant. (Chapter 1).
5   Worn or damaged internal components. Disassembly and overhaul of the transfer case may be necessary (Chapter 7).

44   Transfer case noisy in all gears

Insufficient or incorrect grade of lubricant. Drain and refill (Chapter 1).

45   Noisy or jumps out of four-wheel drive Low range

1   Transfer case not fully engaged. Stop the vehicle, shift into Neutral and then engage 4L.
2   Shift linkage loose, worn or binding. Tighten, repair or lubricate linkage as necessary.
3   Shift fork cracked, inserts worn or fork binding on the rail. Disassemble and repair as necessary (Chapter 7).

46   Lubricant leaks from the vent or output shaft seals

1   Transfer case is overfilled. Drain to the proper level (Chapter 1).
2   Vent is clogged or jammed closed. Clear or replace the vent.
3   Output shaft seal incorrectly installed or damaged. Replace the seal and check contact surfaces for nicks and scoring.

Driveshaft

47   Oil leak at seal end of driveshaft

Defective transmission or transfer case oil seal. See Chapter 7 for replacement procedures. While this is done, check the splined yoke for burrs or a rough condition which may be damaging the seal. Burrs can be removed with crocus cloth or a fine whetstone.

48   Knock or clunk when the transmission is under initial load (just after transmission is put into gear)

1   Loose or disconnected rear suspension components. Check all mounting bolts, nuts and bushings (see Chapter 10).
2   Loose driveshaft bolts. Inspect all bolts and nuts and tighten them to the specified torque.
3   Worn or damaged universal joint bearings. Check for wear (see Chapter 8).

49 Metallic grinding sound consistent with vehicle speed.

Pronounced wear in the universal joint bearings. Check as described in Chapter 8.

50 Vibration

Note: *Before assuming that the driveshaft is at fault, make sure the tires are perfectly balanced and perform the following test.*
1   Install a tachometer inside the vehicle to monitor engine speed as the vehicle is driven. Drive the vehicle and note the engine speed at which the vibration (roughness) is most pronounced. Now shift the transmission to a different gear and bring the engine speed to the same point.
2   If the vibration occurs at the same engine speed (rpm) regardless of which gear the transmission is in, the driveshaft is NOT at fault since the driveshaft speed varies.
3   If the vibration decreases or is eliminated when the transmission is in a different gear at the same engine speed, refer to the following probable causes.
4   Bent or dented driveshaft. Inspect and replace as necessary (see Chapter 8).
5   Undercoating or built-up dirt, etc. on the driveshaft. Clean the shaft thoroughly and recheck.
6   Worn universal joint bearings. Remove and inspect (see Chapter 8).
7   Driveshaft and/or companion flange out of balance. Check for missing weights on the shaft. Remove the driveshaft (see Chapter 8) and reinstall 180-degrees from original position, then retest. Have the driveshaft professionally balanced if the problem persists.

Axles

51 Noise

1   Road noise. No corrective procedures available.
2   Tire noise. Inspect tires and check tire pressures (Chapter 1).
3   Rear wheel bearings loose, worn or damaged (Chapter 8).

52 Vibration

See probable causes under Driveshaft. Proceed under the guidelines listed for the driveshaft. If the problem persists, check the rear wheel bearings by raising the rear of the vehicle and spinning the rear wheels by hand. Listen for evidence of rough (noisy) bearings. Remove and inspect (see Chapter 8).

53 Oil leakage

1   Pinion seal damaged (see Chapter 8).
2   Axleshaft oil seals damaged (see Chapter 8).
3   Differential inspection cover leaking. Tighten the bolts or replace the gasket as required (see Chapters 1 and 8).

Brakes

Note: *Before assuming that a brake problem exists, make sure that the tires are in good condition and inflated properly (see Chapter 1), that the front end alignment is correct and that the vehicle is not loaded with weight in an unequal manner.*

54 Vehicle pulls to one side during braking

1   Defective, damaged or oil contaminated disc brake pads or shoes on one side. Inspect as described in Chapter 9.
2   Excessive wear of brake shoe or pad material or drum/disc on one side. Inspect and correct as necessary.
3   Loose or disconnected front suspension components. Inspect and tighten all bolts to the specified torque (Chapter 10).
4   Defective drum brake or caliper assembly. Remove the drum or caliper and inspect for a stuck piston or other damage (Chapter 9).
5   Inadequate lubrication of front brake caliper slide rails. Remove caliper and lubricate slide rails (Chapter 9).

55 Noise (high-pitched squeal with the brakes applied)

1   Disc brake pads worn out. The noise comes from the wear sensor rubbing against the disc (does not apply to all vehicles) or the actual pad
backing plate itself if the material is completely worn away. Replace the pads with new ones immediately (Chapter 9). If the pad material has worn completely away, the brake discs should be inspected for damage as described in Chapter 9.
2   Missing or damaged brake pad insulators (disc brakes). Replace pad insulators (see Chapter 9).
3   Linings contaminated with dirt or grease. Replace pads or shoes.
4   Incorrect linings. Replace with correct linings.

56 Excessive brake pedal travel

1   Partial brake system failure. Inspect the entire system (Chapter 9) and correct as required.
2   Insufficient fluid in the master cylinder. Check (Chapter 1), add fluid and bleed the system if necessary (Chapter 9).
3   Rear brakes not adjusting properly. Make a series of starts and stops while the vehicle is in Reverse. If this does not correct the situation, remove the drums and inspect the self-adjusters (Chapter 9).

57 Brake pedal feels spongy when depressed

1   Air in the hydraulic lines. Bleed the brake system (Chapter 9).
2   Faulty flexible hoses. Inspect all system hoses and lines. Replace parts as necessary.
3   Master cylinder mounting bolts/nuts loose.
4   Master cylinder defective (Chapter 9).

58 Excessive effort required to stop vehicle

1   Power brake booster not operating properly (Chapter 9).
2   Excessively worn linings or pads. Inspect and replace if necessary (Chapter 9).
3   One or more caliper pistons or wheel cylinders seized or sticking. Inspect and rebuild as required (Chapter 9).
4   Brake linings or pads contaminated with oil or grease. Inspect and replace as required (Chapter 9).
5   New pads or shoes installed and not yet seated. It will take a while for the new material to seat against the drum (or rotor).

59 Pedal travels to the floor with little resistance

1   Little or no fluid in the master cylinder reservoir caused by leaking wheel cylinder(s), leaking caliper piston(s), loose, damaged or disconnected brake lines. Inspect the entire system and correct as necessary.
2   Worn master cylinder seals (Chapter 9).

60 Brake pedal pulsates during brake application

1   Caliper improperly installed. Remove and inspect (Chapter 9).
2   Disc or drum defective. Remove (Chapter 9) and check for excessive lateral runout and parallelism. Have the disc or drum resurfaced or replace it with a new one.

Suspension and steering systems

61 Vehicle pulls to one side

1   Tire pressures uneven (Chapter 1).
2   Defective tire (Chapter 1).
3   Excessive wear in suspension or steering components (Chapter 10).
4   Front end in need of alignment.
5   Front brakes dragging. Inspect the brakes as described in Chapter 9.

62 Shimmy, shake or vibration

1   Tire or wheel out-of-balance or out-of-round. Have professionally balanced.
2   Loose, worn or out-of-adjustment rear wheel bearings (Chapter 1).
3   Shock absorbers and/or suspension components worn or damaged (Chapter 10).

63 Excessive pitching and/or rolling around corners or during braking

1   Defective shock absorbers. Replace as a set (Chapter 10).
2   Broken or weak springs and/or suspension components. Inspect as described in Chapter 10.

64 Excessively stiff steering

1   Lack of fluid in power steering fluid reservoir (Chapter 1).
2   Incorrect tire pressures (Chapter 1).
3   Lack of lubrication at steering joints (see Chapter 1).
4   Front end out of alignment.
5   Lack of power assistance (see Section 62).

65 Excessive play in steering

1   Loose front wheel bearings (Chapters 1 and 10).
2   Excessive wear in suspension or steering components (Chapter 10).
3   Steering gearbox damaged or out of adjustment (Chapter 10).

66 Lack of power assistance

1   Steering pump drivebelt faulty or not adjusted properly (Chapter 1).
2   Fluid level low (Chapter 1).
3   Hoses or lines restricted. Inspect and replace parts as necessary.
4   Air in power steering system. Bleed the system (Chapter 10).

67 Excessive tire wear (not specific to one area)

1   Incorrect tire pressures (Chapter 1).
2   Tires out-of-balance. Have professionally balanced.
3   Wheels damaged. Inspect and replace as necessary.
4   Suspension or steering components excessively worn (Chapter 10).

68 Excessive tire wear on outside edge

1   Inflation pressures incorrect (Chapter 1).
2   Excessive speed in turns.
3   Front end alignment incorrect (excessive toe-in). Have professionally aligned.
4   Suspension arm bent or twisted (Chapter 10).

69 Excessive tire wear on inside edge

1   Inflation pressures incorrect (Chapter 1).
2   Front end alignment incorrect (toe-out). Have professionally aligned.
3   Loose or damaged steering components (Chapter 10).

70 Tire tread worn in one place

1   Tires out-of-balance.
2   Damaged or buckled wheel. Inspect and replace if necessary.
3   Defective tire (Chapter 1).

Chapter 1
Tune-up and routine maintenance

Contents

	Section
Air filter replacement	19
Automatic transmission fluid check/change	8
Automatic transmission shift linkage lubrication	14
Battery check, maintenance and charging	12
Brake system check	26
Chassis lubrication	15
CHECK ENGINE light on	See Chapter 6
Cooling system check	23
Cooling system servicing (draining, flushing and refilling)	30
Differential lubricant level check and change	17
Drivebelt check, adjustment and replacement	11
Driveshaft and driveaxle yoke lubrication (4WD models)	31
Engine oil and filter change	6
Exhaust system check	24
Fluid level checks	3
Front hub lock, spindle bearing and wheel bearing maintenance (1991 through 1994 4WD models)	28

	Section
Front wheel bearing check, repack and adjustment (2WD models)	27
Fuel filter replacement	22
Fuel system check	21
Introduction	1
Manual transmission lubricant level check and change	16
Owner safety checks	5
Positive Crankcase Ventilation (PCV) valve check and replacement	20
Power steering fluid level check	7
Spark plug and wire check and replacement	13
Steering and suspension check	25
Tire and tire pressure checks	4
Tire rotation	9
Transfer case lubricant level check and change	18
Tune-up general information	2
Underhood hose check and replacement	10
Windshield wiper blade check and replacement	29

Specifications

Recommended lubricants and fluids

Engine oil
Type ... API grade SG
Viscosity ... See accompanying chart

OIL VISCOSITY CHART

Power steering fluid type ... Type F automatic transmission fluid
Brake fluid type ... DOT 3 heavy duty brake fluid
Automatic transmission fluid type ... MERCON automatic transmission fluid
Manual transmission lubricant type
  Mitsubishi transmission ... SAE 80W EP gear lubricant
  Mazda transmission ... MERCON automatic transmission fluid
Transfer case lubricant type ... MERCON automatic transmission fluid
Coolant type ... 50/50 mixture of ethylene glycol-based antifreeze and water
Front wheel bearing grease ... NLGI No. 2 lithium base grease containing polyethylene and molybdenum disulfide

Recommended lubricants and fluids

Automatic locking front hubs.. NLGI No. 2 lithium base grease containing polyethylene and molybdenum disulfide

Front spindle and thrust bearings (4WD)................................ NLGI No. 2 lithium base grease containing polyethylene and molybdenum disulfide

Caliper slide rail grease .... Disc brake caliper slide rail grease
Chassis grease .... NLGI No. 2 lithium base grease containing polyethylene and molybdenum disulfide

Differential lubricant* .... API GL-5 SAE 90 Hypoid gear lubricant

Traction-Lok axles add 4 oz. of friction modifier (Ford part no. C8AZ-19B546-A, or equivalent) when oil is changed.

Capacities (approximate)

Engine oil
   With filter change .... 5 qts
   Without filter change .... 4 qts
Cooling system*
   Without air conditioning .... 7.8 qts
   With air conditioning .... 8.6 qts
Transfer case (Warner 13-54) .... 2.5 pints
Front axle differential .... 3.5 pints
Rear axle differential
   1991 through 1994 .... 5.3 pints
   1995 and later .... 5.5 pints
Automatic transmission (drain and refill)
   2WD.. 2.7 qts
   4WD.. 3.0 qts
Manual transmission
   Mazda.. 5.6 pints
   Mitsubishi .... 4.8 pints

Capacity may vary +/- 15% due to equipment variations. Most service refills take only 80% of listed capacity because some coolant remains in the engine.

ENGINE CYLINDERS

IGNITION COIL

FIRING ORDER:
1-4-2-5-3-6

FRONT OF VEHICLE

4.0L ENGINE

Brakes

Disc brake pad thickness (minimum)..................................... 1/8-inch
Drum brake shoe lining thickness (minimum)......................... 1/16-inch above rivet heads

Ignition system

Spark plug
   Type
      1991 through 1993... Motorcraft AWSF-42C or equivalent
      1994 on... Motorcraft AWSF-42PP
   Gap.. 0.054-inch
Ignition timing .... Not adjustable

Fuel system

Idle speed .... Not adjustable

Torque specifications   **Ft-lbs** (unless otherwise indicated)

Wheel lug nuts 100
Front hub adjusting nut (1994 and earlier 2WD models)
   Step 1 .... 17 to 25
   Step 2 .... Back off 1/2-turn
   Step 3 .... 18 to 20 in-lbs
Front hub adjusting nut (1994 and earlier 4WD models)
   Manual locking hubs
      Step 1.. 35
      Step 2.. Back off 1/4-turn
      Step 3.. 16 in-lbs
      Step 4 (outer locknut)... 150
      Endplay.. 0 to 0.003 inch
      Hub turning torque (maximum)................................ 25 in-lbs
   Automatic locking hubs
      Step 1.. 35
      Step 2.. Back-off 1/4-turn
      Step 3.. 16 in-lbs
      Endplay.. 0 to 0.003 inch
      Hub turning torque (maximum)................................ 25 in-lbs
Automatic transmission pan bolts... 96 to 120 in-lbs

Typical engine compartment layout

1	Relays	5	Ignition wires	9	Windshield washer reservoir
2	Air cleaner housing	6	Engine oil dipstick	10	Radiator cap
3	Engine oil filler cap	7	Brake master cylinder reservoir	11	Upper radiator hose
4	Ignition coil pack	8	Engine coolant reservoir	12	Battery

Engine compartment underside components (1991 through 1994 4WD models)

1	Radiator drain	3	Front differential check/fill plug	5	Front driveaxle
2	Lower radiator hose	4	Transmission pan	6	Grease fittings

Typical rear underside components

1	Rear shock absorber	3	Exhaust hanger	5	Rear differential
2	Leaf spring assembly	4	Muffler		

Ford Explorer/Mazda Navajo Maintenance schedule

The following maintenance intervals are based on the assumption that the vehicle owner will be doing the maintenance or service work, as opposed to having a dealer service department do the work. Although the time/mileage intervals are loosely based on factory recommendations, most have been shortened to ensure, for example, that such items as lubricants and fluids are checked/changed at intervals that promote maximum engine/driveline service life. Also, subject to the preference of the individual owner interested in keeping his or her vehicle in peak condition at all times, and with the vehicle's ultimate resale in mind, many of the maintenance procedures may be performed more often than recommended in the following schedule. We encourage such owner initiative.

Because off-road use necessitates more frequent maintenance, a separate schedule is included for vehicles used off road.

When the vehicle is new it should be serviced initially by a factory authorized dealer service department to protect the factory warranty. In many cases the initial maintenance check is done at no cost to the owner (check with your dealer service department for more information).

Every 250 miles or weekly, whichever comes first

Check the engine oil level (Section 3)
Check the engine coolant level (Section 3)
Check the brake fluid level (Section 3)
Check the clutch fluid level (Section 3)
Check the windshield washer fluid level (Section 3)
Check the tires and tire pressures (Section 4)
Perform owner safety checks (Section 5)

Every 3,000 miles or 3 months, whichever comes first

All items listed above, plus . . .
Change the engine oil and oil filter (Section 6)
Check the power steering fluid level (Section 7)
Check the automatic transmission fluid level (Section 8)
Rotate the tires (Section 9)

Every 6,000 miles or 6 months, whichever comes first

All the items listed above, plus . . .
Inspect/replace the underhood hoses (Section 10)
Check/adjust the drivebelt (Section 11)
Check/service the battery (Section 12)
Check/regap the spark plugs (Section 13)
Inspect/lubricate automatic transmission shift linkage (Section 14)
Lubricate the chassis (Section 15)

Every 12,000 miles or 12 months, whichever comes first

All items listed above, plus . . .
Check/replenish the manual transmission lubricant (Section 16)
Check the differential lubricant level (Section 17)
Check the transfer case lubricant level (Section 18)
Replace the air filter (Section 19)
Check/replace the PCV valve (Section 20)
Check the fuel system (Section 21)
Check/replace the fuel filter (Section 22)
Inspect the cooling system (Section 23)
Inspect the exhaust system (Section 24)
Inspect the steering and suspension components (Section 25)
Inspect the brakes and lubricate caliper friction points (Section 26)
Check/lubricate the front wheel bearings (2WD) (Section 27)
Check hub lock, spindle and front wheel bearing lubrication (4WD) (Section 28)
Inspect/replace the windshield wiper blades (Section 29)

Every 24,000 miles or 24 months, whichever comes first

All items listed above plus . . .
Change the automatic transmission fluid and filter (Section 8)
Service the cooling system (drain, flush and refill) (Section 30)
Check/replace the spark plug wires (Section 13)

Every 30,000 miles or 30 months, whichever comes first

Change the differential lubricant (Section 17)
Change the transfer case lubricant (Section 18)
Lubricate the driveshaft slip yokes (Section 31)
Lubricate right front driveaxle slip yoke (4WD) (Section 31)

Every 60,000 miles or 60 months, whichever comes first

Replace platinum type spark plugs (Section 13)

Off-road operation

If the vehicle is driven off road, perform the following maintenance items every 1,000 miles. If the vehicle is driven in mud or water, perform the items daily.
Inspect the brakes (Section 26)
Inspect the front wheel bearings (2WD models) (Section 27)
Check hub lock, spindle and front wheel bearing lubrication (4WD) (Section 28)
Inspect exhaust system (Section 24)
Lubricate driveshaft slip yoke and U-joints (if equipped with grease fittings) (Sections 15 and 31)

3.4a Remove the dipstick, wipe it clean, then reinsert it all the way before withdrawing it for an accurate oil level check

3.4b The oil level should appear between the ADD 1 QT and SAFE marks; don't overfill the crankcase

3.6 To add oil, remove the filler cap from the valve cover

1   Introduction

This Chapter is designed to help the home mechanic maintain his or her vehicle with the goals of maximum performance, economy, safety and reliability in mind.

Included is a master maintenance schedule (page 3), followed by procedures dealing specifically with each item on the schedule. Visual checks, adjustments, component replacement and other helpful items are included. Refer to the accompanying illustrations of the engine compartment and the underside of the vehicle for the locations of various components. Servicing the vehicle, in accordance with the mileage/time maintenance schedule and the step-by-step procedures will result in a planned maintenance program that should produce a long and reliable service life. Keep in mind that it is a comprehensive plan, so maintaining some items but not others at specified intervals will not produce the same results.

As you service the vehicle, you will discover that many of the procedures can - and should - be grouped together because of the nature of the particular procedure you're performing or because of the close proximity of two otherwise unrelated components to one another.

For example, if the vehicle is raised for chassis lubrication, you should inspect the exhaust, suspension, steering and fuel systems while you're under the vehicle. When you're rotating the tires, it makes good sense to check the brakes since the wheels are already removed. Finally, let's suppose you have to borrow or rent a torque wrench. Even if you only need it to tighten the spark plugs, you might as well check the torque of as many critical fasteners as time allows.

The first step in this maintenance program is to prepare yourself before the actual work begins. Read through all the procedures you're planning to do, then gather up all the parts and tools needed. If it looks like you might run into problems during a particular job, seek advice from a mechanic or an experienced do-it-yourselfer.

2   Tune-up general information

The term tune-up is used in this manual to represent a combination of individual operations rather than one specific procedure.

If, from the time the vehicle is new, the routine maintenance schedule is followed closely and frequent checks are made of fluid levels and high wear items, as suggested throughout this manual, the engine will be kept in relatively good running condition and the need for additional work will be minimized.

More likely than not, however, there will be times when the engine is running poorly due to a lack of regular maintenance. This is even more likely if a used vehicle, which has not received regular and frequent maintenance checks, is purchased. In such cases, an engine tune-up will be needed outside of the regular maintenance intervals.

The first step in any tune-up or diagnostic procedure to help correct a poor running engine is a cylinder compression check. A compression check (see Chapter 2, Part B) will help determine the condition of internal engine components and should be used as a guide for tune-up and repair procedures. If, for instance, a compression check indicates serious internal engine wear, a conventional tune-up will not improve the performance of the engine and would be a waste of time and money. Because of its importance, the compression check should be done by someone with the right equipment and the knowledge to use it properly.

The following procedures are those most often needed to bring as generally poor running engine back into a proper state of tune.

Minor tune-up

Clean, inspect and test the battery (see Section 12)
Check all engine related fluids (see Section 3)
Check and adjust the drivebelts (see Section 11)
Replace the spark plugs (see Section 13)
Inspect the spark plug wires (see Section 13)
Check the PCV valve (see Section 20)
Check the air filter (see Section 19)
Check the cooling system (see Section 23)
Check all underhood hoses (see Section 10)

Major tune-up

All items listed under minor tune-up, plus . . .
Check the ignition system (see Chapter 5)
Check the charging system (see Chapter 5)
Check the fuel system (see Chapter 4)
Replace the spark plug wires (see Section 13)

3   Fluid level checks

Refer to illustrations 3.4a, 3.4b, 3.6, 3.9, 3.15, 3.16, 3.23a, 3.23b and 3.23c

Note: *The following are fluid level checks to be done on a 250 mile or weekly basis. Additional fluid level checks can be found in specific maintenance procedures which follow. Regardless of intervals, be alert to fluid leaks under the vehicle which would indicate a fault to be corrected immediately.*

1   Fluids are an essential part of the lubrication, cooling, brake and windshield washer systems. Because the fluids gradually become depleted and/or contaminated during normal operation of the vehicle, they must be periodically replenished. See *Recommended lubricants and fluids* at the beginning of this Chapter before adding fluid to any of the following components. **Note:** *The vehicle must be on level ground when fluid levels are checked.*

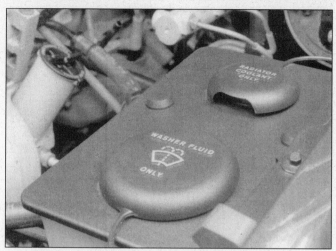

3.9 The coolant recovery reservoir is combined with the windshield washer fluid reservoir (there are separate compartments for the two fluids)

3.15 Clutch fluid is contained in a separate reservoir next to the brake master cylinder - clean the rubber cap before returning it to the reservoir

Engine oil

2   Engine oil is checked with a dipstick, which is located on the side of the engine (refer to the underhood illustration at the front of this Chapter for dipstick location). The dipstick extends through a metal tube down into the oil pan.

3   The engine oil should be checked before the vehicle has been driven, or about 15 minutes after the engine has been shut off. If the oil is checked immediately after driving the vehicle, some of the oil will remain in the upper part of the engine, resulting in an inaccurate reading on the dipstick.

4   Pull the dipstick out of the tube **(see illustration)** and wipe all of the oil away from the end with a clean rag or paper towel. Insert the clean dipstick all the way back into the tube and pull it out again. Note the oil at the end of the dipstick. At its highest point, the oil should be above the ADD mark, in the SAFE range **(see illustration)**.

5   It takes one quart of oil to raise the level from the ADD mark to the FULL or MAX mark on the dipstick. Do not allow the level to drop below the ADD mark or oil starvation may cause engine damage. Conversely, overfilling the engine (adding oil above the FULL or MAX mark) may cause oil fouled spark plugs, oil leaks or oil seal failures.

6   To add oil, remove the filler cap located on the valve cover **(see illustration)**. After adding oil, wait a few minutes to allow the level to stabilize, then pull the dipstick out and check the level again. Add more oil if required. Install the filler cap and tighten it by hand only.

7   Checking the oil level is an important preventive maintenance step. A consistently low oil level indicates oil leakage through damaged seals, defective gaskets or past worn rings or valve guides. The condition of the oil should also be noted. If the oil looks milky in color or has water droplets in it, the cylinder head gasket(s) may be blown or the head(s) or block may be cracked. The engine should be repaired immediately. Whenever you check the oil level, slide your thumb and index finger up the dipstick before wiping off the oil. If you see small dirt or metal particles clinging to the dipstick, the oil should be changed (see Section 6).

Engine coolant

Warning: *Do not allow antifreeze to come in contact with your skin or painted surfaces of the vehicle. Rinse off spills immediately with plenty of water. Antifreeze is highly toxic if ingested. Never leave antifreeze lying around in an open container or in puddles on the floor; children and pets are attracted by it's sweet smell and may drink it. Check with local authorities about disposing of used antifreeze. Many communities have collection centers which will see that antifreeze is disposed of safely.*

8   All vehicles covered by this manual are equipped with a pressurized coolant recovery system. A white plastic coolant reservoir

located at the front of the engine compartment is connected by a hose to the radiator filler neck. If the engine overheats, coolant escapes through a valve in the radiator cap and travels through the hose into the reservoir. As the engine cools, the coolant is automatically drawn back into the cooling system to maintain the correct level.

9   The coolant level in the reservoir **(see illustration)** should be checked regularly. **Warning:** *Do not remove the radiator cap to check the coolant level when the engine is warm!* The level in the reservoir varies with the temperature of the engine. When the engine is cold, the coolant level should be at or slightly above the COLD FULL mark on the reservoir. Once the engine has warmed up, the level should be at or near the FULL HOT mark. If it isn't, allow the engine to cool, then remove the cap from the reservoir and add a 50/50 mixture of ethylene glycol based antifreeze and water. Don't use rust inhibitors or additives.

10   Drive the vehicle and recheck the coolant level. If only a small amount of coolant is required to bring the system up to the proper level, water can be used. However, repeated additions of water will dilute the antifreeze and water solution. In order to maintain the proper ratio of antifreeze and water, always top up the coolant level with the correct mixture. An empty plastic milk jug or bleach bottle makes an excellent container for mixing coolant.

11   If the coolant level drops consistently, there may be a leak in the system. Inspect the radiator, hoses, filler cap, drain plugs and water pump (see Section 23). If no leaks are noted, have the radiator cap pressure tested by a service station.

12   If you have to remove the radiator cap, wait until the engine has cooled completely, then wrap a thick cloth around the cap and turn it to the first stop. If coolant or steam escapes, let the engine cool down longer, then remove the cap.

13   Check the condition of the coolant as well. It should be relatively clear. If it's brown or rust colored, the system should be drained, flushed and refilled. Even if the coolant appears to be normal, the corrosion inhibitors wear out, so it must be replaced at the specified intervals.

Brake and clutch fluid

Warning: *Brake fluid can harm your eyes and damage painted surfaces, so use extreme caution when handling or pouring it. Do not use brake fluid that has been standing open or is more than one year old. Brake fluid absorbs moisture from the air, which can cause a dangerous loss of brake effectiveness. Use only the specified type of brake fluid. Mixing different types (such as DOT 3 or 4 and DOT 5) can cause brake failure.*

14   The brake master cylinder is mounted at the left (driver's side) rear corner of the engine compartment. The clutch fluid reservoir (used on models with manual transmissions) is mounted adjacent to it.

15   To check the clutch fluid level, observe the level through the

3.16 Check the brake fluid level by looking through the translucent plastic reservoir

3.23a To check the rear windshield washer fluid level, lift the tabs and remove the access panel in the luggage compartment . . .

3.23b . . . to expose the reservoir

3.23c To fill the reservoir, lift the cap on the quarter panel above the tail light and pour washer fluid into the hole

translucent reservoir. The level should be at or near the step molded into the reservoir. If the level is low, remove the reservoir cap to add the specified fluid **(see illustration)**.

16   The brake fluid level is checked by looking through the plastic reservoir mounted on the master cylinder. The fluid level should be between the MAX and MIN lines on the reservoir **(see illustration)**. If the fluid level is low, wipe the top of the reservoir and the cap with a clean rag to prevent contamination of the system as the cap is unscrewed. Top up with the recommended brake fluid, but do not overfill.

17   While the reservoir cap is off, check the master cylinder reservoir for contamination. If rust deposits, dirt particles or water droplets are present, the system should be drained and refilled by a dealer service department or repair shop.

18   After filling the reservoir to the proper level, make sure the cap is seated to prevent fluid leakage and/or contamination.

19   The fluid level in the master cylinder will drop slightly as the disc brake pads wear. A very low level may indicate worn brake pads. Check for wear (see Section 26).

20   If the brake fluid level drops consistently, check the entire system for leaks immediately. Examine all brake lines, hoses and connections, along with the calipers, wheel cylinders and master cylinder (see Section 26).

21   When checking the fluid level, if you discover one or both reservoirs empty or nearly empty, the brake or clutch hydraulic system should be checked for leaks and bled (see Chapters 8 and 9).

Windshield washer fluid

22   Fluid for the front windshield washer system is stored in a plastic reservoir in the engine compartment. The front windshield washer

4.2 Use a tire tread depth indicator to monitor tire wear - they are available at auto parts stores and service stations and cost very little

reservoir is combined with the coolant reservoir (there are separate compartments for the two different fluids) **(see illustration 3.9)**.

23   Fluid for the rear windshield washer system is stored in a reservoir in the left quarter panel. To check the fluid level, remove the access cover from the left side of the luggage compartment **(see illustrations)**. To add fluid, locate the filler tube cap on the quarter panel above the tail light **(see illustration)**. Open the cap, add fluid and close the cap.

24   In milder climates, plain water can be used in the reservoir, but it

Condition	Probable cause	Corrective action	Condition	Probable cause	Corrective action
Shoulder wear	• Underinflation (both sides wear) • Incorrect wheel camber (one side wear) • Hard cornering • Lack of rotation	• Measure and adjust pressure. • Repair or replace axle and suspension parts. • Reduce speed. • Rotate tires.	Feathered edge / Toe wear	• Incorrect toe	• Adjust toe-in.
Center wear	• Overinflation • Lack of rotation	• Measure and adjust pressure. • Rotate tires.	Uneven wear	• Incorrect camber or caster • Malfunctioning suspension • Unbalanced wheel • Out-of-round brake drum • Lack of rotation	• Repair or replace axle and suspension parts. • Repair or replace suspension parts. • Balance or replace. • Turn or replace. • Rotate tires.

4.3 This chart will help you determine the condition of the tires, the probable cause(s) of abnormal wear and the corrective action necessary

4.4a If a tire loses air on a steady basis, check the valve core first to make sure it's snug (special inexpensive wrenches are commonly available at auto parts stores)

4.4b If the valve core is tight, raise the corner of the vehicle with the low tire and spray a soapy water solution onto the tread as the tire is turned slowly - leaks will cause small bubbles to appear

should be kept no more than 2/3 full to allow for expansion if the water freezes. In colder climates, use windshield washer system antifreeze, available at any auto parts store, to lower the freezing point of the fluid. This comes in concentrated or pre-mixed form. If you purchase concentrated antifreeze, mix the antifreeze with water in accordance with the manufacturer's directions on the container. **Caution:** *Do not use cooling system antifreeze - it will damage the vehicle's paint.*

4 Tire and tire pressure checks

Refer to illustrations 4.2, 4.3, 4.4a, 4.4b and 4.8

1   Periodic inspection of the tires may save you the inconvenience of being stranded with a flat tire. It can also provide you with vital information regarding possible problems in the steering and suspension systems before major damage occurs.

2   Tires are equipped with 1/2-inch wide bands that will appear when tread depth reaches 1/16-inch, but they don't appear until the tires are worn out. Tread wear can be monitored with a simple, inexpensive device known as a tread depth indicator **(see illustration).**

3   Note any abnormal tire wear **(see illustration).** Tread pattern irregularities such as cupping, flat spots and more wear on one side that the other are indications of front end alignment and/or balance problems. If any of these conditions are noted, take the vehicle to a tire shop or service station to correct the problem.

4   Look closely for cuts, punctures and embedded nails or tacks. Sometimes a tire will hold air pressure for a short time or leak down very slowly after a nail has embedded itself in the tread. If a slow leak persists, check the valve stem core to make sure it is tight **(see illustration).** Examine the tread for an object that may have embedded itself in the tire or for a "plug" that may have begun to leak (radial tire punctures are repaired with a plug that is installed in the puncture). If a puncture is suspected, it can be easily verified by spraying a solution of soapy water onto the puncture **(see illustration).** The soapy solution will bubble if there is a leak. Unless the puncture is unusually large, a tire shop or service station can usually repair the tire.

5   Carefully inspect the inner sidewall of each tire for evidence of brake fluid leakage. If you see any, inspect the brakes immediately.

6   Correct air pressure adds miles to the lifespan of the tires, improves mileage and enhances overall ride quality. Tire pressure cannot be accurately estimated by looking at a tire, especially if it's a radial. A tire pressure gauge is essential. Keep an accurate gauge in the glove compartment. The pressure gauges attached to the nozzles of air hoses at gas stations are often inaccurate.

7   Always check tire pressure when the tires are cold. Cold, in this case, means the vehicle has not been driven over a mile in the three hours preceding a tire pressure check. A pressure rise of four to eight pounds is not uncommon once the tires are warm.

8   Unscrew the valve cap protruding from the wheel or hubcap and push the gauge firmly onto the valve stem **(see illustration)**. Note the reading on the gauge and compare the figure to the recommended tire pressure shown in your owner's manual or on the tire placard on the passenger side door or door pillar. Be sure to reinstall the valve cap to keep dirt and moisture out of the valve stem mechanism. Check all four tires and, if necessary, add enough air to bring them to the recommended pressure.

9   Don't forget to keep the spare tire inflated to the specified pressure (refer to your owner's manual or the placard attached to the door pillar). Note that the pressure recommended for temporary (mini) spare tires is higher than for the tires on the vehicle.

5   Owner safety checks

1   Most of these checks can be easily performed while the vehicle is being driven, simply by paying attention to the specified items. The checks are intended to make the vehicle owner aware of potential safety problems before they occur.

2   Check the seat belts for wear, fraying and cuts. Make sure the buckles latch securely and that the automatic retractors function correctly. Do not try to repair seat belts; always replace them if any problems are found.

3   Make sure the ignition key cannot be removed when the transmission is in any gear other than Park (automatic) or Reverse (manual). Make sure the steering column locks when the key is removed from the ignition. It may be necessary to rotate the steering wheel slightly to lock the steering column.

4   Check the parking brake. The easiest way to do this is to park on a steep hill, set the parking brake and note whether it keeps the vehicle from rolling.

5   If equipped with an automatic transmission, also check the Park mechanism. Place the transmission in Park, release the parking brake and note whether the transmission holds the vehicle from rolling. If the vehicle rolls while in Park, the transmission should be taken to a qualified shop for repairs.

6   If equipped with an automatic transmission, note whether the shift indicator shows the proper gear. If it doesn't, refer to Chapter 7 for linkage adjustment procedures.

7   If equipped with an automatic transmission, make sure the vehicle starts only in Park or Neutral. If it starts in any other gear, refer to Chapter 7 for switch adjustment procedures.

8   If equipped with a manual transmission, the starter should operate only when the clutch pedal is pressed to the floor. If the starter operates when it shouldn't, refer to Chapter 8 for clutch/starter interlock switch service.

9   Make sure the brakes do not pull to one side while stopping. The brake pedal should feel firm, but excessive effort should not be required to stop the vehicle. If the pedal sinks too low, if you have to pump it more than once to get a firm pedal, or if pedal effort is too high, refer to Chapter 9 for repair procedures. A squealing sound from the front brakes may be caused by the pad wear indicators. Refer to Chapter 9 for pad replacement procedures.

10   Rearview mirrors should be clean and undamaged. They should hold their position when adjusted.

11   Sun visors should hold their position when adjusted. They should remain securely out of the way when lifted off the windshield.

4.8 To extend the life of the tires, check the air pressure at least once a week with an accurate gauge (don't forget the spare!)

12   Make sure the defroster blows heated air onto the windshield. If it doesn't, refer to Chapter 3 for heating system service.

13   The horn should sound with a clearly audible tone every time it is operated. If not, refer to Chapter 12.

14   Make sure the windows are clean and undamaged.

15   Turn on the lights, then walk around the car and make sure they work. Check headlights in both the high beam and low beam positions. Check the turn indicators for one side of the vehicle, then for the other side. If possible, have an assistant watch the brake lights while you push the pedal. If no assistant is available, the brake lights can be checked by backing up to a wall or garage door, then pressing the pedal. There should be three distinct patches of red light when the brake pedal is pressed.

16   Make sure locks operate smoothly when the key is turned. Lubricate locks if necessary with Ford Lock Lubricant or an equivalent product. Make sure all latches hold securely.

6   Engine oil and filter change

Refer to illustrations 6.2, 6.7 and 6.16

1   Frequent oil changes are the most important preventive maintenance procedures that can be done by the home mechanic. As engine oil ages, it becomes diluted and contaminated, which leads to premature engine wear.

2   Make sure that you have all the necessary tools before you begin this procedure **(see illustration)**. You should also have plenty of rags or newspapers handy for mopping up oil spills.

3   Start the engine and allow it to reach normal operating temperature - oil and sludge will flow more easily when warm. If new oil, a filter or tools are needed, use the vehicle to go get them and warm up the engine oil at the same time. Park on a level surface and shut off the engine when it's warmed up. Remove the oil filler cap from the valve cover.

4   Access to the oil drain plug and filter will be improved if the vehicle can be lifted on a hoist, driven onto ramps or supported by jackstands. **Warning:** *DO NOT work under a vehicle supported only by a bumper, hydraulic or scissors-type jack - always use jackstands!*

5   Raise the vehicle and support it on jackstands. Make sure it is safely supported!

6   If you haven't changed the oil on this vehicle before, get under it and locate the drain plug and the oil filter. The exhaust components will be hot as you work, so note how they are routed to avoid touching them.

7   Being careful not to touch the hot exhaust components, position a drain pan under the plug in the bottom of the engine. Clean the area around the plug, then remove the plug **(see illustration)**. It's a good idea to wear an old glove while unscrewing the plug the final few turns to avoid being scalded by hot oil. It will also help to hold the drain plug against the threads as you unscrew it, then pull it away from the drain hole suddenly. This will place your arm out of the way of the hot oil, as

6.2 These tools are required when changing the engine oil and filter

1 **Drain pan** - *It should be fairly shallow in depth, but wide to prevent spills*

2 **Rubber gloves** - *When removing the drain plug and filter, you will get oil on your hands (the gloves will prevent burns)*

3 **Breaker bar** - *Sometimes the oil drain plug is tight and a long breaker bar is needed to loosen it*

4 **Socket** - *To be used with the breaker bar or a ratchet (must be the correct size to fit the drain plug - six-point preferred)*

5 **Filter wrench** - *This is a metal band-type wrench, which requires clearance around the filter to be effective*

6 **Filter wrench** - *This type fits on the bottom of the filter and can be turned with a ratchet or breaker bar (different size wrenches are available for different types of filters)*

6.7 Remove the oil pan drain plug with a box-end wrench or socket - an open-end or adjustable wrench shouldn't be used, since it may round off the corners of the drain plug

6.16 Lubricate the oil filter gasket with clean engine oil before installing the filter on the engine

well as reducing the chances of dropping the drain plug into the drain pan.

8   It may be necessary to move the drain pan slightly as oil flow slows to a trickle. Inspect the old oil for the presence of metal particles.

9   After all the oil has drained, wipe off the drain plug with a clean rag. Any small metal particles clinging to the plug would immediately contaminate the new oil.

10   Reinstall the plug and tighten it securely, but don't strip the threads.

11   Move the drain pan into position under the oil filter.

12   Loosen the oil filter by turning it counterclockwise with a filter wrench. Any standard filter wrench will work.

13   Sometimes the oil filter is screwed on so tightly that it can't be loosened. If it is, punch a metal bar or long screwdriver directly through it, as close to the engine as possible, and use it as a T-bar to turn the filter. Be prepared for oil to spurt out of the canister as it's punctured.

14   Once the filter is loose, use your hands to unscrew it from the block. Just as the filter is detached from the block, immediately tilt the open end up to prevent oil inside the filter from spilling out.

15   Using a clean rag, wipe off the mounting surface on the block. Also, make sure that none of the old gasket remains stuck to the mounting surface. It can be removed with a scraper if necessary.

16   Compare the old filter with the new one to make sure they are the same type. Smear some engine oil on the rubber gasket of the new

filter and screw it into place **(see illustration)**. Overtightening the filter will damage the gasket, so don't use a filter wrench. Most filter manufacturers recommend tightening the filter by hand only. Normally, they should be tightened 3/4-turn after the gasket contacts the block, but be sure to follow the directions on the filter or container.

17   Remove all tools and materials from under the vehicle, being careful not to spill the oil in the drain pan, then lower the vehicle.

18   Add new oil to the engine through the oil filler cap in the rocker arm cover. Use a funnel to prevent oil from spilling onto the top of the engine. Pour four quarts of fresh oil into the engine. Wait a few minutes to allow the oil to drain into the pan, then check the level on the dipstick (see Section 3 if necessary). If the oil level is in the SAFE range, install the filler cap.

19   Start the engine and run it for about a minute. While the engine is running, look under the vehicle and check for leaks at the oil pan drain plug and around the oil filter. If either one is leaking, stop the engine and tighten the plug or filter slightly.

20   Wait a few minutes, then recheck the level on the dipstick. Add oil as necessary to bring the level into the SAFE range.

21   During the first few trips after an oil change, make it a point to check frequently for leaks and proper oil level.

22   The old oil drained from the engine cannot be reused in its present state and should be discarded. Oil reclamation centers, auto repair shops and gas stations will normally accept the oil, which can be recycled. After the oil has cooled, it can be drained into a container (plastic jugs, bottles, milk cartons, etc.) for transport to a disposal site.

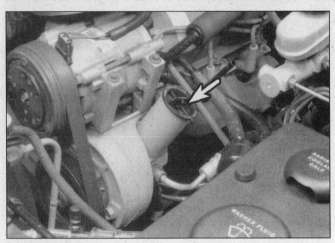

7.2 Location of the power steering pump (arrow)

7.5 Check the power steering fluid level with the engine at normal operating temperature - fluid should not go above the Full Hot mark

7   Power steering fluid level check

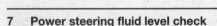

Refer to illustrations 7.2 and 7.5

1   Check the power steering fluid level periodically to avoid steering system problems, such as damage to the pump. **Caution:** *DO NOT hold the steering wheel against either stop (extreme left or right turn) for more than five seconds. If you do, the power steering pump could be damaged.*

2   The power steering pump, located at the left front corner of the engine on all models, is equipped with a twist-off cap with an integral fluid level dipstick **(see illustration)**.

3   Park the vehicle on level ground and apply the parking brake.

4   Run the engine until it has reached normal operating temperature. With the engine at idle, turn the steering wheel back-and-forth several times to get any air out of the steering system. Shut the engine off, remove the cap by turning it counterclockwise, wipe the dipstick clean and reinstall the cap (make sure it is seated).

5   Remove the cap again and note the fluid level. It must be between the two lines designating the FULL HOT range **(see illustration)** (be sure to use the proper temperature range on the dipstick when checking the fluid level - the FULL COLD lines on the reverse side of the dipstick are only usable when the engine is cold).

6   Add small amounts of fluid until the level is correct. **Caution:** *Do not overfill the pump. If too much fluid is added, remove the excess with a clean syringe or suction pump.*

7   Check the power steering hoses and connections for leaks and wear (see Section 10).

8   Check the condition and tension of the serpentine drivebelt (see Section 11).

8   Automatic transmission fluid check/change

Fluid level check

Refer to illustrations 8.5 and 8.6

Caution: *The use of transmission fluid other than the type listed in this Chapter's Specifications could result in transmission malfunctions or failure.*

1   The automatic transmission fluid should be carefully maintained. Low fluid level can lead to slipping or loss of drive, while overfilling can cause foaming and loss of fluid. Either condition can cause transmission damage.

2   Since transmission fluid expands as it heats up, the fluid level should only be checked when the transmission is warm (at normal operating temperature). If the vehicle has just been driven over 20 miles (32 km), the transmission can be considered warm. **Caution:** *If the vehicle has just been driven for a long time at high speed or in city traffic,*

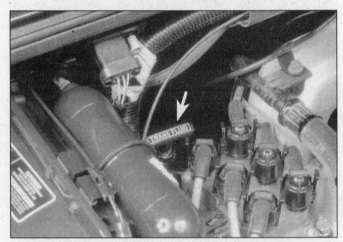

8.5 Make sure the area around the transmission dipstick is clean (arrow), then pull it out of the tube - fluid level is checked with the engine idling

in hot weather, or if it has been pulling a trailer, an accurate fluid level reading cannot be obtained. Allow the transmission to cool down for about 30 minutes. You can also check the transmission fluid level when the transmission is cold. If the vehicle has not been driven for over five hours and the fluid is about room temperature (70 to 95-degrees F), the transmission is cold. However, the fluid level is normally checked with the transmission warm to ensure accurate results.

3   Immediately after driving the vehicle, park it on a level surface, set the parking brake and start the engine. While the engine is idling, depress the brake pedal and move the selector lever through all the gear ranges, beginning and ending in Park.

4   Locate the automatic transmission dipstick tube in the engine compartment (see the illustration at the front of this chapter for dipstick location).

5   With the engine still idling, pull the dipstick away from the tube **(see illustration)**, wipe it off with a clean rag, push it all the way back into the tube and withdraw it again, then note the fluid level.

6   If the transmission is cold, the level should be in the room temperature range on the dipstick (between the two circles); if it's warm, the fluid level should be in the operating temperature range (between the two lines) **(see illustration)**. If the level is low, add the specified automatic transmission fluid through the dipstick tube - use a clean funnel to prevent spills.

7   Add just enough of the recommended fluid to fill the transmission to the proper level. It takes about one pint to raise the level from the

8.6 Follow the directions stamped on the transmission dipstick to get an accurate reading

8.14 Remove the bolts around the front and sides of the transmission . . .

8.16 . . . and let the pan hang down so the fluid can drain

8.19 Once the pan is removed the filter is accessible

low mark to the high mark when the fluid is hot, so add the fluid a little at a time and keep checking the level until it's correct.

8   The condition of the fluid should also be checked along with the level. If the fluid is black or a dark reddish-brown color, or if it smells burned, it should be changed (see below). If you are in doubt about its condition, purchase some new fluid and compare the two for color and smell.

Fluid and filter change

Refer to illustrations 8.14, 8.16 and 8.19

9   At the specified intervals, the transmission fluid should be drained and replaced. Since the fluid will remain hot long after driving, perform this procedure only after the engine has cooled down completely.

10   Before beginning work, purchase the specified transmission fluid (see *Recommended lubricants and fluids* at the front of this Chapter), a new filter and gasket. Never reuse the old filter or gasket!

11   Other tools necessary for this job include jackstands to support the vehicle in a raised position, a drain pan capable of holding at least eight quarts, newspapers and clean rags.

12   Raise the vehicle and support it securely on jackstands. DO NOT crawl under the vehicle when it is supported only by a jack! Place the drain pan beneath the transmission.

13   Pry loose the two clips that secure the catalytic converter heat shield to the edge of the transmission fluid pan. **Note:** *It's impossible to remove the forward clip completely from the pan. For this reason, the pan must be removed toward the driver's side of the vehicle.*

14   With the drain pan in place, remove the mounting bolts from the

front and sides of the transmission fluid pan **(see illustration)**.

15   Loosen the rear pan bolts approximately four turns.

16   Carefully pry the transmission pan loose with a screwdriver. Let the pan hang down so the fluid can drain **(see illustration)**. Don't damage the pan or transmission gasket surfaces or leaks could develop.

17   Remove the remaining bolts, pan and gasket. Carefully clean the gasket surface of the transmission to remove all traces of the old gasket and sealant.

18   Drain the fluid from the transmission pan, clean it with solvent and dry it with compressed air.

19   Remove the filter from the mount inside the transmission **(see illustration)**.

20   Install a new filter and gasket. Tighten the mounting bolt securely.

21   Make sure the gasket surface on the transmission pan is clean, then install a new gasket. Put the pan in place against the transmission and install the bolts. Working around the pan, tighten each bolt a little at a time until the torque listed in this Chapter's Specifications is reached. Don't overtighten the bolts!

22   Lower the vehicle and add automatic transmission fluid through the filler tube. **Caution:** *Refer to the Specifications at the front of this chapter for the correct amount and type of transmission fluid. Use of the wrong type or the wrong amount can cause transmission damage.*

23   With the transmission in Park and the parking brake set, run the engine at a fast idle, but don't race it.

24   Move the gear selector through each range and back to Park. Check the fluid level. Add fluid if needed to reach the correct level.

25   Check under the vehicle for leaks after the first few trips.

FOUR TIRE ROTATION

FRONT OF VEHICLE

LF   RF

LR   RR

FIVE TIRE ROTATION

LF   RF

LR   RR

CONVENTIONAL SPARE TIRE

SIDE-TO-SIDE ROTATION

LF   RF

LR   RR

9.2 Tire rotation diagram

FITTING AND CAP ASSEMBLY

1/4 INCH PORT FOR AUTO. TRANS.

1/4 INCH PORT FOR CCD

1/4 INCH PORT FOR VACUUM RESERVOIR/EGR

1/4 INCH PORT FOR AIR CLEANER (BI-METALLIC)

3/8 INCH PORT FOR POWER BRAKES

1/4 INCH PORT FOR FUEL PRESSURE REGULATOR — NO CAP

5/15 INCH PORT FOR SPEED CONTROL

FRONT OF VEHICLE

10.6 Several vacuum hoses are connected to one fitting on the intake manifold

9   Tire rotation

Refer to illustration 9.2

1   The tires should be rotated at the specified intervals and whenever uneven wear is noticed. Since the vehicle will be raised and the tires checked anyway, check the brakes also (see Section 26). **Note:** *Even if you don't rotate the tires, at least check the lug nut tightness.*

2   It is recommended that the tires be rotated in a specific pattern **(see illustration)**.

3   Refer to the information in Jacking and towing at the front of this manual for the proper procedure to follow when raising the vehicle and changing a tire. If the brakes must be checked, don't apply the parking brake as stated.

4   The vehicle must be raised on a hoist or supported on jackstands to get all four tires off the ground. Make sure the vehicle is safely supported!

5   After the rotation procedure is finished, check and adjust the tire pressures as necessary and be sure to check the lug nut tightness.

10   Underhood hose check and replacement

Caution: *Replacement of air conditioning hoses must be left to a dealer service department or air conditioning shop that has the equipment to depressurize the system safely. Never disconnect air conditioning hoses or components until the system has been depressurized.*

General

1   High temperatures under the hood can cause deterioration of the rubber and plastic hoses used for engine, accessory and emission systems operation. Periodic inspection should be made for cracks, loose clamps, material hardening and leaks.

2   Information specific to the cooling system can be found in Section 23.

3   Most (but not all) hoses are secured to the fitting with clamps. Where clamps are used, check to be sure they haven't lost their tension, allowing the hose to leak. If clamps aren't used, make sure the hose has not expanded and/or hardened where it slips over the fitting, allowing it to leak.

PCV system hose

4   To reduce hydrocarbon emissions, crankcase blow-by gas is vented through the PCV valve to the intake manifold via a rubber hose on most models. The blow-by gases mix with incoming air in the intake manifold before being burned in the combustion chambers.

5   Check the PCV hose for cracks, leaks and other damage. Disconnect it from the valve cover and the intake manifold and check the inside for obstructions. If it's clogged, clean it out with solvent.

Vacuum hoses

Refer to illustration 10.6

6   It's quite common for vacuum hoses, especially those in the emissions system, to be color coded or identified by colored stripes molded into them. Various systems require hoses with different wall thicknesses, collapse resistance and temperature resistance. When replacing hoses, be sure the new ones are made of the same material. A number of hoses connect to a vacuum fitting on the intake manifold **(see illustration)**.

7   Often the only effective way to check a hose is to remove it completely from the vehicle. If more than one hose is removed, be sure to label the hoses and fittings to ensure correct installation.

8   When checking vacuum hoses, be sure to include any plastic T-fittings in the check. Inspect the fittings for cracks and the hose where it fits over each fitting for distortion, which could cause leakage.

9   A small piece of vacuum hose can be used as a stethoscope to detect vacuum leaks. Hold one end of the hose to your ear and probe around vacuum hoses and fittings, listening for the "hissing" sound

4.0L ENGINE BELT INSTALLATION

BELT DRIVE

VIEW A

MAIN VIEW

WITH AIR CONDITIONING
VIEW A

AIR CONDITIONING
ALTERNATOR
TENSIONER
POWER STEERING
IDLER
WATER PUMP
CRANKSHAFT

WITHOUT AIR CONDITIONING
VIEW A

11.2a Serpentine belt routing details

11.2b The belt's pathway is illustrated on a decal on the radiator support

characteristic of a vacuum leak. **Warning:** *When probing with the vacuum hose stethoscope, be careful not to come into contact with moving engine components such as the drivebelt, cooling fan, etc.*

Fuel hoses

Warning: *There are certain precautions which must be taken when servicing or inspecting fuel system components. Work in a well ventilated area and do not allow open flames (cigarettes, appliance pilot lights, etc.) or bare light bulbs near the work area. Mop up any spills immediately and do not store fuel-soaked rags where they could ignite.*
10   The fuel lines are usually under pressure, so if any fuel lines are to be disconnected be prepared to catch spilled fuel. **Warning:** *If your vehicle is equipped with fuel injection, you must relieve the fuel system pressure before servicing the fuel lines.* Refer to Chapter 4 for the fuel system pressure relief procedure.
11   Check all rubber fuel lines for deterioration and chafing. Check especially for cracks in areas where the hose bends and just before fittings, such as where a hose attaches to the fuel pump, fuel filter and carburetor or fuel injection system.
12   High quality fuel line, usually identified by the word *Fluoroelastomer* printed on the hose, should be used for fuel line replacement. Never, under any circumstances, use unreinforced vacuum line, clear plastic tubing or water hose for fuel lines.
13   Spring-type clamps are commonly used on fuel lines. These clamps often lose their tension over a period of time, and can be

"sprung" during removal. Replace all spring-type clamps with screw clamps whenever a hose is replaced.

Metal lines

14   Sections of metal line are often used for fuel line between the fuel pump and carburetor or fuel injection system. Check carefully to make sure the line isn't bent, crimped or cracked.
15   If a section of metal fuel line must be replaced, use seamless steel tubing only, since copper and aluminum tubing do not have the strength necessary to withstand the vibration caused by the engine.
16   Check the metal brake lines where they enter the master cylinder and brake proportioning unit (if used) for cracks in the lines and loose fittings. Any sign of brake fluid leakage calls for an immediate thorough inspection of the brake system.

Nylon fuel lines

17   Nylon fuel lines are used at several points in fuel injection systems. These lines require special materials and methods for repair. Refer to Chapter 4 for details.

Power steering hoses

18   Check the power steering hoses for leaks, loose connections and worn clamps. Tighten loose connections. Worn clamps or leaky hoses should be replaced.

11   Drivebelt check, adjustment and replacement

Refer to illustrations 11.2a, 11.2b, 11.3, 11.5a, 11.5b and 11.6
1   The accessory drivebelt is located at the front of the engine. The single serpentine belt drives the water pump, alternator, power steering pump and air conditioning compressor. The condition and tension of the drivebelt is critical to the operation of the engine and accessories. Excessive tension causes bearing wear, while insufficient tension produces slippage, noise, component vibration and belt failure. Because of their composition and the high stress to which they are subjected, drivebelts stretch and continue to deteriorate as they get older. As a result, they must be periodically checked. The serpentine belt has an automatic tensioner and requires no adjustment for the life of the belt.

Check

2   These vehicles use a single V-ribbed belt to drive all of the accessories. This is known as a "serpentine" belt because of the winding path it follows between various drive, accessory and idler pulleys **(see illustrations)**.

CRACKS RUNNING ACROSS "V" PORTIONS OF BELT

ACCEPTABLE

1/2"

MISSING TWO OR MORE ADJACENT RIBS 1/2" OR LONGER

CRACKS RUNNING PARALLEL TO "V" PORTIONS OF BELT

UNACCEPTABLE

11.3 Small cracks in the underside of a V-ribbed belt are acceptable - lengthwise cracks, or missing pieces that cause the belt to make noise, are cause for replacement

11.5a To loosen the belt, place a wrench on the tensioner nut . . .

11.5b . . . and rotate it against the spring force in the direction shown to lift the tensioner off the belt

3   With the engine off, open the hood and locate the drivebelt at the front of the engine. With a flashlight, check the belt for separation of the rubber plies from each side of the core, a severed core, separation of the ribs from the rubber and torn or worn ribs. Also check for fraying and glazing, which gives the belt a shiny appearance. Cracks in the rib side of V-ribbed belts are acceptable, as are small chunks missing from the ribs. If a V-ribbed belt has lost chunks bigger than 1/2-inch (13 mm) from two adjacent ribs, or if the missing chunks cause belt noise, the belt should be replaced **(see illustration)**. Both sides of the belt should be inspected, which means you'll have to twist it to check the underside. Use your fingers to feel the belt where you can't see it. If any of the above conditions are evident, replace the belt as described below.

Adjustment

4   Tension is set by an automatic tensioner. Manual adjustment is not required.

Replacement

5   To replace a serpentine belt, rotate the tensioner counter-

BELT

PULLEY

CORRECT

NOTE: ENSURE CORRECT SEATING ON ALL PULLEYS. ONE REVOLUTION OF THE ENGINE WITH AN IN-CORRECTLY SEATED BELT MAY SNAP TENSILE MEMBERS IN THE BELT

BELT

PULLEY

INCORRECT

11.6 V-ribbed drivebelts should be centered on the pulleys, not offset

clockwise to lift it off the belt **(see illustrations)**. Slip the belt off the pulleys.
6   Hold the tensioner in the released position. Install a new belt and make sure it is routed correctly **(see illustrations 11.2a and 11.2b)**. Be sure the ribs of the new belt engage the pulley ribs correctly **(see illustration)**. Release the tensioner.

12.4 Remove the cell caps to check the water level in the battery - if the level is low, add distilled water only

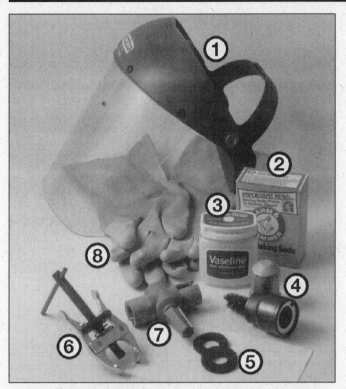

12.1 Tools and materials required for battery maintenance

1 **Face shield/safety goggles** - *When removing corrosion with a brush, the acidic particles can easily fly up into your eyes*
2 **Baking soda** - *A solution of baking soda and water can be used to neutralize corrosion*
3 **Petroleum jelly** - *A layer of this on the battery posts will help prevent corrosion*
4 **Battery post/cable cleaner** - *This wire brush cleaning tool will remove all traces of corrosion from the battery posts and cable clamps*
5 **Treated felt washers** - *Placing one of these on each post, directly under the cable clamps, will help prevent corrosion*
6 **Puller** - *Sometimes the cable clamps are very difficult to pull off the posts, even after the nut/bolt has been completely loosened. This tool pulls the clamp straight up and off the post without damage.*
7 **Battery post/cable cleaner** - *Here is another cleaning tool which is a slightly different version of number 4 above, but it does the same thing*
8 **Rubber gloves** - *Another safety item to consider when servicing the battery; remember that's acid inside the battery!*

12 Battery check, maintenance and charging

Check and maintenance

Refer to illustrations 12.1, 12.4, 12.8a, 12.8b, 12.8c and 12.8d
Warning: *Certain precautions must be followed when checking and servicing the battery. Hydrogen gas, which is highly flammable, is always present in the battery cells, so keep lighted tobacco and all other flames and sparks away from it. The electrolyte inside the battery is actually dilute sulfuric acid, which will cause injury if splashed on your skin or in your eyes. It will also ruin clothes and painted surfaces. When removing the battery cables, always detach the negative cable first and hook it up last!*

1 Battery maintenance is an important procedure which will help ensure that you are not stranded because of a dead battery. Several tools are required for this procedure **(see illustration)**.
2 Before servicing the battery, always turn the engine and all

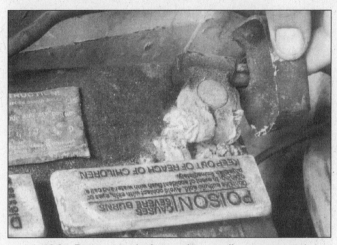

12.8a Battery terminal corrosion usually appears as light, fluffy powder

accessories off and disconnect the cable from the negative terminal of the battery.
3 A sealed (sometimes called maintenance free) battery is standard equipment. The cell caps cannot be removed, no electrolyte checks are required and water cannot be added to the cells. However, if an aftermarket battery has been installed and it is a type that requires regular maintenance, the following procedures can be used.
4 Check the electrolyte level in each of the battery cells **(see illustration)**. It must be above the plates. There's usually a split-ring indicator in each cell to indicate the correct level. If the level is low, add distilled water only, then install the cell caps. **Caution:** *Overfilling the cells may cause electrolyte to spill over during periods of heavy charging, causing corrosion and damage to nearby components.*
5 If the positive terminal and cable clamp on your vehicle's battery is equipped with a rubber protector, make sure that it's not torn or damaged. It should completely cover the terminal.
6 The external condition of the battery should be checked periodically. Look for damage such as a cracked case.
7 Check the tightness of the battery cable clamps to ensure good electrical connections and inspect the entire length of each cable, looking for cracked or abraded insulation and frayed conductors.
8 If corrosion (visible as white, fluffy deposits) is evident, remove the cables from the terminals, clean them with a battery brush and reinstall them **(see illustrations)**. Corrosion can be kept to a minimum by installing specially treated washers available at auto parts stores or by applying a layer of petroleum jelly or grease to the terminals and cable clamps after they are assembled.

12.8b Removing the cable from a battery post with a wrench - sometimes a special battery pliers is required for this procedure if corrosion has caused deterioration of the nut hex (always remove the ground cable first and hook it up last!)

12.8c Regardless of the type of tool used on the battery posts, a clean, shiny surface should be the result

12.8d When cleaning the cable clamps, all corrosion must be removed (the inside of the clamp is tapered to match the taper on the post, so don't remove too much material)

9   Make sure that the battery carrier is in good condition and that the hold-down clamp bolt is tight. If the battery is removed (see Chapter 5 for the removal and installation procedure), make sure that no parts remain in the bottom of the carrier when it's reinstalled. When reinstalling the hold-down clamp, don't overtighten the bolt.

10   Corrosion on the carrier, battery case and surrounding areas can be removed with a solution of water and baking soda. Apply the mixture with a small brush, let it work, then rinse it off with plenty of clean water.

11   Any metal parts of the vehicle damaged by corrosion should be coated with a zinc-based primer, then painted.

12   Additional information on the battery and jump starting can be found in Chapter 5 and the front of this manual.

13.2 Tools required for changing spark plugs

1   Spark plug socket - This will have special padding inside to protect the spark plug's porcelain insulator

2   Torque wrench - Although not mandatory, using this tool is the best way to ensure the plugs are tightened properly

3   Ratchet - Standard hand tool to fit the spark plug socket

4   Extension - Depending on model and accessories, you may need special extensions and universal joints to reach one or more of the plugs

5   Spark plug gap gauge - This gauge for checking the gap comes in a variety of styles. Make sure the gap for your engine is included.

Charging

13   Remove all of the cell caps (if equipped) and cover the holes with a clean cloth to prevent spattering electrolyte. Disconnect the negative battery cable and hook the battery charger leads to the battery posts (positive to positive, negative to negative), then plug in the charger. Make sure it is set at 12-volts if it has a selector switch.

14   If you're using a charger with a rate higher than two amps, check the battery regularly during charging to make sure it doesn't overheat. If you're using a trickle charger, you can safely let the battery charge overnight after you've checked it regularly for the first couple of hours.

15   If the battery has removable cell caps, measure the specific gravity with a hydrometer every hour during the last few hours of the charging cycle. Hydrometers are available inexpensively from auto parts stores - follow the instructions that come with the hydrometer. Consider the battery charged when there's no change in the specific gravity reading for two hours and the electrolyte in the cells is gassing (bubbling) freely. The specific gravity reading from each cell should be very close to the others. If not, the battery probably has a bad cell(s).

16   Some batteries with sealed tops have built-in hydrometers on the top that indicate the state of charge by the color displayed in the hydrometer window. Normally, a bright-colored hydrometer indicates a full charge and a dark hydrometer indicates the battery still needs charging. Check the battery manufacturer's instructions to be sure you know what the colors mean.

17   If the battery has a sealed top and no built-in hydrometer, you can hook up a digital voltmeter across the battery terminals to check the charge. A fully charged battery should read 12.6-volts or higher.

18   Further information on the battery and jump starting can be found in Chapter 5 and at the front of this manual.

13 Spark plug and wire check and replacement

Spark plugs

Refer to illustrations 13.2, 13.5a, 13.5b, 13.6, and 13.10.

1   The spark plugs are located on the sides of the engine.

2   In most cases, the tools necessary for spark plug replacement include a spark plug socket which fits into a ratchet (spark plug sockets are padded inside to prevent damage to the porcelain insulators on the new plugs and to hold the plugs in the socket during removal and installation), various extensions and a gap gauge to check and adjust the gaps on the new plugs **(see illustration)**. A special plug wire removal tool is available for separating the wire boots from the spark plugs, but it isn't absolutely necessary. A torque wrench should

13.5a Spark plug manufacturers recommend using a wire type gauge when checking the gap - if the wire does not slide between the electrodes with a slight drag, adjustment is required

13.5b To change the gap, bend the *side* electrode only, as indicated by the arrows, and be very careful not to crack or chip the porcelain insulator surrounding the center electrode

13.6 When removing the spark plug wires, pull only on the boot and twist it back-and-forth

1

be used to tighten the new plugs.

3   The best approach when replacing the spark plugs is to purchase the new ones in advance, adjust them to the proper gap and replace the plugs one at a time. When buying the new spark plugs, be sure to obtain the correct type for your particular engine. This information can be found on the *Vehicle Emission Control Information* label located under the hood, in the vehicle owner's manual and in this Chapter's Specifications. If differences exist between the plug specified on the emissions label and in the owner's manual, assume the emissions label is correct. **Note:** *These vehicles use platinum-tipped spark plugs. The factory-specified replacement interval for this type of plug is 60,000 miles.*

4   Allow the engine to cool completely before attempting to remove any of the plugs. While you are waiting for the engine to cool, check the new plugs for defects and adjust the gaps.

5   The gap is checked by inserting the proper thickness gauge between the electrodes at the tip of the plug **(see illustration)**. The gap between the plugs should be the same as the one specified on the *Vehicle Emissions Control Information* label or in this Chapter's Specifications. The gauge wire should just slide between the electrodes with a slight amount of drag. If the gap is incorrect, use the adjuster on the gauge body to bend the curved side electrode slightly until the specified gap is obtained **(see illustration)**. If the side electrode is not exactly over the center electrode, bend it with the adjuster until it is. Check for cracks in the porcelain insulator (if any are found, the plug should not be used).

6   With the engine cool, remove the spark plug wire from one spark plug. Pull only on the boot at the end of the wire - do not pull on the wire. A plug wire removal tool should be used if available **(see illustration)**.

7   If compressed air is available, use it to blow any dirt or foreign material away from the spark plug hole. A common bicycle pump will also work. The idea here is to eliminate the possibility of debris falling into the cylinder as the spark plug is removed.

8   Place the spark plug socket over the plug and remove it from the engine by turning in a counterclockwise direction.

9   Compare the spark plug to those shown in the spark plug condition chart on the inside of the back cover to get an indication of the general running condition of the engine.

10   Thread one of the new plugs into the hole until you can no longer turn it with your fingers, then tighten it with a torque wrench (if available) or the ratchet. It's a good idea to slip a short length of rubber hose over the end of the plug to use as a tool to thread it into place, particularly if the cylinder head is made of aluminum **(see illustration)**. The hose will grip the plug well enough to turn it, but will start to slip if the plug begins to cross-thread in the hole - this will prevent damaged

13.10 A length of 3/8-inch ID rubber hose will save time and prevent damaged threads when installing the spark plugs

threads and the accompanying repair costs.

11   Before pushing the spark plug wire onto the end of the plug, inspect it following the procedures outlined below.

12   Attach the plug wire to the new spark plug, again using a twisting motion on the boot until it is seated on the spark plug.

13   Repeat the procedure for the remaining spark plugs, replacing them one at a time to prevent mixing up the spark plug wires.

Spark plug wires

Refer to illustration 13.16

Note: *Every time a spark plug wire is detached from a spark plug, the distributor cap or the coil, silicone dielectric compound (a white grease available at auto parts stores) should be applied to the inside of each boot before reconnection. Use a small standard screwdriver to coat the entire inside surface of each boot with a thin layer of the compound.*

14   The spark plug wires should be checked and, if necessary, replaced at the same time new spark plugs are installed.

15   The easiest way to identify bad wires is to make a visual check while the engine is running. In a dark, well-ventilated garage, start the engine and look at each plug wire. Be careful not to come into contact with any moving engine parts. If there is a break in the wire, you will see arcing or a small spark at the damaged area. If arcing is noticed, make a note to obtain new wires.

16   The spark plug wires should be inspected one at a time, beginning with the spark plug for the number one cylinder (the cylinder closest to the radiator on the right bank), to prevent confusion. Clearly label each original plug wire with a piece of tape marked with the

correct number. The plug wires must be reinstalled in the correct order to ensure proper engine operation **(see illustration)**.

17   Disconnect the spark plug wire from the first spark plug. A removal tool can be used **(see illustration 13.6)**, or you can grab the wire boot, twist it slightly and pull the wire free. Do not pull on the wire itself, only on the rubber boot.

18   Push the wire and boot back onto the end of the spark plug. It should fit snugly. If it doesn't, detach the wire and boot once more and use a pair of pliers to carefully crimp the metal connector inside the wire boot until it does.

19   Using a clean rag, wipe the entire length of the wire to remove built-up dirt and grease.

20   Once the wire is clean, check for burns, cracks and other damage. Do not bend the wire sharply or you might break the conductor.

21   Disconnect the wire from the distributor or ignition coil pack. Again, pull only on the rubber boot. Check for corrosion and a tight fit. Replace the wire in the distributor or coil pack.

22   Inspect each of the remaining spark plug wires, making sure that each one is securely fastened at the distributor or coil pack and spark plug when the check is complete.

23   If new spark plug wires are required, purchase a set for your specific engine model. Pre-cut wire sets with the boots already installed are available. Remove and replace the wires one at a time to avoid mix-ups in the firing order.

4.0L ENGINE

13.16 Firing order and spark plug wire connection points

14   Automatic transmission shift linkage lubrication

Refer to illustrations 14.3a, 14.3b and 14.4

1   Open the hood and locate the shift cable pivot point on the steering column. Also locate the cable end and pivot point on the transmission lever (raise the vehicle and support it securely on jackstands, if necessary).

2   Clean the cable ends and pivot points.

3   Carefully pry the cable ends off the pivot points and lubricate the pivot points with multi-purpose grease **(see illustrations)**.

14.3a Lubricate the automatic transmission shift cable at the points indicated

14.3b The lubrication points are accessible between the transmission and the exhaust pipe on the driver's side of the vehicle

14.4 Carefully pry the kickdown cable end off the ballstud to lubricate the stud

4   Carefully pry the cable end off the kickdown lever ballstud, then lubricate the stud with multi-purpose grease **(see illustration)**. Reconnect the cable.

15 Chassis lubrication

Refer to illustrations 15.1, 15.6a, 15.6b, 15.6c, 15.13, 15.14a and 15.14b
1   Refer to *Recommended lubricants and fluids* at the front of this Chapter to obtain the necessary grease, etc. You'll also need a grease gun **(see illustration)**. Occasionally plugs will be installed rather than grease fittings. If so, grease fittings will have to be purchased and installed.
2   Look under the vehicle and locate the grease fittings or plugs in the tie-rod ends. If there are plugs, remove them and buy grease fittings, which will thread into the component. A dealer or auto parts store will be able to supply the correct fittings. Straight, as well as angled, fittings are available.
3   For easier access under the vehicle, raise it with a jack and place jackstands under the frame. Make sure the vehicle is safely supported - DO NOT crawl under the vehicle when it is supported only by the jack! If the wheels are to be removed at this interval for tire rotation or brake inspection, loosen the lug nuts slightly while the vehicle is still on the ground.
4   Before beginning, force a little grease out of the nozzle to remove any dirt from the end of the gun. Wipe the nozzle clean with a rag.
5   With the grease gun and plenty of clean rags, crawl under the vehicle.
6   Wipe the tie-rod end grease fitting nipple clean and push the nozzle firmly over it. Squeeze the trigger on the grease gun to force grease into the component **(see illustrations)**. They should be lubricated until the rubber seal is firm to the touch. Don't pump too much grease into the fitting as it could rupture the seal. If grease escapes around the grease gun nozzle, the nipple is clogged or the nozzle is

15.1 Materials required for chassis and body lubrication

1   *Engine oil - Light engine oil in a can like this can be used for door and hood hinges*
2   *Graphite spray - Used to lubricate lock cylinders*
3   *Grease - Grease, in a variety of types and weights, is available for use in a grease gun. Check the Specifications for your requirements.*
4   *Grease gun - A common grease gun, shown here with a detachable hose and nozzle, is needed for chassis lubrication. After use, clean it thoroughly!*

15.6a Lubricate the tie-rod ends (one on each side of the vehicle) . . .

15.6b . . . the Pitman arm connection to the steering linkage . . .

15.6c . . . and the steering linkage cross rod

not completely seated on the fitting. Resecure the gun nozzle to the fitting and try again. If necessary, replace the fitting with a new one.

7   Wipe the excess grease from the components and the grease fitting. Repeat the procedure for the remaining fitting(s).

8   Open the hood and smear a little chassis grease on the hood latch mechanism. Have an assistant pull the hood release lever from inside the vehicle as you lubricate the cable at the latch.

9   Lubricate all the hinges (door, hood, etc.) with engine oil to keep them in proper working order.

10   The key lock cylinders can be lubricated with spray graphite or silicone lubricant, which is available at auto parts stores.

11   Lubricate the door weatherstripping with silicone spray. This will reduce chafing and retard wear.

12   Lubricate the parking brake linkage. Note that two different types of grease are required. Use multi-purpose grease on the linkage, adjuster assembly and connectors; use speedometer cable lubricant on parts of the cable that touch other parts of the vehicle. Lubricate the cable twice, once with the parking brake set and once with it released.

13   On manual transmission equipped models, lubricate the clutch linkage pivot points **(see illustration)**.

14   Remove the protective cover from the throttle lever ballstud **(see illustration)**. Carefully unsnap the throttle linkage from the ballstud **(see illustration)**. Lubricate the ballstud with multi-purpose grease, then reconnect the linkage and install the protective cover.

15.13   Clutch linkage lubrication points

15.14a   The throttle linkage protective cover is secured by two screws (and a clip on the underside, which isn't visible in this photo)

15.14b   After the cover is removed, carefully pry the linkage from the stud, grease the stud and reconnect the linkage

16.1   Manual transmission filler plug

17.2a The check/fill plug for the rear differential is located in the differential housing, facing the front of the vehicle

17.2b The check/fill plug for the front differential on 4WD models is located in the axle housing - use an open-end wrench to loosen it (1991 through 1994 model shown)

17.3 Reach into the filler hole with a finger to check the lubricant level

1

16   Manual transmission lubricant level check and change

Refer to illustration 16.1

Note: *The transmission lubricant level and quality should not deteriorate under normal driving conditions. However, it's recommended that you check the level occasionally. The most convenient time would be when the vehicle is raised for another reason, such as an engine oil change.*

Level check

1   The transmission has a check/fill plug which must be removed to check the lubricant level **(see illustration)**. If the vehicle is raised to gain access to the plug, be sure to support it safely on jackstands - DO NOT crawl under a vehicle which is supported only by a jack!

2   Remove the plug from the transmission and use your little finger to reach inside the housing and feel the lubricant level. It should be at or very near the bottom of the plug hole.

3   If it isn't, add the recommended lubricant through the plug hole with a syringe or squeeze bottle.

4   Install and tighten the plug securely and check for leaks after the first few miles of driving.

Lubricant change

5   Manual transmission lubricant does not normally need changing during the life of the vehicle, but if you wish to do so, place a drain pan beneath the drain plug. Remove the filler plug, then remove the drain

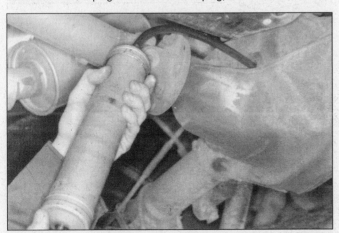

17.7 A suction pump can be used to remove the old lubricant from all differentials - it's the only method for differentials that don't have a drain plug

plug and let the lubricant drain into a pan. Let the lubricant drain for 10 minutes or more, then reinstall the filler plug and tighten securely.

6   Fill the transmission to the bottom of the filler plug hole with recommended lubricant.

7   Install and tighten the filler plug securely and check for leaks after the first few miles of driving.

17   Differential lubricant level check and change

Refer to illustrations 17.2a, 17.2b, 17.3, 17.7, 17.8, 17.11a, 17.11b and 17.12

Note: *This procedure applies to both the front and rear differential.*

Level check

1   The differential has a check/fill plug which must be removed to check the lubricant level. If the vehicle is raised to gain access to the plug, be sure to support it safely on jackstands - DO NOT crawl under the vehicle when it's supported only by the jack!

2   Remove the lubricant check/fill plug from the differential **(see illustrations)**. Use a 3/8-inch drive ratchet and short extension without a socket to unscrew the plug from the rear differential; use an open end wrench to unscrew the plug from the front differential.

3   Use your little finger as a dipstick to make sure the lubricant level is even with the bottom of the plug hole **(see illustration)**. If not, use a syringe to add the recommended lubricant until it just starts to run out of the opening. On some models a tag is located in the area of the plug which gives information regarding lubricant type, particularly on models equipped with a limited slip differential.

4   Install the plug and tighten it securely.

Lubricant change

5   If it is necessary to change the differential lubricant, remove the check/fill plug **(see illustration 17.2a or 17.2b)**, then drain the differential. Some differentials can be drained by removing the drain plug, while on some rear differentials it's necessary to remove the cover plate on the differential housing. As an alternative, a hand suction pump can be used to remove the differential lubricant through the filler hole. This is the only way to drain front axles which don't have a drain plug. If you remove the cover plate, obtain a tube of silicone sealant to be used when reinstalling the differential cover.

6   If equipped with a drain plug, remove the plug and allow the differential lubricant to drain completely. After the lubricant has drained, install the plug and tighten it securely.

7   If a suction pump is being used, insert the flexible hose **(see illustration)**. Work the hose down to the bottom of the differential housing and pump the lubricant out.

17.8 The rear differential can be drained by removing the cover if you don't have a suction pump

17.11b . . . then apply a thick bead all around the inside edge of the cover

8   If the differential is being drained by removing the cover plate, remove all of the bolts except the two near the top. Loosen the remaining two bolts and use them to keep the cover loosely attached. Allow the lubricant to drain into the pan, then completely remove the cover **(see illustration)**.

17.12 Tighten the cover bolts in a criss-cross pattern - don't overtighten the bolts, or the cover may be distorted, causing it to leak

17.11a If you drain the differential by removing the cover, apply a thin film of RTV sealant to the differential cover just before installation . . .

9   Using a lint-free rag, clean the inside of the cover and the accessible areas of the differential housing. As this is done, check for chipped gears and metal particles in the lubricant, indicating that the differential should be more thoroughly inspected and/or repaired.
10   Clean all old gasket material from the cover and differential housing.
11   Apply a thin film of RTV sealant to the cover mating surface, then run a thick bead all the way around inside the cover bolt holes **(see illustrations)**.
12   Place the cover on the differential housing and install the bolts. Tighten the bolts securely in a criss-cross pattern **(see illustration)**. Don't overtighten them or the cover may be distorted and leaks may develop.
13   On all models, use a hand pump, syringe or funnel to fill the differential housing with the specified lubricant until it's level with the bottom of the plug hole.
14   Install the check/fill plug and tighten it securely.

18   Transfer case lubricant level check and change

Refer to illustrations 18.2, 18.6 and 18.7

Level check

1   The transfer case has a check/fill plug which must be removed to check the lubricant level. If the vehicle is raised to gain access to the plug, be sure to support it safely on jackstands - DO NOT crawl under

18.2 If the vehicle has a transfer case damper, unbolt it to gain access to the fill and drain plugs

18.6 If the vehicle's skid plate will obstruct removal of the drain plug, unbolt it from the frame rail to gain access to the plug

18.7 Location of the transfer case drain plug

1

19.2a Loosen the clamp (arrow) and disconnect the air outlet tube and hose

19.2b Unplug the electrical connector for the Mass Air Flow sensor

19.2c Label and disconnect the vacuum lines at the rear of the cover, remove the cover retaining screws and slide the cover sideways out of the retaining tab slots

a vehicle which is supported only by a jack!
2   Remove the transfer case damper (if equipped) to gain access to the fill plug **(see illustration)**.
3   Remove the plug from the transfer case and use your little finger to reach inside the housing and feel the lubricant level. It should be at or very near the bottom of the plug hole.
4   If it isn't, add the recommended lubricant through the plug hole with a syringe or squeeze bottle.

19.3 Lift the cover off and take the element out of the housing

5   Install and tighten the plug securely and check for leaks after the first few miles of driving.

Lubricant change

6   To change the lubricant, first note whether the transfer case skid plate will be in the way when the lubricant is drained. If it will be, remove it **(see illustration)**.
7   Remove the fill plug first. This will speed draining. Remove the drain plug **(see illustration)** and let the lubricant drain.
8   Clean the drain plug threads, then reinstall the plug after the lubricant has finished draining.
9   Fill the transaxle to the bottom of the filler plug threads with the recommended lubricant listed in this Chapter's Specifications.
10   Install the filler plug and tighten it securely.

19   Air filter replacement

Refer to illustrations 19.2a, 19.2b, 19.2c, 19.3, 19.5a and 19.5b
1   Purchase a new filter element.
2   Disconnect the PCV hose from the air outlet tube, then disconnect the air outlet tube from the air cleaner cover. Disconnect the electrical connector from the Mass Air Flow (MAF) sensor. Label and disconnect the vacuum lines at the rear of the cover **(see illustrations)**.
3   Remove the cover retaining screws. Disengage the cover tabs from the slots and lift the cover off **(see illustration)**.

19.5a If necessary, squeeze the hot air hose retainers and push the hose out of the housing . . .

19.5b . . . then remove the mounting screw and lift the housing out

20.1 The PCV valve (arrow) is mounted in the valve cover near the brake booster

4   Remove the filter element.

5   Wipe the inside of the air cleaner housing with a clean cloth. If it's necessary to remove the housing, squeeze the hot air hose and push it out of the housing **(see illustration)**. Remove the mounting screw **(see illustration)** and lift the housing out.

6   Place the new air filter element in the housing. If the element is marked TOP be sure the marked side faces up.

7   Reinstall the cover and retaining screws. Don't overtighten the screws!

8   Reconnect the vacuum hoses, air outlet tube and electrical connector.

20   Positive Crankcase Ventilation (PCV) valve check and replacement

Refer to illustrations 20.1 and 20.2

Note 1: *To maintain the efficiency of the PCV system, clean the hoses and check the PCV valve at the intervals recommended in the mainte-nance schedule. For additional information on the PCV system, refer to Chapter 6.*

Note 2: *Ford will replace the PCV valve at no cost at 60,000 miles on vehicles equipped with U.S. Federal emissions controls.*

1   Locate the PCV valve **(see illustration)**.

2   To check the valve, first pull it out of the grommet in the valve cover. Shake the valve **(see illustration)**. It should rattle, indicating that it is not

clogged with deposits. If the valve does not rattle, replace it with a new one. If it does rattle, reinstall it.

3   Start the engine and allow it to idle, then disconnect the PCV hose. If vacuum is felt, the PCV valve system is working properly (see Chapter 6 for additional PCV system information).

4   If no vacuum is felt, the oil filler cap, hoses or valve cover gasket may be leaking or the PCV valve may be bad. Check for vacuum leaks at the valve, filler cap and all hoses.

5   Pull straight up on the valve to remove it. Check the rubber grommet for cracks and distortion. If it's damaged, replace it.

6   If the valve is clogged, the hose is also probably plugged. Remove the hose and clean with solvent.

7   After cleaning the hose, inspect it for damage, wear and deterio-ration. Make sure it fits snugly on the fittings.

8   If necessary, install a new PCV valve. **Note:** *The elbow (if equipped) is not part of the PCV valve. A new valve will not include the elbow. The original must be transferred to the new valve. If a new elbow is purchased, it may be necessary to soak it in warm water for up to an hour to slip it onto the new valve. Do not attempt to force the elbow onto the valve or it will break.*

9   Install the clean PCV system hose. Make sure that the PCV valve and hose are secure.

20.2 Shake the valve to test it - if it doesn't rattle, the valve is stuck and should be replaced

21   Fuel system check

Warning: *Certain precautions should be observed when inspecting or servicing the fuel system components. Work in a well ventilated area and don't allow open flames (cigarettes, appliance pilot lights, etc.) near the work area. Mop up spills immediately. Do not store fuel soaked rags where they could ignite. It is a good idea to keep a dry chemical (Class B) fire extinguisher near the work area any time the fuel system is being serviced.*

1   If you smell gasoline while driving or after the vehicle has been sitting in the sun, inspect the fuel system immediately.

2   Remove the fuel filler cap and inspect it for damage and corrosion. The gasket should have an unbroken sealing imprint. If the gasket is damaged or corroded, install a new cap.

3   Inspect the fuel feed and return lines for cracks. Make sure that the connections between the fuel lines and the fuel injection system and between the fuel lines and the in-line fuel filter are tight. **Warning:** *The fuel system pressure must be relieved before servicing fuel system components. The fuel system pressure relief procedure is outlined in Chapter 4.*

4   Since some components of the fuel system - the fuel tank and some of the fuel feed and return lines, for example - are underneath the vehicle, they can be inspected more easily with the vehicle raised on a hoist. If that's not possible, raise the vehicle and support it on jackstands.

22.1 The inline fuel filter is mounted in the left frame rail

22.4 Make sure the fuel line fittings (arrow) are clean before disconnecting them - see Chapter 4 for disconnection procedures

1

5   With the vehicle raised and safely supported, inspect the gas tank and filler neck for punctures, cracks or other damage. The connection between the filler neck and the tank is particularly critical. Sometimes a rubber filler neck will leak because of loose clamps or deteriorated rubber. Inspect all fuel tank mounting brackets and straps to be sure the tank is securely attached to the vehicle. **Warning:** *Do not, under any circumstances, try to repair a fuel tank (except rubber components).* A welding torch or any open flame can easily cause fuel vapors inside the tank to explode.

6   Carefully check all rubber hoses and metal or nylon lines leading away from the fuel tank. Check for loose connections, deteriorated hoses, crimped lines and other damage. Repair or replace damaged sections as necessary (see Chapter 4).

22 Fuel filter replacement

Refer to illustrations 22.1 and 22.4

Warning: *Gasoline is extremely flammable, so extra safety precautions must be observed when working on any part of the fuel system. Do not smoke and don't allow open flames or bare light bulbs near the vehicle. Also, don't perform fuel system maintenance procedures in a garage where a natural gas type appliance, such as a water heater or clothes dryer, with a pilot light is present!*

1   The fuel filter is mounted within the left frame rail **(see illustration)**. Periodic fuel filter replacement isn't required and Ford states that the inline filter used on fuel injected models should last the life of the vehicle. Replace the filter if it becomes clogged.

2   Obtain a new fuel filter before starting. **Warning:** *Be sure the new filter is specifically designed for your engine.* Fuel injection system filters are built to withstand high pressure, and as a result, often cost more than filters meant for use in carbureted systems. Filters meant for carbureted systems may burst due to the high pressure. Also, be sure the new filter includes replacement hairpin clips (if used). Ford recommends against reusing the clips. **Warning:** *Before removing the fuel filter, the fuel system pressure must be relieved. See Chapter 4.*

3   Position the front end of the vehicle higher than the rear to prevent fuel siphoning. Remove the gas cap, then reinstall it after relieving the fuel system pressure.

4   Inspect the hose fittings at both ends of the filter to see if they're clean **(see illustration)**. If more than a light coating of dust is present, clean the fittings before proceeding.

5   Disconnect the push-connect fittings from the filter (see Chapter 4).

6   Note which way the arrow on the filter is pointing - the new filter must be installed the same way. Loosen the clamp screw and detach the filter from the bracket.

23.3 The radiator cap seals and the sealing surfaces in the radiator filler neck should be checked for built-up corrosion - the radiator cap should be replaced if the seals are brittle or deteriorated

7   Install the new filter in the bracket with the arrow pointing in the right direction and tighten the clamp screw securely.

8   Carefully connect each hose to the filter (see Chapter 4).

9   Start the engine and check for fuel leaks.

23 Cooling system check

Refer to illustrations 23.3, 23.4a and 23.4b

1   Many major engine failures can be attributed to a faulty cooling system. If the vehicle is equipped with an automatic transmission, the cooling system also plays an important role in prolonging transmission life because it cools the fluid.

2   The engine should be cold for the cooling system check, so perform the following procedure before the vehicle is driven for the day or after it has been shut off for at least three hours.

3   Remove the radiator cap **(see illustration)** and clean it thoroughly, inside and out, with clean water. Also clean the filler neck on the radiator. The presence of rust or corrosion in the filler neck means the coolant should be changed (see Section 30). The coolant inside the radiator should be relatively clean and transparent. If it's rust colored, drain the system and refill with new coolant.

4   Carefully check the radiator hoses and smaller diameter heater

23.4a Radiator and heater hose locations - the lower radiator hose, not shown, is connected to the bottom of the radiator

1 *Heater return*
2 *Heater supply*
3 *Upper radiator hose*
4 *Coolant recovery hose*

ALWAYS CHECK hose for chafed or burned areas that may cause an untimely and costly failure.

SOFT hose indicates inside deterioration. This deterioration can contaminate the cooling system and cause particles to clog the radiator.

HARDENED hose can fail at any time. Tightening hose clamps will not seal the connection or stop leaks.

SWOLLEN hose or oil soaked ends indicate danger and possible failure from oil or grease contamination. Squeeze the hose to locate cracks and breaks that cause leaks.

23.4b Hoses, like drivebelts, have a habit of failing at the worst possible time - to prevent the inconvenience of a blown radiator or heater hose, inspect them carefully as shown here

hoses **(see illustrations)**. Inspect each coolant hose along its entire length, replacing any hose which is cracked, swollen or deteriorated. Cracks will show up better if the hose is squeezed. Pay close attention to hose clamps that secure the hoses to cooling system components. Hose clamps can pinch and puncture hoses, resulting in coolant leaks.

5   Make sure all hose connections are tight. A leak in the cooling system will usually show up as white or rust colored deposits on the area adjoining the leak. If wire-type clamps are used on the hoses, it may be a good idea to replace them with screw-type clamps.

6   Clean the front of the radiator and air conditioning condenser with compressed air, if available, or a soft brush. Remove all bugs, leaves, etc. embedded in the carburetor fins. Be extremely careful not to damage the cooling fins or cut your fingers on them.

7   If the coolant level has been dropping consistently and no leaks are detectable, have the radiator cap and cooling system pressure checked at a service station.

24 Exhaust system check

Refer to illustrations 24.4a, 24.4b, 24.4c and 24.4d

1   With the engine cold (at least three hours after the vehicle has been driven), check the complete exhaust system from the engine to end of the tailpipe. Ideally, the inspection should be done with the

vehicle on a hoist to permit unrestricted access. If a hoist isn't available, raise the vehicle and support it securely on jackstands.

2   Check the exhaust pipes and connections for evidence of leaks, severe corrosion and damage. Make sure that all brackets and hangers are in good condition and are tight.

3   At the same time, inspect the underside of the body for holes, corrosion, open seams, etc. which may allow exhaust gases to enter the passenger compartment. Seal all body openings with silicone or body putty.

4   Rattles and other noises can often be traced to the exhaust system, especially the mounts, hangers and heat shields. Try to move the pipes, muffler and catalytic converter **(see illustrations)**. If the components can come in contact with the body or suspension parts, secure the exhaust system with new mounts.

5   Check the running condition of the engine by inspecting inside

24.4a A catalytic converter is mounted beside the transmission - on automatic transmission models, the heat shield should be securely mounted in its clips

24.4b Also check the heat shields around the rear portion of the catalytic converter assembly

24.4c The main muffler should be securely attached to its brackets . . .

the end of the tailpipe. The exhaust deposits here are an indication of engine state-of-tune. If the pipe is black and sooty or coated with white deposits, the engine may need a tune-up, including a thorough fuel system inspection.

25 Steering and suspension check

Refer to illustrations 25.9a, 25.9b, 25.9c, 25.9d, 25.10a, 25.10b, 25.11a and 25.11b

Note: *The steering linkage and suspension components should be checked periodically. Worn or damaged suspension and steering linkage components can result in excessive and abnormal tire wear, poor ride quality and vehicle handling and reduced fuel economy. For detailed illustrations of the steering and suspension components, refer to Chapter 10.*

Shock absorber check

1   Park the vehicle on level ground, turn the engine off and set the parking brake. Check the tire pressures.

2   Push down at one corner of the vehicle, then release it while noting the movement of the body. It should stop moving and come to rest in a level position with one or two bounces.

3   If the vehicle continues to move up-and-down or if it fails to return to its original position, a worn or weak shock absorber is probably the reason.

4   Repeat the above check at each of the three remaining corners of the vehicle.

5   Raise the vehicle and support it on jackstands.

6   Check the shock absorbers for evidence of fluid leakage. A light film of fluid is no cause for concern. Make sure that any fluid noted is from the shocks and not from any other source. If leakage is noted,

24.4d . . . as should the rear muffler

replace the shocks as a set.

7   Check the shock absorbers to be sure that they are securely mounted and undamaged. Check the upper mounts for damage and wear. If damage or wear is noted, replace the shock absorbers as a set.

8   If the shock absorbers must be replaced, refer to Chapter 10 for the procedure.

Steering and suspension check

9   Visually inspect the steering system components for damage and distortion **(see illustrations)**. Look for leaks and damaged seals, boots and fittings.

25.9a Steering and front suspension components - 1991 through 1994 4WD models

FRONT OF VEHICLE

FRONT AXLE

SHOCK ABSORBER

COIL SPRING

DRAG LINK

PITMAN ARM

TIE ROD END

RADIUS ARM

25.9b Steering and front suspension components - 1991 through 1994 2WD models

DRAG LINK

I-BEAM AXLE

SHOCK ABSORBER

COIL SPRING

STABILIZER BAR

SPINDLE

RADIUS ARM

FRONT OF VEHICLE

TIE ROD END

PITMAN ARM

BALL JOINTS

25.9c Steering and front suspension components -
1995 and later 2WD models

  1   *Frame*
  2   *Upper control arm*
  3   *Not used*
  4   *Torsion bar*
  5   *Nut*
  6   *Bolt*
  7   *Front wheel spindle*
  8   *Not used*
  9   *Nut*
  10   *Cotter pin*
  11   *Nut*
  12   *Front shock absorber*
  13   *Tie-rod end*
  14   *Front stabilizer bar link*
  15   *Lower control arm*
  16   *Not used*
  17   *Front stabilizer bar*

FRONT OF VEHICLE

25.10a To check the suspension balljoints, try to move the lower
edge of each front tire in-and-out while watching/feeling for
movement at the top of the tire . . .

FRONT OF VEHICLE

25.9d Steering and front suspension components - 1995 and
later 4WD models

  1   *Upper control arm*   7   *Nut*
  2   *Frame*   8   *Cotter pin*
  3   *Nut*   9   *Cotter pin*
  4   *Front wheel hub and*   10   *Nut*
       spindle   11   *Front wheel driveshaft*
  5   *Not used*   12   *Not used*
  6   *Hub washer and nut*   13   *Lower control arm*
       assembly

10   Clean the lower end of the steering knuckle. Have an assistant
grasp the lower edge of the tire and move the wheel in-and-out **(see
illustration)** while you look for movement at the steering knuckle-to-
axle arm balljoints **(see illustration)**. If there is any movement, the
balljoint(s) must be replaced.
11   Grasp each front tire at the front and rear edges, push in at the
front, pull out at the rear and feel for play in the steering linkage **(see
illustrations)**. If any freeplay is noted, check the steering gear mounts
and the tie-rod balljoints for looseness. If the steering gear mounts are
loose, tighten them. If the tie-rods are loose, the balljoints may be worn
(check to make sure the nuts are tight). Additional steering and
suspension system illustrations can be found in Chapter 10.

25.10b . . . if there's movement, repeat the test and look for
looseness at the balljoints

25.11a To check the steering gear and idler arm mounts and tie-rod connections for play, grasp each front tire like this and try to move it back-and-forth . . .

25.11b . . . if play is noted, check the steering gear mounts and make sure that they're tight; look for looseness at the tie-rod ends (shown) and the steering linkage connections

26.7a The brake hoses at the front of the vehicle (arrow) should be inspected and replaced if they show any defects

26.7b The rear brake hose meets the metal brake lines at a junction block on the axle housing - they should also be inspected and replaced if they show any defects

Front wheel bearing check

12   Refer to Section 27 (2WD) or Section 28 (4WD) for the wheel bearing check, repack and adjustment procedure.

26   Brake system check

Refer to illustrations 26.7a, 26.7b, 26.7c, 26.7d, 26.11 and 26.18
Warning: *Dust produced by lining wear and deposited on brake components may contain asbestos, which is hazardous to your health. DO NOT blow it out with compressed air and DO NOT inhale it! DO NOT use gasoline or solvents to remove the dust. Brake system cleaner should be used to flush the dust into a drain pan. After the brake components are wiped with a damp rag, dispose of the contaminated rag(s) and brake cleaner in a covered and labeled container. Try to use non-asbestos replacement parts whenever possible.*
Note: *In addition to the specified intervals, the brake system should inspected each time the wheels are removed or a malfunction is indicated. Because of the obvious safety considerations, the following brake system checks are some of the most important maintenance procedures you can perform on your vehicle.*

Symptoms of brake system problems

1   The disc brakes have built-in wear indicators which should make a high-pitched squealing or scraping noise when they're worn to the replacement point. When you hear this noise, replace the pads

immediately or expensive damage to the brake discs could result.
2   Any of the following symptoms could indicate a potential brake system defect. The vehicle pulls to one side when the brake pedal is depressed, the brakes make squealing or dragging noises when applied, brake travel is excessive, the pedal pulsates and brake fluid leaks are noted (usually on the inner side of the tire or wheel). If any of these conditions are noted, inspect the brake system immediately.

Brake lines and hoses

Note: *Steel tubing is used throughout the brake system, with the exception of flexible, reinforced hoses at the front wheels and as connectors at the rear axle. Periodic inspection of these lines is very important.*
3   Park the vehicle on level ground and turn the engine off.
4   Remove the wheel covers. Loosen, but do not remove, the lug nuts on all four wheels.
5   Raise the vehicle and support it securely on jackstands.
6   Remove the wheels (see *Jacking and towing* at the front of this book, or refer to your owner's manual, if necessary).
7   Check all brake lines and hoses for cracks, chafing of the outer cover, leaks, blisters and distortion. Check the brake hoses at front and rear of the vehicle for softening, cracks, bulging, or wear from rubbing on other components **(see illustrations)**. Check all threaded fittings for leaks and make sure the brake hose mounting bolts and clips are secure.
8   If leaks or damage are discovered, they must be fixed immediately. Refer to Chapter 9 for detailed brake system repair procedures.

SOFTENING   CRACKING

SWOLLEN   LEAKAGE

26.7c   Typical brake hose defects

TWISTED

DENTED

CRIMPED

BENT

26.7d   Typical metal brake line defects

26.11   The lining thickness of the front disc brake pads (arrows) can be checked through the caliper inspection hole

Disc brakes

9   If it hasn't already been done, raise the vehicle and support it securely on jackstands. Remove the front wheels.

10   The disc brake calipers, which contain the pads, are now visible. Each caliper has an outer and an inner pad - all pads should be checked.

11   Note the pad thickness by looking through the inspection hole in the caliper **(see illustration)**. If the lining material is 1/8-inch thick or less, or if it is tapered from end-to-end, the pads should be replaced (see Chapter 9). Keep in mind that the lining material is riveted or bonded to a metal plate or shoe - the metal portion is not included in this measurement.

12   Check the condition of the brake disc. Look for score marks, deep scratches and overheated areas (they will appear blue or discolored). If damage or wear is noted, the disc can be removed and resurfaced by an automotive machine shop or replaced with a new one. Refer to Chapter 9 for more detailed inspection and repair procedures.

13   Remove the calipers without disconnecting the brake hoses (see Chapter 9). Lubricate the caliper slide rails and the inner pad slots on the steering knuckles with the special caliper slide grease listed in this Chapter's Specifications.

Drum brakes

14   Refer to Chapter 9 and remove the rear brake drums.

15   Note the thickness of the lining material on the rear brake shoes and look for signs of contamination by brake fluid or grease. If the lining material is within 1/16-inch of the recessed rivets or metal shoes, replace the brake shoes with new ones. The shoes should also be replaced if they are cracked, glazed (shiny lining surfaces), or contaminated with brake fluid or grease. See Chapter 9 for the replacement procedure.

16   Check the shoe return and hold-down springs and the adjusting mechanism to make sure they are installed correctly and in good condition. Deteriorated or distorted springs, if not replaced, could allow the linings to drag and wear prematurely.

17   Check the wheel cylinders for leakage by carefully peeling back the rubber boots **(see illustration)**. Slight moisture behind the boots is acceptable. If brake fluid is noted behind the boots or if it runs out of the wheel cylinder, the wheel cylinders must be overhauled or replaced (see Chapter 9).

18   Check the drums for cracks, score marks, deep scratches and hard spots, which will appear as small discolored areas. If imperfections cannot be removed with emery cloth, the drums must be resurfaced by an automotive machine shop (see Chapter 9 for more detailed information).

19   Refer to Chapter 9 and install the brake drums.

20   Install the wheels, but don't lower the vehicle yet.

Parking brake

Note: *The parking brake cable and linkage should be periodically lubricated (see Section 15). This maintenance procedure helps prevent the parking brake cable adjuster or the linkage from binding and adversely affecting the operation or adjustment of the parking brake.*

21   The easiest, and perhaps most obvious, method of checking the

26.18 Carefully peel back the rubber boot on each end of the wheel cylinder - if the exposed area is covered with brake fluid, or if fluid runs out, the wheel cylinder must be overhauled or replaced

27.7 An exploded view of the front wheel bearing components (2WD models)

parking brake is to park the vehicle on a steep hill with the parking brake set and the transmission in Neutral. If the parking brake doesn't prevent the vehicle from rolling, refer to Chapter 9 and adjust it.

27 Front wheel bearing check, repack and adjustment (2WD models)

Refer to illustrations 27.1, 27.7, 27.9, 27.15, 27.16 and 27.23

1   In most cases the front wheel bearings will not need servicing until the brake pads are changed. However, the bearings should be checked whenever the front of the vehicle is raised for any reason. Several items, including a torque wrench and special grease, are required for this procedure **(see illustration)**.
2   With the vehicle securely supported on jackstands, spin each wheel and check for noise, rolling resistance and freeplay.
3   Move the wheel in-and-out on the spindle **(see illustration 25.11a)**. If there's any noticeable movement, the bearings should be checked and then repacked with grease or replaced if necessary.
4   Remove the wheel.
5   Remove the brake caliper (see Chapter 9) and hang it out of the way on a piece of wire. **Warning:** *DO NOT allow the brake caliper to hang by the rubber hose!*
6   Pry the grease cap out of the hub with a screwdriver or hammer and chisel.
7   Straighten the bent ends of the cotter pin, then pull the cotter pin out of the retaining nut and spindle **(see illustration)**. Discard the cotter pin and use a new one during reassembly.
8   Remove the retainer, the adjusting nut and flat washer from the end of the spindle.
9   Pull the hub assembly out slightly, then push it back into its

27.1 Tools and materials needed for front wheel bearing maintenance

1   **Hammer -** *A common hammer will do just fine*
2   **Grease -** *High-temperature grease that is formulated specially for front wheel bearings should be used*
3   **Wood block -** *If you have a scrap piece of 2 x4, it can be used to drive the new seal into the hub*
4   **Needle-nose pliers -** *Used to straighten and remove the cotter pin in the spindle*
5   **Torque wrench -** *This is very important in this procedure; if the bearing is too tight, the wheel won't turn freely - if it's too loose, the wheel will "wobble" on the spindle. Either way, it could mean extensive damage.*
6   **Screwdriver -** *Used to remove the seal from the hub (a long screwdriver would be preferred)*
7   **Socket/breaker bar -** *Needed to loosen the nut on the spindle if it's extremely tight*
8   **Brush -** *Together with some clean solvent, this will be used to remove old grease from the hub and spindle*

27.9 Pull out on the hub to dislodge the outer bearing

original position. This should force the outer bearing off the spindle enough so it can be removed **(see illustration)**.
10   Pull the hub off the spindle.
11   Use a screwdriver to pry the grease seal out of the rear of the hub. As this is done, note how the seal is installed.

27.15 Pack each wheel bearing by working the grease into the rollers from the back side

27.16 Apply a thin coat of grease to the spindle, particularly where the seal rides

12   Remove the inner wheel bearing from the hub.

13   Use solvent to remove all traces of old grease from the bearings, hub and spindle. A small brush may prove helpful; however make sure no bristles from the brush embed themselves inside the bearing rollers. Allow the parts to air dry.

14   Carefully inspect the bearings for cracks, heat discoloration, worn rollers, etc. Check the bearing races inside the hub for wear and damage. If the bearing races are defective, the hubs should be taken to a machine shop with the facilities to remove the old races and press new ones in. Note that the bearings and races come as matched sets and new bearings should never be installed on old races.

15   Use high-temperature front wheel bearing grease to pack the bearings. Work the grease completely into the bearings, forcing it between the rollers, cone and cage from the back side **(see illustration)**.

16   Apply a thin coat of grease to the spindle at the outer bearing seat, inner bearing seat, shoulder and seal seat **(see illustration)**.

17   Put a small quantity of grease inboard of each bearing race inside the hub. Using your finger, form a dam at these points to provide extra grease availability and to keep thinned grease from flowing out of the bearing.

18   Place the grease-packed inner bearing into the rear of the hub and put a little more grease outward of the bearing.

19   Place a new seal over the inner bearing and tap the seal evenly into place with a hammer and block of wood until it's flush with the hub.

20   Carefully place the hub assembly onto the spindle and push the grease-packed outer bearing into position.

21   Install the flat washer and adjusting nut. Tighten the nut only slightly.

22   Spin the hub in a forward direction to seat the bearings and remove any grease or burrs which could cause excessive bearing play later.

23   While spinning the wheel, tighten the adjusting nut to the specified torque (Step 1 in this Chapter's Specifications) **(see illustration)**.

24   Loosen the nut 1/2-turn, no more.

25   Tighten the nut to the specified torque (Step 3 in this Chapter's Specifications). Install a new cotter pin through the hole in the spindle and retainer nut. If the holes don't line up, don't turn the nut. Instead, remove the retainer and try it in a different position. The notches in the retainer are offset for this purpose. Keep trying the retainer in different positions until the holes line up.

26   Bend the ends of the cotter pin until they're flat against the nut. Cut off any extra length which could interfere with the grease cap.

27   Install the grease cap, tapping it into place with a hammer.

28   Install the caliper (see Chapter 9).

29   Install the wheel and lug nuts. Tighten the lug nuts to the torque listed in this Chapter's Specifications.

30   Check the bearings in the manner described earlier in this Section.

31   Lower the vehicle.

27.23 Wheel bearing adjustment procedure (2WD models)

28   Front hub lock, spindle bearing and wheel bearing maintenance (1991 through 1994 4WD models)

Removal (manual and automatic hubs)

Refer to illustrations 28.1, 28.7a and 28.7b

1   In most cases the front wheel bearings will not need servicing until the brake pads are changed. However, the bearings should be checked whenever the front of the vehicle is raised for any reason. Several items, including a torque wrench and special grease, are required for this procedure **(see illustration 27.1)**. In addition to these tools you'll need a four-pronged spindle nut spanner wrench (Ford part no. T86T-1197-A or equivalent) for manual locking hubs or a 2-3/8 inch hex locknut wrench (Ford part no. T70T-4252-B or equivalent) for automatic locking hubs **(see illustration)**. These may be available at four-wheel drive shops or auto parts stores. You'll also need a pair of snap-ring pliers.

28.1 The tool on the left is used for automatic locking hubs; the tool on the right is used for manual locking hubs

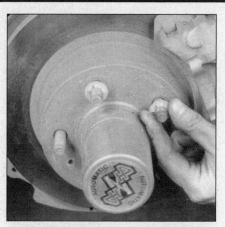

28.7a Pry the retaining washers up slightly to engage the wheel stud threads, then unscrew them from the studs

28.7b Make alignment marks on the locking hub and wheel hub, then take the locking hub off the wheel studs

28.8 An exploded view of the manual locking hub and wheel bearings (1991 through 1994 4WD models)

GREASE SEAL · CUP · ROTOR · **MANUAL LOCKING HUB** · CUP · INNER LOCKNUT · WASHER · AXLE SHAFT SPACER · RETAINER WASHER · SPINDLE · INNER WHEEL BEARING · OUTER WHEEL BEARING · OUTER LOCKNUT · SNAP RING · HUB

28.9 Remove the snap-ring, then the axleshaft spacer

AXLE SHAFT SPACER

28.10 A four-pronged socket is required to remove the outer locknut; the nut is very tight, so don't use makeshift tools

FOUR-PRONG SPINDLE NUT SPANNER WRENCH

2   With the vehicle securely supported on jackstands, spin each wheel and check for noise, rolling resistance and freeplay.

3   Move the wheel in-and-out on the spindle **(see illustration 25.11a)**. If there's any noticeable movement, the bearings should be checked and then repacked with grease or replaced if necessary.

4   The lubrication of hub locks, as well as spindle needle and thrust bearings on vehicles so equipped, should be checked at the intervals specified in the maintenance schedule.

5   Remove the wheel.

6   Remove the brake caliper (see Chapter 9) and hang it out of the way on a piece of wire. **Warning:** *DO NOT allow the brake caliper to hang by the hose!*

7   Remove the retaining washers from the wheel studs **(see illustration)**. Make alignment marks on the locking hub and wheel hub, then take the locking hub off **(see illustration)**.

Manual locking hubs

Refer to illustrations 28.8, 28.9, 28.10, 28.16 and 28.21

8   Using snap-ring pliers, carefully expand the snap-ring just enough to remove it from the end of the spindle shaft **(see illustration)**.

9   Remove the axleshaft spacer **(see illustration)**.

10   Remove the outer wheel bearing locknut with a four-prong spanner wrench (Ford part no. T86T-1197-A or equivalent) **(see illustration)**. **Note:** *This nut is very tight. Don't try to remove it with a makeshift tool.*

28.16 Align the pin in the locknut with one of the holes in the lockwasher; if necessary, adjust the locknut position slightly to align the pin with a hole

28.21 To remove the internal components from a manual locking hub, insert a small screwdriver behind the retaining ring and work it gently out of its groove - DO NOT remove the screw from the plastic dial

28.25a An exploded view of the automatic locking hub and wheel bearings (1991 through 1994 4WD models)

11   Remove the inner wheel bearing locknut with the spanner wrench. Be sure the notch in the wrench is positioned over the locknut pin.

12   Perform Steps 9 through 20 of Section 27 to repack the bearings. Be sure to use the type of grease listed in this Chapter's Specifications.

13   Install the inner locknut on the spindle and tighten it to the specified torque (Step 1 in this Chapter's Specifications).

14   Spin the brake disc several turns in each direction to seat the bearings.

15   Loosen the inner locknut 1/4-turn, then retighten it to the specified torque (Step 3 in this Chapter's Specifications).

16   Install the lockwasher and align the locknut pin with one of the holes in the lockwasher **(see illustration)**. If necessary, turn the inner locknut slightly to align the hole and pin.

17   Install the outer locknut and tighten it to the specified torque (Step 4 in this Chapter's Specifications).

18   Lubricate the needle bearing spacer and needle bearing (if equipped) with the same grease used for the wheel bearings. Install them on the spindle.

19   Install the axleshaft spacer.

20   Install the snap-ring on the spindle.

21   Remove the lock ring that secures the inner components in the locking hub **(see illustration)**. **Caution:** *Don't remove the screw from the plastic dial.*

22   Remove the internal assembly, spring and clutch gear. Lubricate

28.25b The snap-ring can be lifted off with a screwdriver if snap-ring pliers aren't available - hold the center of the snap-ring with a finger as shown so it doesn't fly off

the components with the specified grease.

23   Reassemble the hub and install the lock ring.

24   Install the locking hub on the wheel studs and secure it with the retainer washers. Proceed to Step 35.

28.26 Remove the axleshaft spacer

28.27a Remove the cam from the spindle

28.27b Remove the two plastic thrust spacers

1

28.27c Remove the locking key (arrow) with a pencil magnet - don't try to unscrew the nut before removing the key

28.28 On automatic locking hubs, loosen the wheel bearing adjusting nut with a 2-3/8 inch hex locknut wrench

28.30 Install the wheel bearing adjusting nut

28.33a The adjusting nut has internal slots - line up one of them with the keyway slot

Automatic locking hubs

Refer to illustrations 28.25a, 28.25b, 28.26, 28.27a, 28.27b, 28.27c, 28.28, 28.30, 28.33a, 28.33b and 28.34

25   Using snap-ring pliers, carefully expand the snap-ring just enough to remove it from the end of the spindle shaft **(see illustrations)**. **Note:** *If you don't have snap-ring pliers, carefully pry the snap-ring off with a screwdriver. Hold a finger against the snap-ring as shown in the illustration so the snap-ring doesn't fly off.*

26   Remove the axleshaft spacer **(see illustration)**.
27   Carefully pull the plastic cam assembly from the wheel bearing adjusting nut **(see illustration)**. **Caution:** *Don't pry the cam off or you may damage it. If it's hard to remove, try turning it as you pull. Pull off the two plastic thrust spacers and remove the locking key with a magnet **(see illustrations)**. **Note:** The thrust spacers are thin and flexible, with a tendency to cock sideways and jam on the spindle. Hook your fingernails behind the spacers and pull evenly at two or more points. If necessary, rotate the adjusting nut slightly to relieve pressure on the locking key.*
28   Remove the wheel bearing adjusting nut from the spindle. It may be loose enough to turn with fingers. If not, use a 2-3/8 inch hex socket (Ford part on. T70T-4252-B or equivalent) **(see illustration)**. **Caution:** *Be sure to remove the locking key before you remove the nut or the spindle threads will be damaged.* **Note:** *The socket may be 3/4-inch drive. If so, an adapter can be used so the socket can be turned with a 1/2-inch drive tool.*
29   Perform Steps 9 through 20 of Section 27 to repack the wheel bearings. Be sure to use the correct grease (listed in this Chapter's Specifications).
30   Install the wheel bearing adjusting nut **(see illustration)**. While spinning the brake disc, tighten the nut to the specified torque (Step 1 in this Chapter's Specifications).
31   Loosen the nut 1/4-turn.
32   Retighten the nut to the final torque (Step 3 in this Chapter's Specifications).
33   Line up the center of the spindle keyway slot with the closest slot in the wheel bearing adjusting nut **(see illustration)**. If necessary, tighten the adjusting nut so the next slot aligns with the keyway slot.

28.33b Position the cam over the wheel bearing adjusting nut - use extreme care to align the key accurately with the slot in the spindle

28.34 Align the legs in the automatic locking hub with the pockets on the cam when installing the hub

Be sure the slots line up exactly.
a) Install the locking key in the keyway slot, under the adjusting nut. Don't force the key in or it will be damaged. If it is difficult to insert, make sure the slots are lined up exactly.
b) Install the two thrust spacers **(see illustration 28.27b)**.
c) Line up the key in the fixed cam with the keyway slot in the spindle, then push the cam on over the adjusting nut **(see illustration)**.
d) Install the axleshaft spacer.
e) Install the snap-ring on the end of the spindle.

34   Line up the three legs on the automatic locking hub with the pockets in the cam **(see illustration)**, then install the locking hub and secure it with the retainer washers.

All models

35   Install the wheel and lug nuts. Lower the vehicle and tighten the lug nuts to the torque listed in this Chapter's Specifications.
36   Check the endplay of the wheel on the spindle and measure the amount of torque required to turn the hub. Compare your findings with this Chapter's Specifications. If the measurements are incorrect, readjust the wheel bearings.

---

29 Windshield wiper blade check and replacement

---

1   Road film can build up on the wiper blades and affect their efficiency, so they should be washed regularly with a mild detergent solution.

Check

2   The windshield wiper and blade assembly should be inspected periodically. Even if you don't use your wipers, the sun and elements will dry out the rubber portions, causing them to crack and break apart. If inspection reveals hardened or cracked rubber, replace the wiper blades. If inspection reveals nothing unusual, wet the windshield, turn the wipers on, allow them to cycle several times, then shut them off. An uneven wiper pattern across the glass or streaks over clean glass indicate that the blades should be replaced.
3   The operation of the wiper mechanism can loosen the fasteners, so they should be checked and tightened, as necessary, at the same time the wiper blades are checked (see Chapter 12 for further information regarding the wiper mechanism).

Front wiper blade replacement

Refer to illustrations 29.5a and 29.5b
4   Park the wiper blades in a convenient position to be worked on. To do this, run the wipers, then turn the ignition key to Off when the

29.5a Squeeze the retaining lever . . .

wiper blades reach the desired position.
5   Lift the blade slightly from the windshield. Squeeze the retaining lever to release the blade **(see illustration)**, unhook the wiper arm from the blade **(see illustration)** and take the blade off. **Caution:** *Do not press too hard on the spring lock or it will be distorted.*
6   Slide the new blade onto the wiper arm hook until the blade locks. Make sure the spring lock secures the blade to the pin.

Rear wiper blade replacement

Refer to illustrations 29.8a and 29.8b
7   Park the wiper blades in a convenient position to be worked on. To do this, run the wipers, then turn the ignition key to Off when the wiper blades reach the desired position.
8   Press straight in on the retaining lever with a small screwdriver **(see illustration)**. Lift the blade off the stud on the wiper arm **(see illustration)**.
9   To install, push the blade onto the wiper arm stud until it locks.

Front or rear wiper element replacement

Refer to illustrations 29.10 and 29.13
10   Insert a screwdriver blade between the wiper blade and element **(see illustration)**. Twist the screwdriver clockwise while pressing in and down to separate the element from the end retaining claw.
11   Slide the element out of the remaining retaining claws.

29.5b . . . push the wiper blade down the arm to disengage the hook and separate the blade from the arm

29.8a To remove a rear wiper blade, press on the retaining lever with a small screwdriver . . .

29.8b . . . and pull the blade off the stud on the wiper arm

12 Starting at either end of the blade, slide a new element into the second retaining claw (not the one closest to the end of the blade). Slide it through the other retaining claws until it reaches the end of the blade.

13 Bend the element and slide it back into the claw at the end of the blade (see illustration).

30 Cooling system servicing (draining, flushing and refilling)

Refer to illustrations 30.4a and 30.4b

Warning: *Do not allow antifreeze to come in contact with your skin or painted surfaces of the vehicle. Rinse off spills immediately with plenty of water. Antifreeze is highly toxic if ingested. Never leave antifreeze lying around in an open container or in puddles on the floor; children and pets are attracted by it's sweet smell and may drink it. Check with local authorities about disposing of used antifreeze. Many communities have collection centers which will see that antifreeze is disposed of safely.*

1 Periodically, the cooling system should be drained, flushed and refilled to replenish the antifreeze mixture and prevent formation of rust and corrosion, which can impair the performance of the cooling system and cause engine damage. When the cooling system is serviced, all hoses and the radiator cap should be checked and replaced if necessary.

Draining

2 Apply the parking brake and block the wheels. If the vehicle has just been driven, wait several hours to allow the engine to cool down before beginning this procedure.

3 Once the engine is completely cool, remove the radiator cap.

4 Move a large container under the radiator drain to catch the coolant (see illustration). Attach a 3/8-inch diameter hose to the drain

INSERT SCREWDRIVER 1/8 INCH (3.2mm) OR LESS PAST THE EDGE

FRAME

PRESS DOWN AND IN

SCREWDRIVER

ELEMENT

29.10 To remove a wiper element, pry it out of the retaining claw at either end of the blade

FRAME

ELEMENT

RETAINING CLAW

29.13 To install an element, slide it into three of the retaining claws, then bend it back and slide it into the retaining claw at the end of the blade

30.4a The radiator drain (arrow) is located on the bottom of the radiator

30.4b Connect a length of rubber hose to the drain and let it hang into the drain pan

fitting to direct the coolant into the container **(see illustration)**, then open the drain fitting (a pair of pliers may be required to turn it).

5   While the coolant is draining, check the condition of the radiator hoses, heater hoses and clamps (see Section 23 if necessary).

6   Replace any damaged clamps or hoses (see Chapter 3 for detailed replacement procedures).

Flushing

7   Once the system is completely drained, flush the radiator with fresh water from a garden hose until the water runs clear at the drain. The flushing action of the water will remove sediments from the radiator but will not remove rust and scale from the engine and cooling tube surfaces.

8   These deposits can be removed by the chemical action of a cleaner such as Ford Premium Cooling System Flush, or equivalent. Follow the procedure outlined in the manufacturer's instructions. If the radiator is severely corroded, damaged or leaking, it should be removed (see Chapter 3) and taken to a radiator repair shop.

9   The heater core should be backflushed whenever the cooling system is flushed. To do this, disconnect the heater return hose from the thermostat housing or engine. Slide a female garden hose fitting into the heater hose and secure it with a clamp. This will allow you to attach a garden hose securely.

10   Attach the end of a garden hose to the fitting you installed in the heater hose.

11   Disconnect the heater inlet hose and position it to act as a drain.

12   Turn the water on and off several times to create a surging action through the heater core. Then turn the water on full force and allow it to run for approximately five minutes.

13   Turn off the water and disconnect the garden hose from the female fitting. Remove the fitting from the heater return hose, then reconnect the hoses to the engine.

14   Remove the overflow hose from the coolant recovery reservoir. Drain the reservoir and flush it with clean water, then reconnect the hose.

Refilling

15   Close and tighten the radiator drain. Install and tighten the block drain plug(s).

16   Place the heater temperature control in the maximum heat position.

17   Slowly add new coolant (a 50/50 mixture of water and antifreeze) to the radiator until it is full. Add coolant to the reservoir up to the lower mark.

18   Leave the radiator cap off and run the engine in a well-ventilated area until the thermostat opens (coolant will begin flowing through the radiator and the upper radiator hose will become hot).

19   Turn the engine off and let it cool. Add more coolant mixture to bring the coolant level back up to the lip on the radiator filler neck.

20   Squeeze the upper radiator hose to expel air, then add more coolant mixture if necessary. Replace the radiator cap.

21   Start the engine, allow it to reach normal operating temperature and check for leaks.

31   Driveshaft and driveaxle yoke lubrication (4WD models)

At the specified intervals, the slip yokes on the driveshafts and (on 1994 and earlier models) the right front driveaxle should be lubricated (see this Chapter's Specifications for the correct lubricant). This requires removal of the driveshafts and driveaxle (see Chapter 8 for the procedures).

Chapter 2 Part A
4.0L V6 engine

Contents

	Section
Camshaft - removal, inspection and installation	13
CHECK ENGINE light on	See Chapter 6
Compression check	See Chapter 2B
Crankshaft pulley, front oil seal and timing chain cover - removal and installation	10
Crankshaft oil seals - replacement	16
Cylinder heads - removal and installation	9
Drivebelt check, adjustment and replacement	See Chapter 1
Engine mounts - check and replacement	18
Engine oil and filter change	See Chapter 1
Engine overhaul - general information	See Chapter 2B
Engine - removal and installation	See Chapter 2B
Exhaust manifolds - removal and installation	8
Flywheel/driveplate - removal and installation	17
General information	1

	Section
Intake manifold - removal and installation	7
Oil pump - removal and installation	15
Oil pan and baffle - removal and installation	14
Repair operations possible with the engine in the vehicle	2
Rocker arms and pushrods - removal, inspection and installation	5
Spark plug replacement	See Chapter 1
Timing chain and sprockets - inspection, removal and installation	11
Top Dead Center (TDC) for number one piston - locating	3
Valve lifters - removal, inspection and installation	12
Valve springs, retainers and seals - replacement	6
Valve covers - removal and installation	4
Valves - servicing	See Chapter 2B
Water pump - removal and installation	See Chapter 3

2A

Specifications

General

Displacement	4.0 liters (244 cubic inches)
Cylinder numbers (front-to-rear)	
Left (driver's) side	4-5-6
Right side	1-2-3
Firing order	1-4-2-5-3-6

Camshaft

Lobe lift (intake and exhaust)	0.2756 inch
Allowable lobe lift loss	0.005 inch
Endplay	
Standard	0.0008 to 0.004 inch
Service limit	0.009 inch

Cylinder location and distributor rotation

FRONT OF VEHICLE

ENGINE CYLINDERS

3 6
2 5
1 4

4.0L ENGINE
FIRING ORDER:
1-4-2-5-3-6

IGNITION COIL

3 4
2 6
1 5

Camshaft (continued)

Thrust plate thickness	0.158 to 0.159 inch
Journal-to-bearing (oil) clearance	
Standard	0.001 to 0.0026 inch
Service limit	0.006 inch
Bearing inside diameter (standard)	
No. 1	1.954 to 1.955 inch
No. 2	1.939 to 1.940 inch
No. 3	1.919 to 1.920 inch
No. 4	1.924 to 1.925 inch
Journal diameter (standard)	
No. 1	1.951 to 1.952 inch
No. 2	1.937 to 1.938 inch
No. 3	1.922 to 1.923 inch
No. 4	1.907 to 1.908 inch
Front bearing location	0.040 to 0.060 inch below face of block

Oil pan-to-transmission spacer thicknesses

Coded yellow	0.010 inch
Coded blue	0.020 inch
Coded pink	0.030 inch

Crankshaft rear seal

Dimension from rear face of block	0.413 +0.008 -0.012 inch
Square to crankshaft centerline within	0.015 inch

Torque specifications

	Ft-lbs (unless otherwise indicated)
Camshaft sprocket bolt	44 to 50
Camshaft thrust plate bolts	84 to 120 in-lbs
Crankshaft pulley bolt	
Step 1	30 to 37
Step 2	Turn an additional 80 to 90 degrees
Cylinder head bolts	
Step 1	44
Step 2	Tighten intake manifold to 36 to 72 in-lbs
Step 3	59
Step 4	Tighten intake manifold to 72 to 132 in-lbs
Step 5	Turn cylinder head bolts an additional 80 to 85 degrees
Flywheel/driveplate bolts	59
Engine mount insulator-to-frame nuts	71 to 94
Engine mount insulator-to-bracket nuts	65 to 85
Engine mount bracket-to-block bolts	45 to 60
Exhaust manifold bolts	19
Exhaust pipe-to-manifold nuts	20
Timing chain cover bolts	13 to 15
Intake manifold bolts/nuts	
Step 1	36 to 72 in-lbs
Step 2	72 to 132 in-lbs
Step 3	132 to 180 in-lbs
Step 4	180 to 216 in-lbs*
Intake manifold studs to block	72 to 84 in-lbs
Oil pump drive gear bolt	156 to 180 in-lbs
Oil pump pick-up tube-to-pump bolts	84 to 120 in-lbs
Oil pump-to-block bolts	156 to 180 in-lbs
Oil pan-to-block bolts	60 to 84 in-lbs
Timing chain tensioner bolts	84 to 96 in-lbs
Timing chain guide bolts	84 to 108 in-lbs
Valve cover bolts	
1991 models	
Step 1	30 to 60 in-lbs
Step 2	Wait 2 minutes
Step 3	Retighten to 30 to 60 in-lbs
1992 models	53 to 70 in-lbs
Rocker arm shaft support bolts	
Step 1	24
Step 2	Tighten an additional 90 degrees

*Retighten in sequence to 180 to 216 in-lbs after the engine has been run.

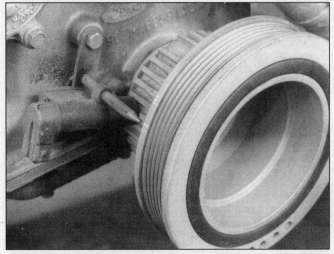

3.5a The crankshaft pulley has a gap at 60-degrees BTDC - TDC is located at the sixth tooth from the gap

3.5b The pointer on the front of the engine lines up with a notch in the crankshaft pulley to indicate TDC

1 General information

This Part of Chapter 2 is devoted to in-vehicle repair procedures for the 4.0L V6 engine, as well as procedures such as timing chain and sprocket and oil pan removal which require removal of the engine from the vehicle. All information concerning engine removal and installation and engine block and cylinder head overhaul can be found in Part B of this Chapter.

The following repair procedures are based on the assumption that the engine is installed in the vehicle. If the engine has been removed from the vehicle and mounted on a stand, many of the steps outlined in this Part of Chapter 2 will not apply.

The Specifications included in this Part of Chapter 2 apply only to the procedures contained in this Part. Part B of Chapter 2 contains the Specifications necessary for cylinder head and engine block rebuilding.

2 Repair operations possible with the engine in the vehicle

Many major repair operations can be accomplished without removing the engine from the vehicle.

Clean the engine compartment and the exterior of the engine with some type of degreaser before any work is done. It will make the job easier and help keep dirt out of the internal areas of the engine.

Depending on the components involved, it may be helpful to remove the hood to improve access to the engine as repairs are performed (refer to Chapter 11 if necessary). Cover the fenders to prevent damage to the paint. Special pads are available, but an old bedspread or blanket will also work.

If vacuum, exhaust, oil or coolant leaks develop, indicating a need for gasket or seal replacement, the repairs can generally be made with the engine in the vehicle. The intake and exhaust manifold gaskets and cylinder head gaskets are all accessible with the engine in place. **Note:** *Removing the oil pan on a 4.0L engine requires removing the engine from the vehicle.*

Exterior engine components, such as the intake and exhaust manifolds, the water pump, the starter motor, the alternator, the distributor and the fuel system components can be removed for repair with the engine in place.

Since the cylinder heads can be removed without pulling the engine, valve component servicing can also be accomplished with the engine in the vehicle. Replacement of the timing chain and sprockets requires removal of the oil pan, so it is not possible with the engine in the vehicle.

3 Top Dead Center (TDC) for number one piston - locating

Refer to illustrations 3.5a and 3.5b
Note: *The 4.0L engine is not equipped with a distributor. Piston position must be determined by feeling for compression at the number one spark plug hole, then aligning the ignition timing marks as described in Step 5.*

1   Top Dead Center (TDC) is the highest point in the cylinder that each piston reaches as it travels up-and-down when the crankshaft turns. Each piston reaches TDC on the compression stroke and again on the exhaust stroke, but TDC generally refers to piston position on the compression stroke.

2   Positioning the piston(s) at TDC is an essential part of many other repair procedures discussed in this manual.

3   Before beginning this procedure, be sure to place the transmission in Neutral and apply the parking brake or block the rear wheels. Remove the spark plugs (see Chapter 1). Disable the ignition system by disconnecting the wiring harness connector from the ignition coil pack, located above the left valve cover.

4   In order to bring any piston to TDC, the crankshaft must be turned using one of the methods outlined below. When looking at the front of the engine, normal crankshaft rotation is clockwise.

a) *The preferred method is to turn the crankshaft with a socket and ratchet attached to the bolt threaded into the front of the crankshaft.*

b) *A remote starter switch, which may save some time, can also be used. Follow the instructions included with the switch. Once the piston is close to TDC, use a socket and ratchet as described in the previous paragraph.*

c) *If an assistant is available to turn the ignition switch to the Start position in short bursts, you can get the piston close to TDC without a remote starter switch. Make sure your assistant is out of the vehicle, away from the ignition switch, then use a socket and ratchet as described in Paragraph a) to complete the procedure.*

5   The crankshaft pulley has 35 teeth, evenly spaced every 10-degrees around the pulley, and a gap where a 36th tooth would be. The gap is located at 60-degrees Before Top Dead Center (BTDC) **(see illustration)**. Turn the crankshaft (see Paragraph 4 above) until you feel compression at the number one spark plug hole, then turn it slowly until the sixth tooth from the missing tooth is aligned with the Variable Reluctance (VR) sensor and the TDC notch is aligned with the pointer (located at the front of the engine) **(see illustration)**.

6   After the number one piston has been positioned at TDC on the compression stroke, TDC for any of the remaining pistons can be located by turning the crankshaft and following the firing order.

4.7 On the passenger's side, disconnect the vacuum hose at the coupling above the valve cover

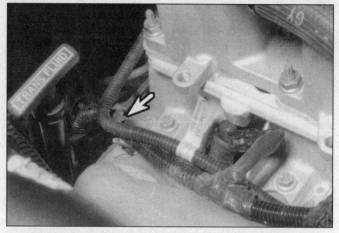

4.8 Lift the wiring harness off the stud with a thumbnail - don't pry it

4   Valve covers - removal and installation

Refer to illustrations 4.7, 4.8, 4.9a, 4.9b, 4.9c, 4.12, 4.16, 4.20 and 4.22

Removal

1   Disconnect the negative cable from the battery.
2   Remove the fresh air intake shield and tube (see Chapter 1). If necessary, disconnect the fuel supply and return lines to provide removal access for the valve covers (see Chapter 4). **Warning:** *Relieve fuel system pressure as described in Chapter 4 before disconnecting any fuel lines.*

Right valve cover

3   Remove the alternator and ignition coil pack (refer to Chapter 5).
4   Remove the bolt that secures the air conditioning tube above the upper intake manifold (if not already done when removing the coil pack).
5   Detach the spark plug wires from the valve cover clips.
6   Carefully pry the two wiring harnesses loose from the valve cover with a tool such as a door panel clip remover (available at auto parts stores).
7   Disconnect the vacuum hose at the coupling above the valve cover **(see illustration)**.

8   Carefully lift the engine wiring harness clip with your thumb at the point shown to separate it from the valve cover **(see illustration)**. Don't pull on the harness.
9   Remove the valve cover bolts and reinforcing plates **(see illustrations)**. Lift the valve cover off **(see illustration)**. Tap it gently with a soft-face hammer if necessary to break the gasket seal.

Left valve cover

10   If you haven't already done so, remove the bolt from the air conditioning tube above the upper intake manifold.
11   Disconnect the electrical connector for the air conditioning compressor clutch. Carefully pry the wiring harness from the back of the compressor with a door panel clip remover or similar tool.
12   Remove the mounting bolts from the air conditioning compressor (see Chapter 3). Lift the air conditioning compressor, then position it out of the way **(see illustration)**. **Warning:** *DO NOT disconnect any refrigerant lines!*
13   Disconnect the brake booster vacuum hose.
14   Label and disconnect the vacuum hoses from the tee on the plenum **(see illustration 10.6 in Chapter 1)**.
15   Detach the PCV hose. Remove the PCV hose and valve (see Chapter 1).
16   Carefully pry the wiring harnesses away from the valve cover with

SEALER APPLICATION

APPLY SILICONE
RUBBER
D6AZ-19562-BA
(ESE-M4G195-A)
IN 4 PLACES
FRONT AND REAR

HEAD

HEAD

BLOCK

INTAKE
MANIFOLD

SCREW (16)   STUD (2)

REINFORCEMENT (12)

COVER   COVER

REINFORCEMENT

GASKET (2)   FRONT

4.9a The valve covers and related components

4.9b Remove the valve cover bolts with a ratchet and extension . . .

4.9c . . . and lift the cover off - you may have to angle it out, as shown here - tap it gently with a soft-face hammer if necessary to break the gasket seal

a door trim panel remover or similar tool **(see illustration)**. Place the harnesses out of the way.

17 Disconnect the driver's side spark plug wires from the plugs and detach them from the clips on the valve cover. Position the wires out of the way.

18 Carefully lift the engine wiring harness clip with your thumb to separate it from the valve cover. Don't pull on the harness.

19 Remove the bolt that secures the fuel line clip to the front of the engine. Move the fuel line just enough to provide access to the front valve cover bolt. DO NOT disconnect any fuel lines without first relieving fuel pressure (see Chapter 4).

20 Remove the valve cover bolts and reinforcing plates **(see illustration 4.9a)**. Lift the valve cover off **(see illustration)**. Tap it gently with a soft-face hammer if necessary to break the gasket seal.

Installation

21 Clean the gasket surfaces on the intake manifold, cylinder head and valve cover. Use a scraper to remove the pieces of old gasket material, then wipe off all residue with lacquer thinner or acetone.

22 Most valve cover gaskets are equipped with self-sticking sealant on the valve cover side. Pull the plastic film off the gasket **(see illustration)** and stick the gasket to the valve cover.

23 **Note:** *In this step, apply silicone sealant to one side of the engine at a time (if both valve covers were removed), then install the valve cover.* Apply silicone sealant to the seam where the cylinder head joins the intake manifold **(see illustration 4.9a)**. Apply a 1/8-inch ball of sealant to the valve cover bolt holes on the outer (exhaust) side of the

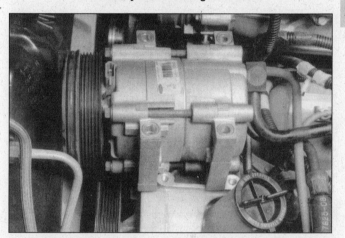

4.12 Disconnect the compressor electrical connector from the back of the compressor, then remove the mounting bolts and shift the compressor forward as shown - DO NOT disconnect any refrigerant lines

cylinder head.

24 The remainder of installation is the reverse of the removal Steps. Tighten the valve cover bolts evenly, starting with the center bolts and working out, to the torque listed in this Chapter's Specifications.

4.16 Wiring harnesses are secured to the valve cover by clips (arrow)

4.20 Move the wiring harnesses out of the way and lift the valve cover off

4.22 Just before installing the new gasket, peel the plastic film off the self-sticking sealant on the valve-cover side of the gasket

NOTE: DRAW BOLTS DOWN
EVENLY AND TORQUE IN
STAGES

5.2a The rocker arm assemblies are secured to the engine by
three bolts each

5   Rocker arms and pushrods - removal, inspection and installation

Removal

Refer to illustrations 5.2a, 5.2b, 5.3, 5.4a and 5.4b

1   Refer to Section 4 and remove the valve cover(s).
2   Loosen the rocker arm shaft support bolts two turns at a time, starting with the center bolt and working out, until the bolts can be removed by hand **(see illustrations)**.
3   Lift the rocker shaft assembly off the cylinder head **(see illustration)**. The pins will hold the components together. Mark each shaft assembly so it can be returned to the same side of the engine.
4   Lift the pushrods out of the engine **(see illustration)**. Place the pushrods in order in a holder **(see illustration)** so they can be returned to their original positions. Be sure to store them so you can reinstall them with the same end facing up.

5.4a Pull the pushrods out of the lifters . . .

5.2b Remove the bolts evenly, two turns at a time, to prevent the
shafts from being bent by valve spring pressure

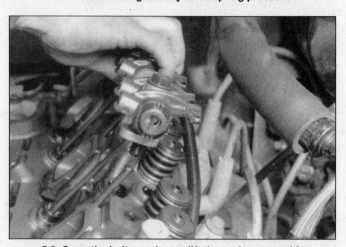

5.3 Once the bolts are loose, lift the rocker assembly
off the engine

Inspection

Refer to illustration 5.5

5   Remove the pins and disassemble the rocker arm assembly **(see illustration)**. Place the parts in order on a clean workbench. Be sure you don't mix up the parts - they must be reassembled in exactly the same order they were before disassembly.

5.4b . . . and place them in a labeled holder so they can be
returned to their original positions

5.5 Rocker arm assembly - exploded view

6 Check each rocker arm for wear, cracks and other damage, especially where the pushrods and valve stems contact the rocker arm faces.
7 Make sure all oil holes are open and not plugged. Plugging can be cleared with a piece of wire.
8 Check each rocker arm bore, and its corresponding position on the rocker shaft, for wear, cracks and galling. If the rocker arms or shaft are damaged, replace them with new ones.
9 Inspect the pushrods for cracks and excessive wear at the ends. Roll each pushrod across a piece of plate glass to see if it's bent (if it wobbles, it's bent).
10 If necessary, remove the plug from each end of the rocker shaft. Drill into one plug and insert a long steel rod through it to knock out the other plug. Knock out the first plug in the same manner.
11 If the rocker arm shaft plugs were removed, tap in new ones with a hammer and suitable drift.
12 Assemble the rocker assembly **(see illustration 5.5)**. Lubricate at

6.4 This is what the air hose adapter that threads into the spark plug hole looks like - they're commonly available from auto parts stores

friction points (pushrod ends, rocker arm bores and ends) with assembly lube.
13 Install new cotter pins in the ends of the rocker shaft. Be sure the rocker shaft oil holes will face down when the shaft is installed. The position of the oil holes is indicated by a notch on the front of each shaft.

Installation

14 Coat each end of each pushrod with assembly lube, then install them in the engine. If you are reinstalling the original pushrods, be sure to return them to their original positions.
15 Coat the rocker arm pads with assembly lube.
16 Install the rocker arm assembly on the engine. The notch on the front end of each shaft should face down.
17 Position the rocker arm ball ends in the pushrods.
18 Tighten the rocker shaft support bolts two turns at a time, working from the center bolt out, to the torque listed in this Chapter's Specifications.
19 The remainder of installation is the reverse of the removal Steps.

6 Valve springs, retainers and seals - replacement

Refer to illustrations 6.4, 6.9a, 6.9b and 6.10
Note: *Broken valve springs and defective valve stem seals can be replaced without removing the cylinder heads. Two special tools and a compressed air source are normally required to perform this operation, so read through this Section carefully and rent or buy the tools before beginning the job. If compressed air isn't available, a length of nylon rope can be used to keep the valves from falling into the cylinder during this procedure.*
1 Refer to Section 4 and remove the valve cover from the affected cylinder head. If all of the valve stem seals are being replaced, remove both valve covers.
2 Remove the spark plug from the cylinder which has the defective component. If all of the valve stem seals are being replaced, all of the spark plugs should be removed.
3 Turn the crankshaft until the piston in the affected cylinder is at top dead center on the compression stroke (refer to Section 3 for instructions). If you're replacing all of the valve stem seals, begin with cylinder number one and work on the valves for one cylinder at a time. Move from cylinder-to-cylinder following the firing order sequence (see this Chapter's Specifications).
4 Thread an adapter into the spark plug hole **(see illustration)** and connect an air hose from a compressed air source to it. Most auto parts stores can supply the air hose adapter. **Note:** *Many cylinder compression gauges utilize a screw-in fitting that may work with your air hose quick-disconnect fitting.*
5 Remove the rocker assembly on the affected side of the engine (see Section 5). If all of the valve stem seals are being replaced, remove both rocker assemblies.
6 Apply compressed air to the cylinder. **Warning:** *The piston may be forced down by compressed air, causing the crankshaft to turn suddenly. If the wrench used when positioning the number one piston at TDC is still attached to the bolt in the crankshaft nose, it could cause damage or injury when the crankshaft moves.*
7 The valves should be held in place by the air pressure. If the valve faces or seats are in poor condition, leaks may prevent air pressure from retaining the valves - refer to the alternative procedure below.
8 If you don't have access to compressed air, an alternative method can be used. Position the piston at a point just before TDC on the compression stroke, then feed a long piece of nylon rope through the spark plug hole until it fills the combustion chamber. Be sure to leave the end of the rope hanging out of the engine so it can be removed easily. Use a large ratchet and socket to rotate the crankshaft in the normal direction of rotation until slight resistance is felt.
9 Stuff shop rags into the cylinder head holes above and below the valves to prevent parts and tools from falling into the engine, then use a valve spring compressor to compress the spring. Remove the

retainer locks with small needle-nose pliers or a magnet **(see illustration)**. **Note:** *A couple of different types of tools are available for compressing the valve springs with the head in place. One type grips the lower spring coils and presses on the retainer as the knob is turned, while the other type, shown here* **(see illustration)**, *utilizes a bar installed in place of the rocker arm shaft for leverage. Both types work very well, although the knob type is more readily available.*

10   Remove the spring retainer and valve spring, then remove the valve stem seal **(see illustration)**. **Note:** *If air pressure fails to hold the valve in the closed position during this operation, the valve face or seat is probably damaged. If so, the cylinder head will have to be removed for additional repair operations.*

11   Wrap a rubber band or tape around the top of the valve stem so the valve won't fall into the combustion chamber, then release the air pressure. **Note:** *If a rope was used instead of air pressure, turn the crankshaft slightly in the direction opposite normal rotation.*

12   Inspect the valve stem for damage. Rotate the valve in the guide and check the end for eccentric movement, which would indicate that the valve is bent.

13   Move the valve up-and-down in the guide and make sure it doesn't bind. If the valve stem binds, either the valve is bent or the guide is damaged. In either case, the head will have to be removed for repair.

14   Reapply air pressure to the cylinder to retain the valve in the closed position, then remove the tape or rubber band from the valve stem. If a rope was used instead of air pressure, rotate the crankshaft in the normal direction of rotation until slight resistance is felt.

15   Lubricate the valve stem with engine oil and install a new stem seal. Ford recommends using tool T90T-6571-A to install the seal.

16   Install the spring in position over the valve.

17   Install the valve spring retainer. Compress the valve spring and carefully position the retainer locks in the groove. Apply a small dab of grease to the inside of each lock to hold it in place.

18   Remove the pressure from the spring tool and make sure the retainer locks are seated.

19   Disconnect the air hose and remove the adapter from the spark plug hole. If a rope was used in place of air pressure, pull it out of the cylinder.

20   Refer to Section 5 and install the rocker arm assembly(ies).

21   Install the spark plug(s) and hook up the wire(s).

22   Refer to Section 4 and install the valve cover(s).

23   Start and run the engine, then check for oil leaks and unusual sounds coming from the valve cover area.

6.9a Compress the valve spring, then remove the retainer locks

---

7   Intake manifold - removal and installation

Refer to illustrations 7.6a, 7.6b, 7.8, 7.9 and 7.11

Removal

1   Disconnect the negative cable from the battery.

2   Remove the upper intake manifold (see Chapter 4).

3   Remove the valve covers (see Section 4).

4   Disconnect the electrical connectors from the coolant temperature sender (see Chapter 3) and EEC-IV system coolant temperature sensor (see Chapter 6) at the front of the intake manifold.

5   Disconnect the heater hose from the front of the intake manifold. Either remove the thermostat and housing (see Chapter 3) or disconnect the upper radiator hose from the outlet fitting.

6   Remove the intake manifold nuts and bolts and lift the manifold off **(see illustrations)**. If it's stuck, tap it lightly with a soft-face hammer to break the gasket seal. If necessary, pry the manifold off, but pry between a casting protrusion and the engine - don't pry against gasket surfaces.

6.9b Here's the lever-type tool and bar used to compress the valve spring - these are special Ford tools, but equivalents may be available from automotive tool companies

6.10 Valves and related components

7.6a Intake manifold installation details

7.6b Remove the eight intake manifold bolts and nuts

Installation

7 Clean away all traces of old gasket material. Remove oil and dirt with a cloth and solvent, such as acetone or lacquer thinner.

8 Apply silicone sealant (Ford specification ESE-M4G195-C or equivalent) around the water jacket ports (the smaller ports at the ends of the heads) and to the front sealing surface. Also apply a bead of sealant to the four corners where the manifold meets the engine **(see the accompanying illustration and illustration 7.6a) Note:** *Install the manifold gasket immediately after applying the sealant. If allowed to set up (approximately 15 minutes), the sealant won't work properly.*

9 Install the manifold gasket **(see illustration)**, then reapply sealant to the four corners.

10 Install the manifold over the studs. Install the nuts and bolts and tighten them finger-tight.

11 Tighten the nuts and bolts in the four stages listed in this Chapter's Specifications, following the sequence **(see illustration)**.

12 The remainder of installation is the reverse of the removal steps.

13 Run the engine and check for oil, coolant and vacuum leaks.

8 Exhaust manifolds - removal and installation

Removal

Left manifold

1 Remove the oil dipstick tube bracket from the engine.

2 If the power steering pump hoses obstruct manifold removal, disconnect them (see Chapter 10). Cap the hoses and fittings to keep out dirt and place the hose ends out of the way.

7.8 Before installing the intake manifold gasket, apply a film of silicone sealant around the water jacket ports as well as the front sealing surface - be sure to apply extra beads to the corners (arrows) at the front and rear of the manifold

7.9 As soon as the sealant is applied, install the gasket and place extra beads of sealant in the corners

7.11 Intake manifold tightening sequence

8.5 Remove the exhaust manifold bolts (arrows)

9.15a Remove the head bolts with a T55 Torx bit - don't use an Allen wrench, since it may round out the bolt heads

Right manifold

3   Detach the heater hose bracket and disconnect the heater hoses (see Chapter 3).

Both manifolds

Refer to illustration 8.5

4   Detach the exhaust pipe from the manifold(s). **Note:** *For access to the exhaust pipe nuts, it may be necessary to raise the vehicle and support it securely on jackstands.*

5   Unbolt the manifold from the cylinder head and take it off **(see illustration).**

Installation

6   Using a scraper, thoroughly clean the mating surfaces on cylinder head, manifold and exhaust pipe. Remove residue with a solvent such as acetone or lacquer thinner.

7   **Note:** *These engines were originally assembled without exhaust manifold gaskets and can be reassembled the same way so long as the mating surfaces are perfectly flat and not damaged in any way. Warped or damaged manifolds may require a gasket or machining.* Apply some graphite grease to the cylinder head mating surface and place the

manifold on the cylinder head. Tighten the bolts evenly to the torque listed in this Chapter's Specifications.

8   Connect the exhaust pipe to the manifold and tighten the nuts evenly to the torque listed in this Chapter's Specifications.

9   The remainder of installation is the reverse of the removal steps. If the heater hoses were disconnected, fill the cooling system (see Chapter 1).

10   Run the engine and check for exhaust leaks.

9   Cylinder heads - removal and installation

Removal

Note: *Head bolt removal requires a Torx bit. Obtain the necessary tool before starting. DO NOT try to use an Allen wrench since it may round out the bolt head.*

1   Disconnect the negative cable from the battery.

2   Drain the cooling system (see Chapter 3).

3   Remove the valve covers (see Section 4).

4   Remove the rocker arms and pushrods (see Section 5).

5   Remove the intake manifold (see Section 7).

9.15b The cylinder head and related components

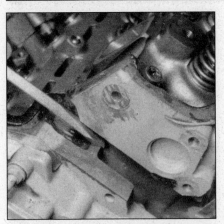

9.16 If necessary, pry the head loose; pry against a casting protrusion so the gasket surfaces won't be damaged

9.17 Remove all traces of the old gasket with a scraper, taking care not to gouge the sealing surfaces

9.20 Be sure the FRONT TOP mark on the head gasket is positioned correctly

2A

Left head

6   Remove the drivebelt (see Chapter 1).
7   If not already done, detach the air conditioning compressor from the engine and place it out of the way **(see illustration 4.12)**. DO NOT disconnect any refrigerant lines!
8   Detach the power steering pump and bracket and set them out of the way (see Chapter 10). Don't disconnect the power steering hoses.
9   There's a wiring harness attached to the rear of the head. The harness is secured to the plastic retainer with tape. Unwrap or cut the tape to detach the harness from the retainer.

Right head

10   Remove the drivebelt (see Chapter 1).
11   Remove the alternator and bracket (see Chapter 5).
12   Remove the ignition coil pack and bracket (see Chapter 5).

Both heads

Refer to illustrations 9.15a, 9.15b and 9.16

13   Remove the spark plugs (see Chapter 1).
14   Remove the exhaust manifolds (see Section 8).
15   Remove and discard the cylinder head bolts **(see illustrations)**. The bolts must be replaced with new ones whenever they are removed. Loosen the bolts in several stages.
16   Lift the cylinder head off the engine. If it's difficult to remove, carefully pry it off. Pry against a casting protrusion, not against gasket surfaces **(see illustration)**.

Installation

Refer to illustrations 9.17, 9.20 and 9.23

17   Thoroughly remove all traces of gasket material with a gasket scraper and clean all parts with solvent **(see illustration)**. Use a rag and acetone or lacquer thinner to remove any traces of oil from the gasket mating surfaces. See Chapter 2 Part B for cylinder head inspection procedures.
18   Use a tap of the correct size to chase the threads in the head bolt holes.

19   Recheck all head bolt holes and cylinder bores for any traces of coolant, oil or other foreign matter. Remove as needed.
20   Position the new gaskets over the dowel pins on the block. Don't use sealant on the gaskets. Be sure the FRONT TOP marks are positioned correctly **(see illustration)**.
21   Install the heads and new head bolts finger tight.
22   Position the intake manifold on the engine (see Section 7).
23   Following the sequence shown **(see illustration)**, tighten the head bolts in three steps to the torque listed in this Chapter's Specifications. **Note:** *The head bolts and intake manifold bolts are tightened in alternate stages to align the manifold with the heads. Be sure to refer to this Chapter's Specifications for the correct tightening stages.*
24   The remainder of installation is the reverse of the removal steps.
25   Run the engine and check for oil, coolant and vacuum leaks.

10 Crankshaft pulley, front oil seal and timing chain cover - removal and installation

Refer to illustrations 10.2, 10.3a and 10.3b

Crankshaft pulley removal and installation

1   Remove the drivebelt (see Chapter 1).
2   Remove the crankshaft pulley bolt **(see illustration)**.

9.23 Cylinder head tightening sequence

10.2 The crankshaft pulley/damper assembly and timing sensor

10.3a To remove the crankshaft pulley, remove the pulley bolt (A) and install a longer bolt that's smaller in diameter (B) into the crankshaft . . .

10.3b . . . so the puller screw (arrow) will have something to push against

10.5 To remove the front cover seal with the cover on the engine, pry it out with a screwdriver, taking care not to gouge the cover

10.13a The timing chain cover - note that the bolts are different lengths and that studs are used in some locations (water pump shown installed, but should be removed for this procedure)

A   Bolt (M8x47)   C   Stud (M8x25)
B   Bolt (M8x25)

10.13b Label the studs and brackets so they can be returned to their original locations

10.14 Remove the cover from the engine - if it's stuck, recheck to make sure all bolts and studs have been removed

3   Insert a longer, smaller-diameter bolt into the crankshaft so the puller will have something to bottom against, then remove the crankshaft pulley with a puller (Ford tool T74P-6316-A or equivalent) (see illustrations). DO NOT pry the pulley off or use an impact puller!
4   Using clean engine oil, lubricate the surface of the pulley where the front seal rides. Install the crankshaft pulley with Ford tool T74P-6316-B or equivalent. Don't hammer the pulley on. Tighten the pulley bolt to the torque listed in this Chapter's Specifications.

Front oil seal replacement

Refer to illustration 10.5
5   Remove the crankshaft pulley (see Steps 1 through 3 above). Carefully pry the oil seal out with a screwdriver (see illustration).
6   Clean the seal bore and check it for nicks or gouges.
7   Coat the lip of the new seal with clean engine oil and drive it into the bore with a socket or large piece of pipe slightly smaller in diameter than the seal. The open side of the seal faces into the engine. Install the crankshaft pulley (see Step 4 above).

Timing chain cover

Removal

Refer to illustration 10.13a, 10.13b and 10.14
8   Remove the crankshaft pulley (see Steps 1 through 3 above). Also remove the crankshaft timing sensor (see Chapter 5).

11.4 To check camshaft endplay, position the dial indicator with its tip against the camshaft sprocket bolt

DIAL INDICATOR BRACKETRY

DIAL INDICATOR

11.7 Unbolt the chain tensioner from the block - when checking timing chain deflection, mark a reference point on the block (arrow)

9   Drain the cooling system (see Chapter 1).
10   Remove the engine cooling fan and radiator (see Chapter 3).
11   Detach the air conditioning compressor and bracket (if equipped) and set them aside (see Chapter 3). DO NOT disconnect any refrigerant lines! Remove the oil pan (see Section 14).
12   Remove the water pump (see Chapter 3). Remove the heater and radiator hoses as needed to provide removal access for the timing chain cover.
13   Remove the brackets, studs and cover bolts **(see illustrations)**.
Note: *The bolts are different lengths, and bolts and studs go in different locations. Label them so they can be installed in the correct holes.*
14   Take the cover off **(see illustration)**. If it's stuck, tap it lightly with a soft-face hammer or pry it carefully to break the gasket seal. Don't use excessive force or you'll crack the cover. If it's difficult to remove, check to make sure you've removed all the bolts.

Installation

15   Thoroughly clean and inspect all parts and use a scraper to remove all traces of gasket material. Remove oil film with a solvent such as lacquer thinner or acetone.
16   Apply RTV sealant to the gasket mating surfaces. Install the guide sleeves (if removed). Install the front cover and start the studs bolts two or three turns by hand. Note that the bolts are different lengths; be sure to install them in the correct holes. If the labels made during

removal are missing or illegible, refer to illustration 10.13a.
17   Tighten the cover bolts evenly to the torque listed in this Chapter's Specifications.
18   Install the crankshaft timing sensor (see Chapter 5).
19   Install the crankshaft pulley (see Step 4 above).
20   The remainder of installation is the reverse of the removal steps.
21   Run the engine and check for oil or coolant leaks.

---

11   Timing chain and sprockets - inspection, removal and installation

Camshaft endplay check

Refer to illustration 11.4
1   Remove the timing chain cover (see Section 10).
2   Remove the rocker arm shafts (see Section 5).
3   Push the camshaft to the rear as far as it will go.
4   Install a dial indicator with its pointer on the camshaft sprocket bolt **(see illustration)**. Set the indicator to zero.
5   Pry the camshaft forward with a large screwdriver or prybar between the camshaft sprocket and the block. Note the dial indicator reading and compare with the endplay listed in this Chapter's Specifications. Replace the camshaft thrust plate (see Section 13) if endplay is excessive.

Timing chain and tensioner inspection

Refer to illustration 11.7
6   Remove the timing chain cover (see Section 10).
7   Remove the timing chain tensioner **(see illustration)**.
8   Rotate the crankshaft counterclockwise (as viewed from the front of the engine) to take up the slack in the right side of the chain.
9   Mark a reference point on the block approximately halfway along the chain and measure from that point to the right side of the chain **(see illustration 11.7)**.
10   Turn the crankshaft clockwise to take up the slack on the left side of the chain.
11   Push the chain out and measure from the reference point to the chain.
12   The difference between the two measurements is deflection. If deflection is excessive, replace the timing chain (see below).
13   Check the tensioner for wear and damage. If tensioner face wear is excessive, replace the tensioner. Before reinstalling the tensioner, it must be retracted (see Step 28). Tighten the tensioner bolts to the torque listed in this Chapter's Specifications.

2A

**11.19 Align the timing marks, then remove the camshaft
Torx bolt and crankshaft key**

11.20a Remove the timing chain and sprockets together

Chain and sprocket

Removal

Refer to illustrations 11.19, 11.20a, 11.20b

14   Drain the cooling system and engine oil (see Chapter 1).

15   Remove the oil pan (see Section 14).

16   Replace the oil filter (see Chapter 1).

17   Remove the drivebelt (see Chapter 1).

18   Remove the timing chain cover (see Section 10).

19   Turn the crankshaft (see Section 3, Step 4) until the timing marks are aligned **(see illustration)**. Remove the camshaft sprocket Torx bolt and the crankshaft sprocket key. Also remove the timing chain tensioner **(see illustration 11.7)**.

20   Remove the sprockets together with the chain **(see illustrations)**. Do not disturb the crankshaft or camshaft while the timing chain and sprockets are removed.

21   If necessary, remove the Torx bolts that secure the chain guide and remove it from the block.

Installation

Refer to illustration 11.28

22   Be sure the crankshaft and camshaft are positioned so the sprocket timing marks will align correctly after the sprockets are installed **(see illustration 11.19)**.

23   If the chain guide was removed, install it. Be sure its pin is inserted into the block oil hole, then tighten the guide bolts to the torque listed in this Chapter's Specifications.

24   Place the sprockets in the chain with their timing marks aligned **(see illustration 11.19)**. Install the sprockets and chain together on the crankshaft and camshaft.

25   Install the crankshaft key.

26   Make sure the sprocket timing marks are still aligned **(see illustration 11.19)**. The guide side of the chain must be straight, without any slack, for the marks to align accurately.

27   Install the camshaft sprocket bolt and tighten to the torque listed in this Chapter's Specifications.

28   Squeeze the tensioner pad with your fingers. At the same time, use a sharp-tipped probe to push the ratchet mechanism down, then in. This will release the latch and let the tensioner retract **(see illustration)**. Retain the tensioner pad in the retracted position by holding it or installing a clip **(see illustration 11.19)** or similar device.

29   Install the timing chain tensioner and tighten its bolts to the torque listed in this Chapter's Specifications.

30   The remainder of installation is the reverse of the removal Steps.

31   Run the engine and check for oil or coolant leaks.

11.20b Timing chain and sprockets - exploded view

**11.28 To retract the timing chain tensioner so it can be installed,
squeeze the tensioner pad and use a sharp-tipped probe to
push the ratchet mechanism down, then in to release
the latch and let the tensioner retract**

12.4 Store the lifters in a marked box so they can be returned to their original positions

12.8a Check the pushrod seat (arrow) in the top of each lifter for wear

12.8b The roller on roller lifters must turn freely - check for wear and excessive play as well

12 Valve lifters - removal, inspection and installation

Refer to illustrations 12.4, 12.8a, 12.8b and 12.11

Removal

1   Remove the intake manifold (see Section 7).

2   Remove the cylinder heads (see Section 9).

3   The lifters protrude from the bores, so if there isn't a lot of varnish buildup, simply pull them out of their bores with your fingers. On engines with a lot of sludge and varnish, work the lifters up and down, using carburetor spray cleaner to loosen the deposits. If the lifters are particularly stubborn, special tools designed to grip and remove lifters (Ford tool no. T70P-14151 or equivalent) are manufactured by many tool companies and are widely available.

4   Before removing the lifters, arrange to store them in a clearly labeled box to ensure that they're installed in their original locations **(see illustration)**.

5   Remove the lifters and store them where they won't get dirty.

Inspection

6   Parts for hydraulic valve lifters are not available separately. The work required to remove them from the engine again if cleaning is unsuccessful outweighs any potential savings from repairing them.

7   Clean the lifters with solvent and dry them thoroughly without mixing them up.

8   Check each lifter wall, pushrod seat and roller for scuffing, score marks and uneven wear. Replace any lifter that shows these conditions. If the lifter walls are worn (which isn't very likely), inspect the lifter bores in the engine block as well. If the pushrod seats are worn **(see illustration)**, check the pushrod ends. Make sure each roller turns freely **(see illustration)**.

9   If new lifters are being installed, a new camshaft must also be installed. If the camshaft is replaced, then use new lifters as well. Ford recommends that the lifters and camshaft be replaced as a set if any lifter needs replacement. Never install used lifters unless the original camshaft is used and the lifters can be installed in their original locations!

10   The original lifters, if they're being reinstalled, must be returned to their original locations.

Installation

11   Install the lifters in the bores. Coat them with moly-based grease or engine assembly lube. Note that when the lifters are installed, the alignment tab must fit in the groove in the lifter bore **(see illustration)**.

12   The remainder of installation is the reverse of the removal Steps.

13 Camshaft - removal, inspection and installation

Endplay check

1   Refer to Section 11 for this procedure.

Lobe lift check

2   In order to determine the extent of cam lobe wear, the lobe lift should be checked prior to camshaft removal. Refer to Section 4 and remove the valve covers. The rocker arm assembly must also be removed (see Section 5), but leave the pushrods in place.

3   Position the number one piston to TDC on the compression stroke (see Section 3).

4   Beginning with the number one cylinder, mount a dial indicator on the engine and position the plunger in-line with and resting on the first pushrod.

5   Zero the dial indicator, then very slowly turn the crankshaft in the normal direction of rotation until the indicator needle stops and begins to move in the opposite direction. The point at which it stops indicates maximum cam lobe lift.

6   Record this figure for future reference, then reposition the piston at TDC on the compression stroke.

7   Move the dial indicator to the remaining number one cylinder pushrod and repeat the check. Be sure to record the results for each valve.

12.11 The alignment tab on each lifter must be positioned in its groove in the lifter bore

ROLLER LIFTER

ALIGNMENT TAB

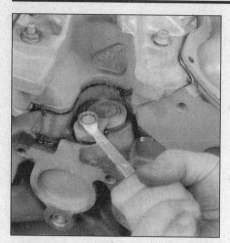

13.17a Remove the oil pump drive gear bolt . . .

13.17b . . . and lift the gear out of the block

13.25 Remove the camshaft thrust plate bolts with a Torx bit and take the thrust plate off - note which end of the thrust plate is up so it can be installed correctly

13.26 As you're withdrawing it, support the camshaft near the block with both hands - be careful not to let the camshaft nick the bearings

8   Repeat the check for the remaining valves. Since each piston must be at TDC on the compression stroke for this procedure, work from cylinder-to-cylinder, following the firing order sequence.
9   After the check is complete, compare the results to this Chapter's Specifications. If camshaft lobe lift is less than specified for any of the lobes, cam lobe wear has occurred and a new camshaft should be installed.

Removal

Refer to illustrations 13.17a, 13.17b, 13.25 and 13.26
Note: *This procedure requires engine removal.*
10   Disconnect the negative cable from the battery.
11   Drain the cooling system and engine oil (see Chapter 1).
12   Remove the radiator and fan (see Chapter 3).
13   Remove the drivebelt (see Chapter 1).
14   Remove the spark plug wires (see Chapter 1). Remove the ignition coil pack and bracket (see Chapter 5).
15   Remove the alternator (see Chapter 5).
16   Remove the engine (see Chapter 2, Part B).
17   On all 1993 models and 1994 Federal emissions models, remove the oil pump drive gear from the block **(see illustrations)**. On 1994 California emissions models and all 1995 and later models, mark the exact orientation of the camshaft position sensor in relation to the block. The camshaft position sensor is installed in the same location as the oil pump drive gear on earlier models. Remove the camshaft position sensor and synchronizer assembly (see Chapter 5).
18   Remove the intake manifold (see Section 7). The upper intake

manifold can be left attached to the lower manifold.
19   Remove the valve covers (see Section 4).
20   Remove the rocker arms and pushrods (see Section 5).
21   Remove the valve lifters (see Section 12).
22   Remove the oil pan (see Section 14).
23   Remove the timing chain cover (see Section 10).
24   Remove the timing chain and sprockets (see Section 11).
25   Remove the camshaft thrust plate bolts with a Torx bit **(see illustration)** and take the thrust plate off the block.
26   Carefully pull the camshaft out of the block, rotating it as you pull **(see illustration)**. Don't let the camshaft lobes or journals nick the camshaft bearings.

Inspection

27   After the camshaft has been removed from the engine, cleaned with solvent and dried, inspect the bearing journals for uneven wear, pits and galling. If the journals are damaged, the bearing inserts in the engine are probably damaged as well. Both the camshaft and bearings will have to be replaced with new ones. Using a telescoping gauge, measure the inside diameter of each camshaft bearing and record the results (take two measurements, 90-degrees apart, at each bearing).
28   Measure the camshaft bearing journals with a micrometer to determine if they're excessively worn or out-of-round. If they're out-of-round, the camshaft should be replaced with a new one. Subtract the bearing journal diameters from the corresponding bearing inside diameter measurements to obtain the oil clearance. If it's excessive, new bearings must be installed. **Note:** *Camshaft bearing replacement requires special tools and expertise that place it outside the scope of the home mechanic. Take the block to an automotive machine shop to ensure that the job is done correctly.*
29   Check the camshaft lobes for heat discoloration, score marks, chopped areas, pitting, flaking and uneven wear. If the lobes are in good condition the camshaft can be reused.
30   Make sure the camshaft oil passages are clear and clean.

Installation

31   Lubricate the camshaft bearing journals and cam lobes with moly-base grease or engine assembly lube.
32   Slide the camshaft into the engine. Support the cam near the block and be careful not to scrape or nick the bearings.
33   Coat both sides of the thrust plate with assembly lube or SAE 50 engine oil, then install it. Tighten its bolts to the torque listed in this Chapter's Specifications.
34   The remainder of installation is the reverse of the removal Steps. On models with a camshaft position sensor, install it as described in Chapter 6.

14.2a The oil pan and related components - exploded view

14.2b Use a Torx driver to remove the two bolts (arrows) adjacent to the crankshaft rear oil seal

14.3 The oil baffle is secured to the main bearing caps

14 Oil pan and baffle - removal and installation

Removal

Refer to illustrations 14.2a, 14.2b and 14.3

1   Remove the engine from the vehicle (see Part B of this Chapter).

2   Remove the oil pan fasteners (see illustration) and remove the pan from the engine. Use a Torx bit to remove the bolt on each side of the crankshaft rear oil seal (see illustration).

3   If necessary, remove the baffle fasteners and remove the baffle (see illustration).

Installation

Refer to illustrations 14.5, 14.9a, 14.9b, and 14.10

Caution: Since two of the oil pan bolts are attached to the transmission, spacers are used between the oil pan and transmission. Failure to select the spacers correctly can cause oil pan damage or oil leaks when the pan is installed.

4   Using a gasket scraper, thoroughly clean all old gasket material from the oil pan and its mounting surface. Remove residue and oil film with a solvent such as acetone or lacquer thinner.

5   Place the pan on the engine. Place a straightedge across the transmission mounting surface on the cylinder block and one of the mounting pads for the oil pan-to-transmission bolts (see illustration).

6   Measure the gap between the mounting pad and straightedge with a feeler gauge.

7   Move the straightedge to the other mounting pad and measure its gap.

8   Select spacers for the mounting pads to compensate for the gap. Spacers are available in three thicknesses (see this Chapter's Specifications).

9   At the rear of the engine, apply a thin bead of RTV sealant to the outside edge of the gasket surface and another bead to the area around

14.5 To select pan-to-transmission spacers, place a straightedge on the transmission mounting surface and each of the pan-to-transmission mounting pads in turn and measure the gap between the straightedge and the mounting pad

14.9a At the rear of the engine, apply thin beads of sealant to the outside edges of the gasket surface (A) and also to the crankshaft rear oil seal corners (B)

14.9b Apply beads of sealant to the corners of the front seal cover (arrows) and at the seams where the timing chain cover meets the engine block

14.10 The long Torx screw next to the crankshaft rear oil seal passes through a boss on the pan, then through the pan flange and into the block

the crankshaft rear oil seal **(see illustration)**. At the front of the engine, apply a bead of sealant to each of the engine block-to-timing-chain cover seams and to the corners of the front seal cover **(see illustration)**.
10   Install a new pan gasket on the engine. Install the pan fasteners and tighten evenly to the torque listed in this Chapter's Specifications. The long screw next to the crankshaft rear oil seal passes through a

boss on the pan, then through the pan flange and into the block **(see illustration)**.
11   Install the spacers on the mounting pads before bolting the engine to the transmission.

15   Oil pump - removal and installation

Removal

Refer to illustrations 15.2, 15.3 and 15.4
1   Remove the oil pan (see Section 14).
2   Remove the oil pump bolts and take the pump off the engine **(see illustration)**.
3   Pull the oil pump intermediate driveshaft out of the engine **(see illustration)**.
4   Unbolt the inlet tube and screen from the pump **(see illustration)**.

Installation

5   Fill one of the pump ports with clean engine oil and rotate the

15.2 Remove the oil pump bolts and lift the pump off the engine

15.3 As you remove the intermediate driveshaft, note the different shapes of its ends and the location of the retainer ring on the shaft

15.4 The oil pump and related components

16.5 Drive the seal in squarely and evenly - a large socket or piece of pipe can be used if a seal driver isn't available

16.11 Thread two sheet metal screws into the crankshaft rear oil seal to pry it out

16.15 Install the crankshaft rear oil seal with the open end facing into the engine - use a socket or large piece of pipe if a seal driver isn't available

pump by hand to prime it.

6   Install the oil pump pick-up tube on the pump, using a new gasket.

7   Insert the intermediate drive shaft into the engine, pointed end first. The pressed-on retaining ring on the shaft should be positioned as shown in illustration 15.4.

8   Install the oil pump on the block, using a new gasket. Install the oil pump bolts and tighten to the torque listed in this Chapter's Specifications.

9   The remainder of installation is the reverse of removal.

10   Run the engine and make sure oil pressure comes up to normal quickly. If it doesn't, stop the engine and find out the cause. Severe engine damage can result from running an engine with insufficient oil pressure!

16 Crankshaft oil seals - replacement

Front seal - timing chain cover in place

1   Refer to Section 10 for this procedure.

Front seal - timing chain cover removed

Refer to illustration 16.5

2   Support the timing chain cover on wooden blocks, then drive out the seal with a punch and hammer.

3   Check the seal bore in the timing chain cover for nicks or burrs.

4   Coat the seal lip and outer circumference with engine oil.

5   Position the new seal with its lip facing IN. Drive in the new seal with a seal driver **(see illustration)**. If a seal driver isn't available, use a socket or piece of pipe the same diameter as the seal.

Rear seal

Refer to illustrations 16.11, 16.15 and 16.16

6   Remove the transmission (see Chapter 7).

7   Remove the clutch (if equipped) (see Chapter 8).

8   Remove the flywheel or driveplate (see Section 17).

9   Remove the engine rear plate.

10   With a sharp awl or similar tool, punch two holes in the seal on opposite sides just above the point where the main bearing cap meets the cylinder block.

11   Thread a sheet metal screw into each hole **(see illustration)**. Pry against the sheet metal screws with two large screwdrivers or small prybars to remove the seal. **Note:** *If you need a fulcrum to pry against, use two small blocks of wood.* **Caution:** *Don't scratch or gouge the crankshaft seal surface.*

12   Clean the oil seal bore in the block and main bearing cap. Check the seal bore and crankshaft sealing surface for nicks or burrs.

13   Apply a thin coat of clean engine oil to the outer diameter of the seal. Apply a thin coat of Lubriplate or equivalent to the contact

surfaces of the seal and crankshaft.

14   Position the seal in the bore with its open end facing IN.

15   Drive the seal in with a seal driver **(see illustration)** until it is securely seated. Use a socket or piece of pipe the same diameter as the seal if a seal driver isn't available.

16   After installation, squareness of the rear seal with the crankshaft centerline and the dimension from the seal to the rear face of the block must be within the tolerances listed in this Chapter's Specifications **(see illustration)**.

17 Flywheel/driveplate - removal and installation

Refer to illustrations 17.3 and 17.4

1   Raise the vehicle and support it securely on jackstands, then refer to Chapter 7 and remove the transmission. If it's leaking, now would be a very good time to replace the front pump seal/O-ring (automatic transmission only).

16.16 The crankshaft rear oil seal must be square with the crankshaft centerline and within the specified dimension from the rear face of the cylinder block

17.3 Paint alignment marks on the flywheel/driveplate and crankshaft - note how deep the paint mark must go to reach the crankshaft

17.4 Remove the mounting bolts and take the flywheel/driveplate off the crankshaft - the manual transmission flywheel is heavy, so be sure to support it during removal

2   Remove the pressure plate and clutch disc (see Chapter 8) (manual transmission equipped vehicles). Now is a good time to check/replace the clutch components and pilot bearing.

3   Paint alignment marks on the flywheel/driveplate and crankshaft to ensure correct alignment during reinstallation **(see illustration)**.

4   Remove the bolts that secure the flywheel/driveplate to the crankshaft **(see illustration)**. If the crankshaft turns, wedge a screwdriver through the starter opening to jam the flywheel.

5   Remove the flywheel/driveplate from the crankshaft. Since the flywheel is fairly heavy, be sure to support it while removing the last bolt.

6   Clean the flywheel to remove grease and oil. Inspect the surface for cracks, rivet grooves, burned areas and score marks. Light scoring can be removed with emery cloth. Check for cracked and broken ring gear teeth. Lay the flywheel on a flat surface and use a straightedge to check for warpage.

7   Clean and inspect the mating surfaces of the flywheel/driveplate and the crankshaft. If the crankshaft rear seal is leaking, replace it before reinstalling the flywheel/driveplate.

8   Position the flywheel/driveplate against the crankshaft. Be sure to align the marks made during removal. Note that some engines have an alignment dowel or staggered bolt holes to ensure correct installation. Before installing the bolts, apply thread locking compound to the threads.

18.8 Engine and transmission mount details

9   Wedge a screwdriver through the starter motor opening to keep the flywheel/driveplate from turning as you tighten the bolts to the torque listed in this Chapter's Specifications.

10   The remainder of installation is the reverse of the removal procedure.

18   Engine mounts - check and replacement

Refer to illustration 18.8

1   Engine mounts seldom require attention, but broken or deteriorated mounts should be replaced immediately or the added strain placed on the driveline components may cause damage or wear.

Check

2   During the check, the engine must be raised slightly to remove the weight from the mounts.

3   Raise the vehicle and support it securely on jackstands, then position a jack under the engine oil pan. Place a large block of wood between the jack head and the oil pan, then carefully raise the engine just enough to take the weight off the mounts. **Warning:** *DO NOT place any part of your body under the engine when it's supported only by a jack!*

4   Check the mounts to see if the rubber is cracked, hardened or separated from the metal plates. Sometimes the rubber will split right down the center.

5   Check for relative movement between the mount plates and the engine or frame (use a large screwdriver or pry bar to attempt to move the mounts). If movement is noted, lower the engine and tighten the mount fasteners.

6   Rubber preservative should be applied to the mounts to slow deterioration.

Replacement

7   Disconnect the negative battery cable from the battery, then raise the vehicle and support it securely on jackstands (if not already done).

8   Remove the fasteners and detach the mount from the frame bracket **(see illustration)**.

9   Raise the engine slightly with a jack or hoist (make sure the fan doesn't hit the radiator or shroud). Remove the mount-to-block bolts and detach the mount.

10   Installation is the reverse of removal. Use thread locking compound on the mount bolts and be sure to tighten them securely.

Chapter 2 Part B
General engine overhaul procedures

Contents

	Section
CHECK ENGINE light on	See Chapter 6
Compression check	3
Crankshaft - inspection	18
Crankshaft - installation and main bearing oil clearance check	22
Crankshaft - removal	13
Cylinder head - cleaning and inspection	9
Cylinder head - disassembly	8
Cylinder head - reassembly	11
Cylinder honing	16
Engine - removal and installation	5
Engine block - cleaning	14
Engine block - inspection	15
Engine overhaul - disassembly sequence	7
Engine overhaul - general information	2
Engine overhaul - reassembly sequence	20
Engine rebuilding alternatives	6
Engine removal - methods and precautions	4
General information	1
Initial start-up and break-in after overhaul	24
Main and connecting rod bearings - inspection	19
Piston rings - installation	21
Pistons/connecting rods - inspection	17
Pistons/connecting rods - installation and rod bearing oil clearance check	23
Pistons/connecting rods - removal	12
Valves - servicing	10

Specifications

General

Displacement ... 4.0 liters
Cylinder compression pressure ... 101 psi min (see accompanying chart)
Oil pressure (engine warm at 2000 rpm) ... 40 to 60 psi

Maximum PSI	Minimum PSI	Maximum PSI	Minimum PSI	Maximum PSI	Minimum PSI	Maximum PSI	Minimum PSI
134	101	164	123	194	145	224	168
136	102	166	124	196	147	226	169
138	104	168	126	198	148	228	171
140	105	170	127	200	150	230	172
142	107	172	129	202	151	232	174
144	108	174	131	204	153	234	175
146	110	176	132	206	154	236	177
148	111	178	133	208	156	238	178
150	113	180	135	210	157	240	180
152	114	182	136	212	158	242	181
154	115	184	138	214	160	244	183
156	117	186	140	216	162	246	184
158	118	188	141	218	163	248	186
160	120	190	142	220	165	250	187
162	121	192	144	222	166		

Cylinder compression variation chart - locate your maximum compression reading on the chart and look to the right to find the minimum acceptable compression (then compare it to your lowest reading)

Cylinder head warpage limit .... 0.003 inch per 6 inches; 0.006 inch overall

Valves and related components

Minimum valve margin width .... 1/32 inch
Intake valve
    Seat angle 45-degrees
    Seat width .... 0.060 to 0.079 inch
    Seat runout limit .... 0.0015 inch total indicator reading
    Stem diameter .... 0.3159 to 0.3167 inch
    Stem-to-guide clearance .... 0.0008 to 0.0025 inch
    Valve face runout limit .... 0.002 inch
    Valve face angle 44-degrees
Exhaust valve
    Seat angle 45-degrees
    Seat width .... 0.060 to 0.079 inch
    Seat runout limit .... 0.0015 inch total indicator reading
    Stem diameter .... 0.3149 to 0.3156 inch
    Stem-to-guide clearance .... 0.0018 to 0.0035 inch
    Valve face runout limit .... 0.002 inch
    Valve face angle 44-degrees
Valve spring
    Pressure .... 60.0 to 68.0 lbs at 1.585 inch
    Service limit .... 10% pressure loss at specified length
    Free length (approximate) .... 1.91 inch
    Installed height .... 1-37/64 to 1-39/64 inch
    Maximum out-of-square .... 5/64 inch
Valve lifter
    Diameter (standard) .... 0.8742 to 0.8755 inch
    Lifter-to-bore clearance
        Standard .... 0.0005 to 0.0022 inch
        Service limit... 0.005 inch

Crankshaft and connecting rods

Connecting rod journal
    Diameter (standard) .... 2.1252 to 2.1260 inches
    Out-of-round limit .... 0.0006 inch
    Taper limit .... 0.0006 inch per inch
    Bearing oil clearance
        Desired .... 0.0005 to 0.0022 inch
        Allowable... 0.0003 to 0.0024 inch
Connecting rod side clearance (endplay)
    Standard... 0.0002 to 0.0025 inch
    Service limit.. 0.014 inch
Main bearing journal
    Diameter .... 2.2433 to 2.2441 inches
    Out-of-round limit .... 0.0006 inch
    Taper limit .... 0.0006 inch per inch
    Bearing oil clearance
        Desired .... 0.0008 to 0.0015 inch
        Allowable... 0.0005 to 0.0019 inch
Crankshaft endplay
    Standard... 0.0016 to 0.0126 inch
    Service limit.. 0.012 inch

Cylinder bore

Diameter .... 3.9527 to 3.9543 inches
Out-of-round service limit .... 0.005 inch
Taper service limit .... 0.010 inch

Pistons and rings

Piston diameter.. 3.9524 to 3.9531 inches
Piston-to-bore clearance.. 0.0008 to 0.0019 inch
Piston ring end gap
    Compression rings .... 0.015 to 0.023 inch
    Oil ring rails.. 0.015 to 0.055 inch
Piston ring side clearance
    Compression rings
        Standard .... 0.0020 to 0.0033 inch
        Service limit... 0.006 inch
    Oil ring .... Snug fit

Torque specifications*

	Ft-lbs
Main bearing cap bolts	66 to 77
Connecting rod cap nuts	18 to 24

Note: Refer to Part A for additional torque specifications.

Cylinder block, crankshaft and related components - exploded view

1 General information

Included in this portion of Chapter 2 are the general overhaul procedures for the cylinder heads and internal engine components.

The information ranges from advice concerning preparation for an overhaul and the purchase of replacement parts to detailed, step-by-step procedures covering removal and installation of internal engine components and the inspection of parts.

The following Sections have been written based on the assumption that the engine has been removed from the vehicle. For information concerning in-vehicle engine repair, as well as removal and installation of the external components necessary for the overhaul, see Part A of this Chapter and Section 7 of this Part.

The Specifications included in this Part are only those necessary for the inspection and overhaul procedures which follow.
Refer to Part A for additional Specifications.

2 Engine overhaul - general information

Refer to illustration 2.4

it's not always easy to determine when, or if, an engine should be completely overhauled, as a number of factors must be considered.

High mileage is not necessarily an indication that an overhaul is needed, while low mileage doesn't preclude the need for an overhaul. Frequency of servicing is probably the most important consideration. An engine that's had regular and frequent oil and filter changes, as well as other required maintenance, will most likely give many thousands of miles of reliable service. Conversely, a neglected engine may require an overhaul very early in its life.

Excessive oil consumption is an indication that piston rings, valve seals and/or valve guides are in need of attention. Make sure that oil leaks aren't responsible before deciding that the rings and/or guides are bad. Perform a cylinder compression check to determine the extent of the work required (see Section 3).

2.4 The oil pressure sending unit is mounted low on the engine, at the front on the driver's side

3.6 A gauge with a threaded fitting for the spark plug hole is preferred over the type that requires hand pressure to maintain the seal during the compression check

Check the oil pressure with a gauge installed in place of the oil pressure sending unit **(see illustration)** and compare it to this Chapter's Specifications. If it's extremely low, the bearings and/or oil pump are probably worn out.

Loss of power, rough running, knocking or metallic engine noises, excessive valve train noise and high fuel consumption rates may also point to the need for an overhaul, especially if they're all present at the same time. If a complete tune-up doesn't remedy the situation, major mechanical work is the only solution.

An engine overhaul involves restoring the internal parts to the specifications of a new engine. During an overhaul, the piston rings are replaced and the cylinder walls are reconditioned (rebored and/or honed). If a rebore is done by an automotive machine shop, new oversize pistons will also be installed. The main bearings, connecting rod bearings and camshaft bearings are generally replaced with new ones and, if necessary, the crankshaft may be reground to restore the journals. Generally, the valves are serviced as well, since they're usually in less-than-perfect condition at this point.

While the engine is being overhauled, other components, such as the starter and alternator, can be rebuilt as well. The end result should be a like-new engine that will give many trouble-free miles. **Note:** *Critical cooling system components such as the hoses, drivebelts, thermostat and water pump MUST be replaced with new parts when an engine is overhauled.* The radiator should be checked carefully to ensure that it isn't clogged or leaking (see Chapter 3). Also, we don't recommend overhauling the oil pump - always install a new one when an engine is rebuilt.

Before beginning the engine overhaul, read through the entire procedure to familiarize yourself with the scope and requirements of the job. Overhauling an engine isn't difficult if you follow all of the instructions carefully, have the necessary tools and equipment and pay close attention to all specifications; however, it is time consuming. Plan on the vehicle being tied up for a minimum of two weeks, especially if parts must be taken to an automotive machine shop for repair or reconditioning. Check on availability of parts and make sure that any necessary special tools and equipment are obtained in advance. Most work can be done with typical hand tools, although a number of precision measuring tools are required for inspecting parts to determine if they must be replaced. Often an automotive machine shop will handle the inspection of parts and offer advice concerning reconditioning and replacement. **Note:** *Always wait until the engine has been completely disassembled and all components, especially the engine block, have been inspected before deciding what service and repair operations must be performed by an automotive machine shop.* Since the block's condition will be the major factor to consider when determining whether to overhaul the original engine or buy a rebuilt one, never purchase parts or have machine work done on other components until the block has been thoroughly inspected. As a general rule, time is the primary cost of an

overhaul, so it doesn't pay to install worn or substandard parts.

As a final note, to ensure maximum life and minimum trouble from a rebuilt engine, everything must be assembled with care in a spotlessly clean environment.

3   Compression check

Refer to illustration 3.6

1   A compression check will tell you what mechanical condition the upper end (pistons, rings, valves, head gaskets) of your engine is in. Specifically, it can tell you if the compression is down due to leakage caused by worn piston rings, defective valves and seats or a blown head gasket. **Note:** *The engine must be at normal operating temperature and the battery must be fully charged for this check.*

2   Begin by cleaning the area around the spark plugs before you remove them (compressed air should be used, if available, otherwise a small brush or even a bicycle tire pump will work). The idea is to prevent dirt from getting into the cylinders as the compression check is being done.

3   Remove all of the spark plugs from the engine (see Chapter 1).

4   Block the throttle wide open.

5   Disable the ignition system by detaching the electrical connector from the coil pack above the left valve cover. The fuel pump circuit should also be disabled (see Chapter 4, Section 2).

6   Install the compression gauge in the number one spark plug hole **(see illustration)**.

7   Crank the engine over at least seven compression strokes and watch the gauge. The compression should build up quickly in a healthy engine. Low compression on the first stroke, followed by gradually increasing pressure on successive strokes, indicates worn piston rings. A low compression reading on the first stroke, which doesn't build up during successive strokes, indicates leaking valves or a blown head gasket (a cracked head could also be the cause). Deposits on the undersides of the valve heads can also cause low compression. Record the highest gauge reading obtained.

8   Repeat the procedure for the remaining cylinders and compare the results to this Chapter's Specifications.

9   Add some engine oil (about three squirts from a plunger-type oil can) to each cylinder, through the spark plug hole, and repeat the test.

10   If the compression increases after the oil is added, the piston rings are definitely worn. If the compression doesn't increase significantly, the leakage is occurring at the valves or head gasket. Leakage past the valves may be caused by burned valve seats and/or faces or warped, cracked or bent valves.

11   If two adjacent cylinders have equally low compression, there's a strong possibility that the head gasket between them is blown. The appearance of coolant in the combustion chambers or the crankcase

5.5a Label each wire before unplugging the connector

5.5b The oil level sensor is mounted in the oil pan, forward of the starter

5.5c The electrical connector for the variable reluctance sensor is located near the crankshaft pulley (arrow)

2B

would verify this condition.

12 If one cylinder is 20-percent lower than the others, and the engine has a slightly rough idle, a worn exhaust lobe on the camshaft could be the cause.

13 If the compression is unusually high, the combustion chambers are probably coated with carbon deposits. If that's the case, the cylinder head(s) should be removed and decarbonized.

14 If compression is way down or varies greatly between cylinders, it would be a good idea to have a leak-down test performed by an automotive repair shop. This test will pinpoint exactly where the leakage is occurring and how severe it is.

4 Engine removal - methods and precautions

If you've decided that an engine must be removed for overhaul or major repair work, several preliminary steps should be taken.

Locating a suitable place to work is extremely important. Adequate work space, along with storage space for the vehicle, will be needed. If a shop or garage isn't available, at the very least a flat, level, clean work surface made of concrete or asphalt is required.

Cleaning the engine compartment and engine before beginning the removal procedure will help keep tools clean and organized.

An engine hoist or A-frame will also be necessary. Make sure the equipment is rated in excess of the combined weight of the engine and accessories. Safety is of primary importance, considering the potential hazards involved in lifting the engine out of the vehicle.

If the engine is being removed by a novice, a helper should be available. Advice and aid from someone more experienced would also be helpful. There are many instances when one person cannot simultaneously perform all of the operations required when lifting the engine out of the vehicle.

Plan the operation ahead of time. Arrange for or obtain all of the tools and equipment you'll need prior to beginning the job. Some of the equipment necessary to perform engine removal and installation safely and with relative ease are (in addition to an engine hoist) a heavy duty floor jack, complete sets of wrenches and sockets as described in the front of this manual, wooden blocks and plenty of rags and cleaning solvent for mopping up spilled oil, coolant and gasoline. If the hoist must be rented, make sure that you arrange for it in advance and perform all of the operations possible without it beforehand. This will save you money and time.

Plan for the vehicle to be out of use for quite a while. A machine shop will be required to perform some of the work which the do-it-yourselfer can't accomplish without special equipment. These shops often have a busy schedule, so it would be a good idea to consult them before removing the engine in order to accurately estimate the amount of time required to rebuild or repair components that may need work.

Always be extremely careful when removing and installing the engine. Serious injury can result from careless actions. Plan ahead, take your time and a job of this nature, although major, can be accomplished successfully.

5 Engine - removal and installation

Removal

Refer to illustrations 5.5a, 5.5b, 5.5c, 5.15 and 5.24

1 Refer to Chapter 4 and relieve the fuel system pressure, then disconnect the negative cable from the battery.

2 Cover the fenders and cowl and remove the hood (see Chapter 11). Special pads are available to protect the fenders, but an old bedspread or blanket will also work.

3 Remove the air cleaner assembly.

4 Drain the cooling system (see Chapter 1).

5 Label the vacuum lines, emissions system hoses, wiring connectors, ground straps and fuel lines to ensure correct reinstallation, then detach them. Pieces of masking tape with numbers or letters written on them work well **(see illustration)**. If there's any possibility of confusion, make a sketch of the engine compartment and clearly label the lines, hoses and wires. Don't forget the following:

  a) *Oil level sensor connector (in the oil pan on the driver's side of the vehicle)* **(see illustration)**.

  b) *Wiring harness at the rear of the driver's side cylinder head.*

  c) *Hose bracket at the lower front corner of the engine on the passenger's side.*

  d) *Variable reluctance sensor connector near the crankshaft pulley* **(see illustration)**.

6 Label and detach all coolant hoses from the engine.

7 Remove the drivebelt (see Chapter 1).

8 Remove the cooling fan, shroud and radiator (see Chapter 3).

9 **Warning:** *Gasoline is extremely flammable, so extra precautions must be taken when working on any part of the fuel system. DO NOT smoke or allow open flames or bare light bulbs near the vehicle. Also, don't work in a garage if a natural gas appliance with a pilot light is present. Disconnect the fuel lines running from the engine to the chassis (see Chapter 4). Plug or cap all open fittings/lines.*

10 Disconnect the throttle linkage (and TV linkage/speed control cable, if equipped) from the engine (see Chapter 4).

11 Unbolt the power steering pump (see Chapter 10). Leave the lines/hoses attached and make sure the pump is kept in an upright position in the engine compartment (use wire or rope to restrain it out of the way).

12 On air-conditioned models, unbolt the compressor (see Chapter 3) and set it aside. DO NOT disconnect the hoses!

13 Drain the engine oil (Chapter 1) and remove the filter.

14 Remove the starter motor (see Chapter 5).

5.15 To remove the alternator bracket, remove the lower idler pulley bolt and pulley (A), but don't remove the drivebelt adjustment pulley (B) - then remove the three bracket bolts (arrows); one bolt is hidden behind the adjustment pulley

5.24 Carefully raise the engine from the engine compartment

15   Remove the alternator (see Chapter 5). Remove the alternator bracket **(see illustration)**.
16   Unbolt the exhaust system from the engine (see Chapter 4).
17   If you're working on a vehicle with an automatic transmission, refer to Chapter 7 and remove the torque converter-to-driveplate fasteners.
18   Support the transmission with a jack. Position a block of wood between the jack head and transmission to prevent damage to the transmission. Special transmission jacks with safety chains are available - use one if possible.
19   Attach an engine sling or a length of chain to the lifting brackets on the engine.
20   Roll the hoist into position and connect the sling to it. Take up the slack in the sling or chain, but don't lift the engine. **Warning:** *DO NOT place any part of your body under the engine when it's supported only by a hoist or other lifting device.*
21   Remove the transmission-to-engine block bolts. Be sure to remove the two bolts that secure the engine oil pan to the transmission.
22   Remove the engine mount-to-frame bolts (see Section 18 of Part A).
23   Recheck to be sure nothing is still connecting the engine to the transmission or vehicle. Disconnect anything still remaining.
24   Raise the engine slightly. It should move easily if it's completely disconnected. If it doesn't, it's stuck - DO NOT try to pry it loose or force it loose with the hoist, since it could shift suddenly and cause injury or damage. Find out why it won't move and fix the problem before continuing. Carefully work the engine forward to separate it from the transmission. If you're working on a vehicle with an automatic transmission, be sure the torque converter stays in the transmission (clamp a pair of vise-grips to the housing to keep the converter from sliding out). If you're working on a vehicle with a manual transmission, the input shaft must be completely disengaged from the clutch. Slowly raise the engine out of the engine compartment **(see illustration)**. Check carefully to make sure nothing is hanging up.
25   Remove the clutch (if equipped - see Chapter 8) and flywheel/driveplate and mount the engine on an engine stand.

Installation

26   Check the engine and transmission mounts. If they're worn or damaged, replace them.
27   If you're working on a manual transmission equipped vehicle, install the clutch and pressure plate (see Chapter 8). Now is a good time to install a new clutch.
28   Carefully lower the engine into the engine compartment - make

sure the engine mounts line up.
29   If you're working on an automatic transmission equipped vehicle, remove the vise grips and guide the torque converter into the crankshaft following the procedure outlined in Chapter 7.
30   If you're working on a manual transmission equipped vehicle, apply a dab of high-temperature grease to the input shaft and guide it into the crankshaft pilot bearing until the bellhousing is flush with the engine block.
31   Install the transmission-to-engine bolts and tighten them securely. **Caution:** *DO NOT use the bolts to force the transmission and engine together!*
32   Reinstall the remaining components in the reverse order of removal.
33   Add coolant, oil, power steering and transmission fluid as needed.
34   Run the engine and check for leaks and proper operation of all accessories, then install the hood and test drive the vehicle.

6   Engine rebuilding alternatives

The do-it-yourselfer is faced with a number of options when performing an engine overhaul. The decision to replace the engine block, piston/connecting rod assemblies and crankshaft depends on a number of factors, with the number one consideration being the condition of the block. Other considerations are cost, access to machine shop facilities, parts availability, time required to complete the project and the extent of prior mechanical experience on the part of the do-it-yourselfer.
Some of the rebuilding alternatives include:
Individual parts - If the inspection procedures reveal that the engine block and most engine components are in reusable condition, purchasing individual parts may be the most economical alternative. The block, crankshaft and piston/connecting rod assemblies should all be inspected carefully. Even if the block shows little wear, the cylinder bores should be surface honed.
Short block - A short block consists of an engine block with a crankshaft, camshaft, timing chain and sprockets and piston/connecting rod assemblies already installed. All new bearings are incorporated and all clearances will be correct. The existing valve train components, cylinder head(s) and external parts can be bolted to the short block with little or no machine shop work necessary.
Long block - A long block consists of a short block plus an oil pump, oil pan, cylinder heads, valve covers, valve train components and timing chain cover. All components are installed with new bearings, seals and gaskets incorporated throughout. The installation of manifolds and external parts is all that's necessary.
Give careful thought to which alternative is best for you and discuss the situation with local automotive machine shops, auto parts dealers and experienced rebuilders before ordering or purchasing replacement parts.

8.2 A small plastic bag, with an appropriate label, can be used to store the valve train components so they can be kept together and reinstalled in the original location

8.3 Use a valve spring compressor to compress the spring, then remove the keepers from the valve stem

8.4 If the valve won't pull through the guide, deburr the edge of the stem end and the area around the top of the keeper groove with a file or whetstone

7 Engine overhaul - disassembly sequence

1   It's much easier to disassemble and work on the engine if it's mounted on a portable engine stand. A stand can often be rented quite cheaply from an equipment rental yard. Before the engine is mounted on a stand, the flywheel/driveplate should be removed from the engine.
2   If a stand isn't available, it's possible to disassemble the engine with it blocked up on the floor. Be extra careful not to tip or drop the engine when working without a stand.
3   If you're going to obtain a rebuilt engine, all external components must come off first, to be transferred to the replacement engine, just as they will if you're doing a complete engine overhaul yourself. These include:

Alternator and brackets (if not removed during engine removal)
Emissions control components
Coil pack, spark plug wires and spark plugs
Thermostat and housing cover
Water pump
EFI components
Intake/exhaust manifolds
Oil filter
Engine mounts
Engine rear plate
Clutch and flywheel/driveplate

Note: When removing the external components from the engine, pay close attention to details that may be helpful or important during installation. Note the installed position of gaskets, seals, spacers, pins, brackets, washers, bolts and other small items.
4   If you're obtaining a short block, which consists of the engine block, crankshaft, pistons and connecting rods all assembled, then the cylinder head, oil pan and oil pump will have to be removed as well. See "Engine rebuilding alternatives" for additional information regarding the different possibilities to be considered.
5   If you're planning a complete overhaul, the engine must be disassembled and the internal components removed in the following order:

Clutch and flywheel or driveplate
Valve covers
Rocker assemblies and pushrods
Intake and exhaust manifolds
Cylinder heads
Oil pan
Oil pump
Timing chain cover and cover plate
Timing chain and sprockets
Valve lifters
Camshaft
Piston/connecting rod assemblies
Crankshaft and main bearings

6   Before beginning the disassembly and overhaul procedures, make sure the following items are available. Also, refer to "Engine overhaul - reassembly sequence" for a list of tools and materials needed for engine reassembly.

Common hand tools
Small cardboard boxes or plastic bags for storing parts
Gasket scraper
Ridge reamer
Vibration damper puller
Micrometers
Telescoping gauges
Dial indicator set
Valve spring compressor
Cylinder surfacing hone
Piston ring groove cleaning tool
Electric drill motor
Tap and die set
Wire brushes
Oil gallery brushes
Cleaning solvent

8 Cylinder head - disassembly

Refer to illustrations 8.2, 8.3 and 8.4
Note: New and rebuilt cylinder heads are commonly available for most engines at dealerships and auto parts stores. Due to the fact that some specialized tools are necessary for the disassembly and inspection procedures, and replacement parts may not be readily available, it may be more practical and economical for the home mechanic to purchase replacement heads rather than taking the time to disassemble, inspect and recondition the originals.
1   Cylinder head disassembly involves removal of the intake and exhaust valves and related components. If they're still in place, remove the rocker arm shaft assemblies (see Part A of this Chapter). Label the parts or store them separately so they can be reinstalled in their original locations.
2   Before the valves are removed, arrange to label and store them, along with their related components, so they can be kept separate and reinstalled in the same valve guides they are removed from (see illustration).
3   Compress the springs on the first valve with a spring compressor and remove the keepers (see illustration). Carefully release the valve spring compressor and remove the retainer and spring.
4   Pull the valve out of the head, then remove the oil seal from the guide. If the valve binds in the guide (won't pull through), push it back into the head and deburr the area around the keeper groove with a fine file or whetstone (see illustration).
5   Repeat the procedure for the remaining valves. Remember to

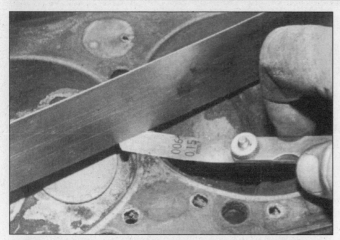

9.12a Check the cylinder head gasket surface for warpage by trying to slip a feeler gauge under the straightedge (see this Chapter's Specifications for the maximum warpage allowed and use a feeler gauge of that thickness)

9.12b Check the cylinder head gasket surface for warpage by trying to slip a feeler gauge under the straightedge (see this Chapter's Specifications for the maximum warpage allowed and use a feeler gauge of that thickness)

keep all the parts for each valve together so they can be reinstalled in the same locations.

6   Once the valves and related components have been removed and stored in an organized manner, the head should be thoroughly cleaned and inspected. If a complete engine overhaul is being done, finish the engine disassembly procedures before beginning the cylinder head cleaning and inspection process.

9   Cylinder head - cleaning and inspection

Refer to illustrations 9.12a, 9.12b, 9.14, 9.15, 9.16, 9.17 and 9.18

1   Thorough cleaning of the cylinder head(s) and related valve train components, followed by a detailed inspection, will enable you to decide how much valve service work must be done during the engine overhaul. **Note:** *If the engine was severely overheated, the cylinder head is probably warped (see Step 12).*

Cleaning

2   Scrape all traces of old gasket material and sealing compound off the head gasket, intake manifold and exhaust manifold sealing surfaces. Be very careful not to gouge the cylinder head. Special gasket removal solvents that soften gaskets and make removal much easier are available at auto parts stores.

3   Remove all built up scale from the coolant passages.

4   Run a stiff wire brush through the various holes to remove deposits that may have formed in them.

5   Run an appropriate size tap into each of the threaded holes to remove corrosion and thread sealant that may be present. If compressed air is available, use it to clear the holes of debris produced by this operation. **Warning:** *Wear eye protection when using compressed air!*

6   Clean the rocker arm pivot stud threads with a wire brush.

7   Clean the cylinder head with solvent and dry it thoroughly. Compressed air will speed the drying process and ensure that all holes and recessed areas are clean. **Note:** *Decarbonizing chemicals are available and may prove very useful when cleaning cylinder heads and valve train components. They are very caustic and should be used with caution. Be sure to follow the instructions on the container.*

8   Clean the rocker arms, fulcrums or shafts, bolts and pushrods with solvent and dry them thoroughly (don't mix them up during the cleaning process). Compressed air will speed the drying process and can be used to clean out the oil passages.

9   Clean all the valve springs, spring seats, keepers and retainers with solvent and dry them thoroughly. Do the components from one valve at a time to avoid mixing up the parts.

10   Scrape off any heavy deposits that may have formed on the valves,

then use a motorized wire brush to remove deposits from the valve heads and stems. Again, make sure the valves don't get mixed up.

Inspection

Note: *Be sure to perform all of the following inspection procedures before concluding that machine shop work is required. Make a list of the items that need attention.*

Cylinder head

11   Inspect the head very carefully for cracks, evidence of coolant leakage and other damage. If cracks are found, check with an automotive machine shop concerning repair. If repair isn't possible, a new cylinder head should be obtained.

12   Using a straightedge and feeler gauge, check the head gasket mating surface for warpage **(see illustrations)**. If the warpage exceeds the limit listed in this Chapter's Specifications, it can be resurfaced at an automotive machine shop. **Note:** *If the heads are resurfaced, the intake manifold flanges will also require machining.*

13   Examine the valve seats in each of the combustion chambers. If they're pitted, cracked or burned, the head will require valve service that's beyond the scope of the home mechanic.

14   Check the valve stem-to-guide clearance by measuring the lateral movement of the valve stem with a dial indicator attached securely to the head **(see illustration)**. The valve must be in the guide and approximately 1/16-inch off the seat. The total valve stem movement indicated by the gauge needle must be divided by two to obtain the actual clearance. After this is done, if there's still some doubt regarding the condition of the valve guides they should be checked by an automotive machine shop (the cost should be minimal).

Valves

15   Carefully inspect each valve face for uneven wear, deformation, cracks, pits and burned areas **(see illustration)**. Check the valve stem for scuffing and galling and the neck for cracks. Rotate the valve and check for any obvious indication that it's bent. Look for pits and excessive wear on the end of the stem. The presence of any of these conditions indicates the need for valve service by an automotive machine shop.

16   Measure the margin width on each valve **(see illustration)**. Any valve with a margin narrower than specified will have to be replaced with a new one.

Valve components

17   Check each valve spring for wear (on the ends) and pits. Measure the free length and compare it to the Specifications **(see illustration)**. Any springs that are shorter than specified have sagged and should not be reused. The tension of all springs should be checked with a

9.14 A dial indicator can be used to determine the valve stem-to-guide clearance (move the valve stem as indicated by the arrows)

9.16 The margin width on each valve must be as specified (if no margin exists, the valve cannot be reused)

9.15 Check for valve wear at the points shown here

1 Valve tip
2 Keeper groove
3 Stem (least worn area)
4 Stem (most worn area)
5 Valve face
6 Margin

2B

9.17 Measure the free length of each valve spring with a dial or vernier caliper

special fixture before deciding that they're suitable for use in a rebuilt engine (take the springs to an automotive machine shop for this check).

18   Stand each spring on a flat surface and check it for squareness **(see illustration)**. If any of the springs are distorted or sagged, replace all of them with new parts.

19   Check the spring retainers and keepers for obvious wear and cracks. Any questionable parts should be replaced with new ones, as extensive damage will occur if they fail during engine operation.

Rocker arm components

20   Check the rocker arm faces (the areas that contact the pushrod ends and valve stems) for pits, wear, galling, score marks and rough spots. Check the rocker arm shafts as well. Look for cracks in each rocker arm and shaft.

21   Inspect the pushrod ends for scuffing and excessive wear. Roll each pushrod on a flat surface, like a piece of plate glass, to determine if it's bent.

22   Any damaged or excessively worn parts must be replaced with new ones.

23   If the inspection process indicates that the valve components are in generally poor condition and worn beyond the limits specified, which is usually the case in an engine that's being overhauled, reassemble the valves in the cylinder head and refer to Section 10 for valve servicing recommendations.

9.18 Check each valve spring for squareness

11.7 Be sure to check the valve spring installed height for each valve (the distance from the top of the seat/shims to the underside of the retainer)

12.1 A ridge reamer is required to remove the ridge from the top of each cylinder - do this before removing the pistons!

10 Valves - servicing

1   Because of the complex nature of the job and the special tools and equipment needed, servicing of the valves, the valve seats and the valve guides, commonly known as a valve job, should be done by a professional.

2   The home mechanic can remove and disassemble the heads, do the initial cleaning and inspection, then reassemble and deliver them to a dealer service department or an automotive machine shop for the actual service work. Doing the inspection will enable you to see what condition the head and valvetrain components are in and will ensure that you know what work and new parts are required when dealing with an automotive machine shop.

3   The dealer service department, or automotive machine shop, will remove the valves and springs, recondition or replace the valves and valve seats, recondition the valve guides, check and replace the valve springs, spring retainers and keepers (as necessary), replace the valve seals with new ones, reassemble the valve components and make sure the installed spring height is correct. The cylinder head gasket surface will also be resurfaced if it's warped.

4   After the valve job has been performed by a professional, the head will be in like-new condition. When the head is returned, be sure to clean it again before installation on the engine to remove any metal particles and abrasive grit that may still be present from the valve service or head resurfacing operations. Use compressed air, if available, to blow out all the oil holes and passages.

11 Cylinder head - reassembly

Refer to illustration 11.7

1   Regardless of whether or not the head was sent to an automotive repair shop for valve servicing, make sure it's clean before beginning reassembly.

2   If the head was sent out for valve servicing, the valves and related components will already be in place. Go to Step 7.

3   Lubricate and install each valve, then install new seals on each of the valve stems, as described in Chapter 2A, Section 6. Don't twist or cock the seals during installation or they won't seat properly on the valve stems.

4   Drop the spring seat or shim(s) over the valve guide and set the valve spring and retainer in place.

5   Compress the springs with a valve spring compressor and carefully install the keepers in the upper groove, then slowly release the compressor and make sure the keepers seat properly. Apply a small dab of grease to each keeper to hold it in place if necessary.

6   Repeat the procedure for the remaining valves. Be sure to return the components to their original locations - don't mix them up!

7   Check the installed valve spring height with a ruler graduated

in 1/32-inch increments or a dial caliper. If the head was sent out for service work, the installed height should be correct (but don't automatically assume that it is). The measurement is taken from the top of each spring seat or shim(s) to the bottom of the retainer **(see illustration)**. If the height is greater than the figure listed in this Chapter's Specifications, shims can be added under the springs to correct it. **Caution:** *Don't, under any circumstances, shim the springs to the point where the installed height is less than specified.*

12 Pistons/connecting rods - removal

Refer to illustrations 12.1, 12.3, 12.4 and 12.6

Note: *Prior to removing the piston/connecting rod assemblies, remove the cylinder head(s), the oil pan and the oil pump by referring to the appropriate Sections in Chapter 2.*

1   Use your fingernail to feel if a ridge has formed at the upper limit of ring travel (about 1/4-inch down from the top of each cylinder). If carbon deposits or cylinder wear have produced ridges, they must be completely removed with a special tool **(see illustration)**. Follow the manufacturer's instructions provided with the tool. Failure to remove the ridges before attempting to remove the piston/connecting rod assemblies may result in piston breakage.

2   After the cylinder ridges have been removed, turn the engine upside-down so the crankshaft is facing up.

3   Before the connecting rods are removed, check the endplay with feeler gauges. Slide them between the first connecting rod and the crankshaft throw until the play is removed **(see illustration)**. The endplay is equal to the thickness of the feeler gauge(s). If the endplay exceeds the service limit, new connecting rods will be required. If new rods (or a new crankshaft) are installed, the endplay may fall under the specified minimum (if it does, the rods will have to be machined to restore it - consult an automotive machine shop for advice if necessary). Repeat the procedure for the remaining connecting rods.

4   Check the connecting rods and caps for identification marks **(see illustration)**. If they aren't plainly marked, use a small center-punch to make the appropriate number of indentations on each rod and cap (1, 2, 3, etc.).

5   Loosen each of the connecting rod cap nuts 1/2-turn at a time until they can be removed by hand. Remove the number one connecting rod cap and bearing insert. Don't drop the bearing insert out of the cap.

6   Slip a short length of plastic or rubber hose over each connecting rod cap bolt to protect the crankshaft journal and cylinder wall as the piston is removed **(see illustration)**.

7   Remove the bearing insert and push the connecting rod/piston assembly out through the top of the engine. Use a wooden hammer handle to push on the upper bearing surface in the connecting rod. If

12.3 Connecting rod side clearance is measured with feeler gauges inserted between the rod cap and crankshaft

12.4 Check the connecting rod and cap for identification marks - if they aren't visible, mark the rods and caps with a hammer and punch to indicate which cylinder they came from (be sure to mark the rod and cap on the same side so they can be reassembled correctly)

12.6 Place short pieces of hose over the connecting rod studs to protect the crankshaft and cylinder walls

13.1 Checking crankshaft endplay with a dial indicator

resistance is felt, double-check to make sure that all of the ridge was removed from the cylinder.
8   Repeat the procedure for the remaining cylinders.
9   After removal, reassemble the connecting rod caps and bearing inserts in their respective connecting rods and install the cap nuts finger tight. Leaving the old bearing inserts in place until reassembly will help prevent the connecting rod bearing surfaces from being accidentally nicked or gouged.
10   Don't separate the pistons from the connecting rods (see Section 17 for additional information).

13   Crankshaft - removal

Refer to illustrations 13.1, 13.3 and 13.4
Note: *The crankshaft can be removed only after the engine has been removed from the vehicle. It's assumed that the flywheel or driveplate, vibration damper, timing chain, oil pan, oil pump and piston/connecting rod assemblies have already been removed.*
1   Before the crankshaft is removed, check the endplay. Mount a dial indicator with the stem in line with the crankshaft and just touching one of the crank throws **(see illustration)**.
2   Push the crankshaft all the way to the rear and zero the dial indicator. Next, pry the crankshaft to the front as far as possible and check the reading on the dial indicator. The distance that it moves is the endplay. If it's greater than the limit listed in this Chapter's Specifications, check the crankshaft thrust surfaces for wear. If no wear is evident, new main bearings should correct the endplay.
3   If a dial indicator isn't available, feeler gauges can be used. Gently

13.3 Checking crankshaft endplay with a feeler gauge

pry or push the crankshaft all the way to the front of the engine. Slip feeler gauges between the crankshaft and the front face of the thrust main bearing (number 3 bearing) to determine the clearance **(see illustration)**.

13.4 The main bearing caps are numbered from the front to the rear of the engine and have cast-in arrows that point to the front of the engine when the caps are installed

14.8 All bolt holes in the block - particularly the main bearing cap and head bolt holes - should be cleaned and restored with a tap (be sure to remove debris from the holes after this is done)

14.10 A large socket on an extension can be used to drive the new core plugs into the bores

14.1 The core plugs should be removed with a puller - if they're driven into the block, they may be impossible to retrieve

4   Check the main bearing caps to see if they're marked to indicate their locations. They should be numbered consecutively from the front of the engine to the rear **(see illustration)**. If they aren't, mark them with number stamping dies or a center-punch. Main bearing caps generally have a cast-in arrow, which points to the front of the engine. Loosen the main bearing cap bolts 1/4-turn at a time each, until they can be removed by hand. Note if any stud bolts are used and make sure they're returned to their original locations when the crankshaft is reinstalled.

5   Gently tap the caps with a soft-face hammer, then separate them from the engine block. If necessary, use the bolts as levers to remove the caps. Try not to drop the bearing inserts if they come out with the caps.

6   Carefully lift the crankshaft out of the engine. It may be a good idea to have an assistant available, since the crankshaft is quite heavy. With the bearing inserts in place in the engine block and main bearing caps, return the caps to their respective locations on the engine block and tighten the bolts finger tight.

14   Engine block - cleaning

Refer to illustrations 14.1, 14.8 and 14.10
Caution: *The core plugs (also known as freeze plugs or soft plugs) may be difficult or impossible to retrieve if they're driven into the block coolant passages.*

1   Drill a small hole in the center of each core plug and pull them out with an auto body type dent puller **(see illustration)**.

2   Using a gasket scraper, remove all traces of gasket material from the engine block. Be very careful not to nick or gouge the gasket sealing surfaces.

3   Remove the main bearing caps and separate the bearing inserts from the caps and the engine block. Tag the bearings, indicating which cylinder they were removed from and whether they were in the cap or the block, then set them aside.

4   Remove all of the threaded oil gallery plugs from the block. The plugs are usually very tight - they may have to be drilled out and the holes retapped. Use new plugs when the engine is reassembled.

5   If the engine is extremely dirty it should be taken to an automotive machine shop to be steam cleaned or hot tanked.

6   After the block is returned, clean all oil holes and oil galleries one more time. Brushes specifically designed for this purpose are available at most auto parts stores. Flush the passages with warm water until the water runs clear, dry the block thoroughly and wipe all machined surfaces with a light, rust preventive oil. If you have access to compressed air, use it to speed the drying process and to blow out all the oil holes and galleries. **Warning:** *Wear eye protection when using compressed air!*

7   If the block isn't extremely dirty or sludged up, you can do an adequate cleaning job with hot soapy water and a stiff brush. Take plenty of time and do a thorough job. Regardless of the cleaning method used, be sure to clean all oil holes and galleries very thoroughly, dry the block completely and coat all machined surfaces with light oil.

15.4a Measure the diameter of each cylinder just under the wear ridge (A), at the center (B) and at the bottom (C)

15.4c The gauge is then measured with a micrometer to determine the bore size

8 The threaded holes in the block must be clean to ensure accurate torque readings during reassembly. Run the proper size tap into each of the holes to remove rust, corrosion, thread sealant or sludge and restore damaged threads (see illustration). If possible, use compressed air to clear the holes of debris produced by this operation. Now is a good time to clean the threads on the head bolts and the main bearing cap bolts as well.

9 Reinstall the main bearing caps and tighten the bolts finger tight.

10 After coating the sealing surfaces of the new core plugs with Permatex no. 2 sealant, install them in the engine block (see illustration). Make sure they're driven in straight and seated properly or leakage could result. Special tools are available for this purpose, but a large socket, with an outside diameter that will just slip into the core plug, a 1/2-inch drive extension and a hammer will work just as well.

11 Apply non-hardening sealant (such as Permatex no. 2 or Teflon pipe sealant) to the new oil gallery plugs and thread them into the holes in the block. Make sure they're tightened securely.

12 If the engine isn't going to be reassembled right away, cover it with a large plastic trash bag to keep it clean.

15 Engine block - inspection

Refer to illustrations 15.4a, 15.4b and 15.4c

1 Before the block is inspected, it should be cleaned as described in Section 14.

2 Visually check the block for cracks, rust and corrosion. Look for stripped threads in the threaded holes. It's also a good idea to have the block checked for hidden cracks by an automotive machine shop that has the special equipment to do this type of work. If defects are found, have the block repaired, if possible, or replaced.

3 Check the cylinder bores for scuffing and scoring.

15.4b The ability to "feel" when the telescoping gauge is at the correct point will be developed over time, so work slowly and repeat the check until you're satisfied the bore measurement is accurate

4 Measure the diameter of each cylinder at the top (just under the ridge area), center and bottom of the cylinder bore, parallel to the crankshaft axis (see illustrations).

5 Next, measure each cylinder's diameter at the same three locations across the crankshaft axis. Compare the results to this Chapter's Specifications.

6 If the required precision measuring tools aren't available, the piston-to-cylinder clearances can be obtained, though not quite as accurately, using feeler gauge stock. Feeler gauge stock comes in 12-inch lengths and various thicknesses and is generally available at auto parts stores.

7 To check the clearance, select a feeler gauge and slip it into the cylinder along with the matching piston. The piston must be positioned exactly as it normally would be. The feeler gauge must be between the piston and cylinder on one of the thrust faces (90-degrees to the piston pin bore).

8 The piston should slip through the cylinder (with the feeler gauge in place) with moderate pressure.

9 If it falls through or slides through easily, the clearance is excessive and a new piston will be required. If the piston binds at the lower end of the cylinder and is loose toward the top, the cylinder is tapered. If tight spots are encountered as the piston/feeler gauge is rotated in the cylinder, the cylinder is out-of-round.

10 Repeat the procedure for the remaining pistons and cylinders.

11 If the cylinder walls are badly scuffed or scored, or if they're out-of-round or tapered beyond the limits given in this Chapter's Specifications, have the engine block rebored and honed at an automotive machine shop. If a rebore is done, oversize pistons and rings will be required.

12 If the cylinders are in reasonably good condition and not worn to the outside of the limits, and if the piston-to-cylinder clearances can be maintained properly, then they don't have to be rebored. Honing is all that's necessary (see Section 16).

16 Cylinder honing

Refer to illustrations 16.3a and 16.3b

1 Prior to engine reassembly, the cylinder bores must be honed so the new piston rings will seat correctly and provide the best possible combustion chamber seal. Note: If you don't have the tools or don't want to tackle the honing operation, most automotive machine shops will do it for a reasonable fee.

2 Before honing the cylinders, install the main bearing caps and tighten the bolts to the torque listed in this Chapter's Specifications.

3 Two types of cylinder hones are commonly available - the flex

hone or "bottle brush" type and the more traditional surfacing hone with spring-loaded stones. Both will do the job, but for the less experienced mechanic the "bottle brush" hone will probably be easier to use. You'll also need some kerosene or honing oil, rags and an electric drill motor. Proceed as follows:

a) *Mount the hone in the drill motor, compress the stones and slip it into the first cylinder* **(see illustration)**. *Be sure to wear safety goggles or a face shield!*

b) *Lubricate the cylinder with plenty of honing oil, turn on the drill and move the hone up-and-down in the cylinder at a pace that will produce a fine crosshatch pattern on the cylinder walls. Ideally, the crosshatch lines should intersect at approximately a 60-degree angle* **(see illustration)**. *Be sure to use plenty of lubricant and don't take off any more material than is absolutely necessary to produce the desired finish.* **Note:** *Piston ring manufacturers may specify a smaller crosshatch angle than the traditional 60-degrees - read and follow any instructions included with the new rings.*

c) *Don't withdraw the hone from the cylinder while it's running. Instead, shut off the drill and continue moving the hone up-and-down in the cylinder until it comes to a complete stop, then compress the stones and withdraw the hone. If you're using a "bottle brush" type hone, stop the drill motor, then turn the chuck in the normal direction of rotation while withdrawing the hone from the cylinder.*

d) *Wipe the oil out of the cylinder and repeat the procedure for the remaining cylinders.*

4   After the honing job is complete, chamfer the top edges of the cylinder bores with a small file so the rings won't catch when the pistons are installed. Be very careful not to nick the cylinder walls with the end of the file.

5   The entire engine block must be washed again very thoroughly with warm, soapy water to remove all traces of the abrasive grit produced during the honing operation. **Note:** *The bores can be considered clean when a lint-free white cloth - dampened with clean engine oil - used to wipe them out doesn't pick up any more honing residue, which will show up as gray areas on the cloth. Be sure to run a brush through all oil holes and galleries and flush them with running water.*

6   After rinsing, dry the block and apply a coat of light rust preventive oil to all machined surfaces. Wrap the block in a plastic trash bag to keep it clean and set it aside until reassembly.

17 Pistons/connecting rods - inspection

Refer to illustrations 17.4a, 17.4b, 17.10 and 17.11

1   Before the inspection process can be carried out, the piston/connecting rod assemblies must be cleaned and the original piston rings removed from the pistons. **Note:** *Always use new piston rings when the engine is reassembled.*

2   Using a piston ring installation tool, carefully remove the rings from the pistons. Be careful not to nick or gouge the pistons in the process.

3   Scrape all traces of carbon from the top of the piston. A handheld wire brush or a piece of fine emery cloth can be used once the majority of the deposits have been scraped away. Do not, under any circumstances, use a wire brush mounted in a drill motor to remove deposits from the pistons. The piston material is soft and may be eroded away by the wire brush.

4   Use a piston ring groove cleaning tool to remove carbon deposits from the ring grooves. If a tool isn't available, a piece broken off the old ring will do the job. Be very careful to remove only the carbon deposits - don't remove any metal and do not nick or scratch the sides of the ring grooves **(see illustrations)**.

5   Once the deposits have been removed, clean the piston/rod assemblies with solvent and dry them with compressed air (if available). Make sure the oil return holes in the back sides of the ring grooves are clear.

6   If the pistons and cylinder walls aren't damaged or worn excessively and if the engine block is not rebored, new pistons won't be necessary. Normal piston wear appears as even vertical wear on the piston thrust surfaces and slight looseness of the top ring in its groove.

16.3a A "bottle brush" hone will produce better results if you've never honed cylinders before

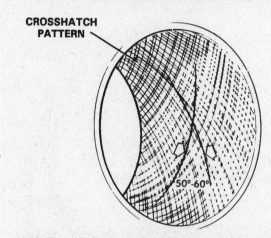

16.3b The cylinder hone should leave a smooth, crosshatch pattern with the lines intersecting at approximately a 60-degree angle

New piston rings, however, should always be used when an engine is rebuilt.

7   Carefully inspect each piston for cracks around the skirt, at the pin bosses and at the ring lands.

8   Look for scoring and scuffing on the thrust faces of the skirt, holes in the piston crown and burned areas at the edge of the crown. If the skirt is scored or scuffed, the engine may have been suffering from overheating and/or abnormal combustion, which caused excessively high operating temperatures. The cooling and lubrication systems should be checked thoroughly. A hole in the piston crown is an indication that abnormal combustion (preignition) was occurring. Burned areas at the edge of the piston crown are usually evidence of spark knock (detonation). If any of the above problems exist, the causes must be corrected or the damage will occur again. The causes may include intake air leaks, incorrect fuel/air mixture, incorrect ignition timing and EGR system malfunctions.

9   Corrosion of the piston, in the form of small pits, indicates that coolant is leaking into the combustion chamber and/or the crankcase. Again, the cause must be corrected or the problem may persist in the rebuilt engine.

10   Measure the piston ring side clearance by laying a new piston ring in each ring groove and slipping a feeler gauge in beside it **(see illustration)**. Check the clearance at three or four locations around each groove. Be sure to use the correct ring for each groove - they are different. If the side clearance is greater than the figure listed in this Chapter's Specifications, new pistons will have to be used.

11   Check the piston-to-bore clearance by measuring the bore (see Section 15) and the piston diameter. Make sure the pistons and bores

17.4a The piston ring grooves can be cleaned with a special tool, as shown here, . . .

17.4b . . . or a section of a broken ring

17.10 Check the ring side clearance with a feeler gauge at several points around the groove

17.11 Measure the piston diameter at a 90-degree angle to the piston pin and in line with it

are correctly matched. Measure the piston across the skirt, at a 90-degree angle to and in line with the piston pin **(see illustration)**. Subtract the piston diameter from the bore diameter to obtain the clearance. If it's greater than specified, the block will have to be rebored and new pistons and rings installed.

12   Check the piston-to-rod clearance by twisting the piston and rod in opposite directions. Any noticeable play indicates excessive wear, which must be corrected. The piston/connecting rod assemblies should be taken to an automotive machine shop to have the pistons and rods resized and new pins installed.

13   If the pistons must be removed from the connecting rods for any reason, they should be taken to an automotive machine shop. While they are there have the connecting rods checked for bend and twist, since automotive machine shops have special equipment for this purpose. **Note:** *Unless new pistons and/or connecting rods must be installed, do not disassemble the pistons and connecting rods.*

14   Check the connecting rods for cracks and other damage. Temporarily remove the rod caps, lift out the old bearing inserts, wipe the rod and cap bearing surfaces clean and inspect them for nicks, gouges and scratches. After checking the rods, replace the old bearings, slip the caps into place and tighten the nuts finger tight. **Note:** *If the engine is being rebuilt because of a connecting rod knock, be sure to install new rods.*

18   Crankshaft - inspection

Refer to illustrations 18.1, 18.2, 18.4, 18.6 and 18.8

1   Remove all burrs from the crankshaft oil holes with a stone, file or scraper **(see illustration)**.

2   Clean the crankshaft with solvent and dry it with compressed air (if available). Be sure to clean the oil holes with a stiff brush **(see illustration)** and flush them with solvent.

18.1 The oil holes should be chamfered so sharp edges don't gouge or scratch the new bearings

18.2 Use a wire or stiff plastic bristle brush to clean the oil passages in the crankshaft

18.4 Rubbing a penny lengthwise on each journal will reveal its condition - if copper rubs off and is embedded in the crankshaft, the journals should be reground

18.6 Measure the diameter of each crankshaft journal at several points to detect taper and out-of-round conditions

18.8 If the seals have worn grooves in the crankshaft journals, or if the seal contact surfaces are nicked or scratched, the new seals will leak

3   Check the main and connecting rod bearing journals for uneven wear, scoring, pits and cracks.

4   Rub a penny across each journal several times **(see illustration)**. If a journal picks up copper from the penny, it's too rough and must be reground.

5   Check the rest of the crankshaft for cracks and other damage. It should be magnafluxed to reveal hidden cracks - an automotive machine shop will handle the procedure.

6   Using a micrometer, measure the diameter of the main and connecting rod journals and compare the results to this Chapter's Specifications **(see illustration)**. By measuring the diameter at a number of points around each journal's circumference, you'll be able to determine whether or not the journal is out-of-round. Take the measurement at each end of the journal, near the crank throws, to determine if the journal is tapered.

7   If the crankshaft journals are damaged, tapered, out-of-round or worn beyond the limits given in the Specifications, have the crankshaft re-ground by an automotive machine shop. Be sure to use the correct size bearing inserts if the crankshaft is reconditioned.

8   Check the oil seal journals at each end of the crankshaft for wear and damage. If the seal has worn a groove in the journal, or if it's nicked or scratched **(see illustration)**, the new seal may leak when the engine is reassembled. In some cases, an automotive machine shop may be able to repair the journal by pressing on a thin sleeve. If repair isn't feasible, a new or different crankshaft should be installed.

9   Refer to Section 19 and examine the main and rod bearing inserts.

19   Main and connecting rod bearings - inspection

Refer to illustration 19.1

1   Even though the main and connecting rod bearings should be replaced with new ones during the engine overhaul, the old bearings should be retained for close examination, as they may reveal valuable information about the condition of the engine **(see illustration)**.

2   Bearing failure occurs because of lack of lubrication, the presence of dirt or other foreign particles, overloading the engine and corrosion. Regardless of the cause of bearing failure, it must be corrected before the engine is reassembled to prevent it from happening again.

3   When examining the bearings, remove them from the engine block, the main bearing caps, the connecting rods and the rod caps and lay them out on a clean surface in the same general position as their location in the engine. This will enable you to match any bearing problems with the corresponding crankshaft journal.

4   Dirt and other foreign particles get into the engine in a variety of ways. It may be left in the engine during assembly, or it may pass

19.1 Typical bearing failures

through filters or the PCV system. It may get into the oil, and from there into the bearings. Metal chips from machining operations and normal engine wear are often present. Abrasives are sometimes left in engine components after reconditioning, especially when parts are not thoroughly cleaned using the proper cleaning methods. Whatever the source, these foreign objects often end up embedded in the soft bearing material and are easily recognized. Large particles will not embed in the bearing and will score or gouge the bearing and journal. The best prevention for this cause of bearing failure is to clean all parts thoroughly and keep everything spotlessly clean during engine assembly. Frequent and regular engine oil and filter changes are also recommended.

5   Lack of lubrication (or lubrication breakdown) has a number of interrelated causes. Excessive heat (which thins the oil), overloading (which squeezes the oil from the bearing face) and oil leakage or throw

21.3 When checking piston ring end gap, the ring must be square in the cylinder bore (this is done by pushing the ring down with the top of a piston as shown)

21.4 With the ring square in the cylinder, measure the end gap with a feeler gauge

21.5 If the end gap is too small, clamp a file in a vise and file the ring ends (from the outside in only) to enlarge the gap slightly

off (from excessive bearing clearances, worn oil pump or high engine speeds) all contribute to lubrication breakdown. Blocked oil passages, which usually are the result of misaligned oil holes in a bearing shell, will also oil starve a bearing and destroy it. When lack of lubrication is the cause of bearing failure, the bearing material is wiped or extruded from the steel backing of the bearing. Temperatures may increase to the point where the steel backing turns blue from overheating.

6   Driving habits can have a definite effect on bearing life. Full throttle, low speed operation (lugging the engine) puts very high loads on bearings, which tends to squeeze out the oil film. These loads cause the bearings to flex, which produces fine cracks in the bearing face (fatigue failure). Eventually the bearing material will loosen in pieces and tear away from the steel backing. Short trip driving leads to corrosion of bearings because insufficient engine heat is produced to drive off the condensed water and corrosive gases. These products collect in the engine oil, forming acid and sludge. As the oil is carried to the engine bearings, the acid attacks and corrodes the bearing material.

7   Incorrect bearing installation during engine assembly will lead to bearing failure as well. Tight fitting bearings leave insufficient bearing oil clearance and will result in oil starvation. Dirt or foreign particles trapped behind a bearing insert result in high spots on the bearing which lead to failure.

20   Engine overhaul - reassembly sequence

1   Before beginning engine reassembly, make sure you have all the necessary new parts, gaskets and seals as well as the following items on hand:

Common hand tools
A 1/2-inch drive torque wrench
Piston ring installation tool
Piston ring compressor
Vibration damper installation tool
Short lengths of rubber or plastic hose
  to fit over connecting rod bolts
Plastigage
Feeler gauges
A fine-tooth file
New engine oil
Engine assembly lube or moly-base grease
Gasket sealant
Thread locking compound

2   In order to save time and avoid problems, engine reassembly must be done in the following general order:

New camshaft bearings (must be done by an automotive
  machine shop)
Piston rings
Crankshaft and main bearings

Piston/connecting rod assemblies
Camshaft
Valve lifters
Timing chain and sprockets
Timing chain cover
Oil pump
Oil pan
Cylinder heads
Intake and exhaust manifolds
Rocker arms and pushrods
Valve covers
Clutch and flywheel or driveplate

21   Piston rings - installation

Refer to illustrations 21.3, 21.4, 21.5, 21.9a, 21.9b and 21.12

1   Before installing the new piston rings, the ring end gaps must be checked. It's assumed that the piston ring side clearance has been checked and verified correct (see Section 17).

2   Lay out the piston/connecting rod assemblies and the new ring sets so the ring sets will be matched with the same piston and cylinder during the end gap measurement and engine assembly.

3   Insert the top (number one) ring into the first cylinder and square it up with the cylinder walls by pushing it in with the top of the piston **(see illustration)**. The ring should be near the bottom of the cylinder, at the lower limit of ring travel.

4   To measure the end gap, slip feeler gauges between the ends of the ring until a gauge equal to the gap width is found **(see illustration)**. The feeler gauge should slide between the ring ends with a slight amount of drag. Compare the measurement to this Chapter's Specifications. If the gap is larger or smaller than specified, double-check to make sure you have the correct rings before proceeding.

5   If the gap is too small, it must be enlarged or the ring ends may come in contact with each other during engine operation, which can cause serious damage to the engine. The end gap can be increased by filing the ring ends very carefully with a fine file. Mount the file in a vise equipped with soft jaws, slip the ring over the file with the ends contacting the file face and slowly move the ring to remove material from the ends. When performing this operation, file only from the outside in **(see illustration)**.

6   Excess end gap isn't critical unless it's greater than 0.040-inch. Again, double-check to make sure you have the correct rings for your engine.

7   Repeat the procedure for each ring that will be installed in the first cylinder and for each ring in the remaining cylinders. Remember to keep rings, pistons and cylinders matched up.

8   Once the ring end gaps have been checked/corrected, the rings can be installed on the pistons.

21.9a Installing the spacer/expander in the oil control ring groove

21.9b DO NOT use a piston ring installation tool when installing the oil ring side rails

21.12 Installing the compression rings with a ring expander - the mark (arrow) must face up

9   The oil control ring (lowest one on the piston) is usually installed first. It's composed of three separate components. Slip the spacer/expander into the groove **(see illustration)**. If an anti-rotation tang is used, make sure it's inserted into the drilled hole in the ring groove. Next, install the lower side rail. Don't use a piston ring installation tool on the oil ring side rails, as they may be damaged. Instead, place one end of the side rail into the groove between the spacer/expander and the ring land, hold it firmly in place and slide a finger around the piston while pushing the rail into the groove **(see illustration)**. Next, install the upper side rail in the same manner.

10   After the three oil ring components have been installed, check to make sure that both the upper and lower side rails can be turned smoothly in the ring groove.

11   The number two (middle) ring is installed next. It's usually stamped with a mark which must face up, toward the top of the piston. **Note:** *Always follow the instructions printed on the ring package or box - different manufacturers may require different approaches.* Do not mix up the top and middle rings, as they have different cross-sections.

12   Use a piston ring installation tool and make sure the identification mark is facing the top of the piston, then slip the ring into the middle groove on the piston **(see illustration)**. Don't expand the ring any more than necessary to slide it over the piston.

13   Install the number one (top) ring in the same manner. Make sure the mark is facing up. Be careful not to confuse the number one and number two rings.

14   Repeat the procedure for the remaining pistons and rings.

22   Crankshaft - installation and main bearing oil clearance check

Refer to illustrations 22.5, 22.11, 22.15, 22.21 and 22.22

1   Crankshaft installation is the first step in engine reassembly. It's assumed at this point that the engine block and crankshaft have been cleaned, inspected and repaired or reconditioned.

2   Position the engine with the bottom facing up.

3   Remove the main bearing cap bolts and lift out the caps. Lay them out in the proper order to ensure correct installation.

4   If they're still in place, remove the original bearing inserts from the block and the main bearing caps. Wipe the bearing surfaces of the block and caps with a clean, lint-free cloth. They must be kept spotlessly clean.

Main bearing oil clearance check

5   Clean the back sides of the new main bearing inserts and lay one in each main bearing saddle in the block. If one of the bearing inserts from each set has a large groove in it, make sure the grooved insert is installed in the block. Lay the other bearing from each set in the corresponding main bearing cap. Make sure the tab on the bearing insert

22.5 The upper main bearing in position (flanged thrust bearing shown) - the oil hole in the bearing must align with the oil hole(s) in the block

fits into the recess in the block or cap. **Caution:** *The oil holes in the block must line up with the oil holes in the bearing insert* **(see illustration)**. Do not hammer the bearing into place and don't nick or gouge the bearing faces. No lubrication should be used at this time.

6   The flanged thrust bearing must be installed in the third cap and saddle (counting from the front of the engine).

7   Clean the faces of the bearings in the block and the crankshaft main bearing journals with a clean, lint-free cloth.

8   Check or clean the oil holes in the crankshaft, as any dirt here can go only one way - straight through the new bearings.

9   Once you're certain the crankshaft is clean, carefully lay it in position in the main bearings.

10   Before the crankshaft can be permanently installed, the main bearing oil clearance must be checked.

11   Cut several pieces of the appropriate size Plastigage (they must be slightly shorter than the width of the main bearings) and place one piece on each crankshaft main bearing journal, parallel with the journal axis **(see illustration)**.

12   Clean the faces of the bearings in the caps and install the caps in their respective positions (don't mix them up) with the arrows pointing toward the front of the engine. Don't disturb the Plastigage.

13   Starting with the center main and working out toward the ends, tighten the main bearing cap bolts, in three steps, to the torque listed in this Chapter's Specifications. Don't rotate the crankshaft at any time during this operation.

14   Remove the bolts and carefully lift off the main bearing caps. Keep them in order. Don't disturb the Plastigage or rotate the crank-

22.11 Lay the Plastigage strips (arrow) on the main bearing journals, parallel to the crankshaft centerline

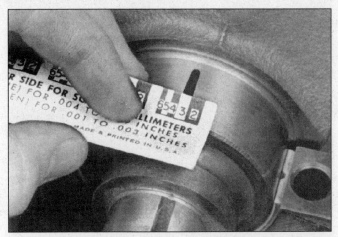

22.15 Compare the width of the crushed Plastigage to the scale on the envelope to determine the main bearing oil clearance (always take the measurement at the widest point of the Plastigage); be sure to use the correct scale - standard and metric ones are included

22.21 The wedge seal (arrow) must be installed on the rear main bearing cap before the cap is installed on the engine

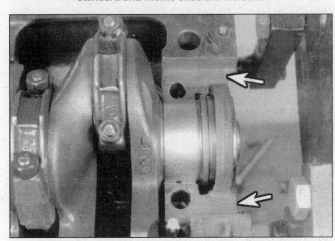

22.22 Before installing the rear main cap, apply sealant to the cap mating surfaces and in the corners where the cap meets the block

2B

crankshaft. If any of the main bearing caps are difficult to remove, tap them gently from side-to-side with a soft-face hammer to loosen them.

15   Compare the width of the crushed Plastigage on each journal to the scale printed on the Plastigage envelope to obtain the main bearing oil clearance (**see illustration**). Check the Specifications to make sure it's correct.

16   If the clearance is not as specified, the bearing inserts may be the wrong size - oversize or undersize - (which means different ones will be required). Before deciding that different inserts are needed, make sure that no dirt or oil was between the bearing inserts and the caps or block when the clearance was measured. If the Plastigage was wider at one end than the other, the journal may be tapered (refer to Section 18).

17   Carefully scrape all traces of the Plastigage material off the main bearing journals and/or the bearing faces. Use your fingernail or the edge of a credit card - don't nick or scratch the bearing faces.

Final crankshaft installation

18   Carefully lift the crankshaft out of the engine.

19   Clean the bearing faces in the block, then apply a thin, uniform layer of moly-base grease or engine assembly lube to each of the bearing surfaces. Be sure to coat the thrust faces as well as the journal face of the thrust bearing.

20   Make sure the crankshaft journals are clean, then lay the crankshaft back in place in the block.

21   Clean the faces of the bearings in the caps, then apply lubricant to them. On the rear main bearing cap, be sure to install the wedge seal (**see illustration**). Also, install the rear main bearing oil seal over

the end of the crankshaft. Be sure it is installed to the correct depth (see Chapter 2A).

22   Install the caps in their respective positions with the arrows pointing toward the front of the engine. Apply sealant into the corners and on the mating surfaces where the rear main cap meets the cylinder block (**see illustration**).

23   Install the bolts.

24   Tighten all except the thrust bearing cap bolts to the specified torque (work from the center out and approach the final torque in three steps).

25   Tighten the thrust bearing cap bolts to 10-to-12 ft-lbs.

26   Tap the ends of the crankshaft forward and backward with a lead or brass hammer to line up the main bearing and crankshaft thrust surfaces.

27   Retighten all main bearing cap bolts to the specified torque, starting with the center main and working out toward the ends.

28   On manual transmission equipped models, install a new pilot bearing in the end of the crankshaft (see Chapter 8).

29   Rotate the crankshaft a number of times by hand to check for any obvious binding.

30   The final step is to check the crankshaft endplay with a feeler gauge or a dial indicator as described in Section 13. The endplay should be correct if the crankshaft thrust faces aren't worn or damaged and new bearings have been installed.

23.5 Compression and oil control ring gap positioning

a) *Oil ring spacer butt connection*
b) *Oil ring side rail gaps*
c) *Compression ring gaps*

23 Pistons/connecting rods - installation and rod bearing oil clearance check

Refer to illustrations 23.5, 23.9a, 23.9b, 23.9c, 23.11, 23.13 and 23.17

1   Before installing the piston/connecting rod assemblies, the cylinder walls must be perfectly clean, the top edge of each cylinder must be chamfered, and the crankshaft must be in place.

2   Remove the cap from the end of the number one connecting rod (refer to the marks made during removal). Remove the original bearing inserts and wipe the bearing surfaces of the connecting rod and cap with a clean, lint-free cloth. They must be kept spotlessly clean.

Connecting rod bearing oil clearance check

3   Clean the back side of the new upper bearing insert, then lay it in place in the connecting rod. Make sure the tab on the bearing fits into the recess in the rod. Don't hammer the bearing insert into place and be very careful not to nick or gouge the bearing face. Don't lubricate the bearing at this time.

4   Clean the back side of the other bearing insert and install it in the rod cap. Again, make sure the tab on the bearing fits into the recess in the cap, and don't apply any lubricant. It's critically important that the mating surfaces of the bearing and connecting rod are perfectly clean and oil free when they're assembled.

5   Position the piston ring gaps at intervals around the piston **(see illustration)**.

6   Slip a section of plastic or rubber hose over each connecting rod cap bolt.

7   Lubricate the piston and rings with clean engine oil and attach a piston ring compressor to the piston. Leave the skirt protruding about 1/4-inch to guide the piston into the cylinder. The rings must be compressed until they're flush with the piston.

8   Rotate the crankshaft until the number one connecting rod journal is at BDC (bottom dead center) and apply a coat of engine oil to the cylinder walls.

9   With the arrow on top of the piston **(see illustration)** facing the front of the engine, gently insert the piston/connecting rod assembly into the number one cylinder bore and rest the bottom edge of the ring compressor on the engine block. Be sure the oil squirt hole in each connecting rod faces the proper direction when the rod is installed **(see illustrations)**. **Caution:** *If the oil squirt hole faces the wrong way when the arrow on the piston points toward the front, the rod and*

23.9a **The arrow in the top of each piston must face the FRONT of the engine as the pistons are installed**

23.9b **Note the direction of the oil squirt hole in the connecting rod - be sure the corresponding hole in the bearing insert aligns with the connecting rod hole**

piston have been assembled incorrectly. Correct the problem before assembling further.

10   Tap the top edge of the ring compressor to make sure it's contacting the block around its entire circumference.

11   Gently tap on the top of the piston with the end of a wooden hammer handle **(see illustration)** while guiding the end of the connecting rod into place on the crankshaft journal. The piston rings may try to pop out of the ring compressor just before entering the cylinder bore, so keep some downward pressure on the ring compressor. Work slowly, and if any resistance is felt as the piston enters the cylinder, stop immediately. Find out what's hanging up and fix it before proceeding. Do not, for any reason, force the piston into the cylinder - you might break a ring and/or the piston.

12   Once the piston/connecting rod assembly is installed, the connecting rod bearing oil clearance must be checked before the rod cap is permanently bolted in place.

13   Cut a piece of the appropriate size Plastigage slightly shorter than the width of the connecting rod bearing and lay it in place on the number one connecting rod journal, parallel with the journal axis **(see illustration)**.

14   Clean the connecting rod cap bearing face, remove the protective hoses from the connecting rod bolts and install the rod cap. Make sure the mating mark on the cap is on the same side as the mark on the connecting rod.

PISTON AND ROD
ASSEMBLY RH

ARROW ON
PISTON TOWARD
FRONT

PISTON AND
ROD ASSEMBLY LH

OIL
SQUIRT
HOLE

OIL SQUIRT
HOLE

VIEWED FROM FRONT OF ENGINE

**23.9c The oil squirt holes in the connecting rods
face in the directions shown**

**23.11 Drive the piston gently into the cylinder bore with the end
of a wooden or plastic hammer handle**

**23.13 Lay the Plastigage strips (arrow) on the main bearing
journals, parallel to the crankshaft centerline**

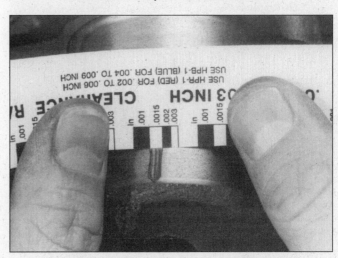

**23.17 Measuring the width of the crushed Plastigage to
determine the rod bearing oil clearance (be sure to use the
correct scale - standard and metric ones are included)**

15   Install the nuts and tighten them to the torque listed in this
Chapter's Specifications, working up to it in three steps. **Note:** *Use a
thin-wall socket to avoid erroneous torque readings that can result if
the socket is wedged between the rod cap and nut. If the socket tends
to wedge itself between the nut and the cap, lift up on it slightly until it
no longer contacts the cap.* Do not rotate the crankshaft at any time
during this operation.
16   Remove the nuts and detach the rod cap, being very careful not
to disturb the Plastigage.
17   Compare the width of the crushed Plastigage to the scale printed
on the Plastigage envelope to obtain the oil clearance **(see illustration)**. Compare it to the Specifications to make sure the clearance is
correct.
18   If the clearance is not as specified, the bearing inserts may be the
wrong size (which means different ones will be required). Before
deciding that different inserts are needed, make sure that no dirt or oil
was between the bearing inserts and the connecting rod or cap when
the clearance was measured. Also, recheck the journal diameter. If the
Plastigage was wider at one end than the other, the journal may be
tapered (refer to Section 18).

Final connecting rod installation

19   Carefully scrape all traces of the Plastigage material off the rod
journal and/or bearing face. Be very careful not to scratch the bearing -
use your fingernail or the edge of a credit card.
20   Make sure the bearing faces are perfectly clean, then apply a
uniform layer of clean moly-base grease or engine assembly lube to
both of them. You'll have to push the piston into the cylinder to expose
the face of the bearing insert in the connecting rod - be sure to slip the
protective hoses over the rod bolts first.
21   Slide the connecting rod back into place on the journal, remove
the protective hoses from the rod cap bolts, install the rod cap and
tighten the nuts to the specified torque. Again, work up to the torque in
three steps.
22   Repeat the entire procedure for the remaining pistons/connecting
rods.
23   The important points to remember are:
a) *Keep the back sides of the bearing inserts and the insides of the
connecting rods and caps perfectly clean when assembling them.*
b) *Make sure you have the correct piston/rod assembly for each
cylinder.*
c) *The notch or mark on the piston must face the front of the engine.*
d) *Lubricate the cylinder walls with clean oil.*
e) *Lubricate the bearing faces when installing the rod caps after the
oil clearance has been checked.*

24   After all the piston/connecting rod assemblies have been properly installed, rotate the crankshaft a number of times by hand to check for any obvious binding.

25   As a final step, the connecting rod endplay must be checked. Refer to Section 12 for this procedure.

26   Compare the measured endplay to the Specifications to make sure it's correct. If it was correct before disassembly and the original crankshaft and rods were reinstalled, it should still be right. If new rods or a new crankshaft were installed, the endplay may be inadequate. If so, the rods will have to be removed and taken to an automotive machine shop for resizing.

24   Initial start-up and break-in after overhaul

Warning: *Have a fire extinguisher handy when starting the engine for the first time.*

1   Once the engine has been installed in the vehicle, double-check the engine oil and coolant levels.

2   With the spark plugs out of the engine and the ignition system disabled (see Section 3), crank the engine until oil pressure registers on the gauge or the light goes out.

3   Install the spark plugs, hook up the plug wires and restore the ignition system functions (see Section 3).

4   Start the engine. It may take a few moments for the fuel system to build up pressure, but the engine should start without a great deal of effort. **Note:** *If backfiring occurs through the carburetor or throttle body, recheck the valve timing and ignition timing.*

5   After the engine starts, it should be allowed to warm up to normal operating temperature. While the engine is warming up, make a thorough check for fuel, oil and coolant leaks.

6   Shut the engine off and recheck the engine oil and coolant levels.

7   Drive the vehicle to an area with minimum traffic, accelerate at full throttle from 30 to 50 mph, then allow the vehicle to slow to 30 mph with the throttle closed. Repeat the procedure 10 or 12 times. This will load the piston rings and cause them to seat properly against the cylinder walls. Check again for oil and coolant leaks.

8   Drive the vehicle gently for the first 500 miles (no sustained high speeds) and keep a constant check on the oil level. It is not unusual for an engine to use oil during the break-in period.

9   At approximately 500 to 600 miles, change the oil and filter.

10   For the next few hundred miles, drive the vehicle normally. Do not pamper it or abuse it.

11   After 2000 miles, change the oil and filter again and consider the engine broken in.

Chapter 3
Cooling, heating and air conditioning systems

Contents

	Section
Air conditioning accumulator - removal and installation	17
Air conditioning compressor - removal and installation	15
Air conditioning condenser - removal and installation	16
Air conditioning system - check and maintenance	14
Antifreeze - general information	2
Coolant level check	See Chapter 1
Coolant reservoir - removal and installation	6
Coolant temperature sending unit - removal and installation	7
Cooling fan and viscous clutch - inspection, removal and installation	5

	Section
Cooling system check	See Chapter 1
Cooling system servicing	See Chapter 1
General information	1
Heater blower motor - replacement	12
Heater control assembly - removal and installation	10
Heater control cables - check and adjustment	11
Heater core - replacement	13
Heater - general information	9
Radiator - removal and installation	4
Thermostat - check and replacement	3
Water pump - check and replacement	8

Specifications

General

Thermostat
Type .... Wax pellet
Opening temperature .... 192-degrees to 199-degrees F
Fully open 226-degrees
Water temperature switch
Lamp on 249-degrees
Air conditioning system refrigerant capacity .... 28 ounces

Torque specifications

Ft-lbs (unless otherwise indicated)

Cooling fan-to-clutch bolt .... 50 to 70 in-lbs
Fan clutch-to-water pump nut .... 30 to 100
Thermostat housing bolts 10
Water pump bolts .... 72 to 108 in-lbs
Accumulator pressure switch
Metal base .... 60 to 120 in-lbs
Plastic base .... Hand tighten only

1   General information

Engine cooling system

All vehicles covered by this manual employ a pressurized engine cooling system with thermostatically controlled coolant circulation. An impeller type water pump mounted on the front of the block pumps coolant through the engine. The coolant flows around each cylinder and toward the rear of the engine. Cast-in coolant passages direct coolant around the intake and exhaust ports, near the spark plug areas and in close proximity to the exhaust valve guides.

A wax pellet type thermostat is located in a housing near the front of the engine. During warm up, the closed thermostat prevents coolant from circulating through the radiator. As the engine nears normal operating temperature, the thermostat opens and allows hot coolant to travel through the radiator, where it's cooled before returning to the engine.

The cooling system is sealed by a pressure type radiator cap, which raises the boiling point of the coolant and increases the cooling efficiency of the radiator. If the system pressure exceeds the cap pressure relief value, the excess pressure in the system forces the spring-loaded valve inside the cap off its seat and allows the coolant to escape through the overflow tube into a coolant reservoir. When the system cools the excess coolant is automatically drawn from the reservoir back into the radiator.

The coolant reservoir serves as both the point at which fresh coolant is added to the cooling system to maintain the proper fluid level and as a holding tank for overheated coolant.

This type of cooling system is known as a closed design because coolant that escapes past the pressure cap is saved and reused.

Heating system

The heating system consists of a blower fan and heater core located in the heater box, the hoses connecting the heater core to the engine cooling system and the heater/air conditioning control head on the dashboard. Hot engine coolant is circulated through the heater core. When the heater mode is activated, a flap door opens to expose the heater box to the passenger compartment. A fan switch on the control head activates the blower motor, which forces air through the core, heating the air.

Air conditioning system

The air conditioning system consists of a condenser mounted in front of the radiator, an evaporator mounted adjacent to the heater core, a compressor mounted on the engine, a filter-drier (accumulator) which contains a high pressure relief valve and the plumbing connecting all of the above components.

A blower fan forces the warmer air of the passenger compartment through the evaporator core (sort of a radiator-in-reverse), transferring the heat from the air to the refrigerant. The liquid refrigerant boils off into low pressure vapor, taking the heat with it when it leaves the evaporator.

2   Antifreeze - general information

Warning: *Do not allow antifreeze to come in contact with your skin or painted surfaces of the vehicle. Rinse off spills immediately with plenty of water. Antifreeze is highly toxic if ingested. Never leave antifreeze lying around in an open container or in puddles on the floor; children and pets are attracted by it's sweet smell and may drink it. Check with local authorities about disposing of used antifreeze. Many communities have collection centers which will see that antifreeze is disposed of safely.*

The cooling system should be filled with a water/ethylene glycol based antifreeze solution, which will prevent freezing down to at least -20-degrees F, or lower if local climate requires it. It also provides protection against corrosion and increases the coolant boiling point.

The cooling system should be drained, flushed and refilled at the specified intervals (see Chapter 1). Old or contaminated antifreeze solutions are likely to cause damage and encourage the formation of rust and scale in the system. It's a good idea to use distilled water with the antifreeze.

Before adding antifreeze, check all hose connections, because antifreeze tends to leak through very minute openings. Engines don't normally consume coolant, so if the level goes down, find the cause and correct it. The exact mixture of antifreeze-to-water which you should use depends on the relative weather conditions. The mixture should contain at least 50-percent antifreeze, but should never contain more than 60-percent antifreeze. Consult the mixture ratio chart on the antifreeze container before adding coolant. Hydrometers are available at most auto parts stores to test the coolant. Use antifreeze which meets specification ESE-M97B44-A (Ford part No. E2FZ-19549-A) or equivalent.

3.8 The thermostat is mounted in a housing at the front of the intake manifold (arrow)

3   Thermostat - check and replacement

Warning: *Do not remove the radiator cap, drain the coolant or replace the thermostat until the engine has cooled completely.*

Check

1   Before assuming the thermostat is to blame for a cooling system problem, check the coolant level, drivebelt tension (see Chapter 1) and temperature gauge (or light) operation.
2   If the engine seems to be taking a long time to warm up (based on heater output or temperature gauge operation), the thermostat is probably stuck open. Replace the thermostat with a new one.
3   If the engine runs hot, use your hand to check the temperature of the upper radiator hose. If the hose isn't hot, but the engine is, the thermostat is probably stuck closed, preventing the coolant inside the engine from escaping to the radiator. Replace the thermostat. **Caution:** *Don't drive the vehicle without a thermostat. The computer may stay in open loop and emissions and fuel economy will suffer.*
4   If the upper radiator hose is hot, it means that the coolant is flowing and the thermostat is open. Consult the Troubleshooting section at the front of this manual for cooling system diagnosis.

Replacement

Refer to illustrations 3.8 and 3.11
5   Disconnect the negative battery cable from the battery.
6   Remove the air cleaner air duct from the throttle body and air cleaner.
7   Drain the cooling system (see Chapter 1). If the coolant is relatively new or in good condition (see Chapter 1), save it and reuse it.
8   Follow the upper radiator hose to the engine to locate the thermostat housing. The housing is located at the front of the intake manifold **(see illustration)**.
9   Loosen the hose clamp, then detach the hose from the fitting. If it's stuck, grasp it near the end with a pair of adjustable pliers and twist it to break the seal, then pull it off. If the hose is old or deteriorated, cut it off and install a new one.
10   If the outer surface of the large fitting that mates with the hose is deteriorated (corroded, pitted, etc.) it may be damaged further by hose removal. If it is, the thermostat housing cover will have to be replaced.
11   Remove the bolts and detach the housing cover. If the cover is stuck, tap it with a soft-face hammer to jar it loose. Be prepared for some coolant to spill out as the gasket seal is broken.
12   Note how it's installed (which end is facing toward the engine), then remove the thermostat **(see illustration)**. It may be necessary to rotate the thermostat to free it.
13   Stuff a rag into the engine opening, then remove all traces of corrosion from the housing and cover with a gasket scraper. Remove

NOTE: SEALING RING MUST BE
PRE-ASSEMBLED TO
THERMOSTAT BEFORE
ASSEMBLY OF CONNECTOR
TO INLET MANIFOLD.
THE AIR RELEASE VALVE ON
THE THERMOSTAT MUST BE
IN THE UPPER POSITION AS
SHOWN.

3.12 Thermostat and related components

4.3a Use a socket or screwdriver to loosen the hose clamp (arrow)

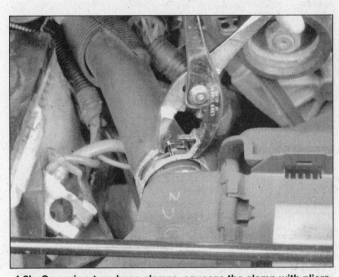

4.3b On spring-type hose clamps, squeeze the clamp with pliers and slide it back along the hose

the rag from the opening and clean the mating surfaces with lacquer thinner or acetone.

14   Make sure the sealing ring is positioned correctly on the thermostat **(see illustration 3.12)**.

15   Install the new thermostat in the housing with the bridge section toward the outlet housing cover. Make sure the air release valve is in the up position **(see illustration 3.12)**.

16   Install the housing cover and bolts. Tighten the bolts to the torque listed in this Chapter's Specifications.

17   Reattach the hose to the fitting and tighten the hose clamp securely.

18   Refill the cooling system (see Chapter 1).

19   Install the air cleaner air duct

20   Start the engine and allow it to reach normal operating temperature, then check for leaks and proper thermostat operation (as described in Steps 2 through 4).

4   Radiator - removal and installation

Refer to illustrations 4.3a, 4.3b, 4.5, 4.6 and 4.8

Warning: *Wait until the engine is completely cool before beginning this procedure.*

1   Disconnect the negative battery cable from the battery.

2   Drain the cooling system (see Chapter 1). If the coolant is relatively new or in good condition, save it and reuse it.

3   Loosen the hose clamps and slide them back on the hoses, then detach the radiator hoses from the fittings **(see illustrations)**. If they're stuck, grasp each hose near the end with a pair of adjustable pliers and twist it to break the seal, then pull it off - be careful not to distort the radiator fittings! If the hoses are old or deteriorated, cut them off and install new ones.

4   Disconnect the reservoir hose from the radiator filler neck.

5   Remove the screws that attach the fan shroud to the radiator and slide the shroud toward the engine **(see illustration)**. Let the shroud rest on the fan.

6   If the vehicle is equipped with an automatic transmission, hold the cooler fittings with a backup wrench and disconnect the lines from the

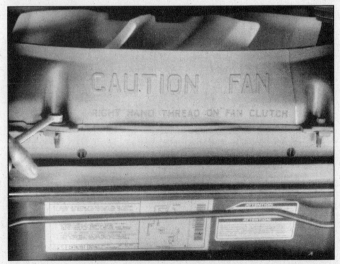

4.5 Remove the shroud mounting bolts and place the shroud over the fan

radiator **(see illustration)**. Use a drip pan to catch spilled fluid.

7   Plug the lines and fittings to avoid spillage and contamination.

8   Remove the radiator mounting bolts **(see illustration)**.

9   Carefully lift the radiator up and out of its lower mounting pads or grommets. Remove the radiator and be careful not to spill coolant on the vehicle or scratch the paint.

10   With the radiator removed, it can be inspected for leaks and damage. If it needs repair, have a radiator shop or dealer service department perform the work as special techniques are required.

11   Bugs and dirt can be removed from the radiator with compressed air and a soft brush. Don't bend the cooling fins as this is done.

12   Check the radiator mounts for deterioration and make sure there's nothing in them when the radiator is installed.

13   Installation is the reverse of the removal procedure with the following additions:

a) *After installation, fill the cooling system with the proper mixture of antifreeze and water (see Chapter 1).*

b) *Start the engine and check for leaks. Allow the engine to reach normal operating temperature, indicated by the upper radiator hose becoming hot. Recheck the coolant level and add more if required.*

c) *If you're working on an automatic transmission equipped vehicle, check and add transmission fluid as needed (see Chapter 1).*

---

5   Cooling fan and viscous clutch - inspection, removal and installation

---

Warning: *To avoid possible injury or damage, DO NOT operate the engine with a damaged fan. Do not attempt to repair fan blades - replace a damaged fan with a new one.*

Viscous clutch inspection

1   Disconnect the negative cable from the battery.

2   Rock the fan back and forth by hand to check for excessive bearing play.

3   With the engine cold, turn the fan blades by hand. The fan should turn freely.

4   Visually inspect for substantial fluid leakage from the clutch

4.6 On automatic transmission models, hold the cooler line fittings with a backup wrench and unscrew the fittings

assembly. If problems are noted, replace the clutch assembly.

5   Reconnect the battery cable and warm up the engine. With the engine completely warmed up, turn off the ignition switch and disconnect the negative battery cable from the battery. Turn the fan by hand. Some drag should be evident. If the fan turns easily, replace the fan clutch.

Removal and installation

Refer to illustrations 5.9a, 5.9b and 5.11

6   Disconnect the negative cable from the battery.

7   Disconnect the reservoir hose from the radiator filler neck.

8   Remove the screws securing the shroud to the radiator and slide the shroud toward the engine (see Section 4).

9   Loosen the clutch hub nut as follows:

a) **Note:** *This nut has standard right-hand threads and must be rotated counterclockwise for removal. Remove the large nut*

4.8 The radiator and related components (typical)

FRONT OF VEHICLE

WINDSHIELD WASHER RESERVOIR

COOLANT RESERVOIR

SCREW AND WASHER

SCREW AND WASHER

INSTALL PAINT STRIPE AT 12:00 POSITION

UPPER HOSE ASSEMBLY

RESERVOIR ASSEMBLY

OVERFLOW HOSE

RADIATOR

INSTALL PAINT STRIPE AT 12:00 POSITION

WATER OUTLET

FAN SHROUD

WATER PUMP

LOWER HOSE

T84T-6312-D

T84T-6312-C

5.9a To loosen the large nut that holds the fan clutch to the water pump, use the Ford tools shown . . .

5.9b . . . hold the pulley from turning (A) and turn the nut counterclockwise to loosen it (B)

securing the clutch hub assembly to the water pump drivebelt hub.
b) *Use special tools Fan Clutch Pulley Holder (Ford part No. T84T-6312-C) and Fan Clutch Nut Wrench (Ford part No. T84T-6312-D), or equivalent* **(see illustrations).**
c) *If the special tools are not available, use a strap wrench to hold the assembly from rotating and use large adjustable pliers to remove the large nut.*

10 Lift the fan/clutch assembly out of the engine compartment.
11 Inspect the fan blades for damage and defects. Replace it if necessary by removing the bolts securing the fan to the clutch assembly **(see illustration).** If the fan clutch is stored, position it with the radiator side facing down.
12 Installation is the reverse of the removal steps. Be sure to tighten the fan and clutch nut evenly and to the torque listed in this Chapter's Specifications.

6 Coolant reservoir - removal and installation

Refer to illustration 6.4
1 Disconnect the radiator overflow hose from the base of the coolant reservoir (see Chapter 1).
2 Connect a hose to the fitting on the coolant reservoir and drain the coolant from the reservoir.
3 Disconnect the electrical connector for the windshield washer pump.
4 Remove the reservoir attachment to the inner fender panel **(see illustration).**
5 Lift the reservoir out of the engine compartment.
6 Installation is the reverse of removal. Refill the reservoir with coolant (see Chapter 1).

7 Coolant temperature sending unit - removal and installation

Refer to illustration 7.2
1 Allow the cooling system to completely cool down, then open the radiator filler cap to relieve any pressure in the cooling system. Install the cap. This will minimize coolant loss during this procedure.

PULLEY

ENGINE COOLING FAN

WATER PUMP

SCREW AND WASHER

FAN CLUTCH

5.11 Exploded view of the fan and clutch assembly

6.4 The coolant reservoir is secured to the inner fender panel by screws

7.2 The temperature sending unit (arrow) is located on the intake manifold - it's on the left when viewed from the front of the vehicle; the larger sending unit on the right is for the EEC-IV system

8.4 If the water pump seal fails, coolant will leak from the weep hole (arrow)

2   Disconnect the electrical connector from the top of the sending unit **(see illustration)**.
3   Wrap the threads of the new sending unit with Teflon tape.
4   Remove the old sending unit from the engine. Place your finger over the hole in the engine to minimize coolant loss.
5   Immediately install the new sending unit and tighten it securely.
6   Connect the sending unit electrical connector.
7   Refill the cooling system (see Chapter 1).
8   Start the engine and check for leaks.

8   Water pump - check and replacement

Check

Refer to illustration 8.4

1   A failure in the water pump can cause serious engine damage due to overheating.
2   There are three ways to check the operation of the water pump while it's installed on the engine. If the pump is defective, it should be replaced with a new or rebuilt unit.
3   With the engine running at normal operating temperature, squeeze the upper radiator hose. If the water pump is working properly, a pressure surge should be felt as the hose is released. **Warning:** *Keep your hands away from the fan blades!*
4   Water pumps are equipped with weep or vent holes. If a failure occurs in the pump seal, coolant will leak from the hole **(see illustration)**. In most cases you'll need a flashlight to find the hole on the water pump from underneath to check for leaks.
5   If the water pump shaft bearings fail there may be a howling sound at the front of the engine while it's running. Shaft wear can be felt if the water pump pulley is rocked up and down. Don't mistake drivebelt slippage, which causes a squealing sound, for water pump bearing failure.

Replacement

Refer to illustration 8.12

Warning: *Wait until the engine is completely cool before beginning this procedure.*

6   Disconnect the negative battery cable from the battery.
7   Drain the cooling system (see Chapter 1). If the coolant is relatively new or in good condition, save it and reuse it.
8   Remove the cooling fan and shroud (see Sections 4 and 5).
9   Remove the drivebelt (see Chapter 1) and the pulley at the end of the water pump shaft.
10   Loosen the clamps and detach the hoses from the water pump. If they're stuck, grasp each hose near the end with a pair of adjustable pliers and twist it to break the seal, then pull it off. If the hoses are

8.12 Locations of the water pump bolts (arrows)

deteriorated, cut them off and install new ones.
11   If necessary, remove the alternator and its mounting bracket from the water pump.
12   Remove the bolts and detach the water pump from the engine **(see illustration)**. Note the locations of the various lengths and different types of bolts as they're removed to ensure correct installation.
13   Clean the bolt threads and the threaded holes in the engine to remove corrosion and sealant.
14   Compare the new pump to the old one to make sure they're identical.
15   Remove all traces of old gasket material from the engine gasket surface with a gasket scraper.
16   Clean the engine and new water pump gasket mating surfaces with lacquer thinner or acetone.
17   Apply a thin coat of RTV sealant to the engine side of the new gasket.
18   Apply a thin layer of RTV sealant to the gasket mating surface of the new pump, then carefully mate the gasket and the pump. Slip a couple of bolts through the pump mounting holes to hold the gasket in place.
19   Carefully attach the pump and gasket to the engine and thread the bolts into the holes finger tight.
20   Install the remaining bolts (if they also hold the alternator bracket in place, be sure to reposition the bracket at this time). Tighten them evenly to the torque listed in this Chapter's Specifications in 1/4-turn increments. Don't overtighten them or the pump may be distorted.
21   Reinstall all parts removed for access to the pump.
22   Refill the cooling system and check the drivebelt tension (see Chapter 1). Run the engine and check for leaks.

10.3 Heater control assembly mounting screws

9 Heater - general information

The heater circulates engine coolant through a small radiator (heater core) in the passenger compartment. Air is drawn in through an opening in the cowl, then blown (by the blower motor) through the heater core to pick up heat. The heated air is blended with varying amounts of unheated air to regulate the temperature. The heated air is then blown into the passenger compartment. Various doors in the heater control the flow of air to the floor and through the instrument panel louvers and defroster outlets.

10 Heater control assembly - removal and installation

Refer to illustration 10.3

Removal

1 Disconnect the negative cable from the battery.
2 Remove the instrument cluster trim panel (see Chapter 12).
3 Remove the four screws securing the control panel to the instrument panel **(see illustration)**.
4 Pull the control assembly through the opening in the instrument panel far enough to allow removal of the electrical connections. Carefully spread the clips on the electrical connectors and disconnect the connectors for the blower switch and illumination light.
5 Use a small screwdriver and remove the two-hose vacuum harness from the vacuum switch on the side of the control assembly.
6 At the back of the control assembly, use a screwdriver or needle-nose pliers and release the temperature and function cable snap-in flag from the white control bracket.
7 At the bottom of the control assembly, remove the temperature

control cable (black cable with a blue snap-in flag) from the control by rotating the cable until the T-pin releases the cable.
8 Pull enough cable through the instrument opening until the function cable (white cable with black snap-in flag) can be held vertical to the control assembly, then remove the cable end from the function lever.
9 Remove the control assembly from the instrument panel.

Installation

10 Pull the control cables through the instrument panel opening by approximately eight inches.
11 Hold the control assembly up to the instrument panel with the control assembly face pointed toward the floor.
12 Carefully bend and attach the function cable (white) to the white plastic lever. Rotate the control assembly back to its normal position for installation, then snap the black cable flag into the control assembly bracket.
13 On the opposite side of the control assembly, attach the black temperature control cable with the blue snap-in flag to the blue plastic lever on the control assembly. Be sure that the end of the cable is seated securely with the T-top pin on the control assembly. Rotate the cable to its operating position and snap the blue cable flag into the control assembly bracket.
14 Install the electrical wire harness connectors.
15 Connect the dual terminal on the vacuum hose to the vacuum switch on the control assembly.
16 Position the control assembly into the instrument panel and install the four mounting screws.
17 Complete the installation by installing the various trim panels and instrument panel items previously removed. Check for proper operation and adjust the cables if necessary (see Section 11).

11 Heater control cables - check and adjustment

Check

1 Move the control lever all the way from left to right.
2 If the control lever stops before the end and bounces back, the cables are out of adjustment.

Adjustment

Refer to illustrations 11.4a and 11.4b

3 Squeeze the tabs on either side of the glove box door to disengage it, then let the door hang down to provide access to the control cables.
4 Working through the glove box opening, remove the cable jacket from its metal attaching clip on top of the heater assembly **(see illustrations)**. The cable ends should remain attached to the door cams and/or crank arms at this time.

11.4a Details of the heater control cables (without air conditioning)

11.4b Details of the heater control cables (with air conditioning)

5   To adjust the temperature control cable, set the temperature lever to the Cool position and hold it there.
6   Push gently on the black cable jacket to seat the blend door (push until you feel resistance).
7   Reinstall the cable to the clip by pushing the jacket into the clip from the top until it snaps in.
8   To adjust the function control cable, set the function control lever to Defrost and hold it there.
9   Pull on the white cam jacket until the cam travel stops.
10   Reinstall the cable to the clip by pushing the jacket into the clip from the top until it snaps in.
11   Run the system on High and actuate the levers, checking for proper operation. Readjust if necessary.
12   Install the glove box door.

12   Heater blower motor - replacement

Refer to illustrations 12.3, 12.6, 12.7 and 12.8
Note: *The blower motor is located in the right side of the engine compartment.*
1   Disconnect the negative cable from the battery.
2   Remove the air cleaner (see Chapter 4).
3   Working in the engine compartment, push down on the electrical connector locking tab and disconnect the connector from the blower motor **(see illustration)**.
4   Models without air conditioning: disconnect the small rubber cooling tube from the blower motor.
5   Models with air conditioning:

   a) *Working in the passenger compartment, remove the single nut*

12.3 Push down on the electrical connector locking tab and disconnect the connector

12.6 Remove the three screws securing the heater blower motor

12.7 Carefully pull the blower assembly from the heater assembly

from the bottom of the plenum. The nut is located just to the right of the heater core access cover.

b) *Working in the engine compartment, disconnect the electrical connector from the blower motor resistor.*

c) *Disconnect the vacuum hose from the check valve.*

d) *Disconnect the vacuum line from the intake manifold and remove it from the routing channel.*

6   Remove the three screws securing the blower motor to the heater blower assembly **(see illustration).**

7   Being very careful not to damage the gasket, pull the blower motor out of the heater assembly **(see illustration).**

8   If necessary, remove the push nut on the motor shaft and remove the blower wheel from the motor **(see illustration).**

9   Installation is the reverse of the removal Steps with the addition of the following:

a) *Replace the gasket between the blower motor and heater assembly if its condition is in doubt. This gasket must be good to prevent moisture from entering the assembly.*

b) *Make sure the electrical connector is fully seated and that it "clicks" into place.*

13 Heater core - replacement

Refer to illustrations 13.5, 13.8 and 13.9

1   Allow the cooling system to completely cool down.

2   Using a thick cloth for protection, turn the radiator filler cap to the

12.8 Exploded view of the blower motor assembly

first stop.

3   Step back and let the pressure release.

4   Once the pressure has been released, tighten the radiator cap.

5   Working within the engine compartment, loosen the clamps on the heater hoses at the engine compartment side of the firewall **(see illustration).** Twist the hoses and carefully separate them from the

3

13.5 Disconnect the heater hoses from the fittings at the firewall

13.8 Heater core installation details

13.9 Pull the heater core to the rear and down to remove it from the plenum

15.3 Unhook the lock-tab and pull the connector off (left arrow); to then pry the retainer (right arrow) out of the compressor with a trim panel removal tool or equivalent

15.5 The refrigerant lines are secured to the rear of the compressor by one bolt (arrow)

heater core tubes.

6   Plug or cap the heater core tubes to prevent coolant from spilling into the passenger compartment when the heater core is removed.

7   Place a plastic sheet on the floor of the vehicle to prevent stains if the coolant spills.

8   Working in the passenger compartment, remove the four screws securing the heater core access cover to the plenum assembly **(see illustration)**.

9   Carefully pull the heater core to the rear and down and remove it from the plenum assembly **(see illustration)**.

10   Installation is the reverse of the removal procedure with the following additions:

a) Fill the cooling system (see Chapter 1).
b) Run the engine, check for leaks and test the heater.

14   Air conditioning system - check and maintenance

Warning: The air conditioning system is under high pressure. Do not loosen any hose fittings or remove any components until after the system has been discharged by a dealer service department or service station. Always wear eye protection when disconnecting air conditioning system fittings.

Note: 1991 through 1994 air conditioning systems use R-12 refrigerant. In 1995 and later models, the air conditioning system was changed to use the new, "environmentally friendly" R-134a refrigerant. Each system uses similar components and locations but components are NOT interchangeable. All discharging of refrigerant, for part replacement or maintenance, should be done by an approved air conditioning facility with the proper refrigerant recovery equipment.

1   The following maintenance checks should be performed on a regular basis to ensure that the air conditioner continues to operate at peak efficiency.

a) Check the compressor drivebelt. If it's worn or deteriorated, replace it (see Chapter 1).
b) Check the system hoses. Look for cracks, bubbles, hard spots and deterioration. Inspect the hoses and all fittings for oil bubbles and seepage. If there's any evidence of wear, damage or leaks, replace the hose(s).
c) Inspect the condenser fins for leaves, bugs and other debris. Use a "fin comb" or compressed air to clean the condenser.
d) Make sure the system has the correct refrigerant charge.

2   It's a good idea to operate the system for about 10 minutes at least once a month, particularly during the winter. Long term non-use

can cause hardening, and subsequent failure, of the seals.

3   Because of the complexity of the air conditioning system and the special equipment necessary to service it, in-depth troubleshooting and repairs are not included in this manual. However, simple checks and component replacement procedures are provided in this Chapter. For more complete information on the air conditioning system, refer to the Haynes Automotive Heating and Air Conditioning Manual.

4   The most common cause of poor cooling is simply a low system refrigerant charge. If a noticeable drop in cool air output occurs, one of the following quick checks will help you determine if the refrigerant level is low.

Checking the refrigerant charge

5   Warm the engine up to normal operating temperature.

6   Place the air conditioning temperature selector at the coldest setting and put the blower at the highest setting. Open the doors (to make sure the air conditioning system doesn't cycle off as soon as it cools the passenger compartment).

7   With the compressor engaged - the clutch will make an audible click and the center of the clutch will rotate - feel the evaporator inlet pipe between the orifice and the accumulator with one hand while placing your other hand on the surface of the accumulator housing.

8   If both surfaces feel about the same temperature and if both feel a little cooler than the surrounding air, the refrigerant level is probably okay. Further inspection of the system is beyond the scope of the home mechanic and should be left to a professional.

9   If the inlet pipe has frost accumulation or feels cooler than the accumulator surface, the refrigerant charge is low. Add refrigerant.

Adding refrigerant

10   Buy an automotive charging kit at an auto parts store. A charging kit includes a 14-ounce can of refrigerant, a tap valve and a short section of hose that can be attached between the tap valve and the system low side service valve. Because one can of refrigerant may not be sufficient to bring the system charge up to the proper level, it's a good idea to buy a couple of additional cans. Make sure that one of the cans contains red refrigerant dye. If the system is leaking, the red dye will leak out with the refrigerant and help you pinpoint the location of the leak. **Warning:** Never add more than two cans of refrigerant to the system.

11   Hook up the charging kit by following the manufacturer's instructions. **Warning:** DO NOT hook the charging kit hose to the system high side!

12   Warm up the engine and turn on the air conditioner. Keep the

15.6 Air conditioning compressor and related components

1 Compressor
2 Mounting bolts
3 Air conditioning compressor and power steering pump bracket
4 Power steering pump support brace
5 Support brace-to-timing chain cover nuts
6 Power steering pump bolts
7 Power steering pump bolts

charging kit hose away from the fan and other moving parts.
13 Add refrigerant to the low side of the system until both the accumulator surface and the evaporator inlet pipe feel about the same temperature. Allow stabilization time between each addition.
14 Once the accumulator surface and the evaporator inlet pipe feel about the same temperature, add the contents remaining in the can.

15 Air conditioning compressor - removal and installation

Refer to illustrations 15.3, 15.5 and 15.6
Warning: *The air conditioning system is under high pressure. DO NOT disassemble any part of the system (hoses, compressor, line fittings, etc.) until after the system has been depressurized by a dealer service department or service station.*
Note: *The accumulator (see Section 17) should be replaced whenever the compressor is replaced.*
1 Have the air conditioning system discharged (see Warning above).
2 Disconnect the negative cable from the battery.
3 Disconnect the electrical connector from the compressor and detach the harness retainer from the back of the compressor **(see illustration).**
4 Remove the drivebelt (see Chapter 1).
5 Remove the bolt that secures the refrigerant lines to the rear of the compressor **(see illustration).** Plug the open fittings to prevent entry of dirt and moisture.
6 Unbolt the compressor from the mounting brackets and lift it out of the vehicle **(see illustration).**
7 If a new compressor is being installed, follow the directions with the

16.6 The air conditioning condenser and related components

1 Condenser
2 U-nut
3 Bolt
4 Stud and washer
5 Nut and washer
6 Seal (some automatic transmission models use two seals)
7 Condenser bottom seal (automatic transmission models only)
8 Condenser top seal
9 Radiator

compressor regarding the draining of excess oil prior to installation.
8 The clutch may have to be transferred from the original to the new compressor.
9 Installation is the reverse of removal with the following additions:
a) *Replace all O-rings with new ones specifically made for air conditioning system use and lubricate them with refrigerant oil.*
b) *Have the system evacuated, recharged and leak tested by the shop that discharged it.*

16 Air conditioning condenser - removal and installation

Refer to illustrations 16.6, 16.10a, 16.10b and 16.10c
Warning: *The air conditioning system is under high pressure. DO NOT disassemble any part of the system (hoses, compressor, line fittings, etc.) until after the system has been depressurized by a dealer service department or service station.*
1 Have the air conditioning system discharged (see Warning above).
2 Remove the battery (see Chapter 5).
3 Drain the cooling system (see Chapter 1).
4 Remove the radiator (see Chapter 3).
5 Disconnect the refrigerant lines from the condenser. This requires a spring lock coupling tool similar to that used for fuel injection lines (see Chapter 4).
6 Working from below, remove the mounting nuts from the condenser studs **(see illustration).**
7 Lift the condenser out of the vehicle and plug the lines to keep dirt and moisture out.
8 If the original condenser will be reinstalled, store it with the line fittings on top to prevent oil from draining out.
9 If a new condenser is being installed, pour one ounce of refrigerant oil into it prior to installation.
10 Reinstall the components in the reverse order of removal. Be sure the rubber pads are in place under the condenser. Be sure the seals

3

16.10a The condenser has two radiator extensions . . .

16.10b . . . two seals between the condenser and the radiator support . . .

are in place around the condenser **(see illustrations)**.

11   Have the system evacuated, recharged and leak tested by the shop that discharged it.

17 Air conditioning accumulator - removal and installation

Warning: *The air conditioning system is under high pressure. DO NOT disassemble any part of the system (hoses, compressor, line fittings, etc.) until after the system has been depressurized by a dealer service department or service station.*

Removal

Refer to illustration 17.4

1   Have the air conditioning system discharged (see Warning above).

2   Disconnect the negative cable from the battery.

3   Unplug the electrical connector from the pressure switch near the top of the accumulator. Unscrew the pressure switch.

4   Disconnect the refrigerant line from the accumulator **(see illustration)**. This requires a spring lock coupling tool of the type used for fuel injection system lines (see Chapter 4).

5   Use a backup wrench to hold the fitting that connects the accumulator to the evaporator core, then disconnect the fitting. Plug the open fittings to prevent entry of dirt and moisture.

6   Remove the mounting bracket screw and the screw that holds the

evaporator tube to the accumulator bracket, then lift the accumulator out.

7   If a new accumulator is being installed, remove the Schrader valve and pour the oil out into a measuring cup, noting the amount. Add fresh refrigerant oil to the new accumulator equal to the amount removed from the old unit, plus one ounce.

Installation

8   Loosely position the bracket on the new accumulator.

9   Connect the accumulator to the evaporator core, using a new O-ring lubricated with clean refrigerant oil. At the same time, align the bracket with the slot between the evaporator case flanges.

10   Using a backup wrench, tighten the fitting securely.

11   Install the screw that holds the bracket between the case flanges.

12   Tighten the accumulator bracket and install the clip that holds the evaporator inlet tube to the bracket.

13   Place a new O-ring, lubricated with clean refrigerant oil, on the pressure switch nipple on the accumulator.

14   Install the pressure switch. If it has a metal base, tighten it to the torque listed in this Chapter's Specifications. If it has a plastic base, tighten it by hand only. Connect the pressure switch electrical connector.

15   Reconnect the negative cable to the battery.

16   Take the vehicle to the shop that discharged the air conditioning system. Have the system recharged and tested for leaks.

16.10c . . . and one vertical seal between the condenser and the radiator

17.4 The accumulator is mounted on the evaporator case in the engine compartment

Chapter 4
Fuel and exhaust systems

Contents

	Section
Air cleaner housing - removal and installation	8
CHECK ENGINE light on	See Chapter 6
Electronic fuel injection - component removal and installation	9
Exhaust system service - general information	10
Fuel lines and fittings - general information	3
Fuel pump/fuel pressure - check	4

	Section
Fuel pump - removal and installation	7
Fuel pressure relief procedure	2
Fuel tank - cleaning and repair	6
Fuel tank - removal and installation	5
General information	1

Specifications

Fuel pressure
Key on, engine off .... 35 to 45 psi
At idle
  With vacuum hose connected .... 30 to 35 psi
  With vacuum hose disconnected .... 35 to 45 psi

Torque specifications
Upper intake manifold nuts .... 15 to 18 ft-lbs
Throttle body bolts .... 76 to 106 in-lbs
Air bypass valve screws .... 72 to 96 in-lbs
Fuel pressure regulator mounting screws .... 72 to 96 in-lbs
Fuel rail mounting bolts (studs) .... 84 to 120 in-lbs

1 General information

Fuel system

The fuel system consists of the fuel tank, the fuel pump, an air cleaner assembly, a fuel injection system and the various Teflon hoses, steel lines and fittings connecting the fuel delivery components together.

Vehicles covered by this manual are equipped with the Ford Electronic Fuel Injection system. This system uses one fuel injector per cylinder.

The fuel pump is a single high pressure electric pump located within the fuel tank.

Exhaust system

All vehicles are equipped with two exhaust manifolds, a catalytic converter, an exhaust pipe and a muffler. Any component of the exhaust system can be replaced. See Chapter 6 for further details regarding the catalytic converter.

2 Fuel pressure relief procedure

Refer to illustration 2.1
Warning: *The fuel supply lines will remain pressurized for a long period of time after the engine is shut down. The pressure within the fuel system must be relieved before servicing any of the fuel delivery*

2.1 The inertia switch is located on the passenger side of the transmission hump on the firewall under the carpet - unplug its electrical connector and crank the engine for 15 to 20 seconds to relieve fuel pressure

1	Inertia switch	2	Transmission hump
1A	Reset button	3	Firewall

components. Gasoline is extremely flammable, so take extra precautions when you work on any part of the fuel system. Don't smoke or allow open flames or bare light bulbs near the work area, and don't work in a garage where a natural gas-type appliance (such as a water heater or clothes dryer) with a pilot light is present. If you spill any fuel on your skin, rinse it off immediately with soap and water. When you perform any kind of work on the fuel system, wear safety glasses and have a Class B type fire extinguisher on hand.

1   The fuel pump switch - sometimes called the "inertia switch" - shuts off fuel to the engine in the event of a collision. This switch provides an easy way to relieve fuel pressure before servicing any fuel injection component. The switch is located in the passenger compartment on the passenger side of the transmission hump **(see illustration)**.

2   Unplug the inertia switch electrical connector.

3   Crank the engine with the starter for 15 to 20 seconds.

4   The fuel system pressure is now relieved. When you're finished working on the fuel system, reconnect the electrical connector back onto the switch and push the reset button on the top of the switch.

5   Even though the pressure has been relieved, it's a good idea to wrap a rag around fuel fittings when they are disconnected.

3   Fuel lines and fittings - general information

Warning: The fuel system pressure must be relieved before disconnecting fuel lines and fittings (see Section 2). Gasoline is extremely flammable, so take extra precautions when you work on any part of the fuel system. Don't smoke or allow open flames or bare light bulbs near the work area, and don't work in a garage where a natural gas-type appliance (such as a water heater or clothes dryer) with a pilot light is present. If you spill any fuel on your skin, rinse it off immediately with soap and water. When you perform any kind of work on the fuel system, wear safety glasses and have a Class B type fire extinguisher on hand.

Spring lock couplings - disassembly and reassembly

Refer to illustrations 3.1a, 3.1b, 3.2 and 3.4a through 3.4e

1   The fuel supply and return lines used on these engines have spring lock couplings at some connections **(see illustration)**. The male end of the spring lock coupling, which is girded by two O-rings, is inserted into a female flared end fitting. The coupling is secured by a garter spring which prevents disengagement by gripping the flared end of the female fitting. A clip and tether assembly provides additional security **(see illustration)**.

3.1a Some fuel lines use spring lock couplings (these are the fuel inlet and return lines in the engine compartment, viewed through the wheel well)

SPRING LOCK COUPLING – FOR FUEL LINE TO ENGINE FUEL RAIL CONNECTIONS

3.1b The lines are secured with tethered clips

2   To disconnect the spring lock coupling supply fitting, you'll need to obtain a spring lock coupling tool or its equivalent **(see illustration)**, as follows:

a) 3/8-inch return fitting, tool D87L-9280-A
b) 1/2-inch supply fitting, tool D87L-9280-B
c) 5/8-inch return fitting, tool T83P-19623-C

3.2 These special tools are required to connect and disconnect engine compartment fuel lines

3.4a Open the tool and place it over the line . . .

3.4b . . . then slide the tool against the fuel line fitting so the lip inside the tool (arrows) . . .

4

3.4c . . . pushes against the garter spring (arrow) . . .

3.4d . . . push the tool against the spring until the spring slides off the flared female end of the line (arrow) the line . . .

3   Before disconnecting the line, unclip the safety clip **(see illustration 3.1b)**.

4   To disconnect and reconnect the line, refer to the accompanying illustrations and follow the information in the captions **(see illustrations)**.

Stainless steel fitting - disassembly and reassembly

Refer to illustrations 3.9 and 3.12

5   All fuel lines outside the engine compartment are either Teflon hose and stainless steel (fuel supply and return lines) or carbon steel (vapor line). These lines are fastened to the frame rails with integral clips and connect with stainless steel fittings. This type of fitting consists of a female tube end with internal retaining "fingers" that grasp a formed male tube end. A safety clip holds the two ends of the fitting together.

6   To disconnect the stainless steel fitting, you'll need to obtain a quick-disconnect tool or its equivalent, as follows:

a) *Pressure regulator fitting, tool T90P-9550-A.*
b) *5/16-inch fitting, tool T90T-9550-B.*
c) *3/8-inch fitting, tool T90T-9550-C.*

7   Release the safety clip from the fitting and install the proper quick-disconnect tool on the fitting body.

8   Align the quick-disconnect tool on the fitting and push the tool

3.4e To reconnect the line, place the flared female end (A) over the O-ring on the male end and push the ends together until the flared end slips under the garter spring (B) - tug on the ends to make sure they're locked, then install the safety clip

3.9 Disconnecting pressure regulator fitting

3.12 Connecting stainless steel fittings

into the fitting body to release the retaining fingers holding the male tube end. Once the fingers are released, pull the male tube end from the female fitting end and remove the tool.

9   Study the accompanying illustration carefully before detaching the fuel return line fitting from the pressure regulator **(see illustration)**.

10   After disassembly, inspect and clean the tube end sealing surfaces. Also inspect the inside of the fitting for any internal damage. If damage is noted, replace the fuel tube.

11   Before reconnecting the fitting, wipe the male tube end with a clean cloth. Check the inside of the fitting to make sure that it's free of dirt and/or obstructions.

12   To reconnect the fitting, align it with the male tube end and push the tube into the fitting. When the fitting is engaged, a definite click will be heard. Pull on the fitting to ensure that it's fully engaged **(see illustration)**.

Fuel lines - Teflon-stainless steel and carbon steel

Warning: *Use only the recommended tubing materials. Other types of tubing could fail in service.*

13   Teflon-stainless steel fuel lines must not be repaired using hose and hose clamps. Should the fittings or steel tubing ends become damaged, approved service parts must be used to replace the lines. Splicing such lines with seamless steel tubing or rubber hose is not recommended.

14   If a length of Teflon hose is damaged, it should be replaced only with an approved service part.

4   Fuel pump/fuel pressure - check

Warning: *Gasoline is extremely flammable, so take extra precautions when you work on any part of the fuel system. Don't smoke or allow open flames or bare light bulbs near the work area, and don't work in a* garage where a natural gas-type appliance (such as a water heater or clothes dryer) with a pilot light is present. If you spill any fuel on your skin, rinse it off immediately with soap and water. When you perform any kind of work on the fuel system, wear safety glasses and have a Class B type fire extinguisher on hand.

Note: *Always make sure there is fuel in the tank before assuming the fuel pump is defective.*

General check

1   An electric fuel pump malfunction will usually result in a loss of fuel flow and/or pressure that is often reflected by a corresponding drop in performance (or a no-run condition).

2   Verify the pump actually runs. Remove the fuel filler cap and have an assistant turn the ignition switch to On - you should hear a brief whirring noise as the pump comes on and pressurizes the system. Have the assistant start the engine (if possible). This time you should hear a constant whirring sound from the pump (but it's more difficult to hear with the engine running).

3   If the pump doesn't run (makes no sound), check the fuel pump fuse (see Chapter 12). If the fuse is okay, check the continuity of the inertia switch with an ohmmeter (see Section 2 for the location of the switch). If the inertia switch is good, proceed to the next Step. If the fuse is blown, replace it and see if the pump works (if it blows again, trace the fuel pump circuit for a short to ground). If the fuse doesn't blow but the fuel pump still doesn't work, proceed to the next Step.

4   With the ignition off, unplug the electrical connector from the fuel pump. Using a jumper wire, ground the negative terminal of the fuel pump. Using a fused jumper wire, apply 12-volts to the fuel pump feed terminal.

5   If the fuel pump doesn't run, replace it (see Section 7). If it does run, the problem lies somewhere in the electrical circuit to the fuel pump (refer to the wiring diagrams at the back of this manual).

Pressure check

6   Relieve the fuel pressure (see Section 2).

U-NUT

HEAT SHIELD
FRONT EXTENSION

STRAP
ASSEMBLY

VIEW A

TANK
ASSEMBLY

REAR STRAP

VIEW A

FRONT
STRAP

FRONT OF VEHICLE

SHIELD AND SKID
PLATE ASSEMBLY

SCREW

FLANGE NUT

SHIELD

5.6 Fuel tank and related components

4

7   Connect a fuel pressure gauge to the Schrader valve on the fuel rail.

8   Turn the ignition switch to the On position. The fuel pump should run for about two seconds, then the pressure should hold steady. Note the reading on the gauge and compare it to the pressure listed in this Chapter's Specifications.

9   Start the engine (if possible) and allow it to idle. The pressure should be lower by 3 to 10 psi (see this Chapter's specifications). Disconnect the vacuum hose from the fuel pressure regulator **(see illustration 9.57)** and compare your reading with the pressure listed in this Chapter's Specifications. If all the pressure readings are within specifications, the system is operating properly.

10   If the pressure did not drop by 3 to 10 psi after starting the engine, apply 10-inches Hg of vacuum to the pressure regulator. If the pressure drops, repair the vacuum source to the regulator. If the pressure doesn't drop, replace the regulator (see Section 9).

11   If the pressure is higher than specified, check for a faulty regulator or a pinched or clogged fuel return hose or pipe.

12   If the pressure is lower than specified:

a) Inspect the fuel filter - make sure it's not clogged.
b) Look for a pinched or clogged fuel hose or line between the fuel tank and the fuel rail.
c) Check the pressure regulator for a malfunction. With the engine running, pinch the fuel return line (if possible). If the pressure rises, replace the fuel pressure regulator.
d) Look for leaks in the fuel feed line.
e) Check for leaking injectors.

13   After the testing is done, relieve the fuel system pressure (see Section 2) and remove the fuel pressure gauge.

5   Fuel tank - removal and installation

Refer to illustrations 5.6 and 5.9

Warning: *Gasoline is extremely flammable, so take extra precautions when you work on any part of the fuel system. Don't smoke or allow open flames or bare light bulbs near the work area, and don't work in a garage where a natural gas-type appliance (such as a water heater or clothes dryer) where a pilot light is present. If you spill any fuel on your skin, rinse it off immediately with soap and water. When you perform any kind of work on the fuel tank, wear safety glasses and have a Class B type fire extinguisher on hand.*

Note: *The following procedure is much easier to perform if the fuel tank is empty. Some tanks have a drain plug for this purpose. If the tank does not have a drain plug, siphon the gasoline into an approved gasoline container.*

1   Remove the fuel tank filler cap to relieve fuel tank pressure.

2   Relieve the fuel system pressure (see Section 2).

3   Detach the negative cable from the battery.

4   If the tank still has fuel in it, you can siphon it out. **Warning:** *Don't start the siphoning action by mouth! Use a siphoning kit, available at most auto parts stores.*

5   Raise the vehicle and place it securely on jackstands.

6   Remove the shield, skid plate and the front retaining strap **(see illustration)**.

7   Support the fuel tank with a floor jack or jackstands. Position a piece of wood between the jack head and the fuel tank to protect the tank.

8   Remove the bolt from the rear retaining strap and pivot the strap down until it is hanging out of the way.

5.9 Filler tube connections

9   Loosen the screw clamps at the fill pipe and the vent pipe. Disconnect the pipes at the tank **(see illustration)**.
10   Lower the tank enough to disconnect the vapor valve and fuel line connectors from the sender unit and vapor valve. **Note:** *The fuel feed and return lines and the vapor return line are three different diameters, so reattachment is simplified. If you have any doubts, however, clearly label the three lines and the fittings. Be sure to plug the hoses to prevent leakage and contamination of the fuel system.*
11   Disconnect the fuel pump and fuel gauge sending unit connectors at the rear of the fuel tank.
12   Remove the tank from the vehicle. **Warning:** *Store the tank in a safe place, away from sparks and open flames (read the Warning at the beginning of this Section).*
13   Installation is the reverse of removal. The manufacturer recommends that new tank retaining strap bolts be used.

6   Fuel tank - cleaning and repair

1   The polyethylene fuel tank cannot be repaired. No reliable repair procedures are available to correct leaks or damage. Fuel tank replacement is the only approved service. **Warning:** *Even after cleaning and flushing of the fuel tank, explosive fumes can remain and ignite.*
3   If the fuel tank is removed from the vehicle, it should not be placed in an area where sparks or open flames could ignite the fumes coming out of the tank. Be especially careful inside garages where a natural gas-type appliance is located, because the pilot light could cause an explosion.
4   Whenever the fuel tank is steam-cleaned or otherwise serviced, the vapor valve assembly should be replaced. All grommets and seals must be replaced to prevent possible leakage.

7.4 The fuel pump is combined with the fuel gauge sending unit and is located within the fuel tank

7   Fuel pump - removal and installation

Refer to illustration 7.4

Warning: *Gasoline is extremely flammable, so take extra precautions when you work on any part of the fuel system. Don't smoke or allow open flames or bare light bulbs near the work area, and don't work in a garage where a natural gas-type appliance (such as a water heater or clothes dryer) where a pilot light is present. If you spill any fuel on your skin, rinse it off immediately with soap and water. When you perform*

any kind of work on the fuel tank, wear safety glasses and have a Class B type fire extinguisher on hand.

1   Remove the fuel tank (refer to Section 5).
2   Remove any dirt that has accumulated where the fuel sender/pump is attached to the fuel tank. Don't allow dirt to enter the fuel tank.
3   Turn the lock ring counterclockwise with lock ring wrench (Ford Part No. T90T-9275-A or equivalent tool) until it's loose. Remove the lock ring.
4   Carefully pull the fuel pump/sending unit assembly from the tank **(see illustration)**. Don't bend the arm for the sending unit float.
5   Remove the old lock ring seal and discard it.
6   Clean the fuel pump mounting flange, the tank mounting surface and seal ring groove.
7   Installation is the reverse of the removal procedure with the following additions:

a) *Apply a thin coat of heavy grease to the new lock ring seal to hold it in place during assembly. Install the seal in the lock ring groove.*
b) *Install the fuel sender/pump unit into the fuel tank so that the tabs of the unit are positioned into the slots in the fuel tank. Make sure to keep the seal in place during installation until the lock ring has been tightened properly.*
c) *Hold the fuel sender/pump unit in place, install and tighten the locking ring clockwise with the lock ring wrench or equivalent until the stop is against the retainer ring tab.*

8   Air cleaner housing - removal and installation

Refer to illustration 8.2

1   Disconnect the negative cable from the battery.
2   Loosen the hose clamps on the air cleaner outlet tube assembly **(see illustration)**. Remove the tube from the throttle body and the air cleaner housing. Cover the throttle body inlet to prevent the entry of foreign matter.

4

8.2   Details of the air cleaner assembly and related ducting

9.8 Unbolt the air conditioning hose bracket from the upper intake manifold and move it aside - DO NOT disconnect any refrigerant lines

9.9a Remove the upper intake manifold nuts with a socket and extension

3   Disconnect the vacuum lines at the bimetal sensor in the air cleaner cover.
4   Disconnect the electrical connector at the Mass Air Flow (MAF) sensor.
5   Remove the screws securing the air cleaner assembly upper half. Label and disconnect the two small hoses from the upper case half and remove the upper half and the air cleaner filter.
6   To remove the remainder of the assembly, perform the following:
   a) *Squeeze the protrusions on the air cleaner hot air tube and disconnect the tube from the air cleaner housing.*
   b) *Remove the bolt securing the air cleaner intake tube assembly to the air cleaner intake deflector next to the radiator panel. Remove the intake tube from the lower half of the air cleaner housing.*
   c) *Remove the screw securing the lower half of the air cleaner housing to the mounting bracket. Remove the lower half of the air cleaner housing.*
7   Installation is the reverse of the removal procedure. Tighten all hose clamps and fittings securely.

9   Electronic fuel injection - component removal and installation

Upper intake manifold and throttle body

Refer to illustrations 9.8, 9.9a, 9.9b, 9.9c and 9.9d

Removal
1   Label and disconnect the electrical connectors and vacuum lines between the upper intake manifold and the engine and body.
2   Remove the snow shield from the accelerator linkage. Remove the accelerator cable bracket and disconnect the accelerator cable from the throttle body.
3   Remove the air inlet tube that connects the air cleaner to the throttle body.
4   Label and disconnect the vacuum lines from the upper intake manifold.
5   Detach the PCV valve from the right valve cover (see Chapter 6).
6   Detach the spark plug wires from the loom at the back of the upper intake manifold.
7   Disconnect the canister purge line at the throttle body fitting.
8   Remove the bolt that secures the air conditioning refrigerant line at the upper rear part of the manifold **(see illustration)**. DO NOT disconnect any refrigerant lines!
9   Remove six nuts that secure the upper intake manifold **(see illustrations)**. Note the cap over the front stud. Lift the upper manifold and throttle body together off the fuel rail **(see illustration)**.

Installation
10   Thoroughly clean all old gasket material from the mating surfaces of upper intake manifold and the fuel rail.
11   Install a new gasket on the fuel rail, then install the upper manifold and tighten the six nuts evenly to the torque listed in this Chapter's Specifications.
12   The remainder of installation is the reverse of the removal steps.

Air intake throttle body

Refer to illustration 9.17

13   Remove the snow shield from the accelerator linkage and disconnect the accelerator cable.
14   Disconnect the electrical connector from the throttle position sensor.
15   Unclamp and disconnect the air inlet duct at the throttle body.
16   Disconnect the canister purge hose from underneath the throttle body.
17   Remove the four throttle body mounting screws **(see illustration)**.

9.9b Details of the upper intake manifold and gasket

9.9c Note the cap over the front stud remove it before unscrewing the nut

9.9d Grasp the upper manifold at front and rear ends and lift it off the engine

Remove the throttle body and gasket from the upper intake manifold.
18   Carefully clean all old gasket material from the mating surface of throttle body and upper intake manifold. **Caution:** *Don't let gasket material fall into the manifold.*
19   Place a new gasket on the manifold, then install the throttle body and tighten the screws to the torque listed in this Chapter's Specifications.
20   The remainder of installation is the reverse of the removal steps.

Throttle Position Sensor (TPS)

Refer to illustration 9.21
21   The throttle position sensor is mounted on the air intake throttle body **(see illustration)**.
22   Disconnect the electrical connector from the throttle position sensor.
23   Remove the throttle position sensor screws. Lift off the TPS and its gasket.
24   Install the TPS, using a new gasket, and tighten the screws securely.

Air bypass valve

Refer to illustration 9.26
25   Disconnect the air bypass valve electrical connector.
26   Remove the two mounting bolts, then take off the valve and gasket **(see illustration)**.
27   Thoroughly clean all old gasket material from the valve and its

9.17 Disconnect the electrical connector and remove the throttle body mounting screws (arrows)

mounting surface. **Caution:** *Don't let gasket material fall into the upper manifold.*
28   Install the valve with a new gasket and tighten its bolts to the torque listed in this Chapter's Specifications.
29   Connect the electrical connector.

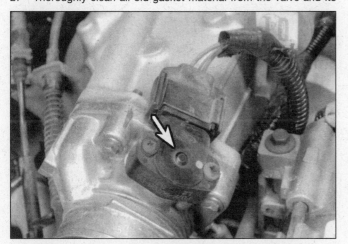

9.21 The Throttle Position Sensor (arrow) is mounted on the throttle body

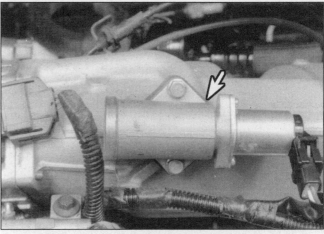

9.26 The air bypass valve (arrow) is mounted on the upper intake manifold

9.30 The Air Charge Temperature sensor (arrow) is screwed
into the intake manifold

9.35 The Mass Air Flow sensor is mounted on the air cleaner
housing and is secured with four screws (arrows)

9.43a Remove the Torx stud bolts that secure the fuel rail
with a Torx socket

9.43b Details of the fuel rail and injectors

Air Charge Temperature (ACT) sensor

Refer to illustration 9.30

30   Disconnect the Air Charge Temperature sensor electrical connector **(see illustration)**.

31   Unscrew the ACT sensor from the intake manifold.

32   Wrap the threads of a new sensor with thread sealing tape to prevent air leaks. Screw in a new sensor and tighten it securely.

Mass Air Flow (MAF) sensor

Refer to illustration 9.35

33   Disconnect the duct from the MAF sensor.

34   Unplug the MAF sensor electrical connector.

35   Remove four screws securing the MAF sensor to the air cleaner housing **(see illustration)**. Take off the sensor and gasket.

36   Install the sensor, using a new gasket, and tighten the screws securely.

Fuel rail and injectors

Refer to illustrations 9.43a, 9.43b, 9.43c, 9.43d and 9.44

Removal

37   It's a good idea to steam clean the engine before starting this procedure to prevent dirt from contaminating exposed fittings and fuel metering orifices.

38   Relieve the fuel system pressure (see Section 2).

39   Disconnect the negative cable from the battery.

40   Remove the air inlet tube the runs between the air cleaner and throttle body.

41   Remove the upper intake manifold as described above.

42   Disconnect the fuel supply and return lines (see Section 3).

43   Remove six Torx stud bolts that secure the fuel rail **(see illustrations)**. Carefully lift the fuel rail and injectors out with a rocking, pulling motion **(see illustrations)**.

44   The injectors may come out with the fuel rail or remain attached to the lower intake manifold. Detach the injectors as follows:

a) *Disconnect the injector electrical connector from the individual injector(s).*

9.43c The fuel injectors (arrows) are mounted between the fuel rail and the lower intake manifold

9.43d Rock the fuel rail to detach the injectors, then lift it off

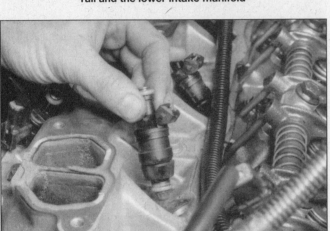

9.44 Detach the fuel injectors with a rocking, pulling motion and take them out

9.46 Each injector uses two O-rings - the injector pintle is protected by a plastic "hat"

b) Remove the injector retaining clip(s).
c) Carefully pull the injector out with a rocking motion **(see illustration)**.

Installation
Refer to illustration 9.46

45 Check the injector O-rings for damage or deterioration and replace as needed.
46 Inspect the plastic "hat" that covers the end of each injector **(see illustration)** (if it's not on the injector, it may be in the intake manifold). Replace the hat if damaged or deteriorated.
47 Lubricate the injector O-rings with a light film of engine oil. Each injector uses two O-rings. **Caution:** *Don't lubricate the injectors with silicone grease. It will clog them.*
48 Install the injectors in the fuel rail with a light rocking motion.
49 The remainder of installation is the reverse of the removal steps.
50 Turn the ignition key On and Off several times (without starting the engine) to pressurize the fuel system. Check all fuel system connections for leaks.

Fuel pressure regulator
Refer to illustrations 9.57, 9.58, 9.62a and 9.62b

51 Disconnect the negative cable from the battery.
52 Remove the snow shield from the throttle linkage.
53 Remove the air inlet tube that connects the air cleaner to the throttle body.

9.57 The fuel pressure regulator is secured by two screws (arrows)

54 Relieve fuel system pressure (see Section 2).
55 Disconnect the vacuum line from the pressure regulator.
56 Disconnect the fuel return line from the pressure regulator (see Section 3).
57 Remove the regulator mounting screws and take the regulator off **(see illustration)**.

9.62a Push the regulator fuel lines together until the shoulder contacts the fitting . . .

9.58 Coat the O-ring with light oil during installation

58   Remove the O-ring and washer **(see illustration)**.
59   Check the O-ring for cracks or deterioration and replace as needed. Replace the washer whenever it's removed.
60   Check the fuel return line for kinks or worn spots and replace as needed.
61   Lubricate the O-ring with a light coat of engine oil.
62   The remainder of installation is the reverse of the removal steps, with the following additions:

a) *Tighten the pressure regulator screws to the torque listed in this Chapter's Specifications.*
b) *To connect the fuel line, push the ends together until the shoulder on the male end touches the fitting on the female end* **(see illustration)**. *Install the retainer and snap its two halves together* **(see illustration)**.

9.62b . . . then snap the retainer halves together

10   Exhaust system service - general information

Warning: *Inspection and repair of exhaust system components should be done only after enough time has elapsed after driving the vehicle to allow the system components to cool completely. Also, when working under the vehicle, make sure it is securely supported on jackstands.*

1   The exhaust system consists of the exhaust manifolds, the catalytic converter, the mufflers, the tailpipe and all connecting pipes, brackets, hangers and clamps. The exhaust system is attached to the body with mounting brackets and rubber hangers. If any of these components are improperly installed, excessive noise and vibration will be transmitted to the body.
2   Conduct regular inspections of the exhaust system to keep it safe and quiet. Look for any damaged or bent parts, open seams, holes, loose connections, excessive corrosion or other defects which could allow exhaust
fumes to enter the vehicle. Deteriorated exhaust system components should not be repaired; they should be replaced with new parts.
3   If the exhaust system components are extremely corroded or rusted together, welding equipment will probably be required to remove them. The convenient way to accomplish this is to have a

muffler repair shop remove the corroded sections with a cutting torch. If, however, you want to save money by doing it yourself (and you don't have a welding outfit with a cutting torch), simply cut off the old components with a hacksaw. If you have compressed air, special pneumatic cutting chisels can also be used. If you do decide to tackle the job at home, be sure to wear safety goggles to protect your eyes from metal chips and work gloves to protect your hands.
4   Here are some simple guidelines to follow when repairing the exhaust system:

a) *Work from the back to the front when removing exhaust system components.*
b) *Apply penetrating oil to the exhaust system component fasteners to make them easier to remove.*
c) *Use new gaskets, hangers and clamps when installing exhaust systems components.*
d) *Apply anti-seize compound to the threads of all exhaust system fasteners during reassembly.*
e) *Be sure to allow sufficient clearance between newly installed parts and all points on the underbody to avoid overheating the floor pan and possibly damaging the interior carpet and insulation. Pay particularly close attention to the catalytic converter and heat shield.*

Chapter 5
Engine electrical systems

Contents

	Section
Alternator - removal and installation	13
Battery check and maintenance	See Chapter 1
Battery - emergency jump starting	3
Battery - removal and installation	2
Battery cables - check and replacement	4
Charging system - check	12
Charging system - general information and precautions	11
CHECK ENGINE light on	See Chapter 6
Crankshaft and camshaft position sensors - removal and installation	8
Drivebelt check, adjustment and replacement	See Chapter 1
General information	1

	Section
Ignition coil pack - removal and installation	7
Ignition module - removal and installation	9
Ignition system - general information	5
Ignition system - check	6
Ignition timing procedure	10
Spark plug replacement	See Chapter 1
Spark plug wire replacement	See Chapter 1
Starting system - general information	14
Starter motor and circuit - in-vehicle check	15
Starter motor - removal and installation	16
Starter relay - removal and installation	17

5

Specifications

Battery voltage
Engine off	12-volts
Engine running	14 to 15-volts

Torque specifications
Starter mounting bolts	15 to 20 ft-lbs

1 General information

The engine electrical systems include all ignition, charging and starting components. Because of their engine-related functions, these components are considered separately from chassis electrical devices like the lights, instruments, etc.

Be very careful when working on the engine electrical components. They are easily damaged if checked, connected or handled improperly. The alternator is driven by an engine drivebelt which could cause serious injury if your hands, hair or clothes become entangled in it with the engine running. Both the starter and alternator are connected directly to the battery and could arc or even cause a fire if mishandled, overloaded or shorted out.

Never leave the ignition switch on for long periods of time with the engine off. Don't disconnect the battery cables while the engine is running. Correct polarity must be maintained when connecting battery cables from another source, such as another vehicle, during jump starting. Always disconnect the negative cable first and hook it up last or the battery may be shorted by the tool being used to loosen the cable clamps.

Additional safety related information on the engine electrical systems can be found in *Safety first* near the front of this manual. It should be referred to before beginning any operation included in this Chapter.

2.1 To remove the battery,
disconnect both cables
(negative first) and remove the
battery hold-down bolts, nuts
and clamp

1   Negative cable
2   Battery
3   Starter relay
4   Felt washer
5   Wiring harness
6   Power network box
    (fuses and relays)
7   Frame member
8   Wiring harness
9   Air cleaner fresh air
    tube

FRONT OF VEHICLE

2   Battery - removal and installation

Refer to illustrations 2.1 and 2.3

1   Disconnect both cables from the battery terminals **(see illustration)**. **Caution:** *Always disconnect the negative cable first and hook
it up last or sparks may occur that can cause the battery to explode.*
2   Locate the battery hold-down clamp at the base of the battery.
Remove the bolt and the hold-down clamp.
3   Lift out the battery. Special straps or clamps that attach to the
battery are available - lifting and moving the battery is much easier if
you use one **(see illustration)**.
4   Installation is the reverse of removal. Make sure the battery
cables and battery posts are free of corrosion. Clean them if necessary
(see Section 4).

3   Battery - emergency jump starting

Refer to the *Booster battery (jump) starting* procedure at the front
of this manual.

4   Battery cables - check and replacement

1   Periodically inspect the entire length of each battery cable for
damage, cracked or burned insulation and corrosion. Poor battery
cable connections can cause starting problems and decreased engine
performance.
2   Check the cable-to-terminal connections at the ends of the
cables for cracks, loose wire strands and corrosion. The presence of
white, fluffy deposits under the insulation at the cable terminal
connection is a sign that the cable is corroded and should be replaced.
Check the terminals for distortion, missing mounting bolts and
corrosion.

3   When replacing the cables, always disconnect the negative cable
first and hook it up last or the battery may be shorted by the tool used
to loosen the cable clamps. Even if only the positive cable is being
replaced, be sure to disconnect the negative cable from the battery
first.
4   Disconnect and remove the cable. Make sure the replacement
cable is the same length and wire size (diameter).
5   Clean the threads of the starter relay or ground connection with a
wire brush to remove rust and corrosion. Apply a light coat of
petroleum jelly to the threads to prevent future corrosion.
6   Attach the cable to the starter relay or ground connection and
tighten the mounting nut/bolt securely.
7   Before connecting the new cable to the battery, make sure that it

BATTERY
CARRIER

2.3 A battery carrier simplifies battery removal

6.2 To use a calibrated ignition tester, simply disconnect a spark plug wire, attach the wire to the tester, clip the tester to a convenient ground (like a valve cover bolt) and operate the starter - if there's enough power to fire the plug, sparks will be visible between the electrode tip and the tester body

7   Before connecting the new cable to the battery, make sure that it reaches the battery post without having to be stretched. Clean the battery posts and cable ends thoroughly and apply a light coat of petroleum jelly to prevent corrosion (see Chapter 1).

8   Connect the positive cable first, followed by the negative cable.

5   Ignition system - general information

The 4.0L V6 engine used in all models is equipped with the Electronic Distributorless Ignition System (EDIS) that is a solid state electronic design. It consists of a crankshaft timing sensor, EDIS module, ignition coil pack, the spark angle portion of the EEC-IV, the spark plug wires and the spark plugs.

This ignition system does not have any moving parts (no distributor) and all engine timing and spark distribution is handled electronically. This system has fewer parts that require replacement and provides more accurate spark timing. During engine operation, the EDIS ignition module and the EEC-IV module calculate spark angle and determine the turn on and firing time of the ignition coil.

The crankshaft timing sensor is a variable reluctance-type consisting of a 36-tooth trigger wheel with one missing tooth that is incorporated into the crankshaft front damper. The signal generated by this sensor is called a Variable Reluctance Sensor (VRS) signal and it provides the base timing and engine RPM information to the EDIS ignition modules. The main function of the EDIS module is to synchronize the ignition coils so they are turned on and off in the proper sequence for accurate spark control.

6   Ignition system - check

Refer to illustration 6.2
Warning: *Because of the very high secondary (spark plug) voltage generated by the ignition system, extreme care should be taken when this check is performed.*

Calibrated ignition tester method

1   If the engine turns over but won't start, disconnect the spark plug lead from any spark plug and attach it to a calibrated ignition tester (available at most auto parts stores). Make sure the tester is designed for Ford ignition systems if a universal tester isn't available (Ford offers

7.2 Squeeze the locking tabs to release the spark plug wires

its own version as tool number D81P-6666-A).

2   Connect the clip on the tester to a bolt or metal bracket on the engine **(see illustration)**, crank the engine and watch the end of the tester to see if bright blue, well-defined sparks occur.

3   If sparks occur, sufficient voltage is reaching the spark plug to fire it (repeat the check at the remaining plug wires to verify that the ignition coil(s) is functioning). However, the plugs themselves may be fouled, so remove and check them as described in Chapter 1 or install new ones.

4   If no sparks or intermittent sparks occur, refer further testing to a Ford dealer or qualified electrical specialist.

7   Ignition coil pack - removal and installation

Refer to illustrations 7.2, 7.3a, 7.3b, 7.5a, 7.5b and 7.5c

1   Disconnect the negative cable from the battery.

2   Using pieces of numbered tape, mark the spark plug wires to the coil terminals (if no numbers are present on the spark plug wires and the coil terminals). Squeeze the locking tab of the wire retainer by hand and remove the spark plug wires from the ignition coil pack with a twisting and pulling motion **(see illustration)**. DO NOT just pull on the wires to disconnect them.

3   Disconnect the engine wiring harness from the ignition coil pack and disconnect the condenser wire **(see illustrations)**.

7.3a Disconnect the electrical connector (arrow) from the coil pack . . .

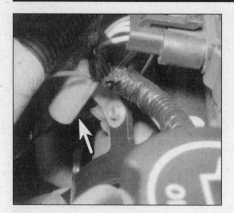

7.3b . . . and from the condenser mounted
on it (arrow)

7.5a Remove the two upper
bolts (arrows) . . .

7.5b . . . and one lower bolt (arrow)

7.5c Ignition coil pack
mounting details

8.3 The crankshaft timing sensor is secured by two screws

4   If necessary, remove the bolt holding the air conditioning hose to
the plenum. Move the air conditioning tube enough to provide working
access to the upper coil pack bolts. **Note:** *It may be possible to
remove the upper coil pack bolts with a socket and universal joint
adapter instead of removing the air conditioning hose bolt.*
5   Remove the three bolts securing the ignition coil pack to the
mounting bracket on the engine **(see illustrations)**.
6   Installation is the reverse of the removal procedure with the
following additions:

a) **Note:** *Whenever a spark plug wire is removed from either the spark
plug or the ignition coil pack, the boot should be coated with
Silicone Dielectric Compound (Ford part No. D7AZ-19A133-A) or
equivalent.*

b) *Insert each spark plug wire into the proper terminal of the ignition
coil pack. Push the wire into the terminal and make sure the boots
are fully seated and both locking tabs are engaged properly (see
Chapter 1, illustration 13.16, if necessary).*

8   Crankshaft and camshaft position sensors - removal and installation

Crankshaft position sensor

Refer to illustration 8.3
1   Disconnect the negative cable from the battery.
2   Disconnect the electrical connector from the crankshaft timing
sensor.
3   Remove the two screws securing the crankshaft timing sensor to
the engine **(see illustration)**. Remove the sensor.
4   Installation is the reverse of the removal procedure. Tighten the
mounting screws securely.

Camshaft position sensor

Refer to illustrations 8.5 and 8.8
Note: *On all models equipped with a camshaft position sensor the
sensor is mounted on a synchronizer assembly, which is essentially a
drive unit for the sensor. If you are simply replacing the cam position
sensor, it is not necessary to remove the synchronizer assembly from
the engine - just remove the screws from the sensor, detach it from the
synchronizer and install the new sensor. However, many engine repair
procedures require removal of the synchronizer assembly, in which
case it will be necessary to perform the following procedure to time the
synchronizer.*
5   Locate the TDC mark on the crankshaft damper. Check for an
additional mark at 26-degrees After Top Dead Center (ATDC). If you
can't find this mark, make one at exactly 34mm (1.34 inches, or 1-
11/32 inches) counterclockwise from the TDC mark **(see illustration)**.
6   Disconnect the cable from the negative terminal of the battery.
Disconnect the electrical connector, remove the hold-down bolt and
clamp and remove the camshaft position sensor.
7   Position the engine at TDC compression for cylinder number 1
(see Chapter 2, Part B).
8   Lubricate the drive gear and the O-ring with clean engine oil. Align
the trailing edge of the sensor vane with the short mark at the left side
of the sensor window **(see illustration)**.
9   Carefully insert the sensor and drive assembly into the engine.
The sensor vane will rotate clockwise as the drive gear meshes with
the gear on the camshaft.
10   Turn the sensor counterclockwise to make room for the hold-
down clamp and bolt. Install the clamp and bolt, but don't tighten the
bolt yet. Now turn the sensor back until it is parallel (lengthwise) with
the centerline of the engine. Reconnect the electrical connector to the
sensor.
11   Rotate the engine two revolutions and return the engine to TDC
compression for cylinder number 1. This will take up any slack in the

8.5 If one is not present, make a mark on the crankshaft damper exactly 34mm (1.34 inches) After Top Dead Center, which is 26-degrees ATDC

8.8 Line up the trailing edge of the sensor vane with the short mark at the left of the sensor window

9.3 Ignition module mounting details

timing chain. Now continue to turn the engine until it is positioned at 26-degrees ATDC.

12   Reconnect the cable to the negative terminal of the battery, then turn the ignition key to the On position. Connect the positive (+) probe of a high-impedance (10-meg ohms) digital voltmeter to the backside of the center terminal of the sensor (the dark blue wire with the orange stripe). **Note:** *If the probes of your voltmeter are too large, you can use a pin or a straightened-out paper clip to backprobe the connector.* Connect the negative probe to a good ground.

13   Rotate the sensor counterclockwise until voltage reads on the voltmeter (it should be approximately battery voltage). Now turn the sensor clockwise until the voltmeter reads 0-volts. Finally, rotate the sensor slowly counterclockwise and stop exactly when the voltmeter reading changes from 0-volts to a positive voltage reading.

14   Detach the voltmeter and tighten the hold-down bolt securely.

9   Ignition module - removal and installation

Refer to illustration 9.3

1   Remove the battery (see Section 2).

2   Disconnect the electrical connector from the ignition module.

3   Remove the screw securing the module to the lower panel adjacent to the radiator **(see illustration)**. Slide the assembly up to remove the positioning rivet from the teardrop hole in the panel and remove it.

4   Installation is the reverse of the removal procedure. Tighten the screw securely.

10   Ignition timing procedure

Note: *No ignition timing adjustments are possible on the vehicles covered by this manual.*

11   Charging system - general information and precautions

The charging system includes the 3G IAR alternator with an integral voltage regulator, a charge indicator light, the battery, a fusible link and the wiring between all the components. The charging system supplies electrical power for the ignition system, the lights, the radio, etc. The alternator is driven by a drivebelt at the front of the engine.

The purpose of the voltage regulator is to limit the alternator's voltage to a preset value. This prevents power surges, circuit overloads, etc., during peak voltage output. On IAR (integral alternator/regulator) systems, a solid state regulator is housed inside the alternator itself.

The charging system doesn't ordinarily require periodic maintenance. However, the drivebelt, battery and wires and connections should be inspected at the intervals outlined in Chapter 1.

Be very careful when making electrical circuit connections to the vehicle and note the following:

a) *When reconnecting wires to the alternator from the battery, be sure to note the polarity.*

b) *Before using arc welding equipment to repair any part of the vehicle, disconnect the wires from the alternator and the battery terminals.*

c) *Never start the engine with a battery charger connected.*

d) *Always disconnect both battery leads before using a battery charger.*

e) *The alternator is turned by the engine drivebelt which could cause serious injury if your hands or clothes become entangled in it with the engine running.*

f) *Because the alternator is connected directly to the battery, it could arc or cause a fire if overloaded or shorted out.*

g) *Wrap a plastic bag over the alternator and secure it with rubber bands before steam cleaning the engine.*

12   Charging system - check

Note: *If the alternator requires service it must be replaced as an assembly. Replacement parts are not available individually.*

1   If a malfunction occurs in the charging circuit, don't automatically assume that the alternator is causing the problem. First check the following items:

a) *The battery cables where they connect to the battery. Make sure the connections are clean and tight (see Chapter 1).*

b) *Check the external alternator wiring harness and the connectors at the alternator and voltage regulator. They must be in good condition, clean, free of corrosion and tight.*

c) *Check the drivebelt condition and tension (refer to Chapter 1).*

d) *Make sure the alternator mounting and adjustment bolts are tight.*

e) *Check the fusible link located between the starter relay and the alternator. If it's burned, determine the cause, repair the circuit and replace the link (refer to Chapter 12).*

f) *Run the engine and check the alternator for abnormal noise.*

2   Turn the headlamps on for 10 to 15 seconds to remove any surface charge from the battery. Wait 3 to 5 minutes for the battery voltage to stabilize before continuing with Step 3.

3   Connect a voltmeter between the battery terminals and check the battery voltage with the engine off. It should be approximately 12-volts.

4   Run the engine at a fast idle (approximately 1500 rpm) and check the battery voltage again after the voltage stops rising. This may take a few minutes. It should now be higher than battery voltage, but not more than 3-volts higher.

5

12.8 Connect an ohmmeter between the A and F terminal screws

12.9 Connect the voltmeter negative lead to the alternator housing and the positive lead to the regulator A terminal screw

12.11 Connect the voltmeter negative lead to the alternator housing and the positive lead to the F terminal screw

12.13 Perform the load test with the voltmeter positive lead connected to the alternator output stud

5   If the voltage reading is less than the specified charging voltage, perform the Under-voltage test in this section. If it is higher, perform the Over-voltage test.

6   Turn on the high beam headlights and turn the heater or air conditioner blower to its highest setting. Run the engine at 2,000 rpm and check the voltage reading. It should now be at least 0.5-volt higher than battery voltage. If not, perform the Under-voltage test.

7   If the voltage readings are correct in the preceding Steps, the charging system is working properly. Use a 12-volt test light and the wiring diagrams (see Chapter 12) to check for a battery drain.

Under-voltage test

Refer to illustrations 12.8, 12.9, 12.11, 12.13 and 12.14

8   Unplug the electrical connector from the voltage regulator. Connect an ohmmeter between the A and F terminal screws **(see illustration)**. The ohmmeter should indicate at least 2.4 ohms.
  a) *If the ohmmeter reading is too low, the regulator is defective.*
  b) *If the ohmmeter reading is within specifications, reconnect the electrical connector to the regulator and perform Step 9.*

9   Connect the voltmeter negative lead to the alternator rear housing and the positive lead to the regulator A terminal screw **(see illustration)**. The voltmeter should indicate battery voltage. If not, check the A circuit for breaks or bad connections.

10   Repeat the load test (see Step 6).

11   If the voltmeter indicates battery voltage in Step 9, place the ignition key in the Off position. Connect the voltmeter negative lead to the alternator frame and the positive lead to the F terminal screw **(see illustration)**.
  a) *If the voltmeter indicates no voltage, replace the alternator.*
  b) *If the voltmeter indicates battery voltage, proceed to Step 12.*

12   Turn the ignition key to the Run position, but don't start the engine. Touch the voltmeter negative lead to the rear of the alternator and the positive lead to the F terminal screw on the regulator.
  a) *If the voltmeter indicates more than two volts, perform the I circuit test in this Section.*
  b) *If the voltmeter indicates two volts or less, proceed to Step 13.*

13   Perform the load test (see Step 6) with the voltmeter positive terminal connected to the alternator output stud **(see illustration)**.

12.14 Using a jumper wire, ground the F terminal to the alternator frame, connect the positive lead of the voltmeter to the alternator output stud and perform the load test described in Step 6

12.16 Connect the voltmeter negative lead to the alternator housing, then connect the positive lead to the A terminal screw and the regulator grounding screw in turn

12.18 Connect the voltmeter negative lead to the alternator housing; connect the positive lead to the A terminal and F terminal in turn

12.22 Connect the voltmeter negative lead to the alternator housing; connect the positive lead to the connector S terminal and A terminal in turn

13.7 Location of the alternator mounting bolts (arrows)

a) If voltage increases to more than 0.5-volt above battery voltage, check the wiring from alternator to starter relay for breaks or bad connections.

b) If the voltage does not increase to more than 0.5 volt above battery voltage, perform Step 14.

14   Connect a jumper wire between the alternator rear housing and the regulator F terminal screw **(see illustration)**. Repeat the load test (see Step 6) with the voltmeter positive lead connected to one of the B+ jumper wire terminals.

a) If voltage increases by more than 0.5-volt, the regulator is defective and the alternator must be replaced.

b) If voltage doesn't increase by more than 0.5-volt, replace the alternator.

Over-voltage test

Refer to illustrations 12.16 and 12.18

15   Turn the key to the On position but leave the engine off.

16   Connect the voltmeter negative lead to the alternator rear housing and connect the positive lead to the alternator output connection at the starter relay, then to the regulator A terminal **(see illustration)**. If the voltage readings differ by more than 0.5-volt, check the A circuit for breaks or bad connections.

17   If Step 16 doesn't correct the problem, check for loose regulator grounding screws and tighten as needed.

18   If the voltage reading is still too high, place the ignition key in the Off position. Connect the voltmeter negative lead to the alternator frame. Connect the voltmeter positive lead to the A terminal screw, then to the F terminal screw **(see illustration)**.

a) If the voltage readings at the two screw heads are different, replace the alternator.

b) If the voltage readings at the two screw heads are the same, the regulator is defective and the alternator must be replaced.

S and/or I circuit test

Refer to illustration 12.22

19   Disconnect the alternator electrical connector.

20   Connect one jumper wire from the alternator A terminal to its corresponding terminal in the electrical connector. Connect another jumper wire from the regulator F screw to the alternator housing.

21   Start the engine and let it idle.

22   Connect the voltmeter negative lead to the alternator housing. Connect the positive lead to the connector S terminal and A terminal in turn **(see illustration)**. Voltage at the A terminal should be approximately double the reading at the S terminal.

a) If the readings are as specified, the regulator is defective and the alternator must be replaced.

b) If there is no voltage, check the wiring for breaks or bad connections. If the wiring is good, replace the alternator.

13   Alternator - removal and installation

Refer to illustration 13.7

1   Disconnect the negative cable from the battery.

2   Remove the snow shield from the throttle linkage.

3   Remove the bolt securing air cleaner intake tube assembly to the air cleaner intake deflector next to the radiator panel. Remove the intake tube from the lower half of the air cleaner assembly.

4   Unplug the electrical connectors from the alternator.

5   Remove the electrical connector bracket.

6   Rotate the drivebelt tensioner counterclockwise and remove the drivebelt (see Chapter 1).

7   Remove the three bolts holding the alternator to its mounting bracket **(see illustration)**.

8   Installation is the reverse of removal.

14   Starting system - general information

The function of the starting system is to crank the engine to start it. The system is composed of the starter motor, starter relay, battery, ignition switch, safety switch and connecting wires.

Turning the ignition key to the Start position actuates the starter relay through the starter control circuit. The starter relay then connects the battery to the starter. The battery supplies the electrical energy to the starter motor, which does the actual work of cranking the engine.

Vehicles equipped with an automatic transmission have a Neutral start switch in the starter control circuit, which prevents operation of the starter unless the shift lever is in Neutral or Park. The circuit on vehicles with a manual transmission prevents operation of the starter motor unless the clutch pedal is depressed.

Never operate the starter motor for more than 15 seconds at a time without pausing to allow it to cool for at least two minutes. Excessive cranking can cause overheating, which can seriously damage the starter.

15   Starter motor and circuit - in-vehicle check

Note: *Before diagnosing starter problems, make sure the battery is fully charged.*

General check

1   If the starter motor doesn't turn at all when the switch is operated, make sure the shift lever is in Neutral or Park (automatic transmission) or the clutch pedal is depressed (manual transmission).

2   Make sure the battery is fully charged and that all cables at the battery and starter relay terminals are not corroded and that they are secure.

5

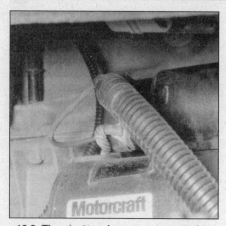

16.3 The starter wires are connected to the terminals at the top of the starter

16.4 Remove the lower mounting nut (arrow) . . .

16.5 . . . and the upper mounting bolt (arrow), then take the starter out

3   If the starter motor spins but the engine doesn't turn over, then the drive assembly in the starter motor is slipping and the starter motor must be replaced (see Section 16).

4   If, when the switch is actuated, the starter motor doesn't operate at all but the starter relay operates (clicks), then the problem lies with either the battery, the starter relay contacts or the starter motor electrical connections.

5   If the starter relay doesn't click when the ignition switch is actuated, the battery could be discharged, or either the starter relay circuit is open or the relay itself is defective. Check the starter relay circuit or replace the relay (see Section 17).

6   To check the starter relay circuit, remove the push-on electrical connector from the relay (red with blue stripe). Make sure that the connection is clean and secure and the relay bracket is grounded. If the connections are good, check the operation of the relay with a jumper wire. To do this, place the transmission in Park (automatic) or Neutral (manual). Remove the push-on connector from the relay. Connect a jumper wire between the battery positive terminal and the relay main terminal (BAT side) on the starter relay. If the starter motor now operates, the starter relay is okay. The problem is in the ignition switch, Neutral start switch, starter/clutch switch, or in the starting circuit wiring (look for open or loose connections). Reconnect the push-on electrical connector.

7   If the starter motor still doesn't operate, replace the starter relay (see Section 17).

8   If the starter motor cranks the engine at an abnormally slow speed, first make sure the battery is fully charged and all terminal connections are clean and tight. Also check the connections at the starter relay and battery ground. Eyelet terminals should not be easily rotated by hand. Also check for a short to ground. If the engine is partially seized, or has the wrong (too heavy) viscosity oil in it, it will crank slowly.

16 Starter motor - removal and installation

Refer to illustrations 16.3, 16.4 and 16.5

1   Disconnect the negative cable from the battery.

2   Raise the vehicle and support it securely on jackstands.

3   Disconnect the starter cable and push-on connector from the starter solenoid terminals **(see illustration). Caution:** *Disconnect the connector at the solenoid S terminal by grasping it and pulling straight off to prevent damage to the connector and terminal.*

4   Remove the starter lower mounting nut **(see illustration)**.

5   Remove the upper bolt. Pull the starter forward, lift the front end of it up to clear the bellhousing and remove the starter from the engine **(see illustration)**.

6   Installation is the reverse of the removal procedure. Tighten the mounting bolts to the torque listed in this Chapter's Specifications.

17.1 The starter relay is mounted in the engine compartment behind the battery

17 Starter relay - removal and installation

Refer to illustration 17.1

1   The starter relay is located in the engine compartment, mounted between the battery and the power network box **(see illustration)**.

2   Disconnect the negative cable from the battery.

3   Label the wires and the terminals on the relay to prevent mix-up during installation.

4   Disconnect the ignition switch and starter neutral start (automatic transmission) or clutch interlock (manual transmission) switch wire from the starter relay.

5   Disconnect the positive battery cable and the feed cable from the starter relay.

6   Disconnect the starter feed cable from the other terminal on the starter relay.

7   Remove the mounting bolts and detach the relay.

8   Installation is the reverse of the removal procedure with the following additions:

a) *Prior to installing the relay, clean the mounting surface with a wire brush or sandpaper to provide a good ground.*

b) *Attach the relay to the inner fender panel and tighten the bolts securely.* **Caution:** *Do not overtighten the bolts - they are self-threading and can easily strip out the holes in the sheet metal.*

c) *Be sure to connect the cables to the correct terminals on the relay. Refer to the labels made in Step 3.*

Chapter 6
Emissions control systems

Contents

	Section
Catalytic converter	6
CHECK ENGINE light on	See Section 2
Electronic Engine Control (EEC-IV) system and trouble codes	2
Fuel evaporative emissions control system	3

	Section
General information	1
Inlet air temperature control system	5
Positive Crankcase Ventilation (PCV) system	4

1 General information

Refer to illustration 1.7

To prevent pollution of the atmosphere from incompletely burned and evaporating gases, and to maintain good driveability and fuel economy, a number of emission control systems are incorporated. They include the:

Electronic Engine Control system
Fuel evaporative emission control system
Positive Crankcase Ventilation (PCV) system
Inlet air temperature control system
Catalytic converter

All of these systems are linked, directly or indirectly, to the emission control system.

The Sections in this Chapter include general descriptions, checking procedures within the scope of the home mechanic and component replacement procedures (when possible) for each of the systems listed above.

Before assuming that an emissions control system is malfunctioning, check the fuel and ignition systems carefully. The diagnosis of some emission control devices requires specialized tools, equipment and training. If checking and servicing become too difficult or if a procedure is beyond your ability, consult a dealer service department. Remember, the most frequent cause of emissions problems is simply a loose or broken vacuum hose or wire, so always check the hose and wiring connections first.

This doesn't mean, however, that emission control systems are particularly difficult to maintain and repair. You can quickly and easily perform many checks and do most of the regular maintenance at home with common tune-up and hand tools. **Note:** *Because of a Federally mandated extended warranty which covers the emission control system components, check with your dealer about warranty coverage before working on any emissions-related systems.* Once the warranty

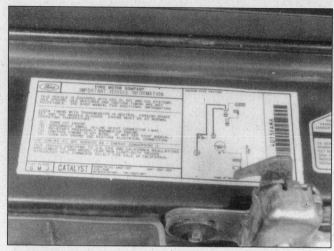

1.7 The Vehicle Emissions Control Information (VECI) label is located in the engine compartment on the radiator support - it contains important emissions specifications and adjustment information, as well as a vacuum hose schematic

has expired, you may wish to perform some of the component checks and/or replacement procedures in this Chapter to save money.

Pay close attention to any special precautions outlined in this Chapter. It should be noted that the illustrations of the various systems may not exactly match the system installed on the vehicle you're working on because of changes made by the manufacturer during production or from year-to-year.

A Vehicle Emissions Control Information label is located in the engine compartment **(see illustration)**. This label contains important emissions specifications and adjustment information, as well as a vacuum hose schematic with emissions components identified. When servicing the engine or emissions systems, the VECI label in your particular vehicle should always be checked for up-to-date information.

---

2 Electronic Engine Control (EEC-IV) system and trouble codes

General description

Refer to illustrations 2.5, 2.19a and 2.19b

1   All models use the Electronic Distributorless Ignition System (EDIS) and the Electronic Engine Control (EEC-IV) system. The EEC-IV system consists of an onboard computer, known as the Powertrain Control Module (PCM), and information sensors, which monitor various functions of the engine and send data to the PCM. Based on the data and the information programmed into the computer's memory, the PCM generates output signals to control various engine functions via control relays, solenoids and other output actuators. **Note:** *1995 models are equipped with a GCM (Generic Control Module). This microprocessor includes programming for the powertrain, the ABS, transmission and 4WD (auto) system.*

2   The PCM, located under the instrument panel, is the "brain" of the EEC-IV system. It receives data from a number of sensors and other electronic components (switches, relays, etc.). Based on the information it receives, the PCM generates output signals to control various relays, solenoids and other actuators. The PCM is specifically calibrated to optimize the emissions, fuel economy and driveability of the vehicle.

3   Because of a Federally-mandated extended warranty which covers the EEC-IV system components and because any owner-induced damage to the PCM, the sensors and/or the control devices may void the warranty, it isn't a good idea to attempt diagnosis or replacement of the PCM at home while the vehicle is under warranty.

Take the vehicle to a dealer service department if the PCM or a system component malfunctions.

Information sensors

4   When battery voltage is applied to the air conditioning compressor clutch, a signal is sent to the PCM, which interprets the signal as an added load created by the compressor and increases engine idle speed accordingly to compensate.

5   The Intake Air Temperature sensor (IAT) **(see illustration)**, threaded into a runner of the intake manifold, provides the PCM with fuel/air mixture temperature information. The PCM uses this information to control fuel flow, ignition timing and EGR system operation.

6   The Engine Coolant Temperature (ECT) sensor, which is threaded into a coolant passage in the intake manifold, monitors engine coolant temperature. The ECT sends the PCM a constantly varying voltage signal which influences PCM control of the fuel mixture, ignition timing and EGR operation.

7   The Heated Exhaust Gas Oxygen (HEGO) sensors, which are threaded into the exhaust manifolds, constantly monitor the oxygen content of the exhaust gases. A voltage signal which varies in accordance with the difference between the oxygen content of the exhaust gases and the surrounding atmosphere is sent to the PCM. The PCM converts this exhaust gas oxygen content signal to the fuel/air ratio, compares it to the ideal ratio for current engine operating conditions and alters the signal to the injectors accordingly.

8   The Throttle Position Sensor (TPS), which is mounted on the side of the throttle body and connected directly to the throttle shaft, senses throttle movement and position then transmits an electrical signal to the PCM. This signal enables the PCM to determine when the throttle is closed, in its normal cruise condition or wide open.

9   The Mass Air Flow (MAF) sensor, which is mounted in the air cleaner intake passage, measures the mass of the air entering the engine. Because air mass varies with air temperature (cold air is denser than warm air), measuring air mass provides the PCM with a very accurate way of determining the correct amount of fuel to obtain the ideal fuel/air mixture.

Output devices

10   The EEC power relay, which is activated by the ignition switch, supplies battery voltage to the EEC-IV system components when the switch is in the Start or Run position.

11   The canister purge solenoid (CANP) switches manifold vacuum to operate the canister purge valve when a signal is received from the PCM. Vacuum opens the purge valve when the solenoid is energized, allowing fuel vapor to flow from the canister to the intake manifold.

12   The solenoid-operated fuel injectors are located above the intake ports (see Chapter 4). The PCM controls the length of time the injector is open. The "open" time of the injector determines the amount of fuel delivered. For information regarding injector replacement, refer to Chapter 4.

13   The fuel pump relay is activated by the PCM with the ignition switch in the ON position. When the ignition switch is turned to the ON position, the relay is activated to supply initial line pressure to the system. For information regarding fuel pump check and replacement, refer to Chapter 4.

14   The EDIS ignition module (see Chapter 5), mounted on a bracket between the upper intake manifold and the valve cover, triggers the ignition coils and determines dwell. The PCM uses a signal from the Profile Ignition Pick-Up (PIP) to determine crankshaft position. Ignition timing is determined by the PCM, which then signals the module to fire the coil. For further information regarding the ignition module, refer to the appropriate Section in Chapter 5.

Obtaining codes

15   The diagnostic codes for the EEC-IV systems are arranged in such a way that a series of tests must be completed in order to extract ALL the codes from the system. If one portion of the test is performed without the others, there may be a chance the trouble code that will pinpoint a problem in your particular vehicle will remain stored in the

Control System Component Locator

2.5 Locations of the EEC-IV information sensors and output actuators (1995 model shown, earlier models similar)

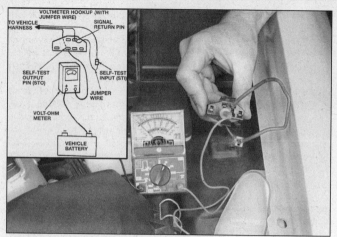

2.19a To read any stored trouble codes, connect a voltmeter to the Diagnostic Test connector as shown, then connect a jumper wire between the self-test input and pin number 2 on the larger connector - turn the ignition key ON (engine not running) and watch the voltmeter needle or CHECK ENGINE light on later models

2.19b The EEC-IV diagnostic connector is located behind the fuse box on the passenger side inner fenderwell

pinpoint a problem in your particular vehicle will remain stored in the PCM without detection. The tests start first with a Key On, Engine Off (KOEO) test followed by a computed timing test then finally a Engine Running (ER) test. Here is a brief overview of the code extracting procedures of the EEC-IV system followed by the actual test:

Quick Test - Key On Engine Off (KOEO)

16   The following tests are all included with the key on, engine off:

Self test codes - These codes are accessed on the test connector by using a jumper wire and an analog voltmeter or the factory diagnostic tool called the Star tester. These codes are also called *Hard Codes*.

Separator pulse codes - After the initial Hard Codes, the system will flash a code 11 (separator pulse) (1991 through 1994) or code 111 (1993 through 1995) and then will flash a series of Soft (or Continuous Memory) Codes.

Continuous Memory Codes - These codes indicate a fault that may or may not be present at the time of testing. These codes usually indicate an intermittent failure. Continuous Memory codes are stored in the system and they will flash after the normal Hard Codes. These codes are either two digit (1991 through 1994) or three digit codes (1993 through 1995). These codes can indicate chronic or intermittent problems. Also called *Soft Codes*.

Fast codes - These codes are transmitted 100 times faster than normal codes and can only be read by a Star Tester from Ford or an equivalent SCAN tool.

Engine running codes (KOER) or (ER)

17   **Running tests** - These tests make it possible for the PCM to pick-up a diagnostic trouble code that cannot be set while the engine is in KOEO. These problems usually occur during driving conditions. Some codes are detected by cold or warm running conditions, some are detected at low rpm or high rpm and some are detected at closed throttle or WOT.

I.D. Pulse codes - These codes indicate the type of engine (4, 6 or 8 cylinder) or the correct module and Self Test mode access.

Computed engine timing test - This engine running test determines base timing for the engine and starts the process of allowing the engine to store running codes.

Wiggle test - This engine running test checks the wiring system to the sensors and output actuators as the engine performs

Cylinder balance test - This engine running test determines injector balance as well as cylinder compression balance. **Note:** *This test should be performed by a dealer service department.*

Beginning the test

18   Position the parking brake ON, Shift lever in PARK, block the drive wheels and turn off all electrical loads (air conditioning, radio, heater fan blower etc.). Make sure the engine is warmed to normal operating temperature (if possible).

19   Perform the KOEO tests:

a)   *Turn the ignition key off for at least 10 seconds.*

b)   *Locate the Diagnostic Test connector inside the engine compartment. Install the voltmeter leads onto the battery and pin number 4 (STO) of the test connector (see illustrations). Install a jumper wire from the test terminal to pin number 2 of the Diagnostic Test terminal (STI).*

c)   *Turn the ignition key ON (engine not running) and observe the needle sweeps on the voltmeter. For example code 23, the voltmeter will sweep once, pause 1/2 second and sweep again. There will be a two second pause between digits and then there will be three distinct sweeps of the needle to indicate the second digit of the code number. On three digit codes, the sequence is the same except there will be an additional sequence of numbers (sweeps) to indicate the third digit in the code. Additional codes will be separated by a four second pause and then the indicated sweeps on the voltmeter. Be aware that the code sequence may continue into the continuous memory codes (read further).* **Note:** *Later models will flash the CHECK ENGINE light on the dash in place of the voltmeter.*

20   Interpreting the continuous memory codes:

a)   *After the KOEO codes are reported, there will be a short pause and any stored Continuous Memory codes will appear in order. Remember that the "Separator" code is 11, or 111 on 1993 through 1995 models. The computer will not enter the Continuous Memory mode without flashing the separator pulse code. The Continuous Memory codes are read the same as the initial codes or "Hard Codes". Record these codes onto a piece of paper and continue the test.*

21   Perform the Engine Running (ER) tests.

a)   *Remove the jumper wires from the Diagnostic Test connector to start the test.*

b)   *Run engine until it reaches normal operating temperature.*

c)   *Turn the engine OFF for at least 10 seconds.*

d)   *Install the jumper wire onto Diagnostic Test connector (see illustration 2.19a and 2.19b) and start the engine.*

e)   *Observe that the voltmeter or CHECK ENGINE light will flash the engine identification code. This code indicates 1/2 the number of cylinders of the engine. For example, 4 flashes represent an 8 cylinder engine, or 3 flashes represent a 6 cylinder engine.*

f) *Within 1 to 2 seconds of the I.D. code, turn the steering wheel at least 1/2 turn and release. This will store any power steering pressure switch trouble codes.*

g) *Depress the brake pedal and release.* **Note:** *Perform the steering wheel and brake pedal procedure in succession immediately (1 to 2 seconds) after the I.D. codes are flashed.*

h) *Observe all the codes and record them on a piece of paper. Be sure to count the sweeps or flashes very carefully as you jot them down.*

22 On some models the PCM will request a Dynamic Response check. This test quickly checks the operation of the TPS, MAF or MAP sensors in action. This will be indicated by a code 1 or a single sweep of the voltmeter needle (one flash on CHECK ENGINE light). This test will require the operator to simply full throttle ("goose") the accelerator pedal for one second. DO NOT throttle the accelerator pedal unless it is requested.

23 The next part of this test makes sure the system can advance the timing. This is called the Computed Timing test. After the last ER code has been displayed, the PCM will advance the ignition timing a fixed amount and hold it there for approximately 2 minutes. Use a timing light to check the amount of advance. The computed timing should equal the base timing plus 20 BTDC. The total advance should equal 27 to 33 degrees advance. If the timing is out of specification, have the system checked at a dealer service department or other repair shop. **Note:** *Remember to remove the SPOUT from the connector as described in the ignition timing procedure in Chapter 5. This will remove the computer from the loop and give base timing.*

24 Finally perform the Wiggle Test. This test can be used to recreate a possible intermittent fault in the harness wiring system.

a) *Use a jumper wire to ground the STI lead on the Diagnostic Test connector* **(see illustration 2.19a)**.

b) *Turn the ignition key ON (engine not running).*

c) *Now deactivate the self test mode (remove the jumper wire) and then immediately reactivate the self-test mode. Now the system has entered Continuous Monitor Test Mode.*

d) *Carefully wiggle, tap or remove any suspect wiring to a sensor or output actuator. If a problem exists, a trouble code will be stored that indicates a problem with the circuit that governs the particular component. Record the codes that are indicated.*

e) *Next, enter Engine Running Continuous Monitor Test Mode to check for wiring problems only when the engine is running. Start first by deactivating the Diagnostic Test connector and turning the ignition key OFF. Now start the engine and allow it to idle.*

f) *Use a jumper wire to ground the STI lead on the Diagnostic Test connector* **(see illustration 2.19a)**. *Wait ten seconds and then deactivate the test mode and reactivate it again (install jumper wire). This will enter Engine Running Continuous Monitor Test Mode.*

g) *Carefully wiggle, tap or remove any suspect wiring to a sensor or output actuator. If a problem exists, a trouble code will be stored that indicates a problem with the circuit that governs the particular component. Record the codes that are indicated.*

25 If necessary, perform the Cylinder Balance Test. This test must be performed by a dealer service department.

Clearing codes

To clear the codes from the PCM memory, start the KOEO self test diagnostic procedure **(see illustration 2.19a)** and install the jumper wire into the Diagnostic Test connector. When the codes start to display themselves on the voltmeter or CHECK ENGINE light, remove the jumper wire from the Diagnostic Test connector. This will erase any stored codes within the system. **Caution:** *Do not disconnect the battery from the vehicle to clear the codes. This will erase stored operating parameters from the KAM (Keep Alive Memory) and cause the engine to run rough for a period of time while the computer relearns the information.*

2 Digit Trouble Codes

Code	Test Condition*	Probable Cause
11	O,C,R	Pass (separator code)
12	R	RPM not within Self-test upper limit
13	R	RPM not within Self-test lower limit
14	C	Profile Ignition Pick-up circuit fault
15	O	Read Only Memory test failed
15	C	Keep Alive Memory test failed
16	R	RPM too low to perform Oxygen Sensor/fuel test
18	C	Loss of TACH input to PCM; SPOUT circuit grounded
18	R	SPOUT circuit open
19	O	Failure in EEC reference voltage
21	O,R	Coolant Temperature Sensor out of range
22	O,C	Manifold Absolute/Baro Pressure Sensor out of range
23	O,R	Throttle Position Sensor out of range
24	O,R	Intake Air Temperature sensor out of range
26	O,R	Mass Air Flow Sensor out of range
29	C	No input from Vehicle Speed Sensor
31	O,C,R	EGR Valve Position Sensor out of range (low)
32	O,C,R	EGR valve not seated; closed voltage low
33	C,R	EGR valve not opening; Insufficient flow detected
34	O,C,R	EGR Valve Pressure Transducer/Position Sensor sonic voltage above closed limit
35	O,C,R	EGR Valve Pressure Transducer/Position Sensor voltage out of range (high)
41	R	Heated Oxygen Sensor circuit indicates system lean, right side
41	C	No Heated Oxygen Sensor switch detected, right side
42	R	Heated Oxygen Sensor circuit indicates system rich, right side
44	R	Secondary Air system inoperative, right side
45	R	Secondary Air upstream during Self-test
45	C	Distributorless Ignition system (DIS) coil pack circuit failure
46	R	Secondary Air not by-passed during Self-test

* *O = Key On, Engine Off; C = Continuous Memory; R = Engine Running*

2 Digit Trouble Codes (Continued)

Code	Test Condition*	Probable Cause
51	O,C	Coolant Temperature sensor circuit open
53	O,C	Throttle Position sensor out of range (high)
54	O,C	Intake Air Temperature sensor circuit open
56	O,C	Mass Air Flow sensor out of range (high)
61	O,C	Coolant Temperature sensor circuit grounded
63	O,C	Throttle Position sensor circuit out of range (low)
64	O,C	Intake Air Temperature sensor circuit grounded
66	C	Mass Air Flow sensor circuit out-of-range (low)
67	O	Neutral Drive Switch circuit open
72	R	Insufficient Mass Air Flow change during Dynamic Response Test
73	R	Insufficient Throttle Position output during Dynamic Response Test
74	R	Brake On/Off switch failure
75	R	Brake On/Off circuit failure
77	R	Wide Open Throttle not sensed during Self-test
79	O	Air conditioning on during self-test
81	O	Secondary Air Injection Diverter (AIRD) circuit failure
82	O	Secondary Air Injection Bypass (AIRB) circuit failure
84	O	EGR Vacuum Regulator circuit failure
85	O	Canister Purge circuit failure
87	O,C	Primary Fuel Pump circuit failure
91	R	Heated oxygen sensor indicates system lean, left side
91	C	No heated oxygen sensor switching indicated, left side
92	R	Heated oxygen sensor indicates system rich, left side
94	R	Torque Converter Clutch (TCC) solenoid circuit failure
95	O,C	Fuel Pump circuit open, PCM to motor
96	O,C	Fuel Pump circuit open, Battery to PCM
98	R	Hard Fault present

* *O = Key On, Engine Off; C = Continuous Memory; R = Engine Running*

3 Digit Trouble Codes

Code	Test Condition*	Probable Cause
111	O,C,R	Pass
112	O,R	Intake Air Temperature sensor circuit indicates circuit grounded/above 245 degrees F
113	O,R	Intake Air Temperature sensor circuit indicates open circuit/below -40 degrees F
114	O,R	Intake Air Temperature sensor out of self-test range
116	O,R	Coolant Temperature sensor out of self-test range
117	O,C	Coolant Temperature circuit below minimum voltage/indicates above 245 degrees F
118	O,C	Coolant Temperature sensor circuit above maximum voltage/ indicates below -40 degrees F
121	O,C,R	Throttle Position sensor out of self-test range
122	O,C	Throttle Position sensor below minimum voltage
123	O,C	Throttle Position sensor above maximum voltage
124	C	Throttle Position Sensor voltage higher than expected
125	C	Throttle Position Sensor voltage lower than expected
126	O,C,R	MAP/BARO sensor higher than expected
128	C	MAP sensor vacuum hose damaged or disconnected
129	R	Insufficient Manifold Absolute Pressure/Mass Air Flow change during Dynamic Response Check
136	R	Heated oxygen sensor indicates lean condition, left side
137	R	Heated oxygen sensor indicates rich condition, left side
139	C	No heated oxygen sensor switching detected, left side
144	C	No heated oxygen sensor switching detected, right side
157	R,C	Mass Air Flow Sensor below minimum voltage
158	O,C,R	Mass Air Flow Sensor above maximum voltage
159	O,R	Mass Air Flow Sensor out of self-test range
167	R	Insufficient Throttle Position Sensor change during Dynamic Response Check
171	C	Heated oxygen sensor unable to switch, right side
172	R,C	Heated oxygen sensor indicates lean condition, right side
173	R,C	Heated oxygen sensor indicates rich condition, right side
174	C	Heated oxygen sensor switching slow, right side
175	C	Heated oxygen sensor unable to switch, left side
176	C	Heated oxygen sensor indicates lean condition, left side
177	C	Heated oxygen sensor indicates rich condition, left side

* *O = Key On, Engine Off; C = Continuous Memory; R = Engine Running*

Code	Test Condition*	Probable Cause
178	C	Heated oxygen sensor switching slow, left side
179	C	Adaptive Fuel lean limit reached at part throttle, system rich, right side
181	C	Adaptive Fuel rich limit reached at part throttle, right side
182	C	Adaptive Fuel lean limit reached at idle, right side
183	C	Adaptive Fuel rich limit reached at idle, right side
184	C	Mass Air Flow higher than expected
185	C	Mass Air Flow lower than expected
186	C	Injector Pulse-width higher than expected
187	C	Injector Pulse-width lower than expected
188	C	Adaptive Fuel lean limit reached, left side
189	C	Adaptive Fuel rich limit reached, left side
211	C	Profile Ignition Pick-up circuit fault
212	C	Ignition module circuit failure/SPOUT circuit grounded
213	R	SPOUT circuit open
214	C	Cylinder identification (CID) circuit failure
215	C	PCM detected coil 1 primary circuit failure
216	C	PCM detected coil 2 primary circuit failure
217	C	PCM detected coil 3 primary circuit failure
218	C	Loss of ignition diagnostic monitor (IDM) signal - left side (dual plug EI)
222	C	Loss of ignition diagnostic monitor (IDM) signal - right side (dual plug)
223	C	Loss of dual plug Inhibit (DPI) control (dual plug)

* *O = Key On, Engine Off; C = Continuous Memory; R = Engine Running*

3 Digit Trouble Codes

Code	Test Condition*	Probable Cause
224	C	PCM detected coil 1,2,3 or 4 primary circuit failure (dual plug EI)
225	C	Knock sensor not detected during dynamic response test KOER
226	O	Ignition Diagnostic Module (IDM) signal not received (EI)
232	C	PCM detected coil 1,2,3 or 4 primary circuit failure (EI)
311	R	Secondary Air System inoperative, right side
312	R	Secondary Air not by-passed
313	R	Secondary Air inoperative, left side
327	O,C,R	EGR Valve Pressure Transducer/Position Sensor circuit below minimum voltage
328	O,C,R	EGR valve position sensor voltage below closed limit
332	C,R	EGR valve opening not detected
334	O,C,R	EGR valve position sensor voltage above closed limit
335	O	EGR Sensor voltage out-of-range
336	R	EGR circuit higher than expected
337	O,C,R	EGR Valve Pressure Transducer/Position Sensor circuit above maximum voltage
341	O	Octane adjust service pin open
411	R	Unable to control RPM during Low RPM Self-test
412	R	Unable to control RPM during High PRM Self-test
452	C	No input from Vehicle Speed Sensor
511	O	Read Only Memory test failed - replace PCM
512	C	Keep Alive Memory test failed
513	O	Internal voltage failure in PCM
519	O	Power steering pressure switch (PSP) circuit open (1993 and 1994 only)
521	R	Power steering pressure switch (PSP) circuit did not change states (1993 and 1994 only)
522	O	Manual Lever Position (MLP) sensor circuit open/vehicle in gear
528	O	Clutch pedal position (CPP) circuit failure
536	C,R	Brake ON/OFF (BOO) circuit failure/not activated during the KOER
538	R	Insufficient change in RPM/operator error in Dynamic Response Check
538	R	Invalid cylinder balance test due to throttle movement during test (1995 models)
538	R	Invalid cylinder balance test due to CID circuit failure (1995 models)
539	O	Air conditioning on during Self-test
542	O,C	Fuel Pump circuit open; PCM to motor
543	O,C	Fuel Pump circuit open; Battery to PCM
551	O	Idle Air Control (IAC) circuit failure KOEO
552	O	Air Management 1 circuit failure
552	O	Secondary Air Injection Bypass (AIRB) circuit failure
553	O	Secondary Air Injection Diverter (AIRB) circuit failure
556	O,C	Primary Fuel Pump circuit failure
558	O	EGR Vacuum Regulator circuit failure

* *O = Key On, Engine Off; C = Continuous Memory; R = Engine Running*

6

3 Digit Trouble Codes (continued)

Code	Test Condition*	Probable Cause
565	O	Canister Purge circuit failure
566	O	3-4 shift solenoid circuit failure KOEO (A4LD transmission)
569	O	Auxiliary Canister Purge (AUX-CANP) circuit failure
617	C	1-2 shift error
618	C	2-3 shift error
619	C	3-4 shift error
621	O,C	Shift Solenoid 1 (SS 1) circuit failure KOEO
622	O	Shift Solenoid 2 (SS2) circuit failure KOEO
624	O,C	Electronic Pressure Control (EPC) circuit failure
625	O,C	Electronic Pressure Control (EPC) driver open in PCM
626	O	Coast Clutch Solenoid (CCS) circuit failure KOEO
628	C	Excessive converter clutch slippage
629	O,C	Torque Converter Clutch (TCC) solenoid circuit failure
631	O	Transmission Control Indicator Lamp (TCIL) circuit failure KOEO
632	R	Transmission Control Switch (TCS) circuit did not change states during KOER
633	O	4X4L switch closed during KOEO
634	O,C,R	Manual Lever Position (MLP) sensor voltage higher or lower than expected
636	O,R	Transmission Fluid Temp (TFT) higher or lower than expected
637	O,C	Transmission Fluid Temp (TFT) sensor circuit above maximum voltage/ -40°F (-40°C) indicated / circuit open
638	O,C	Transmission Fluid Temp (TFT) sensor circuit below minimum voltage/ 290°F (143°C) indicated / circuit shorted
639	C,R	Insufficient input from Transmission Speed Sensor (TSS)
641	O	Shift Solenoid 3 (SS3) circuit failure KOEO
643	O	Coast Clutch Solenoid (CCS) circuit failure KOEO
652	O	Torque Converter Clutch (TCC) solenoid circuit failure
654	O	Transmission Range (TR) sensor not indicating PARK during KOEO
655	O	Transmission Range (TR) sensor not indicating NEUTRAL during KOEO
656	C	Torque Converter Clutch continuous slip error
657	C	Transmission fluid temperature (TFT) overheating
667	C	Transmission range (TR) circuit voltage above minimum voltage
668	C	Transmission range (TR) circuit voltage above maximum voltage
691	C	4X4 LOW switch open or short circuit present (1995 models)
692	C	Transmission state does not match calculated ratio (1995 models)
998	O	Hard fault present

* *O = Key On, Engine Off; C = Continuous Memory; R = Engine Running*

3   Fuel evaporative emissions control system

Refer to illustrations 3.2a and 3.2b

General description

1   This system is designed to prevent hydrocarbons from being released into the atmosphere by trapping and storing fuel vapor from the fuel tank or the fuel injection system.
2   The serviceable parts of the system include a charcoal filled canister and the connecting lines between the fuel tank, fuel tank filler cap and the fuel injection system **(see illustrations)**.
3   Vapor trapped in the gas tank is vented through a valve in the top of the tank. From the valve, the vapor is routed through a single line to a carbon canister located in the engine compartment near the radiator, where it's stored until the next time the engine is started.

System checking

4   There are no moving parts and nothing to wear in the canister. Check for loose, missing, cracked or broken fittings and inspect the canister for cracks and other damage. If the canister is damaged, replace it.
5   Check for fuel smells around the vehicle. Make sure the gas cap is in good condition and properly installed.

Charcoal canister replacement

6   Locate the canister behind the driver's side headlight in the engine compartment **(see illustration 3.2b)**.
7   Reach up above the canister, remove the single mounting bolt and remove the canister.
8   Clearly label the hoses and detach them from the canister.
9   Installation is the reverse of the removal procedure.

All other components

10   Referring to the VECI label of the vehicle, locate the component you intend to replace.
11   Label the hoses, then detach them and remove the component.
12   Installation is the reverse of removal.

4   Positive Crankcase Ventilation (PCV) system

Refer to illustration 4.2

General description

1   The Positive Crankcase Ventilation (PCV) system cycles crankcase vapors back through the engine where they are burned. The

3.2a Evaporative emissions vapor line system (fuel tank-to-canister)

3.2b Engine evaporative emissions vapor line system (canister-to-engine)

4.2 Most of the Positive Crankcase Ventilation (PCV) system components are mounted in the driver's side valve cover - there's also a hose running from the air cleaner outlet tube to the oil filler neck in the passenger side valve cover

valve regulates the amount of ventilating air and blow-by gas to the intake manifold and prevents backfire from traveling into the crankcase.

2   The PCV system consists of a replaceable PCV valve, a crankcase ventilation filter and the connecting hoses **(see illustration)**.

3   The air source for the crankcase ventilation system is in the air cleaner outlet hose. Air passes into the valve cover, then into the rocker arm chamber and the crankcase, from which it circulates up into another section of the rocker arm chamber and finally enters a spring loaded regulator valve (PCV valve) that controls the amount of flow as operating conditions vary. The vapors are routed to the intake manifold through the crankcase vent hose tube and fittings. This process goes on continuously while the engine is running.

Checking

4   Checking procedures for the PCV system components are included in Chapter 1.

Component replacement

5   Component replacement involves simply installing a new valve or hose in place of the one removed during the checking procedure (see Chapter 1, if necessary).

---

5   Inlet air temperature control system

General description

1   The inlet air temperature control system provides heated intake air during warmup, then maintains the inlet air temperature within a 70-degree F to 105-degree F operating range by mixing warm and cool air. This allows leaner fuel/air mixture settings for the EFI system, which reduces emissions and improves driveability.

2   Two fresh air inlets - one warm and one cold - are used. The balance between the two is controlled by intake manifold vacuum, cold weather modulator and a bimetal sensor. A vacuum motor, which operates a heat duct valve in the air cleaner, is controlled by the vacuum switch.

3   When the underhood temperature is cold, warm air radiating off the exhaust manifold is routed by a shroud which fits over the manifold up through a hot air inlet tube and into the air cleaner **(see illustration 8.2 in Chapter 4)**. This provides warm air for the EFI, resulting in better

driveability and faster warmup. As the underhood temperature rises, a heat duct valve is gradually closed by a vacuum motor and the air cleaner draws air through a cold air duct instead. The result is a consistent intake air temperature.

4   A temperature vacuum switch mounted in the air cleaner cover monitors the temperature of the inlet air heated by the exhaust manifold. A bimetal disc in the temperature vacuum switch orients itself in one of two positions, depending on the temperature. One position allows vacuum through a hose to the motor; the other position blocks vacuum.

5   The vacuum motor itself is regulated by a Cold Weather Modulator (CWM), mounted in the side of the air cleaner housing assembly, between the temperature vacuum switch and the motor, which provides the motor with a range of graduated positions between fully open and fully closed.

Checking

Note: *Make sure the engine is cold before beginning this test.*

6   Always check the vacuum source and the integrity of all vacuum hoses between the source and the vacuum motor before beginning the following test. Do not proceed until they're okay.

7   Apply the parking brake and block the wheels.

8   Remove components as necessary from the air intake duct in order to see the vacuum motor door (see Chapter 4).

9   Observe the vacuum motor door position - it should be open. If it isn't, it may be binding or sticking. Make sure it's not rusted in an open or closed position by attempting to move it by hand. If it's rusted, it can usually be freed by cleaning and oiling the hinge. If it fails to work properly after servicing, replace it.

10   If the vacuum motor door is okay but the motor still fails to operate correctly, check carefully for a leak in the hose leading to it. Check the vacuum source to and from the bimetal sensor and the cold weather modulator as well. If no leak is found, replace the vacuum motor (see Step 23).

11   Start the engine. If the duct door has moved or moves to the "heat on" (closed to fresh air) position, go to Step 15.

12   If the door stays in the "heat off" (closed to warm air) position, place a finger over the bimetal sensor bleed. The duct door must move rapidly to the "heat on" position. If the door doesn't move to the "heat on" position, stop the engine and replace the vacuum motor (see Step 23). Repeat this Step with the new vacuum motor.

13   With the engine off, allow the bimetal sensor and the Cold Weather Modulator to cool completely.

14   Restart the engine. The duct door should move to the "heat on" position. If the door doesn't move or moves only partially, replace the bimetal sensor (see Step 18).

15   Start and run the engine briefly (less than 15 seconds). The duct door should move to the "heat on" position.

16   Shut off the engine and watch the duct door. It should stay in the "heat on" position for at least two minutes.

17   If it doesn't stay in the "heat on" position for at least two minutes, replace the CWM.

Component replacement

Refer to illustrations 5.18 and 5.21

Bimetal sensor

18   Clearly label and detach both vacuum hoses from the bimetal sensor (one is coming from the vacuum source at the manifold and the other is going to the vacuum motor underneath the air cleaner housing) **(see illustration)**.

19   Remove the air cleaner housing cover (see Chapter 4).

20   Pry the sensor retaining clip off with a screwdriver **(see illustration 5.18)**.

21   Remove the bimetal sensor **(see illustration)**.

22   Installation is the reverse of removal procedure.

Vacuum motor

23   Remove the air intake duct (see Chapter 1). Place the assembly on a workbench.

5.18 To remove the bimetal sensor, detach the hoses and pry off the retaining clip with a small screwdriver

5.21 The bimetal sensor is mounted inside the air cleaner housing

24   Detach the vacuum hose from the motor.

25   Drill out the vacuum motor retaining strap rivet.

26   Remove the motor.

27   Installation is the reverse of removal. Use a sheet metal screw of the appropriate size to replace the rivet.

---

6   Catalytic converter

Note: *Because of a Federally mandated extended warranty which covers emissions-related components such as the catalytic converter, check with a dealer service department before replacing the converter at your own expense.*

General description

1   The catalytic converter is an emission control device added to the exhaust system to reduce pollutants from the exhaust gas stream. There are two types of converters. The conventional oxidation catalyst reduces the levels of hydrocarbon (HC) and carbon monoxide (CO). The three-way catalyst lowers the levels of oxides of nitrogen (NOx) as well as hydrocarbons (HC) and carbon monoxide (CO).

Check

2   The test equipment for a catalytic converter is expensive and highly sophisticated. If you suspect that the converter on your vehicle is malfunctioning, take it to a dealer or authorized emissions inspection facility for diagnosis and repair.

3   Whenever the vehicle is raised for servicing of underbody components, check the converter for leaks, corrosion, dents and other damage. Check the welds/flange bolts that attach the front and rear ends of the converter to the exhaust system. If damage is discovered, the converter should be replaced.

4   Although catalytic converters don't break too often, they can become plugged. The easiest way to check for a restricted converter is to use a vacuum gauge to diagnose the effect of a blocked exhaust on intake vacuum.

a) *Open the throttle until the engine speed is about 2000 RPM.*

b) *Release the throttle quickly.*

c) *If there is no restriction, the gauge will quickly drop to not more than 2 in Hg or more above its normal reading.*

d) *If the gauge does not show 5 in Hg or more above its normal reading, or seems to momentarily hover around its highest reading for a moment before it returns, the exhaust system, or the converter, is plugged (or an exhaust pipe is bent or dented, or the core inside the muffler has shifted).*

Component replacement

5   The converter is bolted to the exhaust system. Refer to the exhaust system removal and installation section in Chapter 4

6

Notes

Chapter 7 Part A
Manual transmission

Contents

	Section		Section
Extension housing oil seal - replacement	6	Speedometer pinion gear and seal - removal and installation	5
General information	1	Transmission mount - check and replacement	3
Manual transmission - removal and installation	4	Transmission overhaul - general information	7
Shift lever - removal and installation	2		

Specifications

General

Transmission type	5-speed synchromesh
Lubricant type	See Chapter 1

Torque specifications

	Ft-lbs
Transmission-to-clutch housing bolt or nut	18 to 38
Mount-to-crossmember nut	65 to 85
Mount-to-transmission bolt	60 to 80
Crossmember-to-frame bracket nut and bolt	65 to 85

1.1   The 5-speed manual transmission

1   General information

Refer to illustration 1.1

All vehicles covered in this manual come equipped with a 5-speed manual transmission **(see illustration)** or an automatic transmission. All information on the manual transmission is included in this Part of Chapter 7. Information on the automatic transmission can be found in Part B of this Chapter.

Due to the complexity, unavailability of replacement parts and the special tools necessary, internal transmission repair procedures are not recommended for the home mechanic.

Depending on the expense involved in having a faulty transmission overhauled, it may be an advantage to consider replacing the unit with either a new or rebuilt one. Your local dealer or transmission shop should be able to supply you with information concerning cost, availability and exchange policy. Regardless of how you decide to remedy a transmission problem, you can still save a lot of money by removing and installing the unit yourself.

2   Shift lever - removal and installation

1   Place the transmission in Neutral.
2   Carefully pull up the carpeting and remove the shifter boot retaining bolts.
3   Remove the bolt that secures the shift lever to the transmission **(see illustration 1.1)**.

4   Pull the shift lever straight up and off the transmission.
5   Installation is the reverse of the removal Steps.

3   Transmission mount - check and replacement

Refer to illustrations 3.2, 3.3a and 3.3b

1   Insert a large screwdriver or pry bar into the space between the transmission extension housing and the frame crossmember and pry up.
2   The transmission should not move significantly away from the mount **(see illustration)**. If it does, the mount should be replaced.
3   To replace the mount, remove the two nuts securing the mount to the frame crossmember and the two bolts securing the mount to the transmission extension housing **(see illustration)**.
4   Place a jack under the transmission with a piece of wood on top of it to protect the transmission case. Apply a slight amount of jack pressure and raise the transmission. Remove mount and install a new one.
5   Installation is the reverse of the removal Steps.

4   Manual transmission - removal and installation

Refer to illustration 4.7

1   Disconnect the negative cable from the battery.
2   From inside the vehicle, remove the shift lever (see Section 2).

3.2 Pry up on the transmission mount and check for excessive looseness

3.3a Remove the two bolts attaching the transmission mount to the frame crossmember and the two bolts securing the mount to the transmission extension housing

3.3b An exploded view of a typical transmission mount

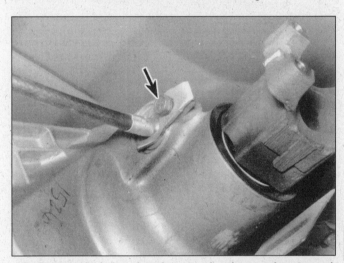

4.7 Remove the bolt and retainer securing the speedometer and disconnect the speedometer cable from the transmission or transfer case

7A

3   Drain the transmission lubricant (see Chapter 1).
4   Raise the vehicle and support it securely on jackstands.
5   Remove the driveshaft (see Chapter 8) and install a plug in the transmission rear extension housing to prevent lubricant leakage.
6   Disconnect the hydraulic fluid line from the clutch release cylinder (see Chapter 8) and plug the line to prevent fluid spillage.
7   Disconnect the speedometer cable from the transfer case or transmission (see illustration).
8   Remove the starter motor (see Chapter 5).
9   Disconnect the electrical connections from the backup lamp and shift indicator switch.
10   Place a jack under the engine and protect the oil pan with a wood block. Apply a slight amount of jack pressure to support the rear of the engine.
11   On 4WD models, remove the transfer case (see Chapter 7 Part C).
12   Remove the exhaust system (see Chapter 4).
13   Place a transmission jack under the transmission. Apply a slight amount of jack pressure to support the transmission. Remove the bolts, lockwashers and plain washers that secure the transmission to the engine.
14   Remove the bolts and nuts securing the transmission mount to the frame crossmember (see illustration 3.3b).
15   Remove the nuts securing the frame crossmember to the frame side rails. Note: If you do not remove the mount from the transmission,

it will be necessary to raise the transmission enough to clear the mount bolts, then slide the crossmember toward the rear.
16   Slowly lower the jack supporting the engine and carefully pull the transmission toward the rear and work it free from the locating dowels. Pull the transmission straight back until the input shaft clears the clutch assembly.
17   Lower the transmission jack and remove the transmission.
18   Installation is the reverse of the removal Steps with the following additions:
   a) Mount the transmission in a transmission jack and position it under the vehicle.
   b) Start the transmission input shaft into the clutch disc. Align the shaft splines with the clutch disc splines and move the transmission forward.
   c) Tighten the bolts and nuts to the torque listed in this Chapter's Specifications.

5   Speedometer pinion gear and seal - removal and installation

Refer to illustrations 5.3 and 5.4
1   Disconnect the speedometer cable from the transmission.

5.3 Pry the retaining clip from the pinion gear and slide the gear off of the cable

5.4 To replace the O-ring, pry off the old O-ring with a small screwdriver

2   Pull the speedometer pinion gear straight out of the transfer case or extension housing.

3   Use a small screwdriver and remove the retaining clip from the pinion gear, then slide the gear off the cable **(see illustration)**.

4   If necessary, use a small screwdriver and remove the O-ring from the retaining groove **(see illustration)**. Discard the O-ring.

5   Lubricate the new O-ring with transmission lubricant and install it in the retaining groove. Make sure it's seated correctly.

6   Install the pinion gear on the cable and install the retaining clip. Make sure the clip is properly seated in the groove.

7   Install the speedometer pinion gear and cable in the transfer case or rear extension housing and secure it with the bolt and bracket.

6   Extension housing oil seal (2WD models) - replacement

1   Raise the vehicle and support it securely on jackstands.

2   Remove the driveshaft (see Chapter 8). Some transmission lubricant may drain out when the driveshaft slip joint is withdrawn from the extension housing.

3   To remove the oil seal from the end of the extension housing use Ford special tool (part No. T74P-77248-A) and withdraw the oil seal. If the special tool is not available, and there is access, use a thin blade screwdriver or chisel and pry the oil seal out.

4   Inspect the sealing surface on the driveshaft slip joint for scoring or burrs that may damage the new oil seal. If the yoke is damaged in any way, replace it.

5   Inspect the extension housing counterbore for burrs. If found, remove them with emery cloth or medium grit wet-and-dry sandpaper. Use a clean cloth dipped in solvent and remove any sanding residue from the counterbore.

6   Apply silicone sealant to the inside diameter of the oil seal and apply grease to the end of the rubber boot portion.

7   Using a seal driver, large socket or section of pipe, install a new

oil seal and make sure it is completely seated in the counterbore.

8   Install the driveshaft (see Chapter 8).

9   Lower the vehicle and check the transmission lubricant level. Top up if necessary (see Chapter 1).

7   Transmission overhaul - general information

Overhauling a manual transmission is a difficult job for the do-it-yourselfer. It involves the disassembly and reassembly of many small parts. Numerous clearances must be precisely measured and, if necessary, changed with select-fit spacers and snap-rings. As a result, if transmission problems arise, it can be removed and installed by a competent do-it-yourselfer, but overhaul should be left to a transmission repair shop. Rebuilt transmissions may be available - check with your dealer parts department and auto parts stores. At any rate, the time and money involved in an overhaul is almost sure to exceed the cost of a rebuilt unit.

Nevertheless, it's not impossible for an inexperienced mechanic to rebuild a transmission if the special tools are available and the job is done in a deliberate step-by-step manner so nothing is overlooked.

The tools necessary for an overhaul include internal and external snap-ring pliers, bearing puller, slide hammer, set of pin punches, dial indicator and possibly a hydraulic press. In addition, a large, sturdy workbench and a large vise or transmission stand will be required.

During disassembly of the transmission, make careful notes of how each piece comes off, where it fits in relation to other pieces and what holds it in place.

Before taking the transmission apart for repair, it will help if you have some idea what area of the transmission is malfunctioning. Certain problems can be closely tied to specific areas in the transmission, which can make component examination and replacement easier. Refer to the *Troubleshooting* section at the front of this manual for information regarding possible sources of trouble.

Chapter 7 Part B
Automatic transmission

Contents

	Section		Section
Automatic transmission - removal and installation	6	Shift cable - adjustment	3
Diagnosis - general	2	Shift cable - removal and installation	4
Extension housing oil seal - replacement	5	Transmission mount - check and replacement	9
General information	1	Vacuum diaphragm - removal and installation	8
Neutral start switch - removal, installation and adjustment	7		

Specifications

General
Transmission type.. A4LD
Fluid type and capacity .... See Chapter 1

Torque specifications   Ft-lbs
Transmission-to-engine bolts.. 28 to 38
Torque converter-to-driveplate nuts.. 20 to 34
Neutral start switch.. 7 to 10

1 General information

All vehicles covered in this manual come equipped with a five-speed manual transmission or an automatic transmission. All information on the automatic transmission is included in this Part of Chapter 7. Information on the manual transmission can be found in Part A of this Chapter.

Due to the complexity of the automatic transmissions covered in this manual and the need for specialized equipment to perform most service operations, this Chapter contains only general diagnosis, routine maintenance, adjustment and removal and installation procedures.

If the transmission requires major repair work, it should be taken to a dealer service department or an automotive or transmission repair shop. You can, however, remove and install the transmission yourself and save the expense, even if the repair work is done by a transmission shop.

2 Diagnosis - general

Note: *Automatic transmission malfunctions may be caused by five general conditions: poor engine performance, improper adjustments, hydraulic malfunctions, mechanical malfunctions or malfunctions in the computer or its signal network. Diagnosis of these problems should always begin with a check of the easily repaired items: fluid level and condition (see Chapter 1) and shift linkage adjustment. Next, perform a road test to determine if the problem has been corrected or if more diagnosis is necessary. If the problem persists after the preliminary tests and corrections are completed, additional diagnosis should be done by a dealer service department or transmission repair shop. Refer to the Troubleshooting section at the front of this manual for information on symptoms of transmission problems.*

Preliminary checks

1   Drive the vehicle to warm the transmission to normal operating temperature.

2   Check the fluid level as described in Chapter 1:

a) *If the fluid level is unusually low, add enough fluid to bring the level within the designated area of the dipstick, then check for external leaks (see below).*

b) *If the fluid level is abnormally high, drain off the excess, then check the drained fluid for contamination by coolant. The presence of engine coolant in the automatic transmission fluid indicates that a failure has occurred in the internal radiator walls that separate the coolant from the transmission fluid (see Chapter 3).*

c) *If the fluid is foaming, drain it and refill the transmission, then check for coolant in the fluid or a high fluid level.*

3   Check the engine idle speed. **Note:** *If the engine is malfunctioning, do not proceed with the preliminary checks until it has been repaired and runs normally.*

4   Inspect the shift linkage (see Section 3). Make sure that it's properly adjusted and that the linkage operates smoothly.

Fluid leak diagnosis

5   Most fluid leaks are easy to locate visually. Repair usually consists of replacing a seal or gasket. If a leak is difficult to find, the following procedure may help.

6   Identify the fluid. Make sure it's transmission fluid and not engine oil or brake fluid (automatic transmission fluid is a deep red color when new and may turn light brown after the vehicle has been driven some distance).

7   Try to pinpoint the source of the leak. Drive the vehicle several miles, then park it over a large sheet of cardboard. After a minute or two, you should be able to locate the leak by determining the source of the fluid dripping onto the cardboard.

8   Make a careful visual inspection of the suspected component and the area immediately around it. Pay particular attention to gasket mating surfaces. A mirror is often helpful for finding leaks in areas that are hard to see.

9   If the leak still cannot be found, clean the suspected area thoroughly with a degreaser or solvent, then dry it.

10   Drive the vehicle for several miles at normal operating temperature and varying speeds. After driving the vehicle, visually inspect the suspected component again.

11   Once the leak has been located, the cause must be determined before it can be properly repaired. If a gasket is replaced but the sealing flange is bent, the new gasket will not stop the leak. The bent flange must be straightened.

12   Before attempting to repair a leak, check to make sure that the following conditions are corrected or they may cause another leak. **Note:** *Some of the following conditions cannot be fixed without highly specialized tools and expertise. Such problems must be referred to a transmission repair shop or a dealer service department.*

Gasket leaks

13   Check the pan periodically. Make sure the bolts are tight, no bolts are missing, the gasket is in good condition and the pan is flat (dents in the pan may indicate damage to the valve body inside).

14   If the pan gasket is leaking, the fluid level or the fluid pressure may be too high, the vent may be plugged, the pan bolts may be too tight, the pan sealing flange may be warped, the sealing surface of the transmission housing may be damaged, the gasket may be damaged or the transmission casting may be cracked or porous. If sealant instead of gasket material has been used to form a seal between the pan and the transmission housing, it may be the wrong sealant.

Seal leaks

15   If a transmission seal is leaking, the fluid level or pressure may be too high, the vent may be plugged, the seal bore may be damaged, the seal itself may be damaged or improperly installed, the surface of the shaft protruding through the seal may be damaged or a loose bearing may be causing excessive shaft movement.

16   Make sure the dipstick tube seal is in good condition and the tube is properly seated. Periodically check the area around the

3.3 Shift cable details

speedometer gear or sensor for leakage. If transmission fluid is evident, check the O-ring for damage.

Case leaks

17   If the case itself appears to be leaking, the casting is porous and will have to be repaired or replaced.

18   Make sure the oil cooler hose fittings are tight and in good condition.

Fluid comes out vent pipe or fill tube

19   If this condition occurs, the transmission is overfilled, there is coolant in the fluid, the case is porous, the dipstick is incorrect, the vent is plugged or the drain back holes are plugged.

---

3   Shift cable - adjustment

Refer to illustration 3.3

1   Raise the vehicle and support it securely on jackstands.

2   Have an assistant position the column shift selector lever in the Drive Overdrive position and hold in place during adjustment. If working by yourself, hang a three-pound weight on the gear selector lever.

3   Working under the vehicle, pull down on the lock tab on the shift cable and remove the fitting from the manual shift lever ball stud with a screwdriver **(see illustration)**.

4   Position the transmission manual shift lever in the Drive Overdrive position by moving the bellcrank lever all the way to the rear (counterclockwise), then forward three detents (clockwise).

5   Connect the cable end fitting to the manual lever ball stud.

5.3a These special tools are available to remove the oil seal and bushing from the transmission extension housing

5.3b Be extremely careful not to damage the sealing surface on the housing when prying out the rear seal

5.7 These special tools are available to install the oil seal and bushing from the transmission extension housing

5.8 Installing the new extension housing oil seal with a punch and hammer - large socket or length of pipe of the proper diameter may also be used to install the oil seal

6   Push the lock tab all the way down to lock the cable in the correctly adjusted position.
7   If used, remove the weight from the gear selector lever.
8   After adjustment, check for Park engagement. The control lever must move to the right when engaged in Park. Check the control lever in all detent positions with the engine running to ensure correct detent/transmission action and adjust and readjust if necessary.
9   Remove the jackstands and lower the vehicle to the ground.
10   Test drive the vehicle slowly at first to make sure the adjustment is correct.

4   Shift cable - removal and installation

1   Use a screwdriver and pry the end fitting from the steering column lever ball stud.
2   Remove the nuts securing the shift cable bracket to the steering column bracket and remove the bracket.
3   Raise the vehicle and support it securely on jackstands.
4   Working under the vehicle, pull down on the lock tab on the shift cable and remove the fitting from the manual lever ball stud with a screwdriver **(see illustration 3.3).**
5   Bend back the retaining tab and disengage the cable from the transmission bracket. Slide the cable down from the transmission bracket and remove the cable.
6   Installation is the reverse of the removal procedure with the following additions:

a) *Adjust the shift linkage (see Section 3).*
b) *Remove the jackstands and lower the vehicle to the ground.*

5   Extension housing oil seal - replacement

Refer to illustrations 5.3a, 5.3b, 5.7 and 5.8
1   Raise the vehicle and support it securely on jackstands.
2   Remove the driveshaft (see Chapter 8). Some transmission fluid may drain out when the driveshaft universal joint is withdrawn from the extension housing.
3   To remove the oil seal from the end of the extension housing use Ford special tool (part No. T71P-7657-A) and withdraw the oil seal **(see illustration).** If the special tool is not available, and there is access, use a thin blade screwdriver or chisel to remove the oil seal **(see illustration).**
4   The extension housing bushing can also be replaced. If the bushing is worn or damaged, removed it with the specified Ford tool or equivalent **(see illustration 5.3a).** Makeshift tools may damage the bushing.
5   Inspect the oil seal contact surface on the universal joint yoke for scoring or burrs that may damage the new oil seal. If the yoke is damaged in any way, replace it.
6   Inspect the extension housing counterbore for burrs. If found, remove them with emery cloth or medium grit wet-and-dry sandpaper. Use a clean cloth dipped in solvent and remove any sanding residue from the counterbore.
7   If the extension housing bushing was removed, install a new one with the recommended Ford tool or equivalent **(see illustration).**
8   Install a new extension housing oil seal and make sure it is completely seated in the counterbore **(see illustration 5.7 and the accompanying illustration).**
9   Install the driveshaft (see Chapter 8).

7B

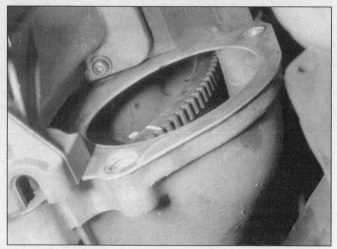

6.6 Mark one of the torque converter studs with white paint and make a corresponding mark on the driveplate so the torque converter and driveplate can be reassembled in the same relative positions

6.9 On 2WD models, remove the speedometer gear retainer bolt and remove the speedometer cable from the transmission

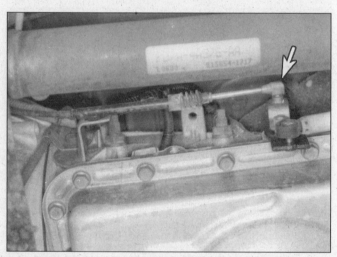

6.10a Disconnect the shift cable from the transmission manual shift lever . . .

6.10b . . . and the kickdown cable from the transmission downshift lever

10   Lower the vehicle and check the transmission fluid level. Top up if necessary (see Chapter 1).

6   Automatic transmission - removal and installation

Refer to illustrations 6.6, 6.9, 6.10a, 6.10b, 6.11, 6.13, 6.15 and 6.18

1   Disconnect the negative cable from the battery.
2   On 4WD models, remove the transfer case (see Chapter 7 Part C).
3   Raise the vehicle and support it securely on jackstands.
4   Drain the transmission fluid (see Chapter 1), then reinstall the pan.
5   Unbolt the starter and tie it up out of the way (see Chapter 5). The starter mounting hole provides access to the torque converter nuts.
6   Mark the torque converter and one of the studs with white paint so they can be installed in the same position **(see illustration)**.
7   Remove the four torque converter-to-driveplate nuts. Turn the crankshaft for access to each nut. Turn the crankshaft in a clockwise direction only (as viewed from the front).
8   On 2WD models, remove the driveshaft (see Chapter 8). Tie a plastic bag over the end of the extension housing to prevent the entry of dirt and to catch any residual transmission fluid.

6.11 Disconnect the electrical connectors for the shift solenoids and neutral start switch

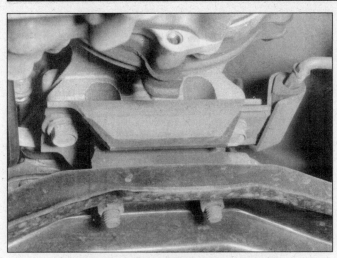

6.13 Detach the transmission mount from the frame crossmember

6.15 Detach the front crossmember from the frame rail on each side of the vehicle

9   On 2WD models, remove the bolt securing the speedometer cable retaining bracket and remove the bracket and bolt as an assembly **(see illustration)**. Disconnect the speedometer cable from the transmission.

10   Disconnect the shift cable from the transmission manual shift lever and the kickdown cable from the transmission kickdown lever **(see illustrations)**.

11   Detach the electrical connectors for the neutral safety switch and torque converter lockup solenoid from the transmission **(see illustration)**.

12   Place a transmission jack beneath the transmission and apply jack pressure to slightly raise the transmission. Use safety chains to help steady the transmission on the jack.

13   Remove the bolts and nuts securing the rear mount and insulator to the frame crossmember **(see illustration)**.

14   Remove the crossmember-to-frame side support mounting bolts and remove the crossmember insulator, support and damper.

15   Remove the bolts and nuts securing the crossmember to the frame rails **(see illustration)**, raise the transmission slightly and remove the crossmember.

16   Support the engine with a jack. Use a block of wood under the oil pan to spread the load.

17   Slightly lower the transmission.

18   Disconnect the transmission oil cooler lines from the transmission and plug them to prevent the entry of dirt. Use a flare nut wrench to avoid rounding off the nuts **(see illustration)**.

19   Remove the lower converter housing-to-engine bolts.

20   Remove the transmission fluid filler (dipstick) tube **(see illustration 6.18)**.

21   Make sure the transmission is securely mounted on the transmission jack. Remove the two upper converter housing-to-engine bolts.

22   Carefully move the transmission to the rear to disengage it from the engine block dowel pins and make sure the torque converter is detached from the driveplate. Secure the torque converter to the transmission so it won't fall out during removal.

23   Installation is the reverse of the removal Steps with the following additions:

a)   Install the converter to the transmission, making sure the converter hub is fully engaged in the pump gear.

b)   Rotate the converter to align the bolt drive lugs and the drain plug with the holes in the driveplate.

c)   With the transmission secured to the jack, raise it into position. Be sure to keep it level so the torque converter does not slide forward and disengage from the pump gear.

6.18 Disconnect the fluid cooler lines and remove the filler tube

d)   Turn the torque converter to line up the studs with the holes in the driveplate. The white paint mark on the torque converter and the stud made in Step 5 must line up.

e)   Move the transmission forward carefully until the dowel pins and the torque converter are engaged.

f)   When installing the driveplate-to-converter nuts, position the driveplate so the pilot hole is in the six o'clock position. First install one nut through the pilot hole and tighten it, then install the remaining nuts. Tighten the nuts to the torque listed in this Chapter's Specifications.

g)   Adjust the shift cable (see Section 3).

h)   Lower the vehicle.

i)   Fill the transmission with the specified fluid (see Chapter 1), run the engine and check for fluid leaks.

7   Neutral start switch - removal, installation and adjustment

Refer to illustration 7.3

1   Disconnect the negative cable from the battery.

2   Disconnect the electrical connector from the switch.

3   Carefully remove the switch **(see illustration)**. **Caution:** *It is easy*

7B

7.3 Neutral start switch - the switch is very fragile and the special Ford tool is recommended for removal and installation

8.2 Details of the vacuum diaphragm and heat shield

1	*Heat shield*	3	*Vacuum diaphragm*
2	*Nut*		

to crush or puncture the walls of the switch. Ford tool (part No. T74P-77247-A) is designed to remove the switch without damaging it.

4   Install the switch and tighten to the torque listed in this Chapter's Specifications. If available, use the same special tool used for removal to avoid damaging the switch.

5   Install the electrical connector.

6   Connect the negative cable to the battery.

7   Check that the engine will start only when the shift selector is in the Neutral or Park positions.

8   Vacuum diaphragm - removal and installation

Refer to illustrations 8.2 and 8.5

1   Raise the vehicle and support it securely on jackstands.

2   Remove the heat shield covering the diaphragm **(see illustration)**.

3   Carefully pry the heat shield from the oil pan, then slide it forward to gain access to the vacuum diaphragm.

4   Disconnect the hose from the vacuum diaphragm.

5   Remove the bolt and the retaining clamp and pull the diaphragm out of the transmission case **(see illustration)**.

6   Remove the control rod from the transmission case.

7   Installation is the reverse of the removal procedure, but be sure to install a new O-ring on the vacuum diaphragm and tighten the clamp bolt securely.

8.5 Remove the retaining bolt and clamp, then pull the vacuum diaphragm out of the transmission

9   Transmission mount - check and replacement

1   Insert a large screwdriver or pry bar into the space between the transmission extension housing and the crossmember and try to pry the transmission up slightly **(see illustration 6.13).**

2   The transmission should not move away from the mount much at all.

3   To replace the mount, remove the nuts attaching the mount to the crossmember and the bolts attaching the mount to the transmission.

4   Raise the transmission slightly with a jack and remove the mount, noting which holes are used in the crossmember for proper alignment during installation.

5   Installation is the reverse of the removal procedure. Be sure to tighten the nuts/bolts securely.

Chapter 7 Part C
Transfer case

Contents

	Section
Electronic control module - removal and installation	5
Electronic shift controls - removal and installation	4
Front output shaft oil seal - removal and installation	6
General information	1

	Section
Linkage adjustment - manual shift transfer case	2
Rear output shaft oil seal - removal and installation	7
Shift lever - removal and installation	3
Transfer case - removal and installation	8

Specifications

Lubricant type .... See Chapter 1

Torque specifications   **Ft-lbs** (unless otherwise indicated)

Cam plate bolt A	70 to 90
Cam plate bolt B	31 to 42
Breather vent	72 to 168 in-lbs
Upper shift control and heat shield bolts	27 to 37
Transfer case-to-transmission bolts	25 to 35
Yoke nut	150 to 180
Skid plate-to-frame bolt	22 to 30
Speedometer cable bolt	20 to 25 in-lbs

1.1a The manually controlled Borg-Warner 13-54 transfer case

1   General information

Refer to illustration 1.1a and 1.1b

Ford Explorers are equipped with either the Borg Warner 13-54 Electronic Shift transfer case or the Borg Warner 44-05 Control Trac (C-Trac) transfer case.

The Borg Warner 13-54 is available in models that are controlled either mechanically or electronically. This model transfer case is equipped onto manual and automatic transmission models. The electronic mode selector is mounted on the dash. The 13-54 transfer case is a part time system **(see illustrations)**. The unit transfers power from the transmission to the rear axle and, when activated, also to the front driveaxle. The unit is lubricated by a positive displacement oil pump that channels oil through drilled holes in the rear output shaft. The pump turns with the rear output shaft and allows towing of the vehicle at maximum legal road speeds for extended distances without disconnecting the front or rear driveshafts.

The Borg Warner 44-05 or C-Trac is controlled either by an electronic shift motor or by the GEM (Generic Electronic Module). This model transfer case is equipped onto manual and automatic transmission models. The electronic mode selector is mounted on the dash. The Borg Warner 44-05 or C-Trac uses an electromechanical clutch to shift the front driveshafts. Sensors determine the driveshaft speed and relay information to the electric clutch to activate the front driveshaft depending upon road conditions (wet, damp, snow, sleet etc.). This

1.1b The electronically controlled Borg-Warner 13-54 transfer case

system uses a GEM (Generic Electronic Module). This automatic selection only occurs in 4WD High. When the electric shift selector on the dash is selected for 4WD Low, a cam selects the proper gear.

Although each of the systems differ internally, the external components on the transfer case are similar.

Due to the complexity of the transfer cases covered in this manual and the need for specialized equipment to perform most service operations, this chapter contains only general diagnosis, routine maintenance, adjustment and removal and installation procedures.

If the transfer case requires major repair work, it should be taken

2.2 Shift linkage adjustment points (manual shift transfer case)

3.4 Manual control transfer case shift lever assembly

to a dealer service department or an automotive or transmission repair shop. You can, however, remove and install the transfer case yourself and save the expense, even if the repair work is done by a transmission shop.

2 Linkage adjustment - manual shift transfer case

Refer to illustration 2.2

1   The linkage should be adjusted if the transfer case won't engage properly or whenever the transfer case control assembly is removed from the vehicle.

2   Lift up the shift boot so the upper surface of the cam plate is visible **(see illustration)**.

3   Loosen bolts A and B one turn each.

4   Move the shift lever on the side of the transfer case to the 4L position (down).

5   Pivot the cam plate clockwise around bolt A until the bottom chamfered corner of the neutral lug just touches the forward right edge of the shift lever on the transfer case.

6   While holding the cam plate from turning, tighten bolt A, then bolt B to the torque listed in this Chapter's Specifications.

7   Move the shift lever inside the vehicle to all positions and check for positive engagement. In the 2H, 4H and 4L positions, there should be clearance between the cam plate and the shift lever on the side of the transfer case.

8   When the linkage is adjusted properly, install the shift lever boot.

3 Shift lever - removal and installation

Refer to illustration 3.4

Removal

1   Place the transfer case shift lever in the 4L position.

2   **Note:** *Don't perform Step 2 unless the shift ball, boot or lever is to be replaced.* Remove the plastic insert from the shift ball. Warm the ball with a heat gun or portable hair dryer to 140 to 180-degrees F and knock the ball off the lever with a piece of wood and a hammer. Be careful not to damage the finish on the shift lever.

3   Remove the rubber boot and the floor pan cover.

4   Disconnect the vent hose from the control lever **(see illustration)**.

5   Unscrew the shift lever from the control lever.

6   Remove the large and small housing bolts securing the shifter to the extension housing. Remove the control lever and bushing.

Installation

7   Adjust the linkage (see Section 2).

8   Install the vent assembly so the white mark on the housing is indexed into the notch in the shifter, if applicable. **Note:** *The upper end of the vent hose should be 3/4-inch above the top of the shifter and positioned just under the vehicle floor.*

9   Install the floor pan cover and the rubber boot.

10   If the shift ball was removed, warm it with a heat gun or portable hair dryer to 140 to 180-degrees F and carefully tap the ball onto the

7C

4.4 Lift the connector latch and pull the electrical connector from the electronic shift control switch

5.2a Location of the shift control module (two door model shown; four door model similar)

5.2b The electronic control module (ECM) is located behind the passenger side kick panel under the dash

lever with a piece of wood and a hammer. Install the plastic insert into the shift ball. **Note:** *The shift ball must be tapped onto the lever until all of the knurled portion of the shaft is covered.*
11   Check the transfer case for proper operation.

4   Electronic shift controls - removal and installation

Refer to illustration 4.4
1   Disconnect the negative cable from the battery.
2   Remove the instrument cluster trim panel (see Chapter 12).
3   Remove the screws securing the shift control assembly and partially pull the assembly out from the instrument panel.
4   Disconnect the electrical connector from the switch assembly and remove the assembly **(see illustration)**.
5   Installation is the reverse of the removal Steps.

5   Electronic control module - removal and installation

Refer to illustration 5.2a, 5.2b and 5.7
Note: *1995 models are equipped with a Generic Electronic Module (GEM). This module incorporates the functions of several different modules into one and offers diagnostic codes to locate any multitude of failures (see Chapter 6).*
1   Disconnect the negative cable from the battery.

1991 through 1994 models
2   Working inside the vehicle, remove the trim panel above the left rear wheel well to gain access to the module. Remove the two bolts securing the control module and the bracket **(see illustration)**.
3   Pull the control module part way out and disconnect the electrical connectors from the module. Remove the control module.
4   Installation is the reverse of removal.

1995 and later models
5   Remove the radio (see Chapter 12).
6   Remove the radio trim panel (see Chapter 12).
7   Slide the GEM off the retaining tabs and toward the front of the vehicle **(see illustration)**.
8   Disconnect the electrical connectors from the GEM and remove the unit from the dash.
9   Installation is the reverse of removal.

6   Front output shaft oil seal - removal and installation

Refer to illustration 6.4

Removal
1   Raise the vehicle and support it securely on jackstands.
2   Drain the transfer case lubricant (see Chapter 1).
3   Remove the front driveshaft from the axle input yoke (see

5.7 Location of the Generic Electronic Module (GEM) on 1995 models

6.4 Front output shaft oil seal components

Chapter 8). Tie it up out of the way.
4   Use a 30 mm thin-walled socket and remove the front output shaft nut, washer, rubber seal and yoke **(see illustration)**.
5   Remove the dust seal from the yoke opening of the transfer case.
6   Carefully pry out the oil seal with a large screwdriver.

Installation

7   Inspect the oil seal contact surface on the housing for scoring or burrs that may damage the new oil seal. If found, remove them with emery cloth or medium grit wet-and-dry sandpaper. Use a clean cloth dipped in solvent and remove any sanding residue from the counterbore.
8   Apply multipurpose grease to the oil seal. Position the seal into the front output shaft housing bore and make sure the oil seal is not cocked in the bore.
9   To drive the front oil seal into the output housing bore use Ford special tool (part No. T83T-7065-B) and driver (part No. T80T-4000-W), or carefully drive the seal into the bore with a hammer and a large socket or piece of pipe of the appropriate size.
10   Clean the transfer case front output female splines and apply multi-purpose grease to them. Insert the front driveshaft splined shaft into the female splines.
11   Install the front yoke onto the splines, then install the rubber seal, steel washer and nut. Tighten the nut to the torque listed in this Chapter's Specifications.
12   Connect the front driveshaft to the axle input yoke (see Chapter 8).
13   Refill the transfer case lubricant (see Chapter 1).
14   Remove the jackstands and lower the vehicle.

7   Rear output shaft oil seal - removal and installation

Removal

1   Raise the vehicle and support it securely on jackstands.
2   Remove the rear driveshaft from the transfer case output shaft yoke and wire the driveshaft out of the way (see Chapter 8).
3   Use a 30 mm thin-walled socket to remove the nut securing the flange **(see illustration 6.4)**.
4   Remove the steel washer and rubber seal, then remove the flange.
5   Carefully pry and pull on the outer curved lip of the oil seal and remove it from transfer case.

Installation

Refer to illustration 7.8
6   Inspect the oil seal contact surface on the housing for scoring or

7.8 A large pipe or socket can be used to install the seal if the special tool isn't available

burrs that may damage the new oil seal. If found, remove them with emery cloth or medium grit wet-and-dry sandpaper. Use a clean cloth dipped in solvent and remove any sanding residue from the counterbore.
7   Apply multi-purpose grease to the oil seal. Position the seal into the front output shaft housing bore and make sure the oil seal is not cocked in the bore.
8   To drive the front oil seal into the output housing bore use Ford special tool (part No. T83T-7065-B) and driver (part No. T80T-4000-W), or carefully drive the seal into the bore with a hammer and a large socket or piece of pipe of the appropriate size **(see illustration)**.
9   Clean the transfer case rear output female splines and apply multi-purpose grease to them.
10   Install the output flange onto the output shaft splines.
11   Install the rubber seal, steel washer and nut. Tighten the nut to the torque listed in this Chapter's Specifications.
12   Connect the front driveshaft to the axle output flange (see Chapter 8).
13   Remove the jackstands and lower the vehicle.

8   Transfer case - removal and installation

Refer to illustrations 8.3, 8.5, 8.6, 8.8, 8.12, 8.14a and 8.14b
1   Raise the vehicle and support it securely on jackstands.
2   On models so equipped, remove the four bolts securing the skid plate to the frame and remove it.

7C

8.3 Some models are equipped with a transfer case damper - this must be removed to remove the transfer case

8.5 Disconnect the shift motor connector (electronic shift models)

8.6 Disconnect the speed sensor connector (if equipped) and speedometer cable

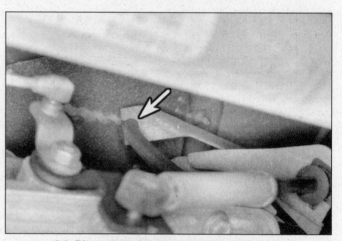

8.8 Disconnect the vent hose from its bracket (electronic shift models)

3　On models so equipped, remove the damper from the transfer case **(see illustration)**.

4　Drain the lubricant from the transfer case (see Chapter 1).

5　On electronically controlled models, squeeze the locking tabs (the part labeled PUSH) toward each other, then pull the electrical connector apart. This may take some effort, but it shouldn't be necessary to use tools to separate the connector halves. Disconnect the electrical connector
from the transfer case motor and from the connector mounting bracket **(see illustration)**.

6　Disconnect the speed sensor electrical connector (if equipped) and speedometer cable from the transfer case **(see illustration)**.

7　Disconnect both driveshafts (see Chapter 8).

8　Disconnect the vent hose from the shift lever bracket (manual shift) or mounting bracket (electronic shift) **(see illustration)**. **Warning:** *The catalytic converter is next to the vent hose and is extremely hot after the engine has been run. Be careful when working around the converter and if possible allow the converter to cool down several hours prior to working around it.*

9　On manually controlled models, remove the nut from the shift lever and remove the shift lever.

10　On manually controlled models, remove the large bolt and the small bolt retaining the shifter to the extension housing. Pull on the control lever unit until the bushing slides off the transfer case shift lever pin.

11　Place a transmission jack beneath the transfer case and apply

jack pressure to slightly raise the transfer case. Use safety chains to steady the transfer case on the jack.

12　Remove the five bolts securing the transfer case to the transmission extension housing **(see illustration)**.

8.12 The transfer case is secured by five bolts

EXTENSION HOUSING

TRANSFER CASE TO EXTENSION HOUSING GASKET

TRANSFER CASE

FRONT OF VEHICLE

TRANSFER CASE RETAINING BOLT

INSTALL HOSE WITH WHITE MARK AT THIS LOCATION

SKID SHIELD

FRAME SIDE RAIL

8.14a Transfer case to extension housing gasket location

13   Slide the transfer case rearward and off the transmission output shaft, then lower the transfer case from the vehicle. Remove and discard the gasket between the transfer case and the extension housing.

14   Installation is the reverse of the removal Steps with the following additions:

a) Install a new gasket between the transfer case and the extension housing (see illustration).

b) Slide the transfer case onto the transmission output shaft, making sure the splines align, until the transfer case seats over the dowel pin.

c) Install the five bolts securing the transfer case and tighten to the torque listed in this Chapter's Specifications and in the torque sequence shown (see illustration). Note: On manually controlled models, always tighten the large bolt securing the shifter to the extension housing before tightening the small bolt.

d) Install the vent assembly so the white marking on the hose is positioned in the notch in the shift lever bracket (manual shift) or mounting bracket (electronic shift). Note: The upper end of the vent hose should be 3/4 inch above the top of the shifter on manually controlled models.

CASE TO EXTENSION —
BOLT TORQUE SEQUENCE

8.14b Tighten the transfer case mounting bolts in the sequence shown.

e) Connect the rear driveshaft to the transfer case output flange. Tighten the bolts to the torque listed in the Chapter 8 Specifications.

f) Refill the transfer case with the proper type of lubricant (see Chapter 1).

7C

Notes

Chapter 8
Clutch and drivetrain

Contents

	Section
Axleshafts (rear), bearings and oil seals - removal and installation	19
Clutch hydraulic line quick-disconnect fittings - general information	7
Clutch pedal - removal and installation	11
Clutch components - removal, inspection and installation	3
Clutch hydraulic system - bleeding	10
Clutch release bearing - removal, inspection and installation	5
Clutch master cylinder and reservoir - removal and installation	9
Clutch - description and check	2
Clutch/starter interlock switch - removal and installation	12
Clutch release cylinder - removal and installation	8
Double cardan type U-joint - overhaul	16
Axleshafts (rear), bearings and oil seals - removal and installation	19
Clutch hydraulic line quick-disconnect fittings - general information	7
Clutch pedal - removal and installation	11
Clutch components - removal, inspection and installation	3
Clutch hydraulic system - bleeding	10

	Section
Clutch release bearing - removal, inspection and installation	5
Clutch master cylinder and reservoir - removal and installation	9
Clutch - description and check	2
Clutch/starter interlock switch - removal and installation	12
Clutch release cylinder - removal and installation	8
Double cardan type U-joint - overhaul	16
Driveshaft and universal joints - description and check	13
Driveshafts - removal and installation	14
Flywheel - inspection	4
Front axle assembly (4WD models) - removal and installation	20
Front axleshaft and joint assembly - removal, component replacement and installation	21
General information	1
Pilot bearing - inspection and replacement	6
Rear axle assembly - removal and installation	18
Rear axle - description and check	17
Right slip yoke and stub shaft assembly, carrier, carrier oil seals and bearings - removal and installation	22
Single cardan type U-joint - overhaul	15

Specifications

Clutch

Fluid type	See Chapter 1
Type	Single dry plate, diaphragm spring
Actuation	Hydraulic
Driveshaft type	One-piece with single or double cardan type joints

Rear axle

Type	Integral carrier
Ring gear size	8.8-inch
Lubricant type	See Chapter 1

Front axle

Type	Dana Model 35 IFS
Hubs	Automatic locking type
Lubricant type	See Chapter 1

Torque specifications   Ft-lbs

Clutch

Pressure plate-to-flywheel bolts	15 to 24
Clutch master cylinder-to-firewall bolts	15 to 20
Release cylinder-to-clutch housing bolts	13 to 19

Rear driveshaft

Driveshaft-to-transfer case bolts (4WD models only)	12 to 16
Driveshaft-to-rear axle bolts	
With double-cardan U-joint	70 to 95
With single-cardan U-joint	8 to 15

Front driveshaft

Driveshaft-to-transfer case flange bolts	70 to 95
Driveshaft-to-differential yoke bolts	10 to 15

Rear axle

Cover bolts	See Chapter 1
Pinion shaft lock-bolt	15 to 30
Leaf spring U-bolt nuts	See Chapter 10
Rear shock absorber-to-axle bracket bolt or nut	See Chapter 10
Brake backing plate nuts	See Chapter 9

Front axle

Pivot bolt	120 to 150
Pivot bracket-to-frame nut	70 to 92
Axle stud	190 to 230
Lower balljoint nut	95 to 110
Upper balljoint nut	85 to 100
Carrier to axle arm bolts	35 to 53
Carrier shear bolt	75 to 95
Front shock absorber-to-radius arm nut	See Chapter 10
Front spring seat nut	See Chapter 10
Front radius arm bracket bolts	See Chapter 10

1   General information

The information in this Chapter deals with the components that transmit power to the wheels, except for the transmission and transfer case, which are dealt with in Chapter 7. For the purposes of this Chapter, these components are grouped into three categories; clutch, driveshaft and axles. Separate Sections within this Chapter offer general descriptions and checking procedures for components in each of the three groups.

Since nearly all the procedures covered in this Chapter involve working under the vehicle, make sure it's securely supported on sturdy jackstands or on a hoist where the vehicle can be easily raised and lowered.

2   Clutch - description and check

Refer to illustration 2.5

1   All models with a manual transmission use a single dry plate, diaphragm spring type clutch. The clutch disc has a splined hub which allows it to slide along the splines of the transmission input shaft. The clutch and pressure plate are held in contact by spring pressure exerted by the diaphragm in the pressure plate.

2   The clutch release system is operated by hydraulic pressure. The hydraulic release system consists of the clutch pedal, a master cylinder and fluid reservoir, the hydraulic line, an internal release cylinder and the clutch release (or throwout) bearing.

3   The internal release cylinder, mounted concentrically on the transmission input shaft, pushes directly on the release bearing. This eliminates the need for a release lever.

4   Terminology can be a problem when discussing the clutch components because common names are in some cases different from those used by the manufacturer. For example, the driven plate is also called the clutch plate or disc, the clutch release bearing is sometimes called a throwout bearing, the release cylinder is sometimes called the operating or slave cylinder.

5   Other than to replace components with obvious damage, some preliminary checks should be performed to diagnose clutch problems.

a) *The first check should be of the fluid level in the clutch master cylinder. If the fluid level is low, add fluid as necessary and inspect the hydraulic system for leaks. If the master cylinder reservoir has run dry, bleed the system as described in Section 10 and retest the clutch operation.*

b) *To check "clutch spin down time," run the engine at normal idle speed with the transmission in Neutral (clutch pedal up - engaged). Disengage the clutch (pedal down), wait several seconds and shift the transmission into Reverse. No grinding noise should be heard. A grinding noise would most likely indicate a problem in the pressure plate or the clutch disc.*

c) *To check for complete clutch release, run the engine (with the parking brake applied to prevent movement) and hold the clutch pedal approximately 1/2-inch from the floor. Shift the transmission between 1st gear and Reverse several times. If the shift is hard or the transmission grinds, component failure is indicated. Check the release bearing travel* **(see illustration)**. *With the clutch pedal depressed completely, the release cylinder should extend substantially. If it doesn't, check the fluid level in the clutch master cylinder (see Chapter 1). Bleed the system (see Section 10).*

d) *Visually inspect the pivot bushing at the top of the clutch pedal to make sure there is no binding or excessive play.*

2.5 Release cylinder and bearing travel can be checked through the inspection port

3 Clutch components - removal, inspection and installation

Warning: *Dust produced by clutch wear and deposited on clutch components may contain asbestos, which is hazardous to your health. DO NOT blow it out with compressed air and DO NOT inhale it. DO NOT use gasoline or petroleum-based solvents to remove the dust. Brake system cleaner should be used to flush the dust into a drain pan. After the clutch components are wiped clean with a rag, dispose of the contaminated rags and cleaner in a covered, marked container.*

Removal
Refer to illustrations 3.3, 3.5a and 3.5b

1   Access to the clutch components is normally accomplished by removing the transmission (and transfer case on 4WD models), leaving the engine in the vehicle. If, of course, the engine is being removed for major overhaul, then check the clutch for wear and replace worn components as necessary. However, the relatively low cost of the clutch components compared to the time and trouble spent gaining access to them warrants their replacement anytime the engine or transmission is removed, unless they are new or in near perfect condition. The following procedures are based on the assumption the engine will stay in place.

2   Referring to Chapter 7 Part A and Part C, remove the transmission from the vehicle. Support the engine while the transmission is out. Preferably, an engine hoist should be used to support it from above. However, if a jack is used underneath the engine, make sure a piece of wood is positioned between the jack and oil pan to spread the load. **Caution:** *The pick-up for the oil pump is very close to the bottom of the oil pan. If the pan is bent or distorted in any way, engine oil starvation could occur.*

3   To support the clutch disc during removal, install a clutch alignment tool through the clutch disc hub **(see illustration)**.

4   Carefully inspect the flywheel and pressure plate for indexing marks. The marks are usually an X, an O or a white letter. If they cannot be found, scribe marks yourself so the pressure plate and the flywheel will be in the same alignment during installation.

5   Turning each bolt only 1/4-turn at a time, loosen the pressure plate-to-flywheel bolts **(see illustration)**. Work in a criss-cross pattern until all spring pressure is relieved evenly. Then hold the pressure plate securely and completely remove the bolts, followed by the pressure plate and clutch disc **(see illustration)**.

Inspection
Refer to illustrations 3.9 and 3.11

6   Ordinarily, when a problem occurs in the clutch, it can be attributed to wear of the clutch driven plate assembly (clutch disc).

3.3 A clutch alignment tool can be purchased at most auto parts stores and eliminates all guesswork when centering the clutch disc in the pressure plate

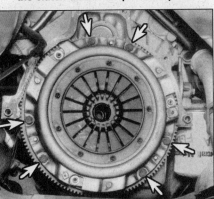

3.5a Loosen the pressure plate bolts (arrows) one turn at a time in rotation until they are free

3.5b An exploded view of the clutch assembly

8

3.9 The clutch disc
1   *Lining* - this will wear down in use
2   *Rivets* - these secure the lining and will damage the flywheel or pressure plate if allowed to contact the surfaces
3   *Marks* - "Flywheel side" or similar

However, all components should be inspected at this time.
7   Inspect the flywheel for cracks, heat checking, grooves and other obvious defects. If the imperfections are slight, a machine shop can machine the surface flat and smooth, which is highly recommended regardless of the surface appearance. Refer to Chapter 2 for the flywheel removal and installation procedure.
8   Inspect the pilot bearing (see Section 6).
9   Inspect the lining on the clutch disc. There should be at least 1/16-inch of lining above the rivet heads. Check for loose rivets, distortion, cracks, broken springs and other obvious damage **(see illustration)**. As mentioned above, ordinarily the clutch disc is routinely replaced, so if in doubt about the condition, replace it with a new one.
10   The release bearing should also be replaced along with the clutch disc (see Section 5).
11   Check the machined surfaces and the diaphragm spring fingers of the pressure plate **(see illustration)**. If the surface is grooved or otherwise damaged, replace the pressure plate. Also check for obvious damage, distortion, cracking, etc. Light glazing can be removed with medium grit emery cloth. If a new pressure plate is required, new and factory-rebuilt units are available.

Installation

12   Before installation, clean the flywheel and pressure plate machined surfaces with lacquer thinner or acetone. It's important that no oil or grease is on these surfaces or the lining of the clutch disc. Handle the parts only with clean hands.
13   Position the clutch disc and pressure plate against the flywheel with the clutch held in place with an alignment tool **(see illustration 3.3)**. Make sure it's installed properly (most replacement clutch plates will be marked "flywheel side" or something similar - if not marked, install the clutch disc with the flat side of the hub toward the flywheel).
14   Tighten the pressure plate-to-flywheel bolts only finger tight, working around the pressure plate.
15   Center the clutch disc by ensuring the alignment tool extends through the splined hub and into the pilot bearing in the crankshaft. Wiggle the tool up, down or side-to-side as needed to bottom the tool in the pilot bearing. Tighten the pressure plate-to-flywheel bolts a little at a time, working in a criss-cross pattern to prevent distorting the cover. After all of the bolts are snug, tighten them to the torque listed in this Chapter's Specifications. Remove the alignment tool.
16   If removed, install the clutch release bearing as described in Section 5.
17   Install the transmission and all components removed previously.

3.11 Replace the pressure plate if excessive or abnormal wear is noted

Tighten all fasteners to the torques listed in this Chapter's Specifications.

4   Flywheel - inspection

1   Inspect the flywheel when the vehicle suffers from excessive transmission gear wear, transmission jumping out of gear, driveline vibration, clutch pedal vibration, clutch slippage, pilot bearing noise or release bearing noise.
2   Visually inspect the flywheel for signs of cracking, warpage, scoring or heat checking. If any of these conditions exist, the flywheel must be removed and resurfaced at an automotive machine shop (see Chapter 2).

5   Clutch release bearing - removal, inspection and installation

Warning: *Dust produced by clutch wear and deposited on clutch components may contain asbestos, which is hazardous to your health. DO NOT blow it out with compressed air and DO NOT inhale it. DO NOT use gasoline or petroleum-based solvents to remove the dust. Brake system cleaner should be used to flush the dust into a drain pan. After the clutch components are wiped clean with a rag, dispose of the contaminated rags and cleaner in a covered, marked container.*

Removal and inspection

Refer to illustration 5.2
1   Remove the transmission (see Chapter 7 Part A).
2   Within the clutch housing, twist the release bearing and carrier assembly until you feel resistance. Keep turning the assembly and the preload spring will push the release bearing off the release cylinder **(see illustration)**.

5.2 Release bearing details

3   Hold the center of the bearing and rotate the outer portion while applying pressure. If the bearing doesn't turn smoothly or it's noisy, replace it with a new one. Wipe the bearing with a clean rag and inspect it for damage, wear and cracks. Don't immerse the bearing in solvent - it's sealed for life and to do so would ruin it.

Installation

4   Apply a light coat of high-temperature lithium based grease to the face of the release bearing, where it contacts the pressure plate diaphragm fingers.
5   Lubricate the inner bore of the bearing and bearing carrier with Ford Premium Long-life Grease (part No. XG-1-C) or equivalent. Don't use petroleum-based grease.
6   Push the release bearing and carrier onto the slave cylinder until it bottoms out **(see illustration 5.2)**.
7   Install the transmission (see Chapter 7 Part A).

6   Pilot bearing - inspection and replacement

Refer to illustrations 6.1 and 6.5
1   The clutch pilot bearing is a needle roller type bearing which is pressed into the rear of the crankshaft **(see illustration)**. It is greased at the factory and does not require additional lubrication. Its primary purpose is to support the front of the transmission input shaft. The pilot bearing should be inspected whenever the clutch components are removed from the engine. Due to its inaccessibility, if you are in doubt as to its condition, replace it with a new one. **Note:** *If the engine has been removed from the vehicle, disregard the following steps which do not apply.*
2   Remove the transmission (refer to Chapter 7 Part A).
3   Remove the clutch components (see Section 3).
4   Inspect for any excessive wear, scoring, lack of grease, dryness or obvious damage. If any of these conditions are noted, the bearing should be replaced. A flashlight will be helpful to direct light into the recess.
5   Removal can be accomplished with a special puller and slide hammer **(see illustration)**, but an alternative method also works.
6   Find a solid steel bar which is slightly smaller in diameter than the bearing. Alternatives to a solid bar would be a wood dowel or a socket with a bolt fixed in place to make it solid.
7   Check the bar for fit - it should just slip into the bearing with very little clearance.

6.1 The pilot bearing seal must face out when the bearing is installed in the crankshaft

6.5 One method of removing the pilot bearing requires an internal puller connected to a slide hammer

8

REMOVAL

DISCONNECT TOOL
T88T-70522-A

7.2 Quick-disconnect hydraulic line fitting

TRANSMISSION
BELL HOUSING

TRANSMISSION
INPUT SHAFT

HYDRAULIC
BLEED SCREW

HYDRAULIC
CLUTCH
LINE
COUPLING

FRONT
OF
VEHICLE

CONCENTRIC
SLAVE
CYLINDER

BOLT

8.4 Clutch release cylinder removal

8   Pack the bearing and the area behind it (in the crankshaft recess) with heavy grease. Pack it tightly to eliminate as much air as possible.
9   Insert the bar into the bearing bore and strike the bar sharply with a hammer which will force the grease to the back side of the bearing and push it out. Remove the bearing and clean all grease from the crankshaft recess.
10   To install the new bearing, lightly lubricate the outside surface with lithium-based grease, then drive it into the recess with a soft-face hammer. The seal must face out **(see illustration 6.1)**.
11   Install the clutch components, transmission and all other components removed previously, tightening all fasteners properly.

7   Clutch hydraulic line quick-disconnect fittings - general information

Refer to illustration 7.2
1   The hydraulic lines are equipped with quick-disconnect fittings and a special tool is required for separation (Ford part No. T88T-70552-A).
2   Depress the white retainer within the quick-disconnect fitting with the special tool while pulling on the hydraulic line, then disconnect the male
connector **(see illustration)**. To install, push the male connector into the female connector until it locks into place.
3   There should be no loss of hydraulic fluid during separation of the fittings so there is no need to bleed the system after a fitting has been disconnected unless shifting is hard or there's a lack of clutch reserve travel.

8   Clutch release cylinder - removal and installation

Refer to illustration 8.4
Note: *Prior to removing the release cylinder, disconnect the master cylinder pushrod from the clutch pedal. If not disconnected, permanent damage to the master cylinder will occur if the clutch pedal is depressed while the release cylinder is disconnected.*
1   Pry off the retainer bushing and disconnect the master cylinder

pushrod from the clutch pedal.
2   Disconnect the hydraulic quick-disconnect fitting from the slave cylinder (see Section 7).
3   Remove the transmission (see Chapter 7 Part A).
4   Remove the bolts securing the release cylinder to the transmission and slide the release cylinder assembly off the transmission input shaft **(see illustration)**.
5   Installation is the reverse of the removal Steps with the following additions:
a) *Install the release cylinder onto the input shaft with the hydraulic line facing toward the left side of the transmission.*
b) *Install the release cylinder mounting bolts and tighten them to the torque listed in this Chapter's Specifications.*
c) *If necessary, bleed the clutch hydraulic system (see Section 10).*

9   Clutch master cylinder and reservoir - removal and installation

Removal

Refer to illustration 9.5
1   Disconnect the negative cable from the battery.
2   Working inside the vehicle, remove the spring clip or retainer bushing and disconnect the pushrod from the top of the clutch pedal.
3   Remove the clutch/starter interlock switch from the pushrod (see Section 12).
4   Disconnect the hydraulic line from the slave cylinder (see Section 7).
5   Within the engine compartment, remove the bolts securing the master cylinder reservoir to the firewall **(see illustration)**. Be careful not to spill any of the fluid.
6   Working in the same area, remove the bolts securing the master cylinder to the firewall. Be careful not to spill any of the fluid.
7   Remove the master cylinder and reservoir from the engine compartment.

Installation

8   Install the master cylinder through the firewall and make sure the pushrod is positioned on the correct side of the clutch pedal so it can be installed onto the pedal's pivot pin.
9   Attach the master cylinder to the firewall and install the mounting bolts. Tighten the bolts to the torque listed in this Chapter's Specifications.

9.5 Clutch master cylinder layout

1)	Clutch pedal	3)	Reservoir bolt
2)	Master cylinder	4)	Clip

10   Attach the master cylinder reservoir to the firewall and install the mounting bolts, tightening them securely.
11   Connect the hydraulic line to the slave cylinder (see Section 7).
12   Working inside the vehicle, connect the pushrod to the clutch pedal and install the clip or retainer bushing.
13   Install the clutch/starter interlock switch (see Section 12).
14   Connect the negative cable to the battery.
15   Fill the clutch master cylinder reservoir with brake fluid conforming to DOT 3 specifications and bleed the clutch system (see Section 10).

10   Clutch hydraulic system - bleeding

Refer to illustration 10.5
1   The hydraulic system should be bled to remove all air whenever air enters the system. This occurs if the fluid level has been allowed to fall so low that air has been drawn into the master cylinder. Under normal circumstances, air should not enter the system when the quick-disconnect hydraulic line fittings are disconnected. The procedure is very similar to bleeding a brake system, but depends mainly on gravity, rather than the pumping action of the pedal, for the bleeding effect.
2   Fill the master cylinder to the top with new brake fluid conforming to DOT 3 specifications. **Caution:** *Do not re-use any of the fluid coming from the system during the bleeding operation and don't use fluid which has been inside an open container for an extended period of time.*
3   Raise the vehicle and place it securely on jackstands to gain access to the bleeder valve, which is located on the left side of the clutch housing.
4   Remove the dust cap which fits over the bleeder valve and push a length of clear plastic hose over the valve. Place the other end of the hose into a clear container.
5   Open the bleeder valve **(see illustration)**. Fluid will run from the master cylinder, down the hydraulic line, into the release cylinder and out through the clear plastic tube. Let the fluid run out until it is free of bubbles. **Note:** *Don't let the fluid level drop too low in the master cylinder, or air will be drawn into the hydraulic line and the whole*

10.5 The bleeder valve is accessible through a port on the left side of the clutch housing

11.5 An exploded view of the clutch pedal

process will have to be started over.
6   Close the bleeder valve.
7   Have an assistant slowly depress the clutch pedal and hold it. Open the bleeder valve on the release cylinder, allowing fluid to flow through the clear plastic hose. Close the bleeder valve when the flow stops. Once closed, have the assistant release the pedal.
8   Slowly press and release the pedal five times, waiting for two seconds each time the pedal is released.
9   Fill the fluid reservoir to the step.
10   The clutch should now be completely bled. If it isn't (indicated by failure to disengage completely), repeat Steps 5 through 9.
11   Continue this process until all air is evacuated from the system, indicated by a solid stream of fluid being ejected from the bleeder valve each time with no air bubbles in the hose or container.
12   Install the dust cap and lower the vehicle. Check carefully for proper operation before placing the vehicle in normal service. Check the fluid level.

11   Clutch pedal - removal and installation

Refer to illustration 11.5
1   Disconnect the negative cable from the battery.
2   Disconnect the barbed end of the clutch/starter interlock switch rod from the clutch pedal. Remove the lockpin and remove the master cylinder pushrod from the clutch pedal. Remove the plastic bushing.
3   Remove the plastic side panel on the driver's sidewall.
4   Unbolt the parking brake and move it aside.
5   Pry the retainer from the clip on the pedal support bracket **(see illustration)**.

8

12.2 Clutch/starter interlock switch

14.3 The rear driveshaft comes from the factory with yellow paint marks that indicate the correct alignment of the driveshaft with the companion flange

6   Slide the pedal out of the bracket.
7   Installation is the reverse of the removal Steps.

12   Clutch/starter interlock switch - removal and installation

Refer to illustration 12.2
1   Disconnect the negative cable from the battery.
2   Disconnect the electrical connector from the switch **(see illustration)**.
3   Rotate the switch so the plastic retainer is visible. Squeeze the retainer tabs together and slide the retainer rearward off the switch.
4   Detach the switch from the master cylinder pushrod and take it out.
5   Installation is the reverse of the removal Steps. Be sure the switch is securely seated on the master cylinder pushrod.

13   Driveshaft and universal joints - description and check

1   The driveshaft is a tube running between the transfer case or transmission and the rear axle or front axle. Universal joints are located at either end of the driveshaft(s) and permit power to be transmitted to the rear (and, on 4WD models the front) wheels at varying angles.
2   Some driveshafts feature a splined slip yoke at one end, which fits into the transmission extension housing. Others incorporate a slip yoke as part of the driveshaft. This arrangement allows the length of the driveshaft to change, which compensates for suspension movement.
3   On models with a slip yoke at the front of the driveshaft, an oil seal is used to prevent leakage of fluid and to keep dirt and contaminants from entering the transmission. If leakage is evident at the front of the driveshaft, replace the oil seal, referring to the procedures in Chapter 7.
4   The driveshaft assembly(ies) requires very little service. The universal joints on models not equipped with grease fittings are lubricated for life and must be replaced if problems develop. The driveshaft(s) must be removed from the vehicle for this procedure.
5   Since the driveshaft is a balanced unit, it's important that no undercoating, mud, etc. be allowed to stay on it. When the vehicle is raised for service it's a good idea to clean the driveshaft(s) and inspect it for any obvious damage. Also check that the small weights used to originally balance the driveshaft(s) are in place and securely attached. Whenever a driveshaft is removed it's important that it be reinstalled in the same relative position to preserve the balance.
6   Problems with the driveshaft(s) are usually indicated by a noise or vibration while driving the vehicle. A road test should verify if the problem is the driveshaft(s) or another vehicle component:

a)   *On an open road, free of traffic, drive the vehicle and note the engine speed (rpm) at which the problem is most evident.*
b)   *With this noted, drive the vehicle again, this time manually keeping the transmission in first, then second, then third gear ranges and running the engine up to the engine speed noted.*
c)   *If the noise or vibration decreased or was eliminated, visually inspect the driveshaft(s) for damage, material on the shaft which would effect balance, missing weights and damaged universal joints. Another possibility for this condition would be tires which are out-of-balance or a bent or damaged wheel(s).*
d)   *If the noise or vibration occurs at the same engine speed regardless of which gear the transmission is in, the driveshaft is not at fault.*

7   To check for worn universal joints:

a)   *On an open road, free of traffic, drive the vehicle slowly until the transmission is in High gear. Let off on the accelerator, allowing the vehicle to coast, then accelerate. A clunking or knocking noise will indicate worn universal joints.*
b)   *Drive the vehicle at a speed of about 10 to 15 mph and then place the transmission in Neutral, allowing the vehicle to coast. Listen for abnormal driveline noises.*
c)   *Raise the vehicle and support it securely on jackstands. With the transmission in Neutral, manually turn the driveshaft(s), watching the universal joints for excessive play.*

14   Driveshafts - removal and installation

Rear driveshaft

Refer to illustrations 14.3 and 14.4
1   Disconnect the negative cable from the battery.
2   Raise the vehicle and support it securely on jackstands. Place the transmission in Neutral with the parking brake off.
3   Look for the yellow paint marks made at the factory on the axle companion flange and the driveshaft flange **(see illustration)**. If these aren't visible, use a scribe, white paint or a hammer and punch to place marks on the driveshaft and the differential flange in line with

14.4 On 4WD models, make alignment marks on the driveshaft and transfer case flanges

each other. This is to make sure the driveshaft is reinstalled in the same position to preserve the balance.

4   On 4WD models, repeat Step 3 for the front end of the driveshaft **(see illustration)**.

5   Remove the bolts and lower the rear of the driveshaft. On 4WD models, remove the bolts and detach the front end from the transfer case. On 2WD models, slide the front end out of the transmission.

6   Installation is the reverse of the removal Steps with the following additions:

a) *On 2WD models, slide the front of the driveshaft into the transmission.*

b) *On 4WD models, position the front end of the driveshaft on the transfer case with the alignment marks lined up.*

c) *Raise the rear of the driveshaft into position, checking to be sure the marks are in alignment. If not, make sure the transmission is still in Neutral, then turn the rear wheels to match the pinion flange and the driveshaft.*

Front driveshaft (4WD models)

Refer to illustrations 14.9 and 14.10

7   Using a scribe, white paint or a hammer and punch, place marks on the driveshaft and differential flanges in line with each other **(see illustration 14.3)**. This is to make sure the driveshaft is reinstalled in the same position to preserve the balance.

8   Make alignment marks on the driveshaft and transfer case flanges.;

9   Unbolt the flange that secures the driveshaft double cardan joint to the transfer case **(see illustration)**.

10   Remove the bolts and straps that secure the front end of the driveshaft to the differential yoke **(see illustration)**.

11   Wrap tape around the universal joint bearings at the axle end of the driveshaft so they won't fall off.

12   Installation is the reverse of the removal Steps with the following additions:

a) *Raise the front of the driveshaft into position, checking to be sure the marks are in alignment. If not, make sure the transmission is still in Neutral, then turn the front wheels to line up the marks.*

b) *Remove the tape securing the bearing cups and install the straps and bolts. Tighten the bolts to the torque listed in this Chapter's Specifications.*

15   Single cardan type U-joint - overhaul

Refer to illustrations 15.2, 15.4a and 15.4b
Note: *A press or large vise will be required for this procedure. It may be*

14.9 Make alignment marks on the front driveshaft and transfer case flanges, then unbolt the driveshaft from the transfer case

14.10 Make alignment marks on the front driveshaft and differential yoke - wrap the universal joint with tape after unbolting it so the bearings won't fall off

a good idea to take the driveshaft to a repair or machine shop where the universal joints can be replaced for you, normally at a reasonable charge.

1   Remove the driveshaft (see Section 14).

2   Place the driveshaft in a sturdy vise and remove the snap-rings from the spider **(see illustration)**.

3   Supporting the driveshaft, place it in position on either an arbor press or on a workbench equipped with a vise.

15.2 Remove the universal joint snap-rings with small pliers

8

15.4a The universal joint bearing cups can be pressed out with a vise and sockets

15.4b The bearing cup can be extracted with locking pliers

4   Place a piece of pipe or a large socket with the same inside diameter over one of the bearing cups. Position a socket which is of slightly smaller diameter than the cup on the opposite bearing cup **(see illustration)** and use the vise or press to force the cup out (inside the pipe or large socket), stopping just before it comes completely out of the yoke. Use the vise or large pliers to work the cup the rest of the way out **(see illustration)**.

5   Transfer the sockets to the other side and press the opposite bearing cup out in the same manner.

6   After the bearings have been removed, lift the spider from the yoke and thoroughly clean all dirt and debris from the yokes on both ends of the driveshaft.

7   Pack the new universal joint bearings with grease. Ordinarily, specific instructions for lubrication will be included with the universal joint servicing kit and should be followed carefully.

8   Position the spider in the yoke and partially install one bearing cup in the yoke.

9   Start the spider into the bearing cup and then partially install the other cup. Align the spider and press the bearing cups into position, being careful not to damage the dust seals.

10   Install the snap-rings. If difficulty is encountered in seating the snap-rings, strike the driveshaft yoke sharply with a hammer. This will spring the yoke ears slightly and allow the snap-rings to seat in the groove. This should also be done if the joint feels tight after assembly.

11   Install the driveshaft (see Section 14).

16   Double cardan type U-joint - overhaul

Note: *A press or large vise will be required for this procedure. It may be a good idea to take the driveshaft to a repair or machine shop where the universal joints can be replaced for you, normally at a reasonable charge.*

1   Remove the driveshaft (see Section 14).

2   Use paint or small punch and hammer and mark the positions of the spiders, the center yoke and the centering socket as related to the stud yoke which is welded to the front of the driveshaft tube. The spiders must be assembled with the bosses in their original position to provide proper clearance.

3   Use a small screwdriver and pry out the snap-rings that attach the bearings in the front of the center yoke.

4   Supporting the driveshaft, place it in position on either an arbor press or on a workbench equipped with a vise.

5   Place a piece of pipe or a large socket with the same inside diameter over one of the bearing cups. Position a socket which is of slightly smaller diameter than the cup on the opposite bearing cup and use the vise or press to force the cup out (inside the pipe or large socket), stopping just before it comes completely out of the yoke **(see illustration 15.4a)**. Use the vise or large pliers to work the cup the rest

of the way out **(see illustration 15.4b)**.

6   Transfer the sockets to the other side and press the opposite bearing cup out in the same manner.

7   Repeat Steps 6 and 7 and remove all bearings from the universal joints.

8   With the front bearing cups removed, remove the spider from the center yoke.

9   Pull the centering socket yoke off the center stud and remove the rubber seal from the centering ball stud.

10   Remove the snap-rings from the center yoke and from the driveshaft yoke.

11   Press or drive the bearing out as previously described.

12   With the bearing cups removed, remove the center yoke from the spider.

13   Remove the spider from the driveshaft yoke.

14   After the bearings have been removed, lift the spider from the yoke and thoroughly clean all dirt and debris from the yokes on both ends of the driveshaft. If using a repair kit, install all of the parts supplied.

15   Pack the new universal joint bearings with grease. Ordinarily, specific instructions for lubrication will be included with the universal joint servicing kit and should be followed carefully.

16   Remove the clamps on the driveshaft dust boot seal and discard the clamps.

17   Note the orientation of the slip yoke to the driveshaft tube for installation during assembly. Mark the relationship of the slip yoke to the driveshaft tube.

18   Carefully pull the slip joint from the driveshaft, be careful not to damage the boot seal.

19   Inspect the spline area and thoroughly clean all foreign matter from the splines with solvent.

20   Lubricate the splines with multi-purpose grease.

21   Install the dust boot seal loosely on the driveshaft tube, then install the yoke into the driveshaft in its original position. Refer to marks made prior to removal.

22   Install new clamps on the dust boot seal and tighten securely.

23   To assemble the double cardan joints, position the spider in the driveshaft yoke. Make sure the spider bosses (or lubricating plugs) are in their original positions.

24   Start the spider into the bearing cup and then partially install the other cup. Align the spider and press the bearing cups into position, being careful not to damage the dust seals.

25   Install new snap-rings. If difficulty is encountered in seating the snap-rings, strike the driveshaft yoke sharply with a hammer. This will spring the yoke ears slightly and allow the snap-rings to seat in the groove.

26   Repeat Step 25 and 26 for the remaining bearings.

27   Pack the socket relief and the ball with multi-purpose grease, then position the center yoke over the spider ends and press in the

bearing.
28   Install new snap-rings.
29   Install a new seal on the centering ball stud and position the centering socket yoke on the stud.
30   Place the front spider in the center yoke and make sure the spider bosses (or lubricating plugs) are in their original positions.
31   Start the spider into the bearing cup and then partially install the other cup. Align the spider and press the bearing cups into position, being careful not to damage the dust seals.
32   Install new snap-rings. If difficulty is encountered in seating the snap-rings, strike the driveshaft yoke sharply with a hammer. This will spring the yoke ears slightly and allow the snap-rings to seat in the groove. This should also be done if the joint feels tight after assembly.

33   If so equipped, lubricate the U-joints through the grease fittings with multi-purpose grease.
34   Install the driveshaft (see Section 14).

17   Rear axle - description and check

Refer to illustration 17.1

Description

1   The rear axle assembly is a hypoid (the centerline of the pinion gear is below the centerline of the ring gear) semi-floating type **(see illustration)**. The differential carrier is a casting with a pressed steel

17.1 An exploded view of a typical rear axle assembly

18.6a Remove the nuts that secure the brake backing plate to the axle housing . . .

18.6b . . . then carefully separate the backing plate from the axle housing and support it with wire - don't bend the brake line or allow the backing plate to hang on the line

cover. The axle tubes are made of steel, pressed and welded into the carrier.

2   An optional Traction-Lok limited slip rear axle is also available. This differential allows for normal operation until one wheel loses traction. The unit utilizes multi-disc clutch packs and a speed sensitive engagement mechanism which locks both axleshafts together, applying equal rotational power to both wheels.

3   In order to undertake certain operations, particularly replacement of the axleshafts, it's important to know the axle identification number. It's located on a small metal tag near one of the cover bolts.

4   Many times a problem is suspected in the rear axle area when, in fact, it lies elsewhere. For this reason, a thorough check should be performed before assuming a rear axle problem.

5   The following noises are those commonly associated with rear axle diagnosis procedures:

a) *Road noise is often mistaken for mechanical faults. Driving the vehicle on different surfaces will show whether the road surface is the cause of the noise. Road noise will remain the same if the vehicle is under power or coasting.*

b) *Tire noise is sometimes mistaken for mechanical problems. Tires which are worn or low on air pressure are particularly susceptible to emitting vibrations and noises. Tire noise will remain about the same during varying driving situations, where rear axle noise will change during coasting, acceleration, etc.*

c) *Engine and transmission noise can be deceiving because it will travel along the driveline. To isolate engine and transmission noises, make a note of the engine speed at which the noise is most pronounced. Stop the vehicle and place the transmission in Neutral and run the engine to the same speed. If the noise is the same, the rear axle is not at fault.*

6   Overhaul and general repair of the rear axle is beyond the scope of the home mechanic due to the many special tools and critical measurements required. Thus, the procedures listed here will involve axleshaft removal and installation, axleshaft oil seal replacement, axleshaft bearing replacement and removal of the entire unit for repair or replacement.

18   Rear axle assembly - removal and installation

Refer to illustrations 18.6a, 18.6b, 18.7, 18.8, 18.9, 18.10a, 18.10b, 18.11 and 18.13

1   Loosen the lug nuts on the rear wheels.

2   Raise the rear of the vehicle, support it securely on jackstands and remove the rear wheels.

18.7   The vent hose is secured to the axle by a crimp-type clamp - you'll need to replace it with a screw-type clamp

3   Remove the axleshafts (see Section 19).

4   Unbolt the brake line junction block from the axle housing and detach the brake lines from the clips on the axle housing. Disconnect the rear anti-lock electrical connector from the sensor on the axle housing (see Chapter 9).

5   Remove the rear brake drums (see Chapter 9).

6   Remove the nuts and bolts that secure the brake backing plate to the axle **(see illustration)**. Separate the backing plates from the axle and tie them up out of the way **(see illustration)**.

7   Detach the vent hose from the axle housing **(see illustration)**.

8   Place a transmission jack beneath the axle housing. Secure the axle housing to the jack with a safety strap or chain **(see illustration)**. **Note:** *You'll need to tilt the axle housing on the jack to remove it. Secure the axle so it can't fall off the jack, but position the strap or chain so the axle can be tilted.*

9   Remove the U-bolt nuts that secure the shock mounting bracket to the axle **(see illustration)**. Don't detach the shock absorber from the bracket.

10   Lower the bracket away from the spring, then remove the U-bolts **(see illustrations)**.

11   Unbolt the stabilizer bar bracket bolts from the axle housing **(see illustration)**. Move the stabilizer bar out of the way.

12   Jack the axle up off the spring. Move it toward the passenger side of the vehicle until the driver's side end of the axle shaft clears the spring.

18.8 Place the axle housing on a transmission jack and secure it firmly - the axle housing is heavy and can cause injury if it falls

18.9 Remove the four nuts that secure the shock mounting bracket to the axle - don't remove the lower shock absorber bolt

18.10a Pull the bracket down off the U-bolts

18.10b then remove the U-bolts from the axle housing and spring

13   Tilt the driver's side of the axle housing down **(see illustration)**. Lower the axle, move it toward the driver's side and remove it from beneath the vehicle.

14   Installation is the reverse of the removal Steps. Be sure to tighten the fasteners to the torque values listed in this Chapter's Specifications. Tighten the wheel lug nuts to the torque listed in the Chapter 1 Specifications.

18.11 Unbolt the stabilizer bar retainer from the axle housing

18.13 Tilt the axle housing a shown to clear the spring, then lower the jack and take it out from under the vehicle

8

19.6a The pinion shaft lock-bolt fits in a recess in the differential housing

19.6b Remove the bolt with a thinwall socket . . .

19.6c . . . then pull the pinion shaft out - on Traction-Lok models, the spacer spring (arrow) need not be removed

19.7a Remove the C-lock from the end of each axleshaft - the differential lubricant is very slippery and makes the C-locks hard to hold with pliers, so be careful not to drop them

19.7b There's a rubber O-ring in the C-lock groove in the end of each axleshaft

19.8 Lift and pull the axleshaft out of the axle housing - be careful not to damage the oil seal

19 Axleshafts (rear), bearings and oil seals - removal and installation

Refer to illustrations 19.6a, 19.6b, 19.6c, 19.7a, 19.7b, 19.8, 19.9 and 19.11

Axleshaft removal

1   Loosen the lug nuts on the rear wheels.
2   Raise the rear of the vehicle, support it securely on jackstands and remove the rear wheels.
3   Remove the rear brake drums (see Chapter 9).
4   Clean all dirt from the area surrounding the carrier cover.
5   Drain the differential lubricant (see Chapter 1).
6   Remove the differential shaft lock-bolt and differential pinion shaft **(see illustrations)**. On Traction-Lok differentials, it isn't necessary to remove the preload spring **(see illustration)**. **Note:** *The pinion gears may be left in place. Once the axleshafts are removed, reinstall the pinion shaft and lock-bolt.*
7   Push the axleshafts toward the center of the vehicle and remove the C-locks from the button end of the axleshafts **(see illustration)**. Don't lose or damage the rubber O-ring which fits in the axle shaft groove under the C-lock **(see illustration)**.
8   Carefully remove the axleshafts from the housing **(see illustration)**. Don't damage the oil seal at the end of the housing.

19.9 Remove the wheel bearing and seal with a puller - the Ford special tool is shown here, but similar pullers can be rented

19.11 The wheel bearing and seal can be installed with a large socket or piece of pipe of the correct diameter if the special tool isn't available

19.14 The O-ring in the C-lock groove goes toward the wheel end of the axleshaft

19.15 Align the lock-bolt hole in the pinion lock shaft with the hole in the differential housing

Oil seal and bearing replacement

9   Insert a rear axle bearing remover, Ford part No. T77F-1102-A and slide hammer, Ford part No. T50T-0100-A or equivalent axle bearing remover with a slide hammer, into the bore of the bearing and position it behind the bearing outer race. Using the slide hammer withdraw the bearing and oil seal as a unit **(see illustration)**.
10   Thoroughly clean the rear axle housing bore with a rag and solvent.
11   Lubricate the new bearing with rear axle lubricant and install the bearing into the housing bore. Use an axle tube bearing driver tool, Ford part No. T78P-1225-A, or large socket that matches the outer bearing race **(see illustration)**. Tap the bearing in until it's into the full depth of its recess. **Caution:** *Do not tap on the inner bearing race while installing the bearing, as it will be damaged.*
12   Apply multi-purpose grease between the lips of the axleshaft seal.
13   Install a new axleshaft seal using the axle tube seal installation tool, Ford part No. Y4T78P-1177-A, or a large socket that matches the seal diameter. **Caution:** *If the seal is installed incorrectly or gets cocked during installation it will be damaged, leading to component failure and an oil leak.*

Axleshaft installation
Refer to illustrations 19.14 and 19.15
14   Make sure the rubber O-ring is in the groove in the end of the

axleshaft. Push the O-ring toward the outer end of the groove (toward the wheel) **(see illustration)**. Carefully insert the axle into the housing and install the C-lock on the button end of the axleshaft splines. Be sure the O-ring is in the axleshaft groove **(see illustration 19.7b)**. Push the shaft out until the C-lock seats in the counterbore of the differential side gear.
15   Position the differential pinion shaft through the case and pinion gears, aligning the hole in the shaft with the lock-bolt hole **(see illustration)**. Apply thread locking compound to the lock-bolt, install the bolt and tighten it to the torque listed in this Chapter's Specifications.
16   Clean the gasket mounting surface on the rear axle housing and cover of all old gasket material residue with lacquer thinner or gasket remover. Apply a continuous bead of silicone sealant, Ford part No. D6AZ-19562-B, or equivalent. Run the bead to the inside of the bolt holes and install the cover and bolts.
17   Tighten the bolts in a criss-cross pattern to the torque listed in this Chapter's Specifications.
18   Refill the axle with the correct quantity and grade of lubricant (see Chapter 1).
19   Install the brake drums (see Chapter 9).
20   Install the wheels and lug nuts.
21   Lower the vehicle and tighten the lug nuts to the value listed in the Chapter 1 Specifications.

20   Front axle assembly (4WD models) - removal and installation

1991 through 1994 models
Refer to illustration 20.7
1   Raise the front of the vehicle and install jackstands under the radius arm brackets.
2   Disconnect the driveshaft from the front axle yoke (see Section 14).
3   Remove the front brake calipers (see Chapter 9). **Caution:** *Tie the calipers up with wire to keep any strain off the flexible brake lines.*
4   Detach the tie-rod ends from the steering linkage (see Chapter 10).
5   Remove the stabilizer bar and its connecting links (see Chapter 10).
6   Position a floor jack under the axle arm and slightly compress the front coil spring. Remove the nut securing the lower portion of the spring to the axle beam.
7   Carefully lower the jack and remove the coil spring, spacer, seat and stud **(see illustration)**. **Caution:** *The axle arm assembly must be*

20.7 The front axle assembly (1991 through 1994 4WD models) - exploded view

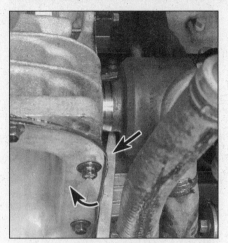

20.21 Use a large screwdriver or prybar (arrow) to carefully pry the CV joint out

20.22 A two jaw puller can be used to push the driveaxle from the hub - do not hammer on the axle

20.23 After the driveaxle has been pushed out of the hub, pull out on the strut/knuckle assembly and free the stub shaft from the hub

and stud **(see illustration)**. **Caution:** *The axle arm assembly must be supported on the jack throughout spring removal and installation. Do not let the arm assembly hang suspended by the brake hose.*

8   Detach the shock absorber from the radius arm bracket.

9   Detach the radius arm and bracket from the axle arm and remove them from the vehicle.

10   Remove the pivot bolt securing the right axle arm assembly to the frame crossmember. Remove the clamps securing the axleshaft boot to the axleshaft slip yoke and axleshaft. Slide the rubber boot over the stub shaft.

11   Once the right driveaxle is disconnected from the slip yoke, lower the floor jack and remove the right axle arm assembly.

12   Position the jack under the differential housing and remove the bolt securing the left axle arm to the frame crossmember. Lower and remove the left axle arm assembly.

13   Installation is the reverse of the removal procedure with the following addition.

14   Tighten all fasteners to the torque listed in this Chapter's Specifications and related Chapters.

1995 models

Refer to illustrations 20.21, 20.22 and 20.23

15   Loosen the wheel lug nuts, raise the vehicle and support it securely on jackstands. Remove the wheel(s).

16   Remove the caliper and brake disc as outlined in Chapter 9.

17   Remove the hub driveaxle/nut. Place a prybar between two of the wheel studs to prevent the hub from turning while loosening the nut. **Warning:** *Discard the wheel hub nut and washer assembly and replace it with a new part. This nut is designed for a single torque sequence and cannot be re-used.*

18   Remove the brake hose support bracket-to-strut bolt.

19   Support the lower control arm with a floor jack, remove the lower control arm balljoint nut and separate the control arm from the steering knuckle (see Chapter 10). **Warning:** *The jack must remain in this position throughout the entire procedure.*

20   Remove the stabilizer bar (see Chapter 10).

21   Using a large screwdriver or prybar, pry the inner CV joint assembly from the front differential **(see illustration)**. Be careful not to damage the front differential. Suspend the axle with a piece of wire - don't let it hang, or damage to the outer CV joint may occur.

22   Push the driveaxle out of the hub with a two-jaw puller **(see illustration)**. **Caution:** *Never use a hammer to remove the driveaxle from the hub or damage to the end of the driveaxle will occur.*

23   Once the driveaxle is loose from the hub splines, pull out on the strut/knuckle assembly and guide the outer CV joint out of the hub. Remove the support wire and carefully detach the driveaxle from the vehicle **(see illustration)**.

20.25 The inner CV joint stub shaft is completely seated when the circlip on the shaft snaps into the groove in the differential side gear

Installation (both driveaxles)

Refer to illustration 20.25

Note: *If both driveaxles were removed, install one at a time, removing the wooden dowel from each side only when the driveaxle is ready for insertion into the transaxle.*

24   Install a **new** circlip on the inner stub shaft splines.

25   Coat the differential seal lips with multi-purpose grease and insert the stub shaft into the differential side gear until the shaft is seated and the circlip snaps into place **(see illustration)**.

26   Pull out on the strut/knuckle assembly and insert the outer CV joint stub shaft into the hub (make sure the splines are aligned). Push the shaft as far into the hub as possible by hand.

27   Support the outer CV joint housing and carefully tap on the hub, using a soft-faced hammer, until enough threads on the stub shaft are exposed to thread the *old* driveaxle/hub nut on. **Caution:** *Don't allow any force to be transmitted to the inner portion of the CV joint.*

28   Tighten the nut until the stub shaft is pulled completely into the hub, then remove the nut and discard it.

29   Install the driveaxle/hub washer and a **new** nut. Tighten the nut to the torque listed in this Chapter's Specifications while preventing the hub from turning by placing a screwdriver between two wheel studs.

30   Insert the balljoint stud into the steering knuckle. Install a **new** nut and tighten it to the torque listed in the Chapter 10 Specifications.

31   Install the stabilizer bar (see Chapter 10).

32   Install the brake disc and caliper (see Chapter 9).

8

21.4 An exploded view of the 4WD front axle (1991 through 1994 models)

33   Install the brake hose support bracket bolt.

34   Install the wheel and lug nuts and lower the vehicle. Tighten the lug nuts to the torque listed in the Chapter 1 Specifications.

35   Check the front differential lubricant level and add, if necessary (see Chapter 1).

21   Front axleshaft and joint assembly - removal, component replacement and installation

1991 through 1994 models

Removal

Refer to illustrations 21.4, 21.5a, 21.5b, 21.6, 21.7a, 21.7b and 21.8

1   Loosen the lug nuts on the front wheels.

2   Raise the front of the vehicle, support it securely on jackstands and remove the front wheels.

3   Remove the front brake calipers (see Chapter 9). Hang the calipers out of the way with pieces of wire. Don't disconnect the brake hoses.

4   Remove the locking hubs, wheel bearings and locknuts **(see illustration)**. Refer to Chapter 1, Section 28, for the hub/brake disc/ wheel bearing removal procedure.

5   Remove the nuts securing the spindle to the steering knuckle. Tap the spindle with a plastic or soft faced hammer to jar it free, then remove it **(see illustrations)**.

6   Remove the spindle seat **(see illustration)**.

7   On the left side of the vehicle, pull the shaft and joint assembly out of the carrier **(see illustration)**. If necessary, tap the slinger off the shaft with a hammer **(see illustration)**. **Note:** *Don't remove the slinger unless necessary. You'll need a press to install it.*

8   Working on the right side, remove the metal clamps from the shaft and joint assembly and the stub shaft. Slide the rubber boot onto the stub shaft and pull the shaft and joint assembly from the splines of the stub shaft **(see illustration)**.

21.5a Remove the spindle securing nuts . . .

21.5b . . . then tap the spindle loose with a soft face hammer and remove it

21.6 Take the spindle seat off

21.7a Take out the left shaft and joint assembly

21.7b If necessary, tap the slinger off with a hammer - a press is needed to reinstall it

21.8 The right shaft and joint assembly - exploded view

Spindle bearing and oil seal replacement

Refer to illustrations 21.12 and 21.13

9   Place the spindle in a padded vise so the vise grips the spindle's second step.

10   Remove the bearing and oil seal with a slide hammer and puller attachment.

11   Clean all dirt and grease from the spindle bore. Make sure there are no nicks or burrs in the bearing bore.

12   Install the new bearing in the bore with the manufacturer's mark out. Install the bearing with Ford spindle bearing replacer T80T-4000-S and driver handle T80T-4000-W or equivalent **(see illustration)**.

21.12 Drive the spindle bearing out with a bearing driver

8

21.13 Drive in a new seal with its lip toward the driver

21.14a Mark the shaft and yoke with paint so they can be reassembled in the same relative positions

13   Use the same tools to install the seal **(see illustration)**. The lip of the seal faces the installer. After installation, coat the lip of the seal with high- temperature lubricant (Ford part no. E8TZ-19590-A/specification no. ESA-M1C198-A or equivalent).

Shaft and joint assembly universal joint replacement

Refer to illustrations 21.14a, 21.14b and 21.15

14   Remove the internal snap-rings from the U-joint with a screwdriver **(see illustration)**.

15   The remainder of the procedure is the same as for driveshaft universal joints, which is described in Section 15 **(see illustration)**.

Installation

16   If the slinger was removed from the spindle, have it pressed on by a machine shop.

17   On the right side of the carrier, install the rubber boot and new metal clamps on the stub shaft slip yoke. There is no blind spline to ensure correct alignment, so pay special attention to the yoke ears and make sure they are in phase. Be sure the assembly is fully seated and crimp the metal clamp.

18   On the left side of the carrier, slide the shaft and joint assembly through the knuckle and engage the splines on the shaft in the carrier.

19   Install the splash shield. Install the spindle on the steering knuckle, then install and tighten the spindle nuts to the torque listed in Chapter 10.

20   Install the front wheel bearings and locking hubs (see Chapter 1).

21   Install the brake caliper (see Chapter 9).

22   Install the front wheels and lower the vehicle.

23   Tighten the lug nuts to the torque listed in Chapter 1.

1995 driveaxle boot replacement and CV joint overhaul

Tripod type

Disassembly

Refer to illustrations 21.24, 21.28, 21.29, 21.30 and 21.31

24   1995 models are equipped with Constant Velocity (CV) joint type driveaxle assemblies **(see illustration)**. The inboard tripod design CV joint and driveaxle boot are serviceable units. The outer CV joint is not serviceable and must be replaced as an assembly. However, the outer driveaxle boot is serviceable with a similar procedure as the inner boot.

25   Remove the driveaxle from the vehicle (see Section 20).

26   Mount the driveaxle in a vise. The jaws of the vise should be lined with wood or rags to prevent damage to the axleshaft.

27   Cut the boot clamps from the boot and discard them.

28   Bend the retaining tabs slightly to allow for tripod removal **(see illustration)**.

29   Remove tripod assembly from outer race **(see illustration)**.

30   Move the inner (exposed) stop ring down the shaft about 1/2-inch **(see illustration)**.

21.14b Push the snap-rings out of the joint with a screwdriver

21.15 Position sockets in a vise to push the bearings out of the joint - the small socket is smaller than the bearing; the large socket is large enough so the bearing will fit into it

Front Wheel Halfshaft and Joint Assemblies

FRONT OF VEHICLE

FRONT WHEEL
HALFSHAFT
AND JOINT

FRONT WHEEL
HALFSHAFT
AND JOINT

FRONT WHEEL
HUB AND SPINDLE

NUT AND
WASHER
ASSEMBLY

**21.24 1995 driveaxle
assembly - exploded view**

1   Nut and washer
     assembly
2   Front wheel hub
3   Excluder seal
4   Driveaxle and outer
     joint assembly
5   Boot clamp
6   Boot
7   Boot clamp
8   Driveshaft
9   Stop ring
10   Circlip
11   Spider assembly
12   Tri-lobe insert
13   Housing
14   Inner CV joint
15   Boot clamp
16   Inner CV joint
17   Circlip
18   Housing
19   Front wheel hub

Front Wheel Halfshaft and Joint Assembly, GKN Design

RIGHT HAND

LEFT HAND

**21.28 Bend the retaining tabs to allow
Tri-pod removal**

TABS

21.29 Removing the Tri-pod assembly

OUTER
RACE

TRIPOD
ASSY

**21.30 Move the stop ring down the
axle shaft**

TRIPOD
ASSY

8

21.31 Remove the circlip and pull off the Tri-pod assembly

21.38a Installing the Tri-pod snap ring

31   Move the tripod down the shaft towards the inner snap-ring until the circlip is visible on the end of the driveaxle. Remove the circlip and remove the tripod assembly off the driveaxle **(see illustration).**

32   No further disassembly of the tripod is possible. Inspect the tripod rollers, roller bearings and races carefully for damage, worn spots and smooth operation. Damaged or worn tripods cannot be rebuilt and must be replaced.

33   Remove the inner stop ring completely and remove the old boot.

Reassembly

Refer to illustrations 21.38a, 21.38b and 21.40

34   Slide new clamp and inner CV joint boot on the axleshaft.

35   Install a new inner stop ring past the second ring groove about 1/2-inch.

36   Install the tripod assembly on the driveaxle with the chamfered side inward.

37   On the four-cylinder engine right side axle, install a new snap-ring onto driveaxle end to secure tripod assembly.

38   Push the tripod assembly down the axle far enough to allow circlip installation. Install the new circlip and push the tripod assembly towards the axle end until the tripod seats on the circlip and the inner stop ring groove is exposed. Next, move the inner stop ring to its groove to secure the tripod assembly **(see illustrations).**

39   On all axles, fill the outer race with CV joint grease and spread some on the inside of the boot as well **(see illustration).** The left axle tripods use about 6.5 ounces of grease and the right axles use about 7 ounces. Push the tripod assembly into outer race and bend the six retaining tabs back to their original shape.

40   Wipe any excess grease from the axle boot groove on the outer race. Seat the small diameter of the boot in the recessed area on the axleshaft and install the clamp. Push the other end of the boot onto the outer race and move the race in-or-out to adjust the axle to the proper length.

41   With the axle set to the proper length, equalize the pressure in the

21.38b Push the Tri-pod assembly toward the axle end and then install the stop ring

boot by inserting a dull screwdriver between the boot and the outer race. Don't damage the boot with the tool.

42   Install the boot clamp. A pair of special clamp-crimping pliers are required.

43   Install a new clip on the stub axle.

44   Install the driveaxle as described in Section 20.

Outer CV joint and boot

Note: *The outer CV joint is a non-serviceable item and is permanently retained to the driveaxle. If any damage or excessive wear occurs to the axle or the outer CV joint, the entire driveaxle assembly must be replaced (excluding the inner CV joint). Service to the outer CV joints is limited to boot replacement and grease repacking only. To replace the outer boot the inner joint must first be removed.*

RIGHT-HAND DRIVEAXLE
438.3MM (17.3 IN)

LEFT-HAND DRIVEAXLE
508.3MM (20.0 IN)

21.40 Driveaxle assembly length specifications

22.7 Push the C-clip off the shaft with a pair of screwdrivers

22 Right slip yoke and stub shaft assembly, carrier, carrier oil seals and bearings - removal and installation

Removal

Refer to illustrations 22.7, 22.9a, 22.9b, 22.10, 22.11, 22.12 and 22.14

1   Loosen the lug nuts on the front wheels.
2   Raise the front of the vehicle, support it securely on jackstands and remove the front wheels.
3   Detach the front driveshaft from the axle yoke (see Section 14). Tie the driveshaft up out of the way.
4   Remove the spindles and the left and right shaft and joint assemblies (see Section 19).
5   Place a transmission jack under the carrier and unbolt the carrier from the left axle arm. Separate the carrier from the arm, let the lubricant drain and remove the carrier.
6   Place the carrier in a vise or on a workbench.
7   Turn the shaft assembly so the open side of the C-clip is exposed, then push the C-clip off with a pair of screwdrivers **(see illustration)**.
8   Pull the slip yoke and shaft assembly out of the carrier.
9   Remove the oil seals with a slide hammer and puller **(see illustrations)**.
10   Remove the caged needle bearings with a slide hammer and puller attachment **(see illustration)**.

22.9a Remove the passenger side oil seal with a slide hammer and a puller that hooks to the inside of the seal

22.9b Remove the driver's side oil seal with a slide hammer and a puller that hooks to the outside of the seal

Installation

11   Clean and inspect the bearing bore for nicks and burrs before installing a new caged bearing. Position the bearing with the manufacturer's marks facing out, then drive the bearing in until it is fully seated in the bore **(see illustration)**.

8

22.10 Remove both caged needle bearings with a slide hammer and puller

22.11 Drive in the bearings with the manufacturer's marking facing toward the driver tool (out)

22.12 After the bearings are installed, drive in the seals

22.14 Push the C-clip into the groove with a screwdriver - don't push on the center section of the C-clip or it may be damaged.

12   Coat the oil seal with high-temperature lubricant (Ford part no. E8TZ-19590-A/specification no. ESA-M1C198-A or equivalent) and drive it into the carrier housing (see illustration).
13   Install the slip yoke and shaft assembly into the carrier so the C-clip groove in the shaft is visible.
14   Push the C-clip into the groove with a screwdriver (see illustration). Make sure it is completely seated in the groove. Caution: Don't push on the center of the C-clip with the screwdriver, as it may be damaged.
15   Clean all traces of gasket sealant from the mating surfaces with lacquer thinner or gasket remover. Apply RTV sealant in an unbroken 1/4-inch wide bead, inboard of the bolt holes.

16   Position the carrier on the transmission jack and install it in position on the support arm. Use the guide pins for alignment. Install and tighten the bolts in a clockwise or counterclockwise pattern to the torque listed in this Chapter's Specifications.
17   Install the shear bolt securing the carrier to the axle arm and tighten to the torque listed in this Chapter's Specifications.
18   Install the shaft and joint assemblies and spindles.
19   Connect the driveshaft to the yoke (see Section 14).
20   Fill the carrier with lubricant (see Chapter 1).
21   Install the front wheels and lower the vehicle.
22   Tighten the lug nuts to the torque listed in Chapter 1.

Chapter 9
Brakes

Contents

	Section
Anti-lock Brake System (ABS) - general information	2
Brake caliper - removal, overhaul and installation	4
Brake disc - inspection, removal and installation	5
Brake fluid level check	See Chapter 1
Brake hoses and lines - inspection and replacement	9
Brake hydraulic system - bleeding	10
Brake light switch - removal and installation	15
Brake pads - replacement	3
Brake shoes (rear) - replacement	6
Brake system check	See Chapter 1

	Section
General information	1
Master cylinder - removal, overhaul and installation	8
Parking brake - adjustment	11
Parking brake cables - replacement	12
Parking brake shoes (rear disc brakes only) - inspection and replacement	13
Power brake booster - check, removal, installation and adjustment	14
Wheel cylinder - removal, overhaul and installation	7

Specifications

Brake fluid type .... See Chapter 1

Drum brakes
Drum wear limit .... Specified on drum
Minimum lining thickness .... 1/16 inch above rivet heads

Disc brakes
Minimum pad lining thickness .... 1/8 inch
Front brake disc
  Standard thickness .... 0.870 inch
  Minimum thickness* .... 0.810 inch
  Runout limit .... 0.010 inch
  Thickness variation (parallelism) .... 0.00035 inch
Rear brake disc
  Standard thickness .... 0.472 inch
  Minimum thickness* .... 0.409 inch
  Runout limit .... 0.003 inch
  Thickness variation (parallelism) .... 0.0005 inch

*Refer to marks stamped on the disc (they supersede information printed here)

9

Torque specifications

	Ft-lbs (unless otherwise indicated)
Backing plate-to-axle housing nuts..	25 to 35
Brake booster-to-firewall nuts..	13 to 25
Brake hose -to-caliper banjo bolt..	29
Caliper mounting bolts (pins)	
Front	38 to 48
Rear	20
Caliper mounting bracket-to-spindle bolts...	73 to 97
Caliper adapter-to-axle flange nuts..	40
Master cylinder-to-brake booster nut...	13 to 25
RABS valve mounting screw	11 to 14
RABS sensor mounting bolt	25 to 30
Rear caliper bolts...	18 to 21

1   General information

Refer to illustration 1.3

General description

All models covered by this manual are equipped with hydraulically operated, power-assisted brake systems. All front brake systems are disc type, while the rear brakes are either disc or drum type. Some models are equipped with an Anti-lock Brake System (ABS), which is described in Section 2.

All brakes are self-adjusting. The front and rear disc brakes automatically compensate for pad wear, while the rear drum brakes incorporate an adjustment mechanism which is activated as the brakes are applied.

The hydraulic system is a split design, meaning there are separate circuits for the front and rear brakes **(see illustration)**. If one circuit fails, the other circuit will remain functional and a warning indicator will light up on the dashboard, showing that a failure has occurred.

Master cylinder

The master cylinder is located under the hood, mounted to the power brake booster, and is best recognized by the large fluid reservoir on top. The removable plastic reservoir is partitioned to prevent total fluid loss in the event of a front or rear brake hydraulic system failure.

The master cylinder is designed for the "split system" mentioned earlier and has separate primary and secondary piston assemblies, the piston nearest the firewall being the primary piston, which applies hydraulic pressure to the front brakes.

Power brake booster

The power brake booster, utilizing engine manifold vacuum and atmospheric pressure to provide assistance to the hydraulically operated brakes, is mounted on the firewall in the engine compartment.

Parking brake

The parking brake mechanically operates the rear brakes only.

On drum brake models the parking brake cables pull on a lever attached to the brake shoe assembly, causing the shoes to expand against the drum. On models with rear disc brakes, the cables operate small parking brake shoes inside the brake disc hub.

Precautions

There are some general cautions and warnings involving the brake system on this vehicle:

a) *Use only brake fluid conforming to DOT 3 specifications.*

b) *The brake pads and linings may contain asbestos fibers which are hazardous to your health if inhaled. Whenever you work on brake system components, clean all parts with brake system cleaner. Do not allow the fine dust to become airborne. Also, wear an approved filtering mask*

1.3 Typical dual master cylinder brake system (non-ABS models)

c) *Safety should be paramount whenever any servicing of the brake components is performed. Do not use parts or fasteners which are not in perfect condition, and be sure that all clearances and torque specifications are adhered to. If you are at all unsure about a certain procedure, seek professional advice. Upon completion of any brake system work, test the brakes carefully in a controlled area before putting the vehicle into normal service.*

If a problem is suspected in the brake system, don't drive the vehicle until it's fixed.

2   Anti-lock Brake System (ABS) - general information

1   Some models are equipped with an Anti-lock Brake System (ABS). Early models are equipped with rear wheel anti-lock brake systems while later models are equipped with 4-wheel anti-lock brake systems. The ABS system is designed to maintain vehicle steerability, directional stability and optimum deceleration under severe braking conditions and on most road surfaces. It does so by monitoring the rotational speed of each wheel and controlling the brake line pressure to each wheel during braking. This prevents the wheel from locking-up and provides maximum vehicle controllability.

Rear wheel Anti-lock Brake System (RABS)

Refer to illustrations 2.2 and 2.4

2   A Rear Anti-lock Brake System (RABS) is used on early models. The system consists of a computer module, anti-lock brake valve, an exciter ring and a sensor **(see illustration)**.

3   Disconnect the cable from the negative battery terminal.

YELLOW REAR ANTI-LOCK
WARNING LAMP

RED BRAKE
WARNING LAMP

VIEW X

VIEW W

REAR ANTI-LOCK BRAKES — EXPLORER

FRONT OF
VEHICLE

SPEED
SENSOR

EXCITOR
RING

SPEED
SENSOR

DIFFERENTIAL
HOUSING

VIEW W

**DIODE/RESISTOR ELEMENT AND SENSOR TEST
CONNECTION**

SENSOR TEST
CONNECTOR

FRONT OF VEHICLE

DIODE/RESISTOR ELEMENT
RABS SELF TEST
CONNECTOR

VIEW X

9

2.2 Rear Anti-lock Brake System (RABS) component layout

2.4 The RABS module is located under the instrument panel; the electro-hydraulic valve is located in the driver's side frame rail near the front of the vehicle

RABS module

4   Working under the instrument panel, press on the plastic tab on the electrical connector and disconnect it from the RABS module **(see illustration)**.

5   Remove the screws securing the RABS module to the instrument panel bracket and remove it.

6   Installation is the reverse of the removal Steps.

RABS valve

7   Disconnect the two brake lines from the RABS valve **(see illustration 2.4)**. Plug the ends of the lines to prevent the loss of hydraulic fluid and the entry of foreign matter and moisture.

8   Disconnect the electrical connector from the RABS valve.

9   Remove the screw securing the RABS valve to the frame rail and take it out.

10 To install, position the RABS valve on the frame rail. Install the screw and tighten it to the torque listed in this Chapter's Specifications.

11 Connect the electrical connector to the valve.

12 Install the brake lines and tighten to the torque listed in this Chapter's Specifications. **Caution:** *Do not overtighten the fittings.*

13 Bleed the hydraulic system.

Speed sensor

Refer to illustration 2.16

14 Disconnect the electrical connector from the sensor located on the rear axle housing.

15 Prior to removing the sensor, thoroughly clean the rear axle housing surrounding the sensor.

16 Remove the bolt securing the sensor and remove it from the rear axle housing **(see illustration)**. Do not allow any dirt to fall into the interior of the rear axle housing.

2.16 The rear wheel speed sensor mounts on the rear axle housing

17 Thoroughly clean the sensor mounting surface on the rear axle housing.

18 Inspect and clean the magnetized sensor pole piece. Remove any small metal particles that could cause erratic system operation.

19 If installing a new sensor, lightly lubricate the O-ring seal with clean engine oil.

2.25 Hydraulic control unit details on 1995 and later models

1	Primary brake tube	*7*	Front brake tube
2	Secondary brake tube		(left side)
3	Pump motor	*8*	Rear brake tube
4	Solenoid control wiring	*9*	Inner fender panel
5	Pump motor wiring		(left side)
6	Front brake tube		
	(right side)		

20   If installing an old sensor, remove the old O-ring seal, install a new one and lubricate it with clean engine oil.

21   Firmly grasp the sides of the sensor (do not apply pressure to the electrical connector) and push it into the mounting hole.

22   Align the mounting flange bolt hole with that on the rear axle housing and install the hold-down bolt. Tighten the bolt to the torque listed in this Chapter's Specifications.

23   Connect the electrical connector to the sensor.

Excitor ring

24   To service the excitor ring the rear axle must be disassembled and the ring gear removed with a press. It is recommended that this procedure be performed by a dealer service department or other repair shop.

Four wheel Anti-lock Brake System

Hydraulic control unit (HCU)

Refer to illustration 2.25

25   The hydraulic control unit is located in the left (driver's side) front corner of the engine compartment. It consists of a brake pressure control valve block, a pump motor and a hydraulic control unit reservoir with a fluid level indicator assembly **(see illustration)**.

26   During normal braking conditions, brake hydraulic fluid from the master cylinder enters the hydraulic control unit through two inlet ports and passes through four normally open inlet valves, one to each wheel.

27   When the anti-lock brake control module senses that a wheel is about to lock up, the anti-lock brake control module closes the appropriate inlet. This prevents any more fluid from entering the affected brake. If the module determines that the wheel is still decelerating, the module opens the outlet valve, which bleeds off pressure in the affected brake.

Wheel sensors

Refer to illustration 2.29

28   The ABS system uses four "variable-reluctance" sensors to monitor wheel speed ("reluctance" is a term used to indicate the amount of resistance to the passage of flux lines - lines of force in a

2.29 ABS front wheel sensor (arrow)

2.30 ABS control module

magnetic field - through a given material). Each sensor contains a small inductive coil that generates an electromagnetic field. When paired with a toothed sensor ring which interrupts this field as the wheels turn, each sensor generates a low-voltage analog (continuous) signal. This voltage signal, which rises and falls in proportion to wheel rotation speed, is continuously sampled (monitored) by the control module, converted into digital data inside the module and processed (interpreted).

29   On 2WD models, the front wheel sensors **(see illustration)** are mounted in the steering knuckle in close proximity to the toothed sensor rings, which are pressed onto the wheel hubs. On 4WD models, the front wheel sensors are an integral part of the front wheel bearings and are not serviceable separately. The rear wheel sensor is mounted in the rear axle housing and the sensor ring is mounted along with the ring gear in the rear axle.

Brake control module

Refer to illustration 2.30

30   The brake control module **(see illustration)**, which is mounted in the front left fenderwell behind the plastic inner liner, is the "brain" of the ABS system. The module (referred to as an Electronic Control Unit or ECU) constantly monitors the incoming analog voltage signals from the four ABS wheel sensors, converts these signals to digital form, processes this digital data by comparing it to the map (program), makes decisions, converts these (digital) decisions to analog form and sends them to the hydraulic control unit, which opens and closes the front and/or rear circuits as necessary.

9

3.3 An exploded view of the front brake caliper components - typical

31   The module also has a self-diagnostic capability which operates during both normal driving as well as ABS system operation. If a malfunction occurs, a red "BRAKE" warning indicator or an amber "CHECK ANTI-LOCK BRAKES" warning indicator will light up on the dash.

a) *If the red BRAKE light glows, the brake fluid level in the master cylinder reservoir has fallen below the level established by the fluid level switch. Top up the reservoir and verify that the light goes out.*

b) *If the amber CHECK ANTI-LOCK BRAKES light glows, the ABS has been turned off because of a symptom detected by the module. Normal power-assisted braking is still operational, but the wheels can now lock up if you're involved in a panic-stop situation. A diagnostic code is also stored in the module when a warning indicator light comes on; when retrieved by a service technician, the code indicates the area or component where the problem is located. Once the problem is fixed, the code is cleared. These procedures, however, are beyond the scope of the home mechanic.*

Relays

32   The main relay and pump motor relay are located in a relay box along with three other relays mounted near the battery on the left side of the engine compartment. Refer to Chapter 12 for the locations and designations for the relays.

Diagnosis and repair

Warning: *If a dashboard warning light comes on and stays on while the vehicle is in operation, the ABS system requires immediate attention!*

33   Although a special electronic ABS diagnostic tester is necessary to properly diagnose the system, the home mechanic can perform a few preliminary checks before taking the vehicle to a dealer who is equipped with this tester.

a) *Check the brake fluid level in the reservoir.*
b) *Verify that the control module electrical connector is securely connected.*
c) *Check the electrical connectors at the hydraulic control unit.*
d) *Check the fuses.*
e) *Follow the wiring harness to each wheel and check that all connections are secure and that the wiring is not damaged.*

If the above preliminary checks do not rectify the problem, the vehicle should be diagnosed by a dealer service department or other qualified repair shop. Due to the rather complex nature of this system,

all actual repair work must be done by the dealer service department or repair shop.

3   Brake pads - replacement

Refer to illustrations 3.3, 3.6a through 3.6l and 3.6m through 3.6r

Warning 1: *Disc brake pads must be replaced on both front wheels or both rear wheels at the same time - never replace the pads on only one wheel. Also, the dust created by the brake system may contain asbestos, which is harmful to your health. Never blow it out with compressed air and don't inhale any of it. An approved filtering mask should be worn when working on the brakes. Do not, under any circumstances, use petroleum-based solvents to clean brake parts. Use brake system cleaner only!*

Warning 2: *1995 and later models use a special lubricating gel on certain parts of the brake caliper. This gel is non-toxic under most conditions. If it is heated to a certain point, however, it can give off toxic fumes which can cause health problems or even death. Never apply heat to these calipers and don't smoke around them, either (the gel might get on your cigarette). Always wash your hands thoroughly after working on the brakes.*

1   Remove the cover from the brake fluid reservoir and siphon out about 1/2 of the brake fluid.

2   Loosen the wheel lug nuts, raise the vehicle and support it securely on jackstands.

3   Remove the wheels. Work on one brake assembly at a time, using the assembled brake for reference if necessary **(see illustration)**.

4   Inspect the brake disc carefully as outlined in Section 5.

5   If machining is necessary, follow the information in that Section to remove the disc, at which time the pads can be removed from the caliper as well.

6   Follow the accompanying photos, beginning with illustration 3.6a, for the front brake pad replacement procedure. Be sure to stay in order and read the caption under each illustration. If you're replacing the rear brake pads, follow the photos beginning with illustration 3.6m.

7   When reinstalling the caliper on 1995 and later models, be sure to tighten the caliper bolts to the torque listed in this Chapter's Specifications.

8   After the job has been completed, firmly depress the brake pedal a few times to bring the pads into contact with the disc.

9   Check the brake fluid level and add some, if necessary, to bring it to the appropriate level (see Chapter 1).

3.6a Use a large C-clamp and push the piston back into the bore just enough to allow the caliper to slide off the brake disc easily - note the one end of the C-clamp is on the flat area of the inner side of the caliper and the other end (screw end) is pressing on the outer pad

3.6b On 1994 and earlier models, use pliers and squeeze the caliper retaining pin while prying the other end until the tabs on the pin enter the spindle groove . . .

3.6c . . . then drive out the pin with a punch and hammer

3.6d On 1995 and later models, remove the two caliper mounting bolts. Note: *Don't wipe the lubricating gel from these pins or the pin boots. At the time of publication there was no substitute for this gel (also read the* Warning *at the beginning of Section 3)*

3.6e If the caliper isn't going to be removed for service, suspend it with a length of wire to relieve any strain on the brake hose

3.6f This spring clip (arrow) holds the outside brake pad to the caliper on 1994 and earlier models - push down on the pad, releasing the locking tabs and slide the pad out of the caliper, then remove the inner pad and the anti-rattle clips. On 1995 and later models, detach the pads from the caliper mount.

3.6g Prior to installing the caliper, lightly lubricate the V-grooves where the caliper slides into the anchor plate with disc brake caliper slide rail grease (1994 and earlier models)

9

3.6h Make sure the tabs on the spring clip are positioned correctly and the clip is fully seated

3.6i Insert a new anti-rattle clip on the lower end of the inner pad

3.6j Compress the anti-rattle clip and slide the upper end of the pad into position

3.6k On 1994 and earlier models, push the outer pad into position on the caliper ears, making sure the torque buttons on the pad seat fully in the retention notches (arrows)

3.6l Place the caliper and outer pad assembly over the disc and inner pad, then drive the caliper pins into their grooves or, on 1995 and later models, install the mounting bolts and tighten them to the torque listed in this Chapter's Specifications

3.6m Remove the two rear caliper bolts (upper and lower arrows) with a Torx Drive bit - DO NOT remove the brake hose banjo bolt (middle arrow) unless you are planning to overhaul the caliper

3.6n Depress the caliper piston by squeezing the old pad with a pair of large water pump pliers

3.6o Pry off the old outer brake pad with a screwdriver

3.6p Remove the old inner brake pad by pulling the retaining clips out of the piston

3.6q To install the new inner brake pad, place it in position like this, then push it all the way in until the retaining clips are fully seated

3.6r To install the new outer brake pad, slide it down like this until the locating pins (arrow) are fully engaged with the holes in the caliper housing; then install the caliper and pads over the disc, install the caliper bolts and tighten them to the torque listed in this Chapter's Specifications

4 Brake caliper - removal, overhaul and installation

Warning 1: *Dust created by the brake system may contain asbestos, which is harmful to your health. Never blow it out with compressed air and don't inhale any of it. An approved filtering mask should be worn when working on the brakes. Do not, under any circumstances, use petroleum-based solvents to clean brake parts. Use brake system cleaner only!*

Warning 2: *1995 and later models use a special lubricating gel on certain parts of the brake caliper. This gel is non-toxic under most conditions. If it is heated to a certain point, however, it can give off toxic fumes which can cause health problems or even death. Never apply heat to these calipers and don't smoke around them, either (the gel might get on your cigarette). Always wash your hands thoroughly after working on the brakes.*

Warning 3: *If the vehicle is equipped with ABS, make sure you plug the brake hose immediately after disconnecting it from the brake caliper, to prevent the fluid from draining out of the line and air entering the Hydraulic Control Unit (HCU). The HCU on an ABS system cannot be bled without a very expensive tool.*

Note: *If an overhaul is indicated (usually because of fluid leakage) explore all options before beginning the job. New and factory-rebuilt calipers are available on an exchange basis, which makes this job quite easy. If it is decided to rebuild the calipers, make sure that a rebuild kit is available before proceeding. Always rebuild the calipers in pairs- never rebuild just one of them.*

Removal

1 Apply the parking brake and block the wheels opposite the end being worked on. Loosen the wheel lug nuts, raise the vehicle and support it securely on jackstands. Remove the wheel.
2 Unscrew the brake hose banjo bolt and detach the hose from the caliper. **Caution:** *On ABS-equipped models, plug the brake hose immediately to prevent air from getting into the hydraulic control unit (HCU). If air gets into the HCU, you will not be able to bleed the brakes properly at home. On non-ABS models, wrap a plastic bag around the end of the hose to prevent fluid loss and contamination.* **Note:** *If the caliper will not be completely removed from the vehicle - as for pad inspection or disc removal - leave the hose connected and suspend the caliper with a length of wire. This will save the trouble of bleeding the brake system.*

3 Refer to the first six steps in Section 3 to separate the caliper from the steering knuckle (front) or the torque plate (rear) - it's part of the brake pad replacement procedure.

Overhaul

Refer to illustrations 4.5, 4.6, 4.7, 4.17, 4.18, 4.19a, 4.19b, 4.20 and 4.21

4 Clean the exterior of the caliper with brake system cleaner. Never use gasoline, kerosene or other petroleum-based cleaning solvents. Place the caliper on a clean workbench.
5 Position a wood block or rags in the center of the caliper as a cushion, then use compressed air to remove the piston from the caliper. **Note:** *1995 and later models have two pistons. Use only enough air to ease the piston out of the bore. If the piston is blown out, even with the cushion in place, it may be damaged.* **Warning:** *Never place your fingers in front of the piston in an attempt to catch or protect it when applying compressed air, as serious injury could occur.*

4.5 With the caliper padded to catch the piston, use compressed air to force the piston out of its bore - make sure your hands and fingers are not between the piston and the caliper!

9

4.6 Remove the dust boot from the caliper bore groove

4.7 To remove the seal from the caliper bore, use a plastic or wooden tool, such as a pencil

4.17 Push the new seal into the groove with your fingers, then check to see that it isn't twisted or kinked

6   Pull the dust boot(s) out of the caliper bore **(see illustration)**. Refer to illustration 3.3 for additional views.

7   Using a wood or plastic tool, remove the piston seal(s) from the caliper bore **(see illustration)**. Metal tools may cause bore damage.

8   Carefully examine the piston for nicks, burrs, cracks, loss of plating, corrosion or any signs of damage. If surface defects are present, the parts must be replaced.

9   Check the caliper bore in a similar way. Light polishing with crocus cloth is permissible to remove light corrosion and stains.

10   Remove the bleeder valve and rubber cap.

11   On 1995 and later models, inspect the caliper pins (bolts) for corrosion and damage. Don't wipe the lubricating gel from the pins or pin boots. At the time of publication there was no suitable substitute for this gel.

12   If the pins (bolts) are in need of addition lubrication, Ford recommends replacing them along with the boots, which come pre-filled with the special lubricating gel. Petroleum or mineral-based greases can destroy the caliper pin boot.

13   Use brake system cleaner to clean all the parts. **Warning:** *Do not, under any circumstances, use petroleum-based solvents to clean brake parts. Allow the parts to dry, preferably using compressed air to blow out all passages. Make sure the compressed air is filtered, as a harmful lubricant residue or moisture may be present in unfiltered systems.*

14   Examine carefully the bore of the caliper. Replace the caliper if the bore is excessively pitted, damaged or scored.

15   Check the fit of the piston in the bore by sliding it into the caliper.

4.18 Install the dust boot in the upper groove in the caliper bore, making sure it's completely seated

The piston should move easily (don't install it yet).

16   Thread the bleeder valve into the caliper and tighten it securely. Install the rubber cap.

17   Lubricate the new piston seal(s) and caliper bore(s) with clean brake fluid. Position the seal in the caliper bore groove, making sure it doesn't twist **(see illustration)**.

4.19a Lubricate the piston and bore with clean brake fluid, insert the piston into the dust boot (NOT the bore) at an angle, then, using a rotating motion, work the piston completely into the dust boot . . .

4.19b . . . and push it straight into the caliper as far as possible by hand

4.20 Use a C-clamp and a block of wood to bottom the piston in the caliper bore - make sure it goes in perfectly straight, or the sides of the piston may be damaged, rendering it useless

4.21 Install the lip of the dust boot in the groove on the caliper piston

5.5a To check disc runout, mount a dial indicator as shown and rotate the disc

5.5b Using a swirling motion, remove the glaze from the disc with sandpaper or emery cloth

1994 and earlier models

18 Fit the new dust boot in the caliper bore upper groove, making sure it's seated **(see illustration)**.
19 Lubricate the caliper piston with clean brake fluid. Push the piston into the caliper, using a turning motion to roll the lip of the dust boot over the piston **(see illustrations)**. Push the piston into the caliper by hand as far as possible.
20 Using a C-clamp and a block of wood, push the piston all the way to the bottom of the bore. Work slowly, keeping an eye on the side of the piston, making sure it enters the bore perfectly straight with no resistance **(see illustration)**.
21 Seat the lip of the dust boot in the groove on the piston **(see illustration)**.

1995 and later models

22 Lubricate the caliper pistons with clean brake fluid. Push the pistons into the caliper bores by hand as far as possible.
23 Using a C-clamp and a block of wood, push the pistons about two-thirds of the way into the bores. Work slowly, keeping an eye on the side of the pistons, making sure they enter the bore perfectly straight with no resistance.
24 Install the dust boots on the pistons and seat the boots in the caliper. Now push the pistons to the bottom of the bores.

Installation

25 Refer to Section 3 for the caliper installation procedure, as it is part of the brake pad replacement procedure.
26 Connect the brake hose to the caliper, using new sealing washers. Tighten the banjo bolt to the torque listed in this Chapter's Specifications.
27 Bleed the brakes as outlined in Section 10. This is not necessary if the banjo bolt was not loosened or removed (if the caliper was removed for access to other components, for example).
28 Install the wheel and lower the vehicle. Tighten the lug nuts to the torque listed in the Chapter 1 Specifications. Pump the brake pedal several times to bring the pads into contact with the disc.
29 Test the operation of the brakes before placing the vehicle into normal service.

5 Brake disc - inspection, removal and installation

Inspection

Refer to illustrations 5.5a, 5.5b, 5.6a and 5.6b
Note: *This procedure applies to front and rear disc brake assemblies.*
1 Loosen the wheel lug nuts, raise the vehicle and support it securely on jackstands. Remove the wheel.

2 Remove the brake caliper as outlined in Section 4. It's not necessary to disconnect the brake hose for this procedure. After removing the caliper bolts, suspend the caliper out of the way with a piece of wire. Don't let the caliper hang by the hose and don't stretch or twist the hose.
3 If you're working on a 1995 or later 4WD model, reinstall three lug nuts (inverted) to hold the disc against the hub. It may be necessary to install washers between the disc and the lug nuts to take up space.
4 Visually check the disc surface for score marks and other damage. Light scratches and shallow grooves are normal after use and may not always be detrimental to brake operation, but deep score marks - over 0.015-inch - require disc removal and refinishing by an automotive machine shop. Be sure to check both sides of the disc. If pulsating has been noticed during application of the brakes, suspect disc runout.
5 To check disc runout, place a dial indicator at a point about 1/2-inch from the outer edge of the disc **(see illustration)**. Set the indicator to zero and turn the disc. The indicator reading should not exceed the specified allowable runout limit. If it does, the disc should be refinished by an automotive machine shop. **Note:** *Professionals recommend resurfacing of brake discs regardless of the dial indicator reading (to produce a smooth, flat surface that will eliminate brake pedal pulsations and other undesirable symptoms related to questionable discs). At the very least, if you elect not to have the discs resurfaced, deglaze the surface with emery cloth or sandpaper (use a swirling motion to ensure a non-directional finish)* **(see illustration)**.
6 The disc must not be machined to a thickness less than the specified minimum refinish thickness. The minimum wear (or discard) thickness is cast into the inside of the disc **(see illustration)**. The disc thickness can be checked with a micrometer **(see illustration)**.

5.6a The minimum thickness limit is cast into the inside of the disc

9

Removal

Refer to illustration 5.7

7   If you're working on a 2WD model, refer to Chapter 1, *Front wheel bearing check, repack and adjustment* for the disc removal procedure. If you're working on a 1994 or earlier 4WD model refer to Chapter 1, *Front hub lock, spindle bearing and wheel bearing maintenance.* If you're working on a 1995 or later 4WD model, simply slide the rotor off of the hub assembly.

5.6b Use a micrometer to measure disc thickness at several points, about 1/2-inch from the edge

Installation

8   Install the disc by reversing the removal procedure.

9   Install the caliper and brake pad assembly over the disc and position it on the steering knuckle (front), or on the torque plate (rear) (see Section 4). Install the caliper bolts and tighten them to the torque listed in this Chapter's Specifications.

10   Install the wheel, then lower the vehicle to the ground. Depress the brake pedal a few times to bring the brake pads into contact with the rotor. Bleeding of the system will not be necessary unless the brake hose was disconnected from the caliper. Check the operation of the brakes carefully before placing the vehicle into normal service.

6   Brake shoes (rear) - replacement

Refer to illustrations 6.4a through 6.4y and 6.5

Warning: *Drum brake shoes must be replaced on both wheels at the same time - never replace the shoes on only one wheel. Also, the dust created by the brake system may contain asbestos, which is harmful to your health. Never blow it out with compressed air and don't inhale any of it. An approved filtering mask should be worn when working on the brakes. Do not, under any circumstances, use petroleum-based solvents to clean brake parts. Use brake system cleaner only!*

Caution: *Whenever the brake shoes are replaced, the retractor and hold-down springs should also be replaced. Due to the continuous heating/cooling cycle that the springs are subjected to, they lose their tension over a period of time and may allow the shoes to drag on the drum and wear at a much faster rate than normal.*

1   Loosen the wheel lug nuts, raise the rear of the vehicle and

5.7 Exploded view of the spindle and hub assembly (1995 and later models)

1	Anti-lock Brake sensor	6	Wheel bearing	12	Nut lock
2	Spindle	7	Brake disc	13	Grease cap
3	Shield	8	Wheel bearing	14	Brake caliper
4	Bolt	9	Washer	15	Caliper mount
5	Grease seal	10	Nut	16	Mount-to-spindle bolts
		11	Cotter pin		

FRONT OF VEHICLE — ANCHOR PIN PLATE — ANCHOR PIN — BRAKE CYLINDER — RETRACTING SPRING — SECONDARY SHOE AND LINING — PARKING BRAKE LINK — RETRACTING SPRING — CABLE GUIDE — PARKING BRAKE LINK SPRING — BRAKE SHOE HOLD DOWN SPRING — SELF-ADJUSTER CABLE — PARKING BRAKE LEVER — PRIMARY SHOE AND LINING — ADJUSTER LEVER SPRING — SOCKET — PIVOT NUT — PIVOT HOOK — ADJUSTING LEVER — PARKING BRAKE CABLE — ADJUSTING SCREW

6.4a Components of the rear brake assembly (left side shown)

6.4b If the drum is difficult to remove, you may have to retract the brake shoes: Remove the rubber plug from the backing plate, insert a screwdriver through the hole, raise the adjusting lever off the star wheel and rotate the star adjuster with a brake adjustment tool or another screwdriver as shown

support it securely on jackstands. Block the front wheels to keep the vehicle from rolling.

2   Release the parking brake.

3   Remove the wheel. **Note:** *All four rear brake shoes must be replaced at the same time, but to avoid mixing up parts, work on only one brake assembly at a time.*

4   Follow the accompanying photos **(illustrations 6.4a through 6.4y)** for the inspection and replacement of the brake shoes. Be sure to stay in order and read the caption under each illustration. **Note:** *If the brake drum cannot be easily pulled off, pry the rubber plug from the backing plate inspection hole and insert a screwdriver and a brake adjusting tool to lift the adjusting lever and rotate the adjusting screw. This will cause the brake shoes to pull together. Spray the assembly with penetrating oil and allow the oil to soak in if the mechanism is difficult to turn. The drum should now come off.*

STANDARD DESIGN DRUM BRAKE — ADJUSTING LEVER — PLUG REMOVED — MOVE HANDLE DOWNWARD TO EXPAND BRAKE SHOES — MOVE HANDLE UPWARD TO RETRACT BRAKE SHOES

6.4c Use a narrow bladed screwdriver to push the adjusting lever away from the adjusting screw star wheel so you can turn the star wheel down with a brake tool (turn the tool handle up) to retract the shoes . . .

6.4d . . . and slide the drum off the shoes

6.4e Use a spring removal tool to remove the shoe retracting springs

6.4f Pull up on the adjusting cable and disconnect the cable eye from the anchor pin

9

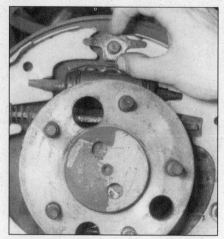

6.4g Remove the anchor pin plate

6.4h Remove the shoe retaining springs and pins (one on each shoe)

6.4i Pull the shoes apart and remove the adjusting screw

6.4j Remove the primary shoe, then slide out the parking brake strut and spring

6.4k Remove the adjuster pawl

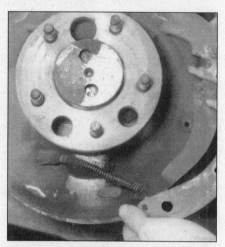

6.4l Pull the secondary shoe away from the backing plate

5   Before reinstalling the drum it should be checked for cracks, score marks, deep scratches and hard spots, which will appear as small discolored areas. If the hard spots cannot be removed with fine emery cloth or if any of the other conditions listed above exist, the drum must be taken to an automotive machine shop to have it turned. **Note:** *Professionals recommend resurfacing the drums whenever a brake job is performed. Resurfacing will eliminate the possibility of out-of-round drums. If the drums are worn so much that they can't be*

6.4m Separate the parking brake cable and spring from the actuating lever

6.4n Remove the retaining clip which holds the parking brake actuating lever to the brake shoes

6.4o Install the parking brake actuator lever on the new brake shoe and install the retaining clip

6.4p Lubricate the threads and end of the adjusting screw assembly with high-temperature brake grease

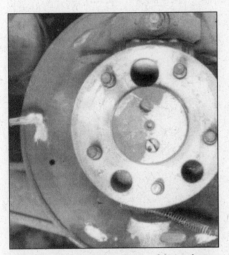

6.4q Lightly coat the shoe guide pads on the backing plate with high-temperature brake grease

6.4r Position the shoes on the backing plate, insert the retaining pins through the backing plate and shoes and put the springs over them

6.4s Install the retaining spring caps

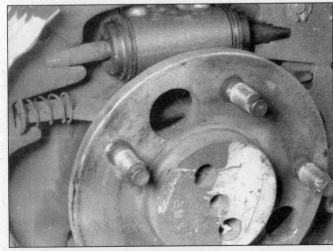

6.4t Make sure the slots in the wheel cylinder pushrods and the parking brake strut properly engage the brake shoes

6.4u Install the adjusting screw with the long end pointing towards the front of the vehicle

9

6.4v Install the adjusting pawl

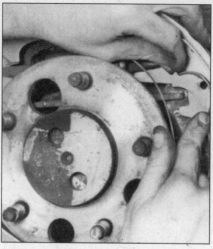

6.4w Install the anchor pin plate, cable guide and cable

6.4x Install the shoe guide and adjusting cable eye to the anchor pin, then install the shoe retracting springs

6.4y Connect the cable and spring to the lever, then install the drum and adjust the brake shoe-to-drum clearance (adjust the shoes so they rub slightly as the drum is turned, then back-off the adjuster until they don't rub)

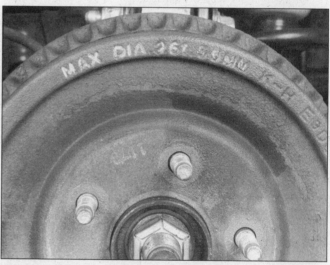

6.5 The maximum permissible diameter specification is cast into the brake drum

resurfaced without exceeding the maximum allowable diameter, which is stamped into the drum (see illustration), then new ones will be required. At the very least, if you elect not to have the drums resurfaced, remove the glazing from the surface with medium-grit emery cloth using a swirling motion.

6   Install the brake drum on the hub.

7   Mount the wheel, install the lug nuts, then lower the vehicle.

8   Make a number of forward and reverse stops to adjust the brakes until satisfactory pedal action is obtained.

7   Wheel cylinder - removal, overhaul and installation

Note: If an overhaul is indicated (usually because of fluid leakage or sticky operation) explore all options before beginning the job. New wheel cylinders are available, which makes this job quite easy. If it's decided to rebuild the wheel cylinder, make sure that a rebuild kit is available before proceeding. Never overhaul only one wheel cylinder - always rebuild both of them at the same time.

7.4 To remove the wheel cylinder, disconnect the brake line fitting (A) and remove the two mounting bolts (B)

BOOT
CYLINDER
CUP
BOOT
CUP
PISTON
BLEEDER SCREW
RETURN SPRING AND CUP EXPANDER ASSY
PISTON

7.7 An exploded view of a typical wheel cylinder assembly

Removal

Refer to illustration 7.4

1   Raise the rear of the vehicle and support it securely on jackstands. Block the front wheels to keep the vehicle from rolling.
2   Remove the brake shoe assembly (see Section 6).
3   Remove all dirt and foreign material from around the wheel cylinder.
4   Disconnect the brake line **(see illustration)**. Don't pull the brake line away from the wheel cylinder.
5   Remove the wheel cylinder mounting bolts.
6   Detach the wheel cylinder from the brake backing plate and place it on a clean workbench. Immediately plug the brake line to prevent fluid loss and contamination.

Overhaul

Refer to illustration 7.7

7   Remove the bleeder screw, cups, pistons, boots and spring assembly from the wheel cylinder body **(see illustration)**.
8   Clean the wheel cylinder with brake fluid, denatured alcohol or brake system cleaner. **Warning:** *Do not, under any circumstances, use petroleum-based solvents to clean brake parts!*
9   Use compressed air to remove excess fluid from the wheel cylinder and to blow out the passages. Make sure the compressed air is filtered and unlubricated.
10   Check the cylinder bore for corrosion and score marks. Crocus cloth can be used to remove light corrosion and stains, but the cylinder must be replaced with a new one if the defects cannot be removed easily, or if the bore is scored.
11   Lubricate the new cups, pistons and cylinder bore with brake fluid.
12   Assemble the brake cylinder components. Make sure the cup lips face in.

Installation

13   Place the wheel cylinder in position, install the mounting bolts and tighten them to the torque listed in this Chapter's Specifications.
14   Connect the brake line and install the brake shoe assembly.
15   Bleed the brakes (see Section 10).

8   Master cylinder - removal, overhaul and installation

Warning: *If the vehicle is equipped with an Anti-lock Brake System (ABS), do not attempt to remove or overhaul the master cylinder. Have the master cylinder removed, rebuilt and installed at a dealer service department or other qualified repair shop. Removing a master cylinder from an ABS system can allow air to get into the ABS hydraulic control unit, which requires a special bleeding procedure impossible to perform at home. And overhauling a master cylinder used with ABS systems is beyond the scope of the average home mechanic because it requires special factory tools.*

Note: *Before deciding to overhaul the master cylinder, check on the availability and cost of a new or factory rebuilt unit and also the availability of a rebuild kit.*

Removal

1   Place rags under the brake line fittings and prepare caps or plastic bags to cover the ends of the lines once they are disconnected. **Caution:** *Brake fluid will damage paint. Cover all body parts and be careful not to spill fluid during this procedure.*
2   Unscrew the tube nuts at the ends of the brake lines where they enter the master cylinder. To prevent rounding off the flats on these nuts, a flare-nut wrench, which wraps around the fitting, should be used.
3   Pull the brake lines away from the master cylinder slightly and plug the ends to prevent contamination.
4   Disconnect the brake warning light electrical connector, remove the two master cylinder mounting nuts, and detach the master cylinder from the vehicle.
5   Remove the reservoir cap, then discard any fluid remaining in the reservoir.

Overhaul

Refer to illustrations 8.7a, 8.7b, 8.8, 8.9, 8.10, 8.14 and 8.19

6   Mount the master cylinder in a vise with the vise jaws clamping on the mounting flange.
7   Remove the primary piston snap-ring by depressing the piston and extracting the ring with a pair of snap-ring pliers **(see illustrations)**.

PLASTIC RESERVOIR
MASTER CYLINDER
SPRING SEAT
SECONDARY PISTON
SPRING
PISTON CUP
PRIMARY PISTON
PISTON CUP
SNAP RING
PISTON CUP
SPRING RETAINER
SPRING
SPRING SEAT
PISTON CUP

8.7a An exploded view of the master cylinder assembly

9

8.7b   Use a Phillips head screwdriver to push the primary piston into the cylinder, then remove the snap-ring

8.8   Remove the primary piston assembly from the cylinder

8.9   Tap the master cylinder against a block of wood to eject the secondary piston assembly

8.10   If you must remove the fluid reservoir to replace leaking seals or a broken reservoir, gently pry it off with a screwdriver or small prybar

8.14   Coat the secondary piston with clean brake fluid and install it in the master cylinder, spring end first

8   Remove the primary piston assembly from the cylinder bore **(see illustration)**.

9   Remove the secondary piston assembly from the cylinder bore. It may be necessary to remove the master cylinder from the vise and invert it, carefully tapping it against a block of wood to expel the piston **(see illustration)**.

10   If fluid has been leaking past the reservoir grommets, pry the reservoir from the cylinder body with a screwdriver **(see illustration)**. Remove the grommets. Clean the master cylinder body and components with brake system cleaner. **Warning:** *DO NOT use petroleum-based solvents to clean brake parts - use brake system cleaner only.*

11   Inspect the cylinder bore for corrosion and damage. If any corrosion or damage is found, replace the master cylinder body with a new one, as abrasives cannot be used on the bore.

12   Lubricate the new reservoir grommets with silicone grease and press them into the master cylinder body. Make sure they're properly seated. **Note:** *If silicone grease is not available, use clean brake fluid.*

13   Lay the reservoir on a hard surface and press the master cylinder body onto the reservoir, using a rocking motion.

14   Lubricate the cylinder bore and primary and secondary piston assemblies with clean brake fluid. Insert the secondary piston assembly into the cylinder **(see illustration)**.

15   Install the primary piston assembly in the cylinder bore, depress it and install the snap-ring. If equipped with a stop bolt, install it now, using a new sealing washer and tightening it securely.

16   Inspect the reservoir cap and diaphragm for cracks and deformation. Replace any damaged parts with new ones and attach

PLUGS

SECONDARY OUTLET PORT

8.19   When bench bleeding the master cylinder, start with the secondary outlet port

the diaphragm to the cap.

17   **Note:** *Whenever the master cylinder is removed, the complete hydraulic system must be bled. The time required to bleed the system can be reduced if the master cylinder is filled with fluid and bench bled (refer to Steps 18 through 22) before the master cylinder is installed on the vehicle.*

18   Insert threaded plugs of the correct size into the cylinder outlet holes and fill the reservoirs with brake fluid. The master cylinder should be supported in such a manner that brake fluid will not spill during the

8.23 **Check the master cylinder-to-booster pushrod clearance**

9.2 **To disconnect the fitting that attaches the flexible brake hose to the metal brake line at the bracket in the wheel well, use a backup wrench on the hose fitting to ensure that the metal line doesn't get twisted**

9.3 **Once the fitting has been unscrewed, remove this large retainer clip and separate the hose from the bracket**

bench bleeding procedure.

19   Loosen one plug at a time, starting with the secondary outlet port first, and push the piston assembly into the bore to force air from the master cylinder **(see illustration)**. To prevent air from being drawn back into the cylinder, the appropriate plug must be replaced before allowing the piston to return to its original position.

20   Stroke the piston three or four times for each outlet to ensure that all air has been expelled.

21   Since high pressure is not involved in the bench bleeding procedure, an alternative to the removal and replacement of the plugs with each stroke of the piston assembly is available. Before pushing in on the piston assembly, remove one of the plugs completely. Before releasing the piston, however, instead of replacing the plug, simply put your finger tightly over the hole to keep air from being drawn back into the master cylinder. Wait several seconds for the brake fluid to be drawn from the reservoir to the piston bore, then repeat the procedure. When you push down on the piston it will force your finger off the hole, allowing the air inside to be expelled. When only brake fluid is being ejected from the hole, replace the plug and go on to the other port.

22   Refill the master cylinder reservoirs and install the diaphragm and cap assembly.

Installation

Refer to illustration 8.23

23   Using a hand-held vacuum pump, apply a vacuum of about 20-in. Hg to the power booster and check the distance from the outer end of the booster pushrod to the front face of the brake booster assembly **(see illustration)**. Turn the pushrod adjusting screw in or out as required to obtain the correct length.

24   Carefully install the master cylinder by reversing the removal steps, then bleed the brakes (see Section 10).

9   Brake hoses and lines - inspection and replacement

Caution: *If the vehicle is equipped with ABS, make sure you plug the brake line immediately after disconnecting it from the brake hose, to prevent the fluid from draining out of the line and air entering the HCU. The HCU on an ABS system cannot be bled without a very expensive tool.*

Inspection

1   About every six months, with the vehicle raised and supported securely on jackstands, the rubber hoses which connect the steel brake lines with the front and rear brake assemblies should be

inspected for cracks, chafing of the outer cover, leaks, blisters and other damage. These are important and vulnerable parts of the brake system and inspection should be complete. A light and mirror will be helpful for a thorough check. If a hose exhibits any of the above conditions, replace it with a new one.

Replacement

Flexible hose

Refer to illustrations 9.2 and 9.3

2   Using a flare nut wrench, disconnect the brake line from the hose fitting, being careful not to bend the frame bracket or brake line. Hold the fitting on the hose with a wrench to prevent the metal line from twisting and the frame bracket from bending **(see illustration)**.

3   Remove the large retaining clip **(see illustration)** and detach the hose from the bracket and the body. **Caution:** *Plug the metal brake line immediately to prevent air from getting into the hydraulic control unit (HCU). If air gets into the HCU, you will not be able to bleed the brakes properly at home.*

4   Remove the banjo bolt from the caliper and discard the sealing washers.

5   Connect the hose to the caliper, using new sealing washers. Tighten the banjo bolt to the torque listed in this Chapter's Specifications.

6   Without twisting the hose, connect the other end of the line to the bracket on the chassis.

7   Connect the metal brake line to the hose fitting by hand, then, using a flare nut wrench, tighten the fitting securely. Be sure to use a wrench on the hose fitting to prevent the bracket from bending or the metal line from twisting.

8   When the brake hose installation is complete, there should be no kinks in the hose. Make sure the hose doesn't contact any part of the suspension. Check this by turning the wheels to the extreme left and right positions. If the hose makes contact, remove it and correct the installation as necessary.

Metal brake line

9   When replacing brake lines be sure to use the correct parts. Don't use copper tubing for any brake system components. Purchase steel brake lines from a dealer or auto parts store.

10   Prefabricated brake line, with the tube ends already flared and fittings installed, is available at auto parts stores and dealers. These lines are also sometimes bent to the proper shapes.

11   When installing the new line make sure it's securely supported in the brackets and has plenty of clearance between moving or hot components.

9

12   After installation, check the master cylinder fluid level and add fluid as necessary. Bleed the brake system as outlined in the next Section and test the brakes carefully before driving the vehicle in traffic.

10   Brake hydraulic system - bleeding

Refer to illustration 10.8
Warning: *Wear eye protection when bleeding the brake system. If the fluid comes in contact with your eyes, immediately rinse them with water and seek medical attention.*
Note: *Bleeding the hydraulic system is necessary to remove any air that manages to find its way into the system when it's been opened during removal and installation of a hose, line, caliper or master cylinder.*

Conventional brakes (non-ABS)

1   It will probably be necessary to bleed the system at all four brakes if air has entered the system due to low fluid level, or if the brake lines have been disconnected at the master cylinder.
2   If a brake line was disconnected only at a wheel, then only that caliper or wheel cylinder must be bled.
3   If a brake line is disconnected at a fitting located between the master cylinder and any of the brakes, that part of the system served by the disconnected line must be bled.
4   Remove any residual vacuum from the brake power booster by applying the brake several times with the engine off.
5   Remove the master cylinder reservoir cover and fill the reservoir with brake fluid. Reinstall the cover. **Note:** *Check the fluid level often during the bleeding operation and add fluid as necessary to prevent the fluid level from falling low enough to allow air bubbles into the master cylinder.*
6   Have an assistant on hand, as well as a supply of new brake fluid, an empty clear plastic container, a length of 3/16-inch plastic, rubber or vinyl tubing to fit over the bleeder valve and a wrench to open and close the bleeder valve.
7   Beginning at the right rear wheel, loosen the bleeder valve slightly, then tighten it to a point where it is snug but can still be loosened quickly and easily.
8   Place one end of the tubing over the bleeder valve and submerge the other end in brake fluid in the container **(see illustration)**.
9   Have the assistant pump the brakes slowly a few times to get pressure in the system, then hold the pedal firmly depressed.
10   While the pedal is held depressed, open the bleeder valve just enough to allow a flow of fluid to leave the valve. Watch for air bubbles to exit the submerged end of the tube. When the fluid flow slows after a couple of seconds, close the valve and have your assistant release the pedal.
11   Repeat Steps 9 and 10 until no more air is seen leaving the tube,

10.8 When bleeding the brakes, a hose is connected to the bleed screw at the caliper or wheel cylinder and then submerged in brake fluid - air will be seen as bubbles in the tube and container (all air must be expelled before moving to the next wheel)

then tighten the bleeder valve and proceed to the left rear wheel, the right front wheel and the left front wheel, in that order, and perform the same procedure. Be sure to check the fluid in the master cylinder reservoir frequently.
12   Never use old brake fluid. It contains moisture which will deteriorate the brake system components.
13   Refill the master cylinder with fluid at the end of the operation.
14   Check the operation of the brakes. The pedal should feel solid when depressed, with no sponginess. If necessary, repeat the entire process. **Warning:** *Do not operate the vehicle if you are in doubt about the effectiveness of the brake system.*

Anti-lock brake system (ABS)

15   ABS-equipped models cannot be bled at home if air gets into the master cylinder and/or the hydraulic control unit (HCU). The first step in the bleeding procedure for these two components requires a special anti-lock test adapter which must be plugged into the control module. Any attempt to bleed the master cylinder and HCU without this special device will trap air in the HCU, which will result in a spongy brake pedal.
16   However, as long as no air has gotten into the master cylinder or the HCU, the brake lines and the calipers can be bled in the conventional manner. Refer to Steps 1 through 14 above.

11   Parking brake - adjustment

1991 and 1992 models

Note: *Adjust the rear brakes prior to adjusting the parking brake cable.*
1   The parking brake is a cable system that incorporates a tension

11.4 Hold the tension limiter and tighten the equalizer nut up the rod to adjust the parking brake

11.8 Scribe a mark on the threaded rod to indicate the position of the equalizer nut

limiter. If the parking brake system is in normal operating condition, depressing the parking brake pedal to the floor will automatically set the proper tension. **Note:** *The brake drums must be cold for this adjustment to be correct.*

Initial adjustment
Refer to illustration 11.4

2   Perform this procedure only if a new tension limiter is installed.

3   Fully apply the parking brake.

4   Hold the threaded rod on the end of the right-hand brake cable from turning and turn the nut 2-1/2-inches up the rod **(see illustration)**. As you turn the nut, keep an eye on the cinch strap. It should slip.

5   After the nut is tightened, dimension A **(see illustration 11.4)** should be less than 1-3/8-inch.

Field adjustment
Refer to illustration 11.8

6   This procedure is used to correct looseness in the system when a new tension limiter isn't installed.

7   Fully apply the parking brake.

8   Scribe a mark on the threaded rod at the equalizer nut to note the original position **(see illustration)**.

9   Grip the threaded rod to prevent it from turning and tighten the equalizer nut six full turns past its original position.

10   Release the parking brake and check for rear wheel drag. The

cables should be tight enough to provide full application of the rear brake shoes with the pedal fully applied. The cable should be loose enough to ensure complete release of the brake shoes when the lever is in the released position.

1993 and 1994 models

11   These models use a parking brake control assembly with an automatic tensioning device. No adjustment of the cable is necessary.

1995 and later models

12   The adjustment on the rear disc brake systems depends on the inner diameter of the rotor/parking brake drum housing and the thickness of the parking brake lining. Refer to the parking brake shoes in Section 13 for the check and replacement procedure.

---

12   Parking brake cables - replacement

1991 and 1992 models
Front cable
Refer to illustrations 12.1 and 12.11

1   Raise the vehicle and support it securely on jackstands. Release the parking brake completely, then loosen the equalizer nut and remove the cable end from the tension limiter **(see illustration)**. Refer

12.1 Parking brake details on 1991 and 1992 models

12.11 Press the retainer fingers and pass the assembly through the backing plate

to illustration 11.4 for additional views.

2   Remove the intermediate cable from the front cable.

3   From inside the vehicle, disconnect the cable from the pedal assembly.

4   Working in the passenger compartment, remove the cable from the vehicle pulling it into the passenger compartment.

5   To install, pull the assembly through the cable housing from the passenger compartment to the cable equalizer.

6   From underneath the vehicle, fasten the cable to the adjuster bracket.

Rear cable

7   Raise the vehicle and support it securely on jackstands. Release the parking brake completely, then remove the hubcap, the wheel and tire, and brake drum.

8   Remove the locknut on the threaded rod at the equalizer.

9   Disconnect the cable end from the equalizer.

10   Depress the prongs that retain the cable housing to the frame bracket and pull out the cable and housing from the crossmember.

11   On the wheel side of the backing plate, compress the retainer fingers so the retainer passes through the hole in the backing plate **(see illustration)**.

12   Lift the cable out of the slot in the parking brake lever attached to the secondary brake shoe and remove the cable through the backing plate hole.

13   Installation is the reverse of removal.

1992 and 1993 models

Front and intermediate cable

Refer to illustration 12.14

14   Raise the vehicle and support it securely on jackstands. Relieve the tension on the parking brake cable by pulling on the front cable and inserting 5/32 drill bit or pin into the hole provided in the parking brake control assembly **(see illustration)**.

15   Disconnect the front cable from the intermediate and then the rear cable and conduit from the intermediate cable. Refer to view Z and view T in illustration 12.14

16   From inside the vehicle, disconnect the cable from the pedal assembly.

17   Working in the passenger compartment, remove the cable from the vehicle pulling it into the passenger compartment.

18   To install, pull the assembly through the cable housing from the passenger compartment to the cable equalizer.

19   From underneath the vehicle, fasten the cable to the adjuster bracket. Refer to View Z in **illustration 12.14**.

Rear cable

20   Raise the vehicle and support it securely on jackstands. Release the parking brake completely, then remove the hubcap, the wheel and tire, and brake drum.

21   Disconnect the rear cable from the intermediate cable and separate the cable and housing from the bracket.

22   Disconnect the rear cable from the rear bracket.

23   On the wheel side of the backing plate, compress the retainer fingers so the retainer passes through the hole in the backing plate.

24   Lift the cable out of the slot in the parking brake lever attached to the secondary brake shoe and remove the cable through the backing plate hole.

25   Installation is the reverse of removal.

1995 and later models

Front cable

26   The front cable is connected to the parking brake mechanism, which is located in the extreme left corner of the area under the dash, where the firewall meets the kick panel. You need to fabricate a special tool to disconnect the front cable from the automatic spring-loaded automatic take-up reel. Unfortunately, you can't really see what you're doing until you have removed the parking brake mechanism. But a module hanging down from the dash is installed in very close proximity to the parking brake mechanism, making removal of the parking brake assembly extremely difficult. For all these reasons, we don't recommend trying to replace the front cable. If the cable breaks or the parking brake mechanism fails, take the vehicle to a dealer or other repair shop and have the cable or mechanism replaced by a professional with the right tools and know-how.

Intermediate and rear cables

Removal

Refer to illustrations 12.28a, 12.28b, 12.28c, 12.28d, 12.29, 12.30, 12.31 and 12.32

Note: *The following procedure applies to the intermediate cable (the short cable between the front cable and the two rear cables) and to either rear cable.*

27   Make sure the parking brake is released. Raise the rear of the vehicle and place it securely on jackstands.

28   Disconnect the rear cable. On models with rear drum brakes,

12.14 Parking brake details on 1993 and 1994 models

1	Parking brake control assembly	8	Bolt	15	Right side cable assembly

1 Parking brake control assembly
2 Bolt
3 Front parking brake cable
4 Parking brake intermediate cable
5 Grommet
6 Bracket
7 Nut

8 Bolt
9 Rear guide bracket
10 Rear parking brake cable retainer
11 Parking brake retainer clip
12 Screw
13 Clip
14 Screw

15 Right side cable assembly
16 Left side cable assembly
17 Parking brake cable equalizer
A Cable end assembly
B Rotate cable down
C Pull pin to adjust cable

9

12.28a Parking brake details on 1995 and later models

1	Parking brake cable and housing	7	Parking brake rear cable	14	Bolt
2	Parking brake control assembly	8	Grommet	15	Parking brake cable
3	Parking brake rear cable and conduit	9	Parking brake intermediate cable	16	Nut
4	Rear parking brake cable retainer	10	Bolt	17	Bolt
5	Cable insulator	11	Clamp	18	Cable end assembly
6	Bracket	12	Parking brake handle	19	Pull pin to adjust cable
		13	Bolt		

12.28b On models with rear disc brakes, remove this retaining clip from the bracket on the torque plate . . .

12.28c . . . pull the cable forward (toward the front of the vehicle) and guide it out of the bracket . . .

12.28d . . . then disconnect the cable from the parking brake lever

12.29 To disconnect the left rear cable from the intermediate cable, pry open this locking tang with a small screwdriver

12.30 To disconnect the right rear cable from the intermediate cable, pry open this locking tang with a small screwdriver

you'll need to remove the brake drum and disassemble the brake (see Steps 14 through 24). Connect the parking brake cable from the actuating lever **(see illustration)**. On models with rear disc brakes, simply follow the accompanying procedure **(see illustrations)**

29   Disconnect the left rear cable from the intermediate cable **(see illustration)**.

30   Disconnect the right rear cable from the intermediate cable **(see illustration)**.

31   If you need to replace the intermediate cable, simply disconnect the front end of the intermediate cable from the connector at the rear end of the front cable **(see illustration)**.

32   Installation is the reverse of removal. When you reattach the two rear cables to the intermediate cable, make sure that the left cable is on top **(see illustration)**.

12.31 If you are replacing the intermediate cable, disconnect it from the front cable by prying it out of this connector with two pair of pliers (you'll find this connector under the crossmember for the transmission extension housing mount)

12.32 When you reattach the two rear parking brake cables to the intermediate cable, make sure the left rear cable (arrow) is on top, and attached to the forward end of the cable connector; the right rear cable should be under the left rear cable, and should be attached to the rear end of the connector

9

13.5a Remove the parking brake leading shoe hold-down spring with an Allen bit . . .

13.5b . . . and remove the trailing shoe hold-down spring

13.5c Rotate the star adjuster to its shortest length, then spread the parking brake shoes apart and remove the adjuster

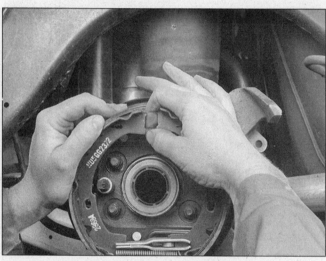

13.5d Detach the upper return spring from the parking brake shoes (it's in the back)

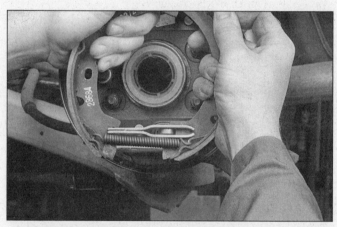

13.5e Remove the parking brake shoes, the lower return springs and the parking brake lever as a single assembly; make sure you don't damage the rubber grommet that lines the hole in the backing plate for the parking brake lever

13   Parking brake shoes (rear disc brakes only) - inspection and replacement

Refer to illustrations 13.5a through 13.5h

Warning: *Dust created by the brake system may contain asbestos, which is hazardous to your health. Never blow it out with compressed air and don't inhale any of it. An approved filtering mask should be worn when working on the brakes. Do not, under any circumstances, use petroleum-based solvents to clean brake parts. Use brake system cleaner only!*

1   Loosen the rear wheel lug nuts. Raise the rear of the vehicle and place it securely on jackstands. Remove the rear wheels.
2   Remove the caliper (see Section 4) and the brake disc (see Section 5). It's not necessary to disconnect the brake hose from the caliper; but hang the caliper out of the way with a piece of wire to prevent damage to the hose.
3   Inspect the thickness of the lining material on the shoes. If the lining has worn down to 3/64-inch or less, the shoes must be replaced.
4   Disconnect the rear parking brake cable from the parking brake lever (see Section 12).
5   Follow the accompanying photos (see illustrations 13.5a through 13.5h) for the parking brake shoe replacement procedure. Be sure to stay in order and read the caption under each illustration.
6   Install the brake disc. Temporarily thread three of the wheel lug

13.5f Finish disassembling the parking brake assembly on the bench: The two lower return springs (one in front of the shoes, one behind them) and the parking brake lever are shown bottom center

13.5g Here's a close-up of the correctly assembled parking brake lever and the lower return springs

13.5h A correctly assembled parking brake shoe assembly (on the bench)

14.10 Working in the passenger compartment, disconnect the brake light switch and booster pushrod . . .

nuts onto the studs to hold the disc in place.

7   Remove the rubber access plug from the backside of the brake torque plate. Adjust the parking brake shoe clearance by turning the adjuster star wheel with a brake adjusting tool or screwdriver until the shoes contact the disc and the disc can't be turned. Back-off the adjuster eight notches, then install the hole plug.

8   Install the brake caliper. Be sure to tighten the bolts to the torque listed in this Chapter's Specifications.

9   Install the wheel and tighten the lug nuts to the torque listed in the Chapter 1 Specifications.

10   To bed the shoes to the drum, drive the vehicle at approximately 30 mph on a dry, level road. Depress the parking brake pedal with about 20 pounds of force. **Note:** *The vacuum release mechanism will prevent the parking brake from setting, if it is operating properly. Be sure to check the function of the vacuum release before performing the bedding-in procedure.* Drive the vehicle for 1/4-mile with the parking brake applied like this.

11   Repeat this procedure two or three times, allowing the brakes to cool between applications.

14 Power brake booster - check, removal, installation and adjustment

1   The power brake booster unit requires no special maintenance apart from periodic inspection of the vacuum hose and the case.

2   Dismantling of the brake booster requires special tools and is not ordinarily done by the home mechanic. If a problem develops, install a new or factory rebuilt unit.

Check

3   Begin the power booster check by depressing the brake pedal several times with the engine off and make sure that there is no change in the pedal reserve distance. The reserve distance is the distance between the pedal and the floor when the pedal is fully depressed.

4   Now, depress the pedal and start the engine. If the pedal goes down slightly, operation is normal. Release the brake pedal and let the engine run for a couple of minutes.

5   Turn off the engine and depress the brake pedal several times slowly. If the pedal goes down farther the first time but gradually rises after the second or third depression, the booster is airtight.

6   Start the engine and depress the brake pedal, then stop the engine with the pedal still depressed. If there is no change in the reserve distance after holding the pedal for about 30-seconds, the booster is airtight.

7   If the pedal feels "hard" when the engine is running, the booster isn't operating properly or there is a vacuum leak in the hose to the booster.

14.11 . . . then pull down the floorboard padding and remove the four booster mounting nuts

Removal

Refer to illustrations 14.10 and 14.11

8   Remove the nuts attaching the master cylinder to the booster (see Section 8) and carefully pull the master cylinder forward until it clears the mounting studs. Use caution so as not to bend or kink the brake lines.

9   Detach the manifold vacuum hose from the booster check valve.

10   Working in the passenger compartment under the steering column, unplug the electrical connector from the brake light switch **(see illustration)**, then remove the pushrod retaining clip and nylon washer from the brake pedal pin. Slide the pushrod off the pin.

11   Remove the nuts attaching the brake booster to the firewall **(see illustrations)**.

12   Carefully detach the booster from the firewall and lift it out of the engine compartment.

Installation

13   Place the booster into position on the firewall and tighten the mounting nuts to the torque listed in this Chapter's Specifications. Connect the pushrod and brake light switch to the brake pedal. Install the retaining clip in the brake pedal pin.

14   Install the master cylinder to the booster, tightening the nuts to the torque listed in this Chapter's Specifications.

15   Carefully check the operation of the brakes before driving the vehicle in traffic.

9

15.2 Installation details of a typical earlier model brake light switch assembly

Adjustment

16   Some boosters feature an adjustable pushrod. They are matched to the booster at the factory and most likely will not require adjustment, but if a misadjusted pushrod is suspected, a gauge can be fabricated out of heavy gauge sheet metal **(see illustration 8.23)**.

17   Some common symptoms caused by a misadjusted pushrod include dragging brakes (if the pushrod is too long) or excessive brake pedal travel accompanied by a groaning sound from the brake booster (if the pushrod is too short).

18   To check the pushrod length, unbolt the master cylinder from the booster and position it to one side. It isn't necessary to disconnect the hydraulic lines, but be careful not to bend them.

19   Apply vacuum to the booster with a hand-held vacuum pump, then place the pushrod gauge against the end of the pushrod, exerting a force of approximately five pounds to seat the pushrod in the power unit **(see illustration 8.23)**. The rod measurement should fall somewhere between the minimum and maximum cutouts on the gauge. If it doesn't, adjust it by holding the knurled portion of the pushrod with a pair of pliers and turning the end with a wrench.

20   When the adjustment is complete, reinstall the master cylinder and check for proper brake operation before driving the vehicle in traffic.

15   Brake light switch - removal and installation

Removal

Refer to illustrations 15.2 and 15.3

1   Remove the under dash panel.

2   Locate the brake light switch assembly **(see illustration)** near the top of the brake pedal and disconnect the switch from the brake pedal by removing the retaining clip.

3   Use a small screwdriver to unlock the electrical connector, then unplug the connector from the brake light switch **(see illustration)**.

Installation

4   Install the switch to the electrical connector by snapping the clip into place.

5   Reconnect the assembly to the brake pedal.

6   Install the under dash panel.

7   Check the brake lights for proper operation.

15.3 Use a small screwdriver to disengage the clip inside the electrical connector

Chapter 10
Suspension and steering systems

Contents

	Section		Section
Axle pivot bracket (1991 through 1994 models) - removal and installation	11	Power steering line quick disconnect fittings	26
Axle pivot bushing (1991 through 1994 models) - removal and installation	10	Radius arm (1991 through 1994 models - removal and installation	7
Balljoints - removal and installation	5	Radius arm insulators (1991 through 1994 models) - replacement	8
Camber adjustment	4	Rear stabilizer bar - removal and installation	18
Coil spring (1991 through 1994 models) - removal and installation	6	Rear leaf spring - removal and installation	17
Drag link (1991 through 1994 models) - removal and installation	21	Rear shock absorbers - inspection, removal and installation	16
Front axle arm (1991 through 1994 models) - removal and installation	9	Steering angles and wheel alignment - general information	28
Front shock absorbers - inspection, removal and installation	2	Steering gear - removal and installation	24
Front stabilizer bar - removal and installation	15	Steering connecting rod (1991 through 1994 models) - removal and installation	22
Front wheel spindle - removal and installation	3	Steering wheel - removal and installation	20
General information	1	Steering system - general information	19
Lower control arm (1995 and later models) - removal, inspection and installation	12	Tie-rod ends - removal and installation	23
Power steering system bleeding	27	Torsion bar (1995 and later models) - removal and installation	14
Power steering pump - removal and installation	25	Upper control arm (1995 and later models) - removal, inspection and installation	13
		Wheels and tires - general information	29

Specifications

General

Front suspension	
1991 through 1994 models	Twin I-beam with coil springs
1995 and later models	Upper and lower control arms with torsion bars
Rear suspension	Leaf spring
Steering	
1991 through 1994 models	Ford integral power steering
1995 and later models	Rack and pinion steering
Power steering pump	Ford Model C-II
Power steering gear	
Gear ratio	17:1
Fluid type and capacity	See Chapter 1

Torque specifications

Ft-lbs (unless otherwise indicated)

1991 through 1994 2WD models

Front suspension	
Shock absorber-to-radius arm nut	39 to 53
Shock absorber upper nut	25 to 35
Spring retainer bolt	191 to 231
Stabilizer bar bolts	16 to 24
Stabilizer bar end nuts	108 to 144 in-lbs
Radius arm-to-frame nut	81 to 120
Radius arm bracket-to-frame bolt	77 to 110
Radius arm front bracket-to-axle arm bolt	191 to 231
Axle pivot bolt	120 to 150
Axle pivot bracket nuts	77 to 90
Jounce bumper bolt	18 to 26
Balljoint pinch bolt	48 to 65

Torque specifications (continued)   **Ft-lbs** (unless otherwise indicated)

1991 through 1994 2WD models

Rear suspension

Rear leaf spring U-bolt nut	88 to 108
Shock-to-lower bracket nut	39 to 53
Shock-to-upper bracket nut	39 to 53
Shackle-to-spring nut	74 to 115
Spring-to-front bracket bolt	64 to 91
Spring shackle-to-rear bracket bolt	74 to 114
Stabilizer-to-mounting bracket bolt	30 to 42
Stabilizer-to-link nut	50 to 68
Stabilizer link-to-frame bolt	50 to 68

1991 through 1994 4WD models

Front suspension

Shock absorber-to-radius arm nut	39 to 53
Shock absorber upper nut	25 to 35
Spring retainer nut	70 to 100
Stabilizer bar bolts	35 to 50
Stabilizer bar link nuts	30 to 44
Radius arm-to-rear bracket nut	80 to 120
Radius arm front bracket front bolts	27 to 37
Radius arm front bracket lower bolt	190 to 230
Radius arm-to-front bracket upper stud	190 to 230
Axle pivot bolt	120 to 150
Axle pivot bracket bolts	
Left bracket (right axle arm)	155
Right bracket (left axle arm)	77 to 110
Jounce bumper bolt	18 to 26
Balljoint pinch bolt	65 to 85

Steering linkage

Drag link-to-Pitman arm nut	51 to 73
Drag link-to-steering connecting rod nut	51 to 73
Tie-rod adjusting sleeve nut	30 to 42
Tie-rod to spindle nut	51 to 73
Pitman arm-to-steering gear nut	170 to 228

Steering system

Flex coupling-to-steering gear input shaft bolt	25 to 34
Steering gear-to-flex coupling bolt	25 to 34
Power steering gear hoses to gear	20 to 30
Power steering gear-to-frame bolt	50 to 61
Power steering pump-to-bracket bolts	35 to 47
Steering wheel bolt	23 to 33

1995 and later models (2WD and 4WD)

Front suspension

Shock absorber-to-lower control arm	
Without ARC	15 to 21
With ARC	18 to 24
Shock absorber upper nut	
Without ARC	30 to 40
With ARC	25 to 34
Upper spindle bolt	30 to 40
Lower balljoint nut	83 to 113
Wheel hub nut	157 to 213
Lower control arm pivot bolts	111 to 148
Front stabilizer bar nut	120 to 156 in-lbs
Front stabilizer bar bracket-to-frame	65 to 91
Tie rod end to spindle	77 to 103

Rear suspension

Rear leaf spring U-bolt nut	65 to 87
Shock absorber-to-lower bracket nut	39 to 53
Shock absorber-to-upper bracket nut	
Without ARC	39 to 53
With ARC	15 to 21
Rear shackle-to-spring nut	74 to 115
Spring-to-front bracket bolt	50 to 68
Spring shackle-to-rear bracket bolt	74 to 114

Torque specifications (continued)

1995 and later models (2WD and 4WD)
Rear suspension
Stabilizer-to-mounting bracket bolt .... 30 to 40
Stabilizer-to-link nut .... 50 to 68
Stabilizer link-to-frame bolt.. 44 to 59

Ft-lbs (unless otherwise indicated)

1   General information

Refer to illustrations 1.6 and 1.7

Front suspension

1991 through 1994 models

The front suspension on 1991 through 1994 2WD models is a twin I-beam type, which is composed of coil springs, I-beam axle arms, radius arms, upper and lower balljoints and spindles, tie-rods, shock absorbers and an optional stabilizer bar. The 4WD model is basically the same except the front driveline system is composed of a two-piece driveaxle assembly.

The front suspension consists of two independent axle arm assemblies **(see illustration 25.9a in Chapter 1)**. One end of the assembly is anchored to the frame and the other is supported by the coil spring and radius arm. The spindle is connected to the axle by upper and lower balljoints. The balljoints are constructed of a lubricated-for-life special bearing material. Lubrication points are found on the tie-rods and steering linkage. Movement of the spindles is controlled by the tie-rods and the steering linkage.

Two adjustments can be performed on the axle assembly. Camber is adjusted by removing and replacing an adapter between the upper balljoint stud and the spindle on 2WD models. 4WD models require replacing the camber adapter on the upper balljoint stud. Adapters are available in 0-degree, 1/2-degree, 1-degree and 1-1/2-degree increments. Toe-in adjustment is accomplished on both models by turning the tie-rod adjusting sleeve.

1995 and later models

The front suspension on 1995 and later models consists of upper and lower control arms, shock absorbers, torsion bars and a front stabilizer bar **(see illustration 12.6 and 13.4)**. The inner ends are attached to the frame; the outer ends are attached to the control arms steering. The upper control arms pivot on a bushing and shaft assembly bolted to the frame. The lower control arms pivot on two separate bolts. The shocks and springs are mounted between the lower control arms and the frame. The front stabilizer bar is attached to the frame with mounting clamps.

The hydraulic shock absorbers are of the direct, double acting type, with later models having low pressure gas shocks. Both shock absorbers are of the telescoping design and come equipped with rubber grommets at the mounting points for quiet operation. The low pressure gas shock absorbers are sealed and charged with nitrogen gas to reduce shock absorber fade and improve ride. The shock absorbers are nonadjustable. The shock absorbers are not rebuildable and must be replaced as complete assemblies.

Rear suspension

The rear suspension uses shock absorbers and semi-elliptical leaf springs. The forward end of each spring is attached to the bracket on the frame side rail **(see illustration)**. The rear of each spring is shackled to a bracket on the frame rail. The rear shock absorbers are direct, double acting units with staggered mounting positions. The right shock is mounted forward of the axle and the left mounted behind it.

Some later 4WD models are equipped with the Automatic Ride

FRONT OF VEHICLE

1.6 Schematic of the rear suspension

1	Shackle	4	Spring plate
2	Leaf spring	5	Spring hanger
3	Stabilizer bar	6	Shock absorber

10

1.7 Schematic of the Automatic Ride Control (ARC) system

1   Front gate solenoid
2   Front shock absorber
3   Generic Electronic Module
4   Powertrain Control Module
5   Automatic Ride Control
6   Message Center Indicator
7   Vehicle Speed Sensor
8   Steering sensor
9   Ignition switch
10 Rear height sensor
11 Rear fill solenoid
12 Air compressor
13 ARC service switch
14 Rear gate solenoid
15 Rear shock absorber
16 Air line
17 Front fill solenoid
18 Stoplight switch
19 Front height sensor
20 Compressor relay

Control (ARC) **(see illustration)**. This system allows the driver to control the ride of the suspension (hard or soft) depending upon the road conditions and the load of the vehicle. ARC system is a computer-controlled suspension system that uses unique suspension components to provide a smooth ride for normal driving conditions without sacrificing handling performance. An air spring integral with each shock absorber, provides automatic load leveling and allows the vehicle height to be adjusted over a span of 2 inches.

The ARC system adjusts the vehicle height on the front axles separately through the use of five solenoid valves, an air compressor and air lines. Four system-specific shock absorbers are used to move the height setting of the chassis using hydraulic pistons and valves.

Since most procedures that are dealt with in this chapter involve jacking up the vehicle and working underneath it, a good pair of jackstands will be needed. A hydraulic floor jack is the preferred type of jack to lift the vehicle, and it can also be used to support certain components during various operations. **Warning:** *Never, under any circumstances, rely on a jack to support the vehicle while working under it.*
Warning: *Whenever any of the suspension or steering fasteners are loosened or removed they must be inspected and, if necessary, replaced with new ones of the same part number or of original equipment quality and design. Torque specifications must be followed for proper reassembly and component retention.*
Caution: *If the vehicle is equipped with Automatic Ride Control (ARC), make sure the air suspension switch is turned to the OFF position before the vehicle is raised, towed or jump started to prevent damage to the system components.*

2   Front shock absorbers - inspection, removal and installation

Caution: *If the vehicle is equipped with Automatic Ride Control (ARC), make sure the air suspension switch is turned to the OFF position before the vehicle is raised, towed or jump started to prevent damage to the system components.*

Inspection

1   The common test of shock damping is simply to bounce the corners of the vehicle several times and observe whether or not the vehicle stops bouncing once you let go if it. A slight rebound and settling indicates good damping, but if the vehicle continues to bounce several times, the shock absorbers must be replaced.
2   If the shock absorbers stand up to the bounce test, visually inspect the shock body for signs of fluid leakage, punctures or deep dents in the metal of the body. Replace any shock absorber which is leaking or damaged, even if it passed the bounce test in Step 1.
3   After removing the shock absorber, pull the piston rod out and push it back in several times to check for smooth operation throughout the travel of the piston rod. Replace the shock absorber if it gives any signs of hard or soft spots in the piston rod travel.
4   Prior to installing the new shock absorbers, pump the piston rod fully in and out several times to lubricate the seals and fill the hydraulic sections of the unit.

Removal and installation

Refer to illustrations 2.8, 2.9, 2.10a and 2.10b
Warning: *On models equipped with the Automatic Ride Control (ARC), turn OFF the ARC service switch before proceeding with any repairs.*
Caution: *The low pressure gas shock absorbers are pressurized to 135 PSI with nitrogen gas. Do not attempt to open, puncture or apply heat to the shock absorbers.*
5   Loosen the front wheel lug nuts on the side to be dismantled. Raise the front of the vehicle, support it securely on jackstands, block the rear wheels and set the parking brake. Remove the front wheel.
6   On vehicles equipped with the ARC system, disconnect the electrical connectors from the shock absorbers and pry the harness retainers from their grommets in the frame.
7   Also, on vehicles equipped with the ARC system, disconnect the air line from the shock absorber. Push IN and hold the plastic ring on the shock absorber. While holding the ring, pull out on the air line.
8   Remove the top nut with a deep socket while holding the shaft with an open end wrench **(see illustration)**. Lift off the washer.
9   On ARC systems, remove the front left height sensor from the

2.8   Hold the shock absorber shaft while turning the top retainer nut

2.10a   The shock absorber lower mounting bracket is attached to the radius arm

upper bracket. Release the spring clip and pull the sensor from the lower ball stud **(see illustration)**.
10   On 1991 through 1994 models, remove the bolt and nut securing the shock absorber to the radius arm **(see illustration)**. On 1995 models, remove the nuts from the lower control arm **(see illustration)**.
11   To remove the shock absorber, slightly compress the shock and remove it from its brackets.
12   Installation is the reverse of the removal steps with the following additions.

a) Install and tighten the new nuts and bolts to the torque listed in this Chapter's Specifications.
b) Install the wheel and lug nuts, lower the vehicle and tighten the lug nuts to the torque listed in Chapter 1.

---

3   Front wheel spindle - removal and installation

Refer to illustrations 3.3 and 3.6
Caution: If the vehicle is equipped with Automatic Ride Control (ARC), make sure the air suspension switch is turned to the OFF position before the vehicle is raised, towed or jump started to prevent damage to the system components.

2.9   On ARC systems, remove the height sensor from the chassis

1 Frame
2 Front height sensor upper bracket
3 Bolt
4 Front height sensor
5 Front height sensor lower bracket
6 Front suspension lower arm

2.10b   Exploded view of the shock absorber in an ARC system

1 Nut, washer and insulator assembly
2 Plastic release ring
3 Electrical connector
4 Front shock absorber
5 Nut
6 Front suspension lower arm
7 Tie-rod end
8 Air line
9 Frame

10

3.3 1991 through 1994 2WD front spindle - exploded view

3.6 Separate the upper balljoint with the Ford special tool, then strike the edge of the front spindle (arrows) with a hammer to break it loose from the balljoint studs

1991 through 1994 2WD models

Removal

1   Remove the front wheel and brake disc (see Chapter 1).

2   Remove the brake dust shield.

3   Remove the cotter pin and nut and disconnect the tie-rod end from the spindle **(see illustration)**.

4   Remove the cotter pin from the lower balljoint stud nut, then remove the nut.

5   Remove the clamp bolt from the upper balljoint.

6   Remove the camber adjuster from the upper balljoint **(see illustration)**.

7   Strike the inside of the spindle near the balljoint to break the spindle loose from the balljoint studs **(see illustration 3.6)**. **Caution:** *Don't use a fork-type separator to detach the balljoint. This will damage the balljoint seal.*

8   Remove the spindle together with the balljoints.

Installation

9   Before installation, check that the upper and lower balljoint seals were not damaged during spindle removal and that they are positioned correctly. Replace if necessary.

10   Position the spindle and balljoints in the axle arm.

11   Install the camber adjuster on the upper balljoint, making sure it's aligned correctly.

12   Tighten the lower balljoint nut to the torque listed in this Chapter's Specifications, then tighten further until a cotter pin hole lines up. Install a new cotter pin and bend it to secure the nut.

13   Install the clamp bolt on the upper balljoint and tighten it to the torque listed in this Chapter's Specifications.

14   Install the dust shield.

15   Install the brake disc and the front wheel (see Chapter 1).

1991 through 1994 4WD models

16   Refer to Chapter 8 for the axleshaft removal procedure, then refer to the 2WD spindle removal and installation procedure described above.

1995 2WD models

Refer to illustration 3.26

17   Place the steering wheel in the center position.

18   Loosen the wheel lug nuts. Raise the vehicle and support it securely on jackstands. Remove the wheel.

19   Remove the disc brake caliper (see Chapter 9). Wire the caliper to the underbody to prevent damage to the brake hose.

20   Remove the brake disc (see Chapter 9).

21   Remove the ABS sensor, if equipped, then remove the dust shield from the spindle.

22   Disconnect the tie-rod end from the spindle.

23   Place a jack under the lower arm of the balljoint area. Raise the jack until it supports the spring load on the lower arm. The jack must remain in this position throughout the remainder of this procedure. **Warning:** *Failure to perform this step could result in serious injury.*

24   Remove the lower balljoint nut and the upper balljoint pinch bolt from the spindle.

25   Unload the torsion bar using a special tool (T95T-53-10-A).

26   Remove the spindle **(see illustration)**.

27   Installation is the reverse of removal. Be sure to tighten all fasteners to the torque values listed in this Chapter's Specifications.

1995 4WD models

Note: *On 4WD models the spindle is referred to as the steering knuckle.*

28   Place the steering wheel in the center position.

29   Loosen the wheel lug nuts. Raise the vehicle and support it securely on jackstands. Remove the wheel.

30   Remove the disc brake caliper (see Chapter 9). Wire the caliper to the underbody to prevent damage to the brake hose.

31   Remove the brake disc (see Chapter 9).

32   Remove the wheel hub nut from the front driveaxle (see Chapter 8). Separate the driveaxle from the wheel hub.

33   Remove the ABS sensor, if equipped, then remove the dust shield from the steering knuckle.

34   Disconnect the tie-rod end from the steering knuckle.

35   Place a jack under the lower arm of the balljoint area. Raise the jack until it supports the spring load on the lower arm. The jack must remain in this position throughout the remainder of this procedure. **Warning:** *Failure to perform this step could result in serious injury.*

36   Remove the lower balljoint nut and the upper balljoint pinch bolt from the steering knuckle.

37   Unload the torsion bar using a special tool (T95T-53-10-A).

38   Remove the steering knuckle.

39   Installation is the reverse of removal. Be sure to tighten all fasteners to the torque values listed in this Chapter's Specifications.

3.26 Exploded view of the spindle on 1995 models with 2WD

1	Upper spindle bolt	7	Cotter pin
2	Nut	8	Nut
3	Spindle	9	Tie rod end
4	Not used	10	Front suspension
5	Nut		lower arm
6	Cotter pin		

4 Camber adjustment

On 1994 and earlier models the camber can be adjusted by replacing the camber adjuster in the upper balljoint socket. On 1995 and later models the camber (as well as caster) is adjusted by repositioning the cams on the upper control arm pivot. Due to the requirement for special alignment tools, this job beyond the scope of the home mechanic. Have this work performed by a Ford dealer or a front end alignment specialist.

5 Balljoints - removal and installation

Warning: *Do not heat the axle or balljoint to aid removal since the temper may be removed from the component(s), leading to premature failure.*

Caution: *If the vehicle is equipped with Automatic Ride Control (ARC), make sure the air suspension switch is turned to the OFF position before the vehicle is raised, towed or jump started to prevent damage to the system components.*

1991 through 1994

2WD models

Refer to illustrations 5.3, 5.4, 5.5 and 5.7

1   Remove the spindle (see Section 3).

2   Remove the snap-ring from the lower balljoint. **Note:** *Remove the lower balljoint first.*

3   Install the C-frame assembly tool (Ford part No. T74P-4635-C and the appropriate size receiving cup) on the lower balljoint **(see illustration)**. Tighten the special tool and press the balljoint out of the spindle. **Note:** *If the C-frame assembly tool and receiver tool are not available or will not remove the balljoint, take the spindle assembly to a*

5.3 Using the Ford special tools to remove the balljoints (2WD models)

5.4 Removing the upper balljoint (2WD models)

5.5 Note the additional receiver cup required to install the upper balljoint - install the upper balljoint first (2WD models)

dealer service department or machine shop and have the balljoints pressed out.

4   Use the same tool setup used in Step 3 on the upper balljoint and press the balljoint out **(see illustration)**.

5   Install the upper balljoint with the C-frame assembly, balljoint receiver cup and installation cup **(see illustration)**. **Note:** *Always install*

10

INSTALLING LOWER BALL JOINT

C-FRAME ASSEMBLY

INSTALLATION CUP

RECEIVER CUP

5.7 Installing the lower balljoint (2WD models)

SNAP RING

CAMBER ADJUSTER

PINCH BOLT

5.12 Remove the snap-ring and pinch bolt

the upper balljoint first since the special tool must pass through the lower balljoint receptacle in the axle.

6   Turn the screw in the C-frame clockwise and press the balljoint into the axle until it is completely seated. **Caution:** *Don't heat the axle or balljoint to aid in installation since the temper may be removed from the component(s) leading to premature failure.*

7   Install the lower balljoint with the C-frame assembly, balljoint receiver cup and installation cup **(see illustration).**

8   Turn the screw in the C-frame clockwise and press the balljoint into the axle until it is completely seated. **Caution:** *Don't heat the axle or balljoint to aid in installation since the temper may be removed from the component(s) leading to premature failure.*

9   Install the lower balljoint snap-ring.

4WD models

Refer to illustrations 5.12, 5.13, 5.18, 5.19 and 5.22

10   Remove the spindle and shaft and joint assembly (see Chapter 8).

11   Remove the cotter pin and nut securing the tie-rod (see Section 20).

12   Remove the snap-ring from the upper balljoint, then remove the pinch bolt **(see illustration).**

13   Remove the cotter pin from the lower balljoint, then loosen the nut to the end of the stud (but no farther) **(see illustration).**

14   Hit the inside of the steering knuckle near each balljoint with a hammer. This will break the axle arm loose from the balljoint studs. Remove the steering knuckle from the axle arm.

15   Remove the camber adjuster sleeve **(see illustration 5.12).** Mark the position of the slot in the camber adjuster. It should be installed in its original position to maintain the correct alignment. **Note:** *If the*

CAMBER ADAPTER

PINCH BOLT

PIVOT BUSHING

LEFT AXLE ARM

SNAP RING

UPPER BALL JOINT

COTTER PIN

STEERING KNUCKLE

NUT

SNAP RING

LOWER BALL JOINT

5.13 Steering knuckle and balljoint (4WD) (driver's side shown)

C-FRAME T74P-4635-C

RECEIVER CUP T83T-3050-A

5.18 Using the Ford special tools to remove the balljoints (4WD models)

5.19 Removing the upper balljoint (4WD models)

5.22 Note the additional receiver cup required to install the upper balljoint; install the lower balljoint first (4WD models)

camber adjuster is difficult to remove, use a Pitman arm puller. These can be rented.

16   Remove the nut from the lower balljoint.

17   Place the steering knuckle in a vise. Remove the snap ring (if equipped) from the lower balljoint socket. **Note:** *Always remove the lower balljoint first.*

18   Install the C-frame assembly tool (Ford part No. T74P-4635-C), forcing screw (Ford part No. D79T-3010-BE) and balljoint remover (Ford part No. D79T-3010-BE) on the lower balljoint **(see illustration)**. Tighten the special tool and press the lower balljoint out of the steering knuckle. **Note:** *If the C-frame assembly tool and receiver tool are not available or won't remove the balljoint, take the knuckle assembly to a dealer service department and have the balljoints pressed out.*

19   Use the same tool setup used in Step 18 on the upper balljoint and press the balljoint out **(see illustration)**.

20   Clean the steering knuckle balljoint bores.

21   Insert the lower balljoint into the knuckle as straight as possible. **Note:** *Always install the lower balljoint first since the special tool must pass through the upper balljoint receptacle in the axle.*

22   Position the C-frame assembly, balljoint receiver cup and installation cup on the lower balljoint **(see illustration)**.

23   Turn the screw in the C-frame clockwise and press the balljoint into the steering knuckle until it is completely seated. **Caution:** *Don't heat the axle or balljoint to ease installation since the temper may be removed from the component(s) leading to premature failure. If the balljoint won't go in all the way, realign the C-frame and receiver cup.*

24   Install the lower balljoint snap-ring (if equipped).

25   Position the C-frame assembly, balljoint receiver cup and installation cup on the upper balljoint **(see illustration 5.22)**.

26   Turn the screw in the C-frame clockwise and press the balljoint into the axle until it is completely seated. **Caution:** *Don't heat the axle or balljoint to aid in installation since the temper may be removed from the component(s) leading to premature failure.*

27   Install the camber adjuster into the axle arm. Place the slot in the original position noted during removal. **Note:** *Install the camber adjuster with the arrow pointing toward the outside for positive camber or with the arrow pointing toward the inside of the vehicle for negative camber. Zero camber bushings do not have an arrow and may be rotated in either direction as long as the lugs on the yoke engage the slots in the bushing.* **Caution:** *The following tightening sequence must be followed exactly when securing the steering knuckle. Excessive spindle turning effort may result in reduced steering returnability if this procedure is not followed.*

28   Install the steering knuckle in the axle arm. Do not disrupt the camber adjuster during installation.

29   Install a new nut on the lower balljoint stud and tighten to the torque listed in this Chapter's Specifications, then advance the nut until a cotter pin slot lines up. Install a new cotter pin and bend the

ends over completely.

30   Install the snap-ring on the upper balljoint stud. Install the pinch bolt and tighten to the torque listed in this Chapter's Specifications. **Note:** *The camber adjuster will position itself in the knuckle during adjustment. DO NOT try to change its position.*

31   Attach the tie-rod end to the knuckle. Tighten the nut to the torque listed in this Chapter's Specifications, install a new cotter pin and bend the ends over completely.

32   The remainder of installation is the reverse of the removal steps.

33   For proper front end alignment, take the vehicle to a dealer or alignment shop.

1995 models

34   The balljoints on upper and lower control arms are not removable or serviceable. If a balljoint is damaged or worn, replace the control arm.

6   Coil spring (1991 through 1994 models) - removal and installation

Note: *1995 models are not equipped with coil springs. Instead, the front suspension uses torsion bars while the rear suspension uses leaf springs.*

Removal

Refer to illustrations 6.2, 6.5a, 6.5b and 6.5c

1   Loosen the front wheel lug nuts on the side to be dismantled. Raise the front of the vehicle, support it securely on jackstands, block the rear wheels and set the parking brake. Remove the front wheel.

10

6.2 With the vehicle supported on jackstands, use a floor jack to raise and lower the front axle

6.5a Remove the lower spring retainer nut

6.5b Front spring and related components (2WD models)

6.5c Front spring and related components (4WD models)

2   Place a floor jack under the axle **(see illustration)**.
3   Remove the bolt and nut securing the shock absorber to the radius arm **(see illustration 2.8)**.
4   Remove the brake caliper assembly and suspend it with a length of wire to relieve any strain on the brake hose (see Chapter 9).
5   At the lower end of the spring, remove the retaining nut and the retainer securing the spring to the front axle **(see illustration)**. **Note:** *The nut is attached to a stud on 4WD models and on 2WD models it is attached to a bolt that runs through the axle* **(see illustrations)**.
6   On models so equipped, remove the through bolt securing the stabilizer bar to the front axle.
7   The front axle should now be free to allow spring removal.
8   If necessary, use a pry bar and lift the spring up and over the bolt or stud that passes through the lower spring seat. Rotate the spring so the upper built-in spring seat retainer is cleared, then remove the spring.

Installation

9   Install the spring lower seat and insulator onto the front axle.

10   Push the front axle down to allow installation of the spring. Install the upper end of the spring into the upper seat and rotate the spring into place.
11   If necessary, use a pry bar and lift the lower end of the spring up and over the bolt or stud on the axle and into place on the lower spring seat and insulator.
12   Apply slight pressure on the floor jack and lift the front axle until the spring is correctly seated.
13   Install the lower spring retainer and new nut. Tighten the nut to the torque listed in this Chapter's Specifications.
14   Install the brake caliper assembly (see Chapter 9).
15   Install the bolt and new nut securing the shock absorber to the radius arm. Tighten the nut to the torque listed in this Chapter's Specifications.
16   Install the wheel and lug nuts, lower the vehicle and tighten the lug nuts to the torque listed in Chapter 1.

7.2 Remove the two bolts (arrows) securing the radius arm to the front bracket

7.3 The radius arm (exploded view (4WD models)

7   Radius arm (1991 through 1994 models) - removal and installation

Removal

Refer to illustrations 7.2, 7.3 and 7.4

1   Remove the spring assembly (see Section 6).
2   On 2WD models, perform the following:
  a) *Remove the spring lower seat from the radius arm.*
  b) *Remove the bolt and nut securing the radius arm to the front axle and front bracket* **(see illustration)**.
3   On 4WD models, perform the following:
  a) *Remove the spring lower seat and stud.*
  b) *Remove the bolts securing the radius arm to the front axle bracket* **(see illustration)**.
4   From the rear side of the radius arm bracket, remove the nut, rear washer, shield (passenger side only) and insulator **(see illustration)**.
5   Remove the radius arm and remove the inner insulator and retainer from the radius arm threaded end **(see illustration 7.2 or 7.3)**.

Installation

6   Install the front end of the radius arm onto the front axle.
7   On 2WD models, from underneath the axle, install the attaching bolt and a new nut. Tighten the nut only finger tight at this time.
8   On 4WD models, position the front end of the radius arm onto the bracket and axle. Install the bolts and stud (and washer on the left axle only) in the bracket. Tighten the bolts and stud only finger tight at this time.
9   Install the rear retainer and insulator onto the threaded end of the radius arm.
10   Install the radius arm into the rear bracket and install the rear insulator, washer and new nut. Tighten the nut to the torque listed in this Chapter's Specifications.
11   Tighten the bolts and nuts installed in Step 7 and Step 8 to the torque listed in this Chapter's Specifications.
12   On 2WD models, install the spring lower seat onto the radius arm.
13   On 4WD models, install the spring lower seat and insulator onto the left radius arm.
14   Install the spring assembly (see Section 6).

7.4 Remove the nut, washer and insulator and remove the rear radius arm support

8   Radius arm insulators (1991 through 1994 models) - replacement

1   Remove the front spring (see Section 6).
2   Loosen the axle arm pivot bolt.
3   Remove the shock absorber upper nut and compress the shock.
4   From the rear side of the radius arm bracket, remove the nut, rear washer, insulator, shield (right side only) and spacer **(see illustration 7.2 or 7.3)**.
5   Raise the front axle arm with a floor jack until the radius arm is level.
6   Push the radius arm forward until it is free of the radius arm bracket. **Note:** *If necessary on 4WD models, detach the driveshaft from the front axle flange.*
7   Remove the front insulator from the radius arm threaded end.
8   Installation is the reverse of the removal steps with the following additions:
  a) *Install new insulators and nut.*
  b) *Tighten the bolts and nut to the torque listed in this Chapter's Specifications.*

10

EXPLORER (4x2)

NUT AND RETAINER

NUT

BOLT AND RETAINER ASSEMBLY

NUT

SPRING

INSULATOR

AXLE PIVOT BRACKET

SPRING SEAT

NUT

BOLT

NUT

NUT

BOLT

NUT FLANGE

STEERING ROD AND LINK ASSEMBLY

BOLT

SPINDLE

9.5 Front axle arm - 2WD models (driver's side shown)

9   Front axle arm (1991 through 1994 models) - removal and installation

Refer to illustration 9.5

Note: *Front axle arm removal and installation for 4WD models is covered in Chapter 8.*

Removal

1   Raise the front of the vehicle, support it securely on jackstands, block the rear wheels and set the parking brake. Position the front wheels in the straight ahead position.
2   Remove the coil spring (see Section 6) and front spindle (see Section 3).
3   Remove the radius arm (see Section 7).
4   Remove the front stabilizer bar (see Section 15).
5   Remove the bolt and nut securing the axle arm to the frame pivot bracket **(see illustration)**. Remove the axle arm.

Installation

6   Install the axle arm to the frame pivot bracket with a new retaining bolt and nut. Tighten the nut finger-tight.
7   Install the front stabilizer bar (see Section 15).
8   Install the front axle arm onto the radius arm (see Section 7).
9   Install the front spindle (see Section 3) and the coil spring (see Section 6).

10   Install the axle arm retaining bolt and nut and tighten them slightly. Don't torque them to specifications yet.
11   Install the wheel and lug nuts. Lower the vehicle and tighten the lug nuts to torque listed in Chapter 1.
12   Tighten the axle arm retaining bolt and nut to the torque listed in this Chapter's Specifications.
13   Have the front end alignment checked by a dealer service department or an alignment shop.

10   Axle pivot bushing (1991 through 1994 models) - removal and installation

Removal

2WD models

Refer to illustration 10.4

1   Remove the front spring (see Section 6).
2   To remove the left axle pivot bushing, remove the retaining bolt and nut, then pull the pivot end of the axle down until the bushing is exposed.
3   To remove the right axle pivot bushing, remove the axle arm from the frame (see Section 9).
4   Install the forcing tool (Ford part No. T78P-5638-A1), bushing remover (Ford part No. T80T-5638-A2) and receiver cup (Ford part No.

10.4 Removing the pivot bushing (2WD models)

10.6 Removing the pivot bushing (4WD models)

T78P-5638-A3) or equivalent bushing removal tools onto the bushing. Position the spacer between the walls of the axle, then turn the forcing screw and press the bushing out of the axle **(see illustration)**.

4WD models

Refer to illustration 10.6

5   Remove the front axle assembly (see Chapter 8).

6   Install the forcing tool (Ford part No. T78P-5638-A1), bushing remover (Ford part No. T80T-5638-A2) and receiver cup (Ford part No. T78P-5638-A4) or equivalent bushing removal tools onto the bushing. Turn the forcing screw and press the bushing out of the axle **(see illustration)**.

Installation

Refer to illustrations 10.7a, 10.7b and 10.8

7   Insert the bushing in the axle receptacle. Install the receiver cup, forcing tool and bushing replacer (Ford No. T82T-3006-A1) onto the axle. Turn the forcing screw and press the bushing into the axle **(see illustrations)**.

8   The new bushing must be flared to prevent movement within the axle. Install the forcing screw (Ford No. T78P-5638-A1), receiving cup (Ford No. T82T-3006-A1 and flaring tool (Ford No. T82T-3006-A1), or equivalent. Turn the forcing screw and flare the lip of the bushing **(see illustration)**.

9   The remainder of installation is the reverse of the removal Steps.

10.7a Installing the pivot bushing (2WD models)

10.7b Installing the pivot bushing (4WD models)

10.8 Flaring the bushing to prevent it from moving within the axle

10

11.9 Exploded view of the right pivot bracket (which supports the left axle arm)

11.10 Exploded view of the left axle pivot bracket (which supports the right axle arm)

11 Axle pivot bracket (1991 through 1994 models) - removal and installation

2WD models

Removal

1   Loosen the front wheel lug nuts on the side to be dismantled. Raise the front of the vehicle, support it securely on jackstands, block the rear wheels and set the parking brake. Remove the front wheel.

2   Remove the front spring (see Section 6), the radius arm (see Section 7), the wheel spindle (see Section 3) and the front axle arm (see Section 9).

3   Remove the bolts and nuts securing the axle pivot bracket to the frame and remove the bracket from the frame crossmember (see illustration 9.5).

Installation

4   Position the front axle bracket onto the frame crossmember. Install the new bolts from within the frame crossmember and out through the bracket, then install the new nuts. After all of the bolts and nuts have been installed, tighten them to the torque listed in this Chapter's Specifications.

5   The remainder of installation is the reverse of the removal Steps.

4WD models

Removal

Refer to illustrations 11.9 and 11.10

6   Loosen the wheel lug nuts on the side to be dismantled, raise the front of the vehicle and support it securely on jackstands. Block the rear wheels and apply the parking brake. Remove the wheel.

7   Remove the front spring (see Section 6).

8   Place a jack beneath the axle arm near the pivot bracket to support it.

9   On the right axle pivot bracket (which supports the left axle arm), remove the nuts and the upper and side bolts and retainers. Discard the lower bolt and retainer. Remove the axle pivot bracket from the

frame crossmember **(see illustration)**.

10   On the left axle pivot bracket (which supports the right axle arm), use a 9/16-inch drill bit and drill out the rivets securing the bracket to the frame. Remove the axle bracket from the frame crossmember **(see illustration)**.

Installation

11   Install the left axle pivot bracket onto the frame crossmember and align the 9/16 inch holes of the bracket and frame. Install 9/16-12x1-1/2-inch Grade 8 bolts **(see illustration 11.10)**. **Caution:** *Be sure to use Grade 8 bolts, not a lesser grade. Install the washer and nuts onto the bolts and tighten to the torque listed in this Chapter's specifications.*

12   To install the right axle pivot bracket, perform the following:

a) *Install the right axle pivot bracket onto the frame crossmember* **(see illustration 11.9)**. *Install all bolts in the direction shown in the illustration. The side bolt heads must face the engine oil pan to give maximum clearance. Install new nuts and tighten to the torque listed in this Chapter's specifications.*

b) *Use a 9/16-inch drill bit and drill out the lower mounting hole bracket and frame crossmember.*

c) *Install a 9/16-inch Grade 8 replacement bolt with two flat washers and a new retaining nut. Tighten the nut to the torque listed in this Chapter's Specifications.*

13   The remainder of installation is the reverse of the removal Steps.

12 Lower control arm (1995 and later models) - removal, inspection and installation

Caution: *If the vehicle is equipped with Automatic Ride Control (ARC), make sure the air suspension switch is turned to the OFF position before the vehicle is raised, towed or jump started to prevent damage to the system components.*

Removal

Refer to illustration 12.6

1   Loosen the wheel lug nuts. Raise the front of the vehicle and support it securely on jackstands. Remove the front wheel.

2   Remove the shock absorber (see Section 2).

3   Disconnect the stabilizer bar (see Section 15).

4   Position the floor jack directly under the lower control arm to give support during removal.

12.6 Exploded view of the front suspension on 1995 and later 2WD models

1	Stabilizer bar stud and bushing	7	Nut	13	Nut
2	Nut, washer and insulator assembly	8	Nut and washer	14	Stabilizer bar link
3	Bolt	9	Lower control arm	15	Stabilizer bar
4	Frame	10	Not used	16	Stabilizer bar bushing
5	Torsion bar (left side)	11	Tie-rod end	17	Stabilizer bar bracket
6	Upper control arm	12	Nut	18	Bolt

5   Remove the torsion bar (see Section 14).

6   Remove and discard the cotter pin from the balljoint stud **(see illustration)**. Loosen the castle nut on the stud one or two turns. Rap the spindle sharply in the immediate vicinity of the stud to relieve stud pressure and loosen the stud in the knuckle. If the stud won't come loose, you might have to resort to a "picklefork" type of balljoint stud separator. **Caution:** *The use of a picklefork balljoint separator will usually result in balljoint boot damage.* **Note:** *It may be necessary to purchase a special Ford tool to remove the balljoint (T64P-3590-F).*

7   Loosen the two control arm pivot bolts.

8   Remove the balljoint stud nut, separate the pivot bolts from the control arm and remove the lower control arm.

Inspection

9   Inspect the bushings for cracks and tears. If they're damaged or worn, take the control arm to an automotive machine shop to have new bushings installed. This procedure requires a number of specialized tools, so it's not worth tackling at home. If the balljoint is worn out the entire control arm must be replaced.

Installation

10   Install the lower control arm pivot bolts and nuts. Don't fully tighten the nuts at this time.

11   Install the torsion bar (see Section 15).

12   Place a floor jack under the lower control arm, raise the lower control arm and guide it into position.

13   Insert the balljoint stud into the spindle, install the castle nut and tighten it to the torque listed in this Chapter's Specifications. Continue to tighten the nut, if necessary, until the hole in the stud is in line with

the slot in the nut. Install a new cotter pin.

14   Install the shock absorber (see Section 2).

15   Attach the stabilizer bar (see Section 15).

16   Install the wheel, remove the jackstands, lower the vehicle and tighten the wheel lug nuts to the torque listed in this Chapter's Specifications.

17   Tighten the lower control arm pivot bolt nuts to the torque listed in this Chapter's Specifications.

18   Adjust the vehicle ride height by turning the torsion bar bolt.

13 Upper control arm (1995 and later models) - removal, inspection and installation

Caution: *If the vehicle is equipped with Automatic Ride Control (ARC), make sure the air suspension switch is turned to the OFF position before the vehicle is raised, towed or jump started to prevent damage to the system components.*
Note: *The upper control arm and ball joint cannot be separated and must be replaced as a single unit.*

Removal

Refer to illustration 13.4

1   Loosen the wheel lug nuts, raise the vehicle, support it securely on jackstands and remove the wheel.

2   Place a floor jack under the lower control arm and raise it slightly. The jack must remain in this position during the entire operation.

3   Remove the pinch bolt that secures the upper balljoint stud to the spindle/steering knuckle.

10

FRONT OF VEHICLE

LH BALL JOINT AND ARM ASSEMBLY

FRONT OF VEHICLE

**RH BALL JOINT AND ARM ASSEMBLY
(TWO-PIECE DESIGN)**

13.4 Upper control arm details on 1995 and later models

1 Nut	4 Frame
2 Front suspension upper adjuster cam	5 Upper control arm ball joint
3 Front suspension upper adjuster cam bolt	6 Upper control arm
	7 Nut

4   Remove the upper control arm pivot bolts **(see illustration)** and detach the arm from the frame.

Inspection

5   Inspect the control arm bushings for cracks and tears. If they're damaged or worn, take the control arm to an automotive machine shop to have new bushings installed. This procedure requires a number of specialized tools, so it's not worth tackling at home. If the balljoint is worn out, the control arm must be replaced.

Installation

6   Position the control arm on the frame and install the two pivot bolts, cams and nuts. Tighten the bolts to the torque listed in this Chapter's Specifications.
7   Insert the upper balljoint stud into the spindle and install the pinch bolt and nut. Tighten the nut to the torque listed in this Chapter's Specifications.
8   Install the wheel and tighten the lug nuts to the torque listed in this Chapter's Specifications.
9   Drive the vehicle to an alignment shop and have the caster, camber and toe-in adjusted as required.

14   Torsion bar (1995 and later models) - removal and installation

Refer to illustrations 14.4 and 14.5
Caution: *If the vehicle is equipped with Automatic Ride Control (ARC), make sure the air suspension switch is turned to the OFF position before the vehicle is raised, towed or jump started to prevent damage*

**14.4 Raise the adjuster assembly using special tool number
T95T-5310-A**

FRONT OF VEHICLE

14.5 Torsion bar mounting details

1	Frame	6	Not used
2	Nut	7	Adjuster
3	Bolt	8	Adjuster bolt
4	Torsion bar protector	9	Torsion bar support nut
5	Torsion bar		

to the system components.
1   Raise the front of the vehicle, support it securely on jackstands, block the rear wheels and set the parking brake. Position the front wheels in the straight ahead position.
2   Disconnect the torsion bar protector from the frame.
3   Unscrew the bolt from the torsion bar nut while counting the number of turns to remove the bolt (for installation purposes). Record this number on a piece of paper.
4   Use a special tool (Torsion Bar Tool T95T-5310-A) to raise the adjuster **(see illustration)**.
5   Remove the torsion bar nut **(see illustration)**. Lower the adjuster.
6   Slide the torsion bar into the lower control arm and remove the adjuster.
7   Remove the torsion bar from the lower control arm.

15.2a Stabilizer bar
(2WD model shown, 4WD similar)

FRONT OF VEHICLE

15.2b Stabilizer bar mounting details on (1995 and later models)

1	Front stabilizer bar bolt	6	Front stabilizer bar bushing
2	Nut		
3	Lower control arm	7	Front stabilizer bar bracket
4	Front stabilizer bar link		
5	Front stabilizer bar	8	Bolt
		9	Frame

8   Installation is the reverse of removal, with the following points:

a) Be sure to lubricate the threads of the adjuster nut and the tip of the adjuster bolt with grease.

b) When installing the adjuster bolt, screw it in the same number of turns it took to remove it, plus two more turns.

c) If necessary, turn the torsion bar adjuster bolt in or out to adjust the ride height so the vehicle is level from side-to-side. If the vehicle is equipped with Automatic Ride Control (ARC), disconnect the air lines from the shock absorbers before

attempting adjustment. Also, roll the vehicle back and forth and jounce the suspension before adjusting and in between adjustments.

15   Front stabilizer bar - removal and installation

Refer to illustration 15.2a and 15.2b

Caution: If the vehicle is equipped with Automatic Ride Control (ARC), make sure the air suspension switch is turned to the OFF position before the vehicle is raised, towed or jump started to prevent damage to the system components.

1   Raise the front of the vehicle, support it securely on jackstands, block the rear wheels and set the parking brake. Position the front wheels in the straight ahead position.

2   Detach the stabilizer bar from the axle arms (1994 and earlier models) or from the link attached to the lower control arm (1995 and later models), then from the frame **(see illustrations)**.

3   Remove the stabilizer bar assembly.

4   Installation is the reverse of the removal steps. Tighten the bolts and nuts to the torque listed in this Chapter's Specifications.

16   Rear shock absorbers - inspection, removal and installation

Caution: If the vehicle is equipped with Automatic Ride Control (ARC), make sure the air suspension switch is turned to the OFF position before the vehicle is raised, towed or jump started to prevent damage to the system components.

Inspection

1   Refer to Section 3 for inspection procedures.

Removal and installation

Refer to illustrations 16.3 and 16.5

2   If the vehicle is equipped with an Automatic Ride Control (ARC) system, turn the ARC switch OFF. Place a floor jack under the axle adjacent to shock absorber being removed. Apply just enough jack

10

16.3 Details of the rear shock absorber on an ARC system

16.5 Remove the shock absorber lower bolt and nut (arrow)

17.4 The rear leaf springs are secured to the axle housing by U-bolts

pressure to take the load off the shock absorber.

3   Disconnect the electrical connector from the shock absorber harness **(see illustration)**.

4   Also, on ARC systems, disconnect the air line from the shock. Push in on the plastic ring on the shock absorber and while holding the ring in, pull out the air line.

5   Remove the nut and bolt securing the lower end of the shock absorber to the spring plate **(see illustration)**.

6   Remove the nut securing the top of the shock absorber to the upper mounting bracket on the frame.

7   Installation is the reverse of the removal steps. Tighten the nuts and bolts to the torque listed in this Chapter's Specifications.

17 Rear leaf spring - removal and installation

Refer to illustrations 17.4, 17.5a, 17.5b and 17.6

Caution: *If the vehicle is equipped with Automatic Ride Control (ARC), make sure the air suspension switch is turned to the OFF position before the vehicle is raised, towed or jump started to prevent damage to the system components.*

Removal

1   Raise the rear of the vehicle until the weight is off the rear springs but the tires are still touching the ground.

2   Support the vehicle securely on jackstands and support the rear axle with a jack. DO NOT get under a vehicle that's supported only by a jack, even if the tires are still installed.

3   Remove the nut and bolt securing the lower end of the shock absorber to the spring plate **(see illustration 16.5)**. Compress the shock up and out of the way.

4   Remove the nuts from the U-bolts and remove the U-bolts and the spring plate from the spring **(see illustration)**.

5   Remove the bolts and nuts securing the shackle assembly at the rear of the spring **(see illustrations)**. Let the spring pivot down and rest on the floor.

6   Remove the spring hanger bolt and nut at the front of the spring **(see illustration)**. Remove the spring.

7   Inspect the spring eye bushings for wear or distortion. If worn or damaged have them replaced by a dealer service department or properly equipped shop.

17.5a To undo the rear shackle, hold the bolts with a wrench . . .

17.5b . . . and remove the shackle nuts

Installation

8   Place the spring in the rear shackle. Install the bolt and nut and tighten them finger-tight.

9   Install the spring in the front bracket. Tighten the bolt and nut finger-tight.

10   Position the rear shackle on the frame. Install the bolt and nut and tighten them finger-tight.

11   Position the axle on the spring and install the spring seat. Make sure the spring tie-bolt is positioned in the hole in the spring, then install the U-bolts and nuts. Tighten the nuts finger-tight.

12   Lower the vehicle to the ground so its weight is resting on the tires. Tighten the spring bracket bolt and nut, shackle bolts and nuts and U-bolt nuts to the torques listed in this Chapter's Specifications.

---

18   Rear stabilizer bar - removal and installation

Refer to illustrations 18.1, 18.2 and 18.3

Caution: *If the vehicle is equipped with Automatic Ride Control (ARC), make sure the air suspension switch is turned to the OFF position before the vehicle is raised, towed or jump started to prevent damage to the system components.*

Removal

1   Remove the nut and washer securing the rear stabilizer bar ends to the link at each end **(see illustration)**.

18.1 Remove the link nut . . .

18.2 . . . and retainer bolts, then remove the stabilizer bar

17.6 The leaf spring front bracket

2   Unbolt the retainers from the rear axle housing **(see illustration)**.

3   Remove the mounting brackets, retainer and the stabilizer bar from the vehicle **(see illustration)**.

4   Inspect the rubber isolators on the stabilizer bar and replace if necessary.

Installation

5   Position the stabilizer bar onto the rear axle assembly. Position the retainer with the UP mark facing up.

6   Install the stabilizer bar and retainer onto the mounting brackets. Make sure the UP mark on the retainer is facing up toward the floor pan or bed.

7   Install the U-bolts and nuts. Tighten the nuts finger-tight.

8   Move the stabilizer bar ends up into position and connect them to the links. Install the bolt, washer and nut on each end. Tighten the bolts and nuts to the torque listed in this Chapter's Specifications.

9   Tighten the retainer bolts and link nuts to the torque listed in this Chapter's Specifications.

18.3 Rear stabilizer bar components

10

19.1 Conventional steering system on 1991 through 1994 models

19   Steering system - general information

Refer to illustrations 19.1 and 19.2

The steering system on 1991 through 1994 models consists of a Pitman arm, drag link, steering connecting rod and tie-rods **(see illustration)**. The Pitman arm transfers the steering gear movements through the drag link and steering connecting rod to the tie-rods at each end. The tie-rods move the spindles (or knuckle) and front wheels to the desired steering movement. The tie-rods are equipped with an adjusting sleeve for setting the toe-in. All models are equipped with the Ford Integral Power Steering gear that consists of a belt-driven Ford C-II pump and associated lines and hoses. The power steering pump reservoir fluid level should be checked periodically (see Chapter 1). The steering wheel operates the steering shaft, which actuates the steering gear through universal joints and the intermediate shaft. Looseness in the steering can be caused by wear in the steering shaft universal joints, the steering gear, the tie-rod ends and loose retaining bolts.

The steering system on 1995 models consists of integral power steering rack-and-pinion gear that incorporates a constant diameter rack **(see illustration)**. The steering gear is mounted to the front of the crossmember. The steering gear is a hydraulic mechanical unit which uses an integral piston and rack design to provide power assisted steering.

Caution: *If the vehicle is equipped with Automatic Ride Control (ARC), make sure the air suspension switch is turned to the OFF position before the vehicle is raised, towed or jump started to prevent damage to the system components.*

20   Steering wheel - removal and installation

Warning 1: *Some models have airbags. Always disconnect the negative battery cable, then the positive battery cable and wait two minutes before working in the vicinity of the impact sensors, steering column or instrument panel to avoid the possibility of accidental deployment of the airbag, which could cause personal injury (see Chapter 12).*

Warning 2: *On models equipped with a driver's side airbag, put the wheels in the straight ahead position and lock the steering column. The steering column must not be rotated while the steering wheel is removed.*

19.2 Rack-and-pinion steering system on 1995 and later models

20.2a Remove the horn pad screws and take the horn pad off

20.2b Remove the plugs from the sides of the steering wheel

20.3a Remove the bolt from each side of the steering wheel

Caution: *If the vehicle is equipped with Automatic Ride Control (ARC), make sure the air suspension switch is turned to the OFF position before the vehicle is raised, towed or jump started to prevent damage to the system components.*

Removal

Refer to illustrations 20.2a, 20.2b, 20.3a, 20.3b, 20.5, 20.6, 20.7 and 20.8

1   Disconnect the negative cable from the battery (and from the positive terminal if equipped with an airbag).

2   On non-airbag systems, remove the screws securing the horn pad to the steering wheel **(see illustration)**. On airbag systems, pry the two plugs covering the driver's side airbag module screws **(see illustration)** on the sides of the steering wheel.

3   On non-airbag systems, partially pull the horn pad away from the steering wheel, unplug the electrical connector then remove the horn pad. On models with airbags, remove the two screws from the side of the steering wheel, lift the airbag off and detach the electrical

connector **(see illustrations)**. Store the airbag in a safe place until needed. **Warning:** *Whenever handling an airbag module, always keep the airbag opening pointed away from your body. Never place the airbag module on a bench of other surface with the airbag opening facing the surface. Always place the airbag module in a safe location with the airbag opening facing up.*

4   Remove the steering wheel bolt.

5   Lift off the damper (if equipped) **(see illustration)**.

AIR BAG CONNECTOR
STEERING WHEEL
AIR BAG MODULE
AIR BAG CONNECTOR

20.3b Disconnect the airbag electrical connector

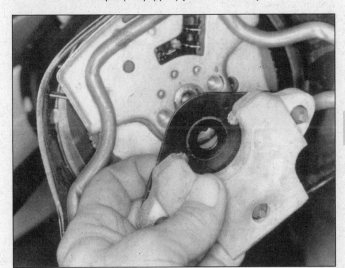

20.5 Lift the damper off the steering wheel (if equipped)

10

20.6 There should be factory alignment marks on the steering wheel and shaft; if not, make your own

20.7 Thread the steering wheel bolt part-way in so the puller will have something to push against, then remove the steering wheel with a puller like the one shown here - DO NOT pound on the wheel to remove it

20.8 Make sure the horn spring is in position before installing the wheel

6   Look for factory alignment marks on the steering wheel and column **(see illustration)**. If they aren't visible, use white paint and make your own marks. These marks will be used during installation to line up the wheel and column.

7   Use a puller to remove the steering wheel **(see illustration)**. **Caution:** *Don't hammer on the shaft to remove the steering wheel. Discard original steering wheel bolt.*

Installation

8   Make sure the horn spring is in position **(see illustration)**. Align the mark on the steering wheel hub with the mark on the steering shaft and slip the wheel onto the shaft. Install the new mounting bolt and tighten it to the torque listed in this Chapter's Specifications.

9   The remainder of installation is the reverse of the removal Steps. **Caution:** *On airbag systems, make sure the airbag wiring does not get trapped between the airbag sliding contact and the steering wheel.*

21   Drag link (1991 through 1994 models)- removal and installation

Refer to illustrations 21.2a, 21.2b and 21.2c

Removal

1   Raise the front of the vehicle, support it securely on jackstands, block the rear wheels and set the parking brake. Position the front wheels in the straight ahead position.

2   Remove the cotter pins and nuts securing the drag link to the steering connecting arm and to the Pitman arm **(see illustrations)**.

3   Loosen the clamp bolts on the tie-rod adjusting sleeve.

4   Unscrew the adjusting sleeve. Count and record the number of turns it takes to back the sleeve off the drag link.

5   Remove the drag link.

21.2a Steering linkage components (1994 and earlier 2WD models)

21.2b Steering linkage components (1994 and earlier 4WD models)

1   Tie-rod
2   Cotter pin
3   Nut

4   Front axle arm
5   Pitman arm
6   Steering drag link

Installation

6   Loosely install the drag link ball stud into the Pitman arm. Position the steering connecting arm ball end into the drag link. Make sure the front wheels and steering wheel are in the straight ahead position. Make sure the ball ends are seated in the taper to prevent them from rotating while tightening the nuts.

7   Install the drag link onto the tie-rod adjusting sleeve and turn it the same number of turns noted during removal in Step 4. Tighten the clamp bolts on the tie-rod adjusting sleeve to the torque listed in this Chapter's Specifications.

8   Install new nuts on the studs of the Pitman arm and steering connecting arm and tighten to the torque listed in this Chapter's Specifications. Install new cotter pins and bend the ends over completely.

9   Install the wheel and lug nuts. Lower the vehicle and tighten the lug nuts to torque listed in Chapter 1.

10   Have the front end alignment checked by a dealer service department or an alignment shop.

22 Steering connecting rod (1991 through 1994 models)- removal and installation

Removal

1   Raise the front of the vehicle, support it securely on jackstands, block the rear wheels and set the parking brake. Position the front wheels in the straight ahead position.

2   Remove the cotter pin and nut from the ball end of the steering connecting rod **(see illustration 21.2a or 21.2b)**.

3   Use a Pitman arm puller and remove the ball end from the drag link **(see illustration 21.2c)**.

4   Loosen the clamp bolts on the tie-rod adjusting sleeve.

5   Unscrew the connecting rod from the tie-rod adjusting sleeve. Count and record the number of turns it takes to remove the connecting rod from the tie-rod adjusting sleeve.

6   Remove the steering connecting rod.

Installation

7   Install the steering connecting rod onto the tie-rod and turn it the same number of turns noted during removal in Step 5. Tighten the clamp bolts on the tie-rod adjusting sleeve to the torque listed in this

21.2c Disconnect the steering linkage joints with a Pitman arm puller - these can be rented

Chapter's Specifications.

8   Install the steering connecting rod end into the drag link. Make sure the front wheels and steering wheel are in the straight ahead position. Make sure the ball end is seated in the taper to prevent them from rotating while tightening the nut.

9   Install a new nut on the stud and tighten to the torque listed in this Chapter's Specifications. Install a new cotter pin and bend the ends over completely.

10   Install the wheel and lug nuts. Lower the vehicle and tighten the lug nuts to torque listed in Chapter 1.

11   Have the alignment checked by a dealer service department or an alignment shop.

23 Tie-rod ends - removal and installation

Warning: *Whenever any of the suspension or steering fasteners are loosened or removed they must be replaced with new ones - discard the originals and don't re-use them. They must be replaced with new*

10

ones of the same part number or of original equipment quality and design. Torque specifications must be followed for proper reassembly and component retention.
Caution: *If the vehicle is equipped with Automatic Ride Control (ARC), make sure the air suspension switch is turned to the OFF position before the vehicle is raised, towed or jump started to prevent damage to the system components.*

Removal

1   Loosen the front wheel lug nuts on the side to be dismantled. Raise the front of the vehicle, support it securely on jackstands, block the rear wheels and set the parking brake.
2   Remove the front wheel.
3   Remove the cotter pin and loosen the nut on the tie-rod end stud. Discard the cotter pin.
4   Loosen the clamp bolts on the tie-rod adjusting sleeve.
5   Unscrew the adjusting sleeve. Count and record the number of turns it takes to back the sleeve off the tie-rod end.
6   Disconnect the tie-rod from the steering spindle with a Pitman arm puller **(see illustration 21.2c). Note:** *On 4WD models the tie-rod end is inserted in from the top of the spindle. On 2WD models the tie-rod is inserted from the bottom of the spindle* **(see illustrations 21.2a and 21.2b).**

24.4 The power steering gear line fittings are accessible through the wheel well

Installation

7   Install the tie-rod onto the steering spindle. Make sure the front wheels and steering wheel are in the straight ahead position. Make sure the tie-rod stud is seated in the taper to prevent it from rotating while tightening the nut.
8   Install a new nut on the stud and tighten it to the torque listed in this Chapter's Specifications. Install a new cotter pin and bend the ends over completely.
9   Install the adjusting sleeve onto the tie-rod end the same number of turns noted during removal in Step 5.
10   Tighten the clamp bolts on the tie-rod adjusting sleeve to the torque listed in this Chapter's Specifications. Make sure the tie-rod is positioned correctly in the same position as when it was removed.
11   Install the steering connecting rod and the drag link.
12   Install the wheel and lug nuts. Lower the vehicle and tighten the lug nuts to the torque listed in Chapter 1.
13   Have the front end alignment checked by a dealer service department or an alignment shop.

---

24   Steering gear - removal and installation

Warning 1: *On models equipped with airbags, make sure the steering shaft is not turned while the steering gear or box is removed or you could damage the airbag system. To prevent the shaft from turning, turn the ignition key to the lock position before beginning work or run the seat belt through the steering wheel and clip the seat belt into place. Due to the possible damage to the airbag system, we recommend only experienced mechanics attempt this procedure.*
Warning 2: *Whenever any of the suspension or steering fasteners are loosened or removed they must be replaced with new ones - discard the originals and don't re-use them. They must be replaced with new ones of the same part number or of original equipment quality and design. Torque specifications must be followed for proper reassembly and component retention.*
Caution: *If the vehicle is equipped with Automatic Ride Control (ARC), make sure the air suspension switch is turned to the OFF position before the vehicle is raised, towed or jump started to prevent damage to the system components.*

BOLT

STEERING GEAR SHAFT
U-JOINT SHIELD

STEERING GEAR SHAFT
U-JOINT SHIELD

STEERING GEAR INTERMEDIATE
SHAFT ASSEMBLY

STEERING GEAR

WASHER

BOLT

24.6 Power steering gear and related components

WASHER

NUT

PITMAN ARM

24.9 Remove the Pitman arm from the gear with a Pitman arm puller - these can be rented

24.10 The power steering gear is secured to the frame member by three bolts

1991 through 1994 models

Removal

Refer to illustrations 24.4, 24.6, 24.9 and 24.10

1   Set the front wheels to the straight-ahead position.
2   Disconnect the cable from the negative battery terminal.
3   Turn the ignition key to the Run position to unlock the steering wheel.
4   Place a pan under the steering gear. Remove the power steering hoses/lines and cap the ends and the ports to prevent excessive fluid loss and contamination (**see illustration** and Section 26).
5   Remove the upper and lower U-joint shaft coupling shield from the steering gear.
6   Remove the bolt securing the flex coupling to the steering gear **(see illustration)**.
7   Loosen the front wheel lug nuts. Raise the front of the vehicle, support it securely on jackstands, block the rear wheels and set the parking brake. Remove both front wheels.
8   Remove the large nut and washer securing the Pitman arm to the sector shaft.
9   Use a Pitman arm puller (Ford part No. T64P-3590-F) or an equivalent puller and remove the Pitman arm from the sector shaft **(see illustration). Caution:** *Don't hammer on the end of the puller as the steering gear will be damaged.*
10   Loosen all three bolts securing the steering gear box to the frame **(see illustration)**. Hold onto the steering gear and remove the bolts and washers and remove the steering gear.

Installation

11   Make sure the steering gear is centered. Turn the input gear shaft (wormshaft) to full lock in one direction, then count and record the number of turns required to rotate it to the opposite full lock position. Turn the pinion shaft back through one half of the number of turns just counted to center the assembly.
12   Check that the front wheels are in the straight ahead position.
13   Install the steering gear input shaft lower shield onto the steering gear box. Install the upper shield onto the intermediate shaft.
14   Position the flat on the gear input shaft so it is facing down. Position the flex coupling on the steering gear input shaft, aligning the flat with the flat on the input shaft.
15   Install all three bolts securing the steering gear box to the frame. Tighten the bolts to the torque listed in this Chapter's Specifications.
16   Align the two blocked teeth on the Pitman arm with the four missing teeth on the steering gear sector shaft and install the Pitman arm. Install the washer and nut and tighten the nut to the torque listed in this Chapter's Specifications.
17   Install the bolt securing the flex coupling to the steering gear input shaft. Tighten the bolt to the torque listed in this Chapter's Specifications.

24.28 Remove the pinch bolt and separate the lower steering column shaft from the steering gear

18   Move the flex coupling shield into place on the steering gear input shield.
19   Install the front wheel(s) and lug nuts.
20   Lower the vehicle and remove the floor jack. Tighten the lug nuts to the torque listed in Chapter 1.
21   Connect the pressure and return lines to the steering gear assembly and tighten to the torque listed in this Chapter's Specifications (see Section 26).
22   Turn the ignition key Off and connect the negative battery cable.
23   Fill the fluid reservoir with the specified fluid and refer to Section 27 for the power steering bleeding procedure.
24   Have the front end alignment checked by a dealer service or front end specialist.

1995 models

Removal

Refer to illustrations 24.28, 24.31, 24.32 and 24.33

25   Set the front wheels to the straight-ahead position.
26   Disconnect the cable from the negative battery terminal.
27   Turn the ignition key to the OFF position to lock the steering wheel. Remove the key from the ignition.
28   Remove the bolt retaining the lower steering column shaft to the steering gear input shaft **(see illustration). Note:** *Do not rotate the steering wheel when the intermediate shaft is disconnected from the steering column or damage to the clockspring will result.*

10

24.31 Power steering pump, power steering cooler and rack (gear) mounting details

1 Power steering pump
2 Power steering pressure hose
3 Power steering cooler and hose assembly
4 Steering gear
5 Frame

24.33 Power steering rack (gear) assembly

1 Bolt
2 Washer
3 Steering gear insulator
4 Steering gear
5 Nut
6 Front crossmember
7 Steering gear insulator

FRONT WHEEL SPINDLE CONNECTING ROD OR END

PITMAN ARM PULLER

FRONT WHEEL SPINDLE

24.32 Remove the tie-rod end using a Pitman arm puller

29 Remove the stabilizer bar from the chassis (see Section 18).
30 Unscrew the disconnect fittings from the power steering hoses at the power steering pump. Plug all the lines and the power steering pump to avoid any entry of dirt or contamination.
31 Remove the power steering cooler from the engine compartment **(see illustration)**.
32 Separate the tie-rod ends from the wheel spindle using a Pitman arm puller **(see illustration)**.
33 Remove the nuts and bolts that retain the steering gear to the front crossmember **(see illustration)**.
34 Remove the steering gear from the vehicle.
35 Check all the mounting bracket insulators and grommets and replace any that are worn or damaged.

Installation

36 Install the steering gear mounting insulators into the steering gear housing.
37 Position the steering gear onto the front crossmember and install the nuts, bolts and washers that retain the unit.
38 Install the power steering cooler.
39 Install the tie rod ends onto the steering arms.
40 Verify that the steering wheel has not rotated from its original position and install the steering column lower intermediate shaft over the steering gear input shaft.
41 Replace the front wheel and tires and lower the vehicle.
42 The remaining installation is the reverse of removal.

25 Power steering pump - removal and installation

Refer to illustrations 25.4, 25.6, 25.7 and 25.10
Caution: If the vehicle is equipped with Automatic Ride Control (ARC), make sure the air suspension switch is turned to the OFF position before the vehicle is raised, towed or jump started to prevent damage to the system components.
Note: Refer to Section 26 for information on quick disconnect fittings used on the power steering system.

Removal

1 Disconnect the cable from the negative battery terminal.

25.4 The power steering pump pressure and return lines (viewed through the wheel well)

25.6 This special tool is needed to remove the power steering pump pulley

25.7 Power steering pump mounting details

2   Remove the drivebelt from the power steering pulley (see Chapter 1).

3   Loosen the front wheel lug nuts. Raise the front of the vehicle, support it securely on jackstands, block the rear wheels and set the parking brake. Remove both front wheels.

4   Disconnect the return hose at the pump **(see illustration)** and drain the fluid into a container.

5   Disconnect the pressure hose from the pump.

6   Remove the drivebelt pulley as follows:

a) *Install the pump pulley removal tool (Ford part No. T69L-10300-B) or equivalent onto the pulley* **(see illustration)**.

b) *Hold onto the pump and rotate the tool nut counterclockwise and remove the pulley from the pump.* **Caution:** *Do not apply excessive force on the pulley shaft as it may damage the internal parts of the pump.*

7   Remove the bolts securing the pump to the mounting bracket **(see illustration)**.

8   Remove the pump and pulley through the mounting bracket.

Installation

9   Place the pump in the bracket and install the mounting bolts. Tighten the bolts to the torque listed in this Chapter's Specifications.

10   Install the pulley onto the pump using Ford tool T65P-3A733-C or equivalent **(see illustration)**. Be sure the pulley removal groove is toward the front of the vehicle and is flush with the end of the shaft

(within 0.010-inch).

11   Install the pump drive belt (see Chapter 1).

12   Install the pressure and return hoses to the proper fittings on the pump (see Section 26).

13   Fill the pump reservoir with the specified fluid and bleed the system (see Section 27).

25.10 This tool is used to install the power steering pump pulley

10

NOTE: IF LEAK OCCURS HERE, REPLACE HOSE ASSEMBLY

O-RING

TUBE NUT

TEFLON SEAL

NOTE: IF LEAK OCCURS HERE, TIGHTEN NUT TO SPECIFICATION. REPLACE TEFLON SEAL IF NECESSARY.

SNAP RING

PUMP OUTLET

NOTE: ALWAYS REPLACE THIS SEAL WHEN A LINE IS REMOVED

26.1 Quick disconnect fitting components

26.3 To install a new Teflon washer, stretch it with a center punch or similar tool until it fits over the flare nut - it will slowly shrink to its original size

26 Power steering line quick disconnect fittings

Refer to illustrations 26.1 and 26.3

1   If a fitting leaks, note whether the leak is between the tubing and the flare nut or between the flare nut and the pump **(see illustration)**. If it's between the tubing and the flare nut, replace the hose as an assembly. If it's between the flare nut and the pump, repair the leak (see Steps 2 and 3 below).

2   Make sure the nut is tightened to the torque listed in this Chapter's Specifications.

3   If the fitting still leaks, unscrew the nut and check the Teflon washer. Replace the washer if its condition is in doubt. **Note:** *It may be necessary to stretch the washer with a center punch or similar tapered tool so it will fit over the flare nut* **(see illustration)**. The washer will slowly return to its original size after being stretched.

4   The O-ring in the fitting can't be replaced. If it's causing the leak, the hose must be replaced as an assembly.

5   If a quick-disconnect fitting disconnects while the pump is in operation, replace the hose as an assembly.

27 Power steering system bleeding

1   The power steering system must be bled whenever a line is disconnected. Bubbles can be seen in power steering fluid which has air in it and the fluid will often have a tan or milky appearance. On later models, low fluid level can cause air to mix with the fluid, resulting in a noisy pump as well as foaming of the fluid.

2   Open the hood and check the fluid level in the reservoir, adding the specified fluid necessary to bring it up to the proper level (see Chapter 1).

3   Start the engine and slowly turn the steering wheel several times from left-to-right and back again. Do not turn the wheel completely from lock-to-lock. Check the fluid level, topping it up as necessary until it remains steady and no more bubbles are visible.

28 Steering angles and wheel alignment - general information

Proper wheel alignment is essential for safe steering and even tire wear. Symptoms of alignment problems are pulling of the steering to one side or the other and uneven tire wear.

If these symptoms are present, check for the following before having the alignment adjusted:

Loose steering gear mounting bolts
Damaged or worn steering gear mounts
Worn or damaged wheel bearings
Bent tie-rods
Worn balljoints
Improper tire pressures
Mixing tires of different construction

Front wheel alignment should be left to a dealer service department or an alignment shop.

29 Wheels and tires - general information

Refer to illustrations 29.8a and 29.8b

1   Check the tire pressures (cold) weekly (see Chapter 1).

2   Inspect the sidewalls and treads periodically for damage and signs of abnormal or uneven wear.

3   Make sure the wheel lug nuts are properly tightened.

4   Don't mix radial and bias ply tires or tires with different tread patterns on the same axle.

5   Periodically inspect the wheels for elongated or damaged lug holes, distortion and nicks in the rim. Replace damaged wheels.

6   Clean the wheels inside and out and check for rust and corrosion, which could lead to wheel failure.

7   If the wheel and tire are balanced on the vehicle, one wheel stud and lug hole should be marked whenever the wheel is removed so it can be reinstalled in the original position. If balanced on the vehicle, the wheel should not be moved to a different axle position.

8   To remove alloy wheels, carefully pry off the center cap to expose the lug nuts.

Chapter 11   Body

Contents

	Section
Body - maintenance	2
Body repair - major damage	6
Body repair - minor damage	5
Door hinge - removal and installation	11
Door latch striker - removal, installation and adjustment	12
Door lock cylinder - removal and installation	15
Door - removal, installation and alignment	10
Door trim panel and watershield - removal and installation	16
Front bumper and valance - removal and installation	26
Front door window glass - replacement and adjustment	17
Front door window regulator - replacement	18
Front fender - removal and installation	25
General information	1
Hinges and locks - maintenance	7
Hood latch control cable - removal and installation	9
Hood - removal, installation and adjustment	8

	Section
Inner door handle and latch assembly - removal and installation	13
Liftgate panel, lock cylinder and latches - removal and installation	22
Liftgate - removal and installation	21
Liftgate glass and hinge - removal and installation	23
Outer door handle - removal and installation	14
Radiator grille - removal and installation	24
Rear bumper - removal and installation	27
Rear door window glass - replacement	19
Rear door window regulator - replacement	20
Seat belt check	30
Seats - removal and installation	29
Upholstery and carpets - maintenance	4
Vinyl trim - maintenance	3
Windshield glass - removal and installation	28

11

1   General information

These models feature a welded body that is attached to a separate frame. Certain components are particularly vulnerable to accident damage and can be unbolted and repaired or replaced. Among these parts are the body moldings, bumpers, hood, doors, liftgate and all glass.

Only general body maintenance procedures and body panel repair procedures within the scope of the do-it-yourselfer are included in this Chapter.

2   Body - maintenance

1   The condition of your vehicle's body is very important, because the resale value depends a great deal on it. It's much more difficult to repair a damaged body than it is to repair mechanical components. The hidden areas of the body, such as the fenderwells, the frame and the engine compartment, are equally important, although they don't require as frequent attention as the rest of the body.

2   Once a year, or every 12,000 miles, it's a good idea to have the underside of the body steam cleaned. All traces of dirt and oil will be

removed and the area can then be inspected carefully for rust, damaged brake lines, frayed electrical wires, damaged cables and other problems. The front suspension components should be greased after completion of this job.

3   At the same time, clean the engine and the engine compartment with a steam cleaner or water soluble degreaser.

4   The fenderwells should be given close attention, since undercoating can peel away and stones and dirt thrown up by the tires can cause the paint to chip and flake, allowing rust to set in. If rust is found, clean down to the bare metal and apply an anti-rust paint.

5   The body should be washed about once a week (or when dirty). Wet the vehicle thoroughly to soften the dirt, then wash it down with a soft sponge and plenty of clean soapy water. If the surplus dirt is not washed off very carefully, it can wear down the paint.

6   Spots of tar or asphalt thrown up from the road should be removed with a cloth soaked in solvent.

7   Once every six months, wax the body and chrome trim. If a chrome cleaner is used to remove rust from any of the vehicle's plated parts, remember that the cleaner also removes part of the chrome, so use it sparingly.

3   Vinyl trim - maintenance

Don't clean vinyl trim with detergents, caustic soap or petroleum-based cleaners. Plain soap and water works just fine, with a soft brush to clean dirt that may be ingrained. Wash the vinyl as frequently as the rest of the vehicle.

After cleaning, application of a high quality rubber and vinyl protectant will help prevent oxidation and cracks. The protectant can also be applied to weatherstripping, vacuum lines and rubber hoses, which often fail as a result of chemical degradation, and to the tires.

4   Upholstery and carpets - maintenance

1   Every three months remove the carpets or mats and clean the interior of the vehicle (more frequently if necessary). Vacuum the upholstery and carpets to remove loose dirt and dust.

2   Leather upholstery requires special care. Stains should be removed with warm water and a very mild soap solution. Use a clean, damp cloth to remove the soap, then wipe again with a dry cloth. Never use alcohol, gasoline, nail polish remover or thinner to clean leather upholstery.

3   After cleaning, regularly treat leather upholstery with a leather wax. Never use car wax on leather upholstery.

4   In areas where the interior of the vehicle is subject to bright sunlight, cover leather seats with a sheet if the vehicle is to be left out for any length of time.

5   Body repair - minor damage

See photo sequence

Repair of minor scratches

1   If the scratch is superficial and does not penetrate to the metal of the body, repair is very simple. Lightly rub the scratched area with a fine rubbing compound to remove loose paint and built up wax. Rinse the area with clean water.

2   Apply touch-up paint to the scratch, using a small brush. Continue to apply thin layers of paint until the surface of the paint in the scratch is level with the surrounding paint. Allow the new paint at least two weeks to harden, then blend it into the surrounding paint by rubbing with a very fine rubbing compound. Finally, apply a coat of wax to the scratch area.

3   If the scratch has penetrated the paint and exposed the metal of the body, causing the metal to rust, a different repair technique is

required. Remove all loose rust from the bottom of the scratch with a pocket knife, then apply rust inhibiting paint to prevent the formation of rust in the future. Using a rubber or nylon applicator, coat the scratched area with glaze-type filler. If required, the filler can be mixed with thinner to provide a very thin paste, which is ideal for filling narrow scratches. Before the glaze filler in the scratch hardens, wrap a piece of smooth cotton cloth around the tip of a finger. Dip the cloth in thinner and then quickly wipe it along the surface of the scratch. This will ensure that the surface of the filler is slightly hollow. The scratch can now be painted over as described earlier in this Section.

Repair of dents

Warning: *Some models are equipped with airbags. Always disconnect the negative battery cable, then the positive battery cable and wait two minutes before working in the vicinity of the impact sensors, steering column or instrument panel to avoid the possibility of accidental deployment of the airbag, which could cause personal injury.*

4   When repairing dents, the first job is to pull the dent out until the affected area is as close as possible to its original shape. There is no point in trying to restore the original shape completely as the metal in the damaged area will have stretched on impact and cannot be restored to its original contours. It is better to bring the level of the dent up to a point about 1/8-inch below the level of the surrounding metal. In cases where the dent is very shallow, it is not worth trying to pull it back out at all.

5   If the back side of the dent is accessible, it can be hammered out gently from behind using a soft-face hammer. While doing this, hold a block of wood firmly against the opposite side of the metal to absorb the hammer blows and prevent the metal from being stretched.

6   If the dent is in a section of the body which has double layers, or some other factor makes it inaccessible from behind, a different technique is required. Drill several small holes through the metal inside the damaged area, particularly in the deeper sections. Screw long, self tapping screws into the holes just enough for them to get a good grip in the metal. Now the dent can be pulled out by pulling on the protruding heads of the screws with locking pliers.

7   The next stage of repair is the removal of the paint from the damaged area and from an inch or so of the surrounding metal. This is easily done with a wire brush or sanding disk in a drill motor, although it can be done just as effectively by hand with sandpaper. To complete the preparation for filling, score the surface of the bare metal with a screwdriver or the tang of a file or drill small holes in the affected area. This will provide a good grip for the filler material. To complete the repair, see the Section on filling and painting.

Repair of rust holes or gashes

8   Remove all paint from the affected area and from an inch or so of the surrounding metal using a sanding disk or wire brush mounted in a drill motor. If these are not available, a few sheets of sandpaper will do the job just as effectively.

9   With the paint removed, you will be able to determine the severity of the corrosion and decide whether to replace the whole panel, if possible, or repair the affected area. New body panels are not as expensive as most people think and it is often quicker to install a new panel than to repair large areas of rust.

10   Remove all trim pieces from the affected area except those which will act as a guide to the original shape of the damaged body, such as headlight shells, etc. Using metal snips or a hacksaw blade, remove all loose metal and any other metal that is badly affected by rust. Hammer the edges of the hole inward to create a slight depression for the filler material.

11   Wire brush the affected area to remove the powdery rust from the surface of the metal. If the back of the rusted area is accessible, treat it with rust inhibiting paint.

12   Before filling is done, block the hole in some way. This can be done with sheet metal riveted or screwed into place, or by stuffing the hole with wire mesh.

13   Once the hole is blocked off, the affected area can be filled and painted. See the following subsection on filling and painting.

Filling and painting

14 Many types of body fillers are available, but generally speaking, body repair kits which contain filler paste and a tube of resin hardener are best for this type of repair work. A wide, flexible plastic or nylon applicator will be necessary for imparting a smooth and contoured finish to the surface of the filler material. Mix up a small amount of filler on a clean piece of wood or cardboard (use the hardener sparingly). Follow the manufacturer's instructions on the package, otherwise the filler will set incorrectly.

15 Using the applicator, apply the filler paste to the prepared area. Draw the applicator across the surface of the filler to achieve the desired contour and to level the filler surface. As soon as a contour that approximates the original one is achieved, stop working the paste. If you continue, the paste will begin to stick to the applicator. Continue to add thin layers of paste at 20-minute intervals until the level of the filler is just above the surrounding metal.

16 Once the filler has hardened, the excess can be removed with a body file. From then on, progressively finer grades of sandpaper should be used, starting with a 180-grit paper and finishing with 600-grit wet-or-dry paper. Always wrap the sandpaper around a flat rubber or wooden block, otherwise the surface of the filler will not be completely flat. During the sanding of the filler surface, the wet-or-dry paper should be periodically rinsed in water. This will ensure that a very smooth finish is produced in the final stage.

17 At this point, the repair area should be surrounded by a ring of bare metal, which in turn should be encircled by the finely feathered edge of good paint. Rinse the repair area with clean water until all of the dust produced by the sanding operation is gone.

18 Spray the entire area with a light coat of primer. This will reveal any imperfections in the surface of the filler. Repair the imperfections with fresh filler paste or glaze filler and once more smooth the surface with sandpaper. Repeat this spray-and-repair procedure until you are satisfied that the surface of the filler and the feathered edge of the paint are perfect. Rinse the area with clean water and allow it to dry completely.

19 The repair area is now ready for painting. Spray painting must be carried out in a warm, dry, windless and dust free atmosphere. These conditions can be created if you have access to a large indoor work area, but if you are forced to work in the open, you will have to pick the day very carefully. If you are working indoors, dousing the floor in the work area with water will help settle the dust which would otherwise be in the air. If the repair area is confined to one body panel, mask off the surrounding panels. This will help minimize the effects of a slight mismatch in paint color. Trim pieces such as chrome strips, door handles, etc. will also need to be masked off or removed. Use masking tape and several thicknesses of newspaper for the masking operations.

20 Before spraying, shake the paint can thoroughly, then spray a test area until the spray painting technique is mastered. Cover the repair area with a thick coat of primer. The thickness should be built up using several thin layers of primer rather than one thick one. Using 600-grit wet-or-dry sandpaper, rub down the surface of the primer until it is very smooth. While doing this, the work area should be thoroughly rinsed with water and the wet-or-dry sandpaper periodically rinsed as well. Allow the primer to dry before spraying additional coats.

21 Spray on the top coat, again building up the thickness by using several layers of paint. Begin spraying in the center of the repair area and then, using a circular motion, work outward until the whole repair area and about two inches of the surrounding original paint is covered. Remove all masking material 10 to 15 minutes after spraying on the final coat of paint. Allow the new paint at least two weeks to harden, then use a very fine rubbing compound to blend the edges of the new paint into the existing paint, Finally, apply a coat of wax.

6 Body repair - major damage

1 Major damage must be repaired by an auto body shop. These shops have the specialized equipment required to do the job properly.

2 If the damage is extensive, the frame must be checked for proper alignment or the vehicle's handling characteristics may be adversely affected and other components may wear at an accelerated rate.

3 Due to the fact that all of the major body components (hood, fenders, etc.) are separate and replaceable units, any seriously damaged components should be replaced rather than repaired. Sometimes the components can be found in a wrecking yard that specializes in used vehicle components, often at a considerable savings over the cost of new parts.

7 Hinges and locks - maintenance

Once every 3,000 miles, or every three months, the hinges and latch assemblies on the doors, hood and the tailgate or the liftgate should be given a few drops of light oil or lock lubricant. The door latch strikers should also be lubricated with a thin coat of grease to reduce wear and ensure free movement. Lubricate the door and the liftgate locks with spray-on graphite lubricant.

8 Hood - removal, installation and adjustment

Refer to illustration 8.3
Warning: *Some models are equipped with airbags. Always disconnect the negative battery cable, then the positive battery cable and wait two minutes before working in the vicinity of the impact sensors, steering column or instrument panel to avoid the possibility of accidental deployment of the airbag, which could cause personal injury.*
Note: *The hood is heavy and somewhat awkward to remove and install - at least two people should perform this procedure.*

Removal and installation

1 Open the hood and support it in the open position with a long piece of wood.

2 Cover the fenders and cowl with blankets or heavy cloths to protect the paint.

3 Scribe or draw alignment marks around the bolt heads to ensure proper alignment on reinstallation **(see illustration)**.

4 Disconnect the underhood light connector on the driver's side and the ground strap on the passenger side of the hood.

5 Have an assistant hold onto the hood on one side while you hold the other side.

6 Remove the hood-to-hinge assembly bolts on your side of the hood, then hold your side of the hood while your assistant removes the hood-to-hinge bolts on the other side.

7 Lift the hood off.

8.3 Scribe or draw alignment marks on the hood to ensure proper alignment on reinstallation

11

These photos illustrate a method of repairing simple dents. They are intended to supplement *Body repair - minor damage* in this Chapter and should not be used as the sole instructions for body repair on these vehicles.

1   If you can't access the backside of the body panel to hammer out the dent, pull it out with a slide-hammer-type dent puller. In the deepest portion of the dent or along the crease line, drill or punch hole(s) at least one inch apart . . .

2   . . . then screw the slide-hammer into the hole and operate it. Tap with a hammer near the edge of the dent to help 'pop' the metal back to its original shape. When you're finished, the dent area should be close to its original contour and about 1/8-inch below the surface of the surrounding metal

3   Using coarse-grit sandpaper, remove the paint down to the bare metal. Hand sanding works fine, but the disc sander shown here makes the job faster. Use finer (about 320-grit) sandpaper to feather-edge the paint at least one inch around the dent area

4   When the paint is removed, touch will probably be more helpful than sight for telling if the metal is straight. Hammer down the high spots or raise the low spots as necessary. Clean the repair area with wax/silicone remover

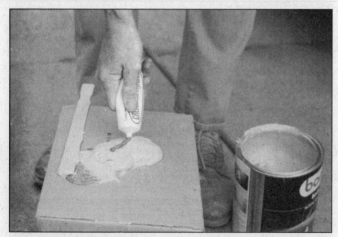

5   Following label instructions, mix up a batch of plastic filler and hardener. The ratio of filler to hardener is critical, and, if you mix it incorrectly, it will either not cure properly or cure too quickly (you won't have time to file and sand it into shape)

6   Working quickly so the filler doesn't harden, use a plastic applicator to press the body filler firmly into the metal, assuring it bonds completely. Work the filler until it matches the original contour and is slightly above the surrounding metal

7   Let the filler harden until you can just dent it with your fingernail. Use a body file or Surform tool (shown here) to rough-shape the filler

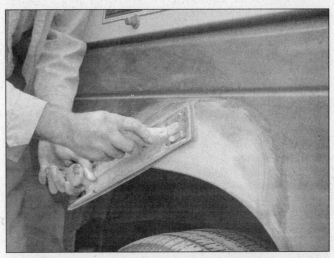

8   Use coarse-grit sandpaper and a sanding board or block to work the filler down until it's smooth and even. Work down to finer grits of sandpaper - always using a board or block - ending up with 360 or 400 grit

9   You shouldn't be able to feel any ridge at the transition from the filler to the bare metal or from the bare metal to the old paint. As soon as the repair is flat and uniform, remove the dust and mask off the adjacent panels or trim pieces

10   Apply several layers of primer to the area. Don't spray the primer on too heavy, so it sags or runs, and make sure each coat is dry before you spray on the next one. A professional-type spray gun is being used here, but aerosol spray primer is available inexpensively from auto parts stores

11   The primer will help reveal imperfections or scratches. Fill these with glazing compound. Follow the label instructions and sand it with 360 or 400-grit sandpaper until it's smooth. Repeat the glazing, sanding and respraying until the primer reveals a perfectly smooth surface

12   Finish sand the primer with very fine sandpaper (400 or 600-grit) to remove the primer overspray. Clean the area with water and allow it to dry. Use a tack rag to remove any dust, then apply the finish coat. Don't attempt to rub out or wax the repair area until the paint has dried completely (at least two weeks)

9.2 Mark the position of the hood latch location for proper installation

9.3 The hood latch is secured by two bolts

9.4 Hood release cable routing and details

8   Installation is the reverse of the removal Steps with the following additions:

a) *Align the hood and hinges using the alignment marks made in Step 3.*

b) *Be sure to tighten the bolts securely.*

Adjustment

9   The hood can be adjusted to obtain a flush fit between the hood and fenders.

10   Loosen the hood retaining bolts.

11   Move the hood from side-to-side or front-to-rear until the hood is properly aligned with the fenders at the front. Tighten the bolts securely.

12   Loosen the bolts securing the hood latch assembly.

13   Move the latch until alignment is correct with the hood latch striker. Tighten the latch bolt securely.

9   Hood latch control cable - removal and installation

Refer to illustrations 9.2, 9.3 and 9.4

Warning: *Some models are equipped with airbags. Always disconnect the negative battery cable, then the positive battery cable and wait two minutes before working in the vicinity of the impact sensors, steering column or instrument panel to avoid the possibility of accidental deployment of the airbag, which could cause personal injury.*

1   Open the hood and support it in the open position with a long piece of wood.

2   Scribe or draw alignment marks around the hood latch to ensure proper alignment on reinstallation **(see illustration)**.

3   Remove the bolts securing the hood latch and take the latch out **(see illustration)**.

4   Detach the cable bushing and lift the cable eye off the anchor post **(see illustration)**.

5   Remove the cable clips from the radiator support bracket and apron.

6   Remove the screws that secure the hood release handle to the instrument panel.

7   Remove the tie wrap that secures the cable to the steering column bracket.

8   Working in the passenger compartment, remove the cable grommet from the firewall, then pull the cable through.

9   Installation is the reverse of the removal Steps with the following additions:

a) *Insert the cable through the grommet in the firewall and make sure the grommet is properly seated within the firewall hole.*

b) *Before closing the hood, operate the control cable and make sure the latch control operates correctly.*

10   Door - removal, installation and alignment

Removal and installation

Refer to illustrations 10.4a and 10.4b

1   With the door in the open position, place a jack under the door or have an assistant hold the door while the hinge bolts are removed. **Note:** *Place thick padding on top of the jack to protect the door's painted finish.*

2   On models so equipped, remove the upper and lower hinge access cover plates. Disconnect the electrical connectors to the door wiring harness.

3   Scribe or paint lines around the door hinges to ensure proper alignment on reinstallation.

4   Remove the hinge-to-door bolts **(see illustrations)** and carefully

10.4a Remove the door hinge bolts and lift the door off

10.4b Door hinges - exploded view

lift off the door.

5   Installation is the reverse of the removal steps. Align the door.

Alignment

6   Check the alignment of the door all around the edge. The door should be evenly spaced in the opening and should be flush with the body.

7   Adjust if necessary as follows:

a) *Note how the door is misaligned and determine which bolts need to be loosened to correct it.*

b) *Loosen the bolts just enough so the door can be moved with a padded pry bar. Reposition the door as necessary, then tighten the bolts securely.*

c) *The door lock striker can also be adjusted both up-and-down and sideways to provide positive engagement with the lock mechanism (see Section 12).*

8   Tighten the hinge-to-body bolts securely.

11   Door hinge - removal and installation

Note: *If both hinges are to be replaced, it is easier to leave the door in place and replace one hinge at a time.*

1   With the door in the open position, place a jack under the door or have an assistant hold the door while the door hinge bolts are removed. **Note:** *If a jack is used, place thick padding on top of the jack to protect the door's painted finish.*

2   On models so equipped, remove the upper and lower hinge access cover plates.

3   Scribe or draw lines around the door hinges to ensure proper

alignment on reinstallation.

4   Remove the hinge-to-door bolts, then the hinge-to-body bolts **(see illustrations 10.4a and 10.4b)**. Carefully remove the hinge(s) or lift off the door.

5   Installation is the reverse of the removal Steps with the following additions:

a) *Apply a sealant (Ford specification ESB-M2G150-A or equivalent) to the hinge before installing it onto the body panel.*

b) *Adjust the door if necessary (see Section 10).*

12   Door latch striker - removal, installation and adjustment

Refer to illustration 12.1

Removal and installation

1   Use a Torx bit to unscrew the door latch striker stud from the door jamb **(see illustration)**.

2   Installation is the reverse of removal. Adjust if necessary.

12.1 The door striker can be adjusted by repositioning it and by adding or removing a shim - don't use more than one shim per door

11

13.2a Front door latch and inside handle (four-door models shown)

Adjustment

3   The door latch striker can be adjusted vertically and laterally as well as fore-and-aft. **Note:** *Don't use the door latch striker to compensate for door misalignment.*

4   The door latch striker can be shimmed to obtain the correct clearance between the latch and the striker. Don't use more than one shim per door.

5   To check the clearance between the latch jamb and the striker area, spread a layer of dark grease on the striker.

6   Open and close the door several times and note the pattern in the grease.

7   Move the door striker assembly laterally to provide a flush fit at the door and pillar or at the quarter panel.

8   Securely tighten the door latch striker after adjustment is complete.

13 Inner door handle and latch assembly - removal and installation

Refer to illustrations 13.2a and 13.2b

1   Remove the door trim panel and watershield (see Section 16).

2   Remove the screws securing the inner door handle assembly to the door **(see illustrations)**.

3   Disconnect the handle link from the handle and lock cylinder.

4   Detach the rods from the latch, then remove the latch screws and

13.2b Rear door latch and inside handle

14.2 Details of the outer door handle assembly

take it out.

5   Installation is the reverse of the removal steps, plus the following additions:
   a) If a new latch is being installed, install the rod retaining clips in it.
   b) Attach the control rod and lock cylinder rod to the latch before installing the latch.
   c) Tighten the latch screws securely.
   d) Check operation of the handle and lock before installing the watershield and door panel.

14   Outer door handle - removal and installation

Refer to illustration 14.2

1   Remove the door trim panel and pull away the watershield (see Section 16).
2   Disconnect the door latch actuator rod from the latch (see illustration).
3   Support the door handle in the open position.
4   Drill out both rivets that secure the handle to the door and remove the handle.
5   Installation is the reverse of the removal steps. Position the handle in the door and install the two pop-rivets.

15   Door lock cylinder - removal and installation

Refer to illustration 15.3

1   Raise the window all the way.

15.3 The lock cylinder is secured to the door by a slide-in retainer

2   Remove the door trim panel and watershield (see Section 16).
3   Disconnect the door latch control-to-cylinder rod (see illustration).
4   Use a pair of pliers and slide the cylinder retainer clip away from the lock cylinder and door.
5   Remove the lock cylinder from the door.
6   Install the lock cylinder into the door opening from the outside and push the retainer clip into place. Make sure it's seated correctly.
7   Reconnect the lock cylinder rod-to-door latch control.
8   Check for proper lock operation, then install the watershield and the door trim panel.

16   Door trim panel and watershield - removal and installation

Front door trim panel

Hi-Series models

Refer to illustrations 16.1 through 16.11

1   Remove two screws that secure the door handle trim (see illustration).

16.1 Remove two screws that secure the door handle trim . . .

11

16.2 . . . and one screw that secures the upper front corner of the panel

16.3 Carefully pry the trim piece out

16.4 Carefully pry out the switch panel, using the notch made for this purpose

16.5 Separate the window and door lock switches from the plate after removing the two screws (arrows)

16.6 Disconnect the power mirror connector from the switch and remove the plate

16.7 Carefully pry the trim clips out of the door with a wide-bladed screwdriver or panel removal tool - don't pull on the panel

2   Remove one screw at the upper front part of the trim panel **(see illustration)**.

3   Carefully pry out the door handle trim with a screwdriver **(see illustration)**. Flex the trim piece and take it out.

4   Insert a screwdriver into the pry notch in the window switch panel **(see illustration)**. Pry the plate up and pull it out.

5   Remove two screws and separate the window and door lock switches from the plate **(see illustration)**.

6   Release the locking finger on the power mirror connector and disconnect the connector from the switch **(see illustration)**.

7   Insert a wide-bladed screwdriver or trim removal tool between the door panel and door **(see illustration)**. Carefully pry the trim clips out of the door.

8   Pull the panel out and remove the door light socket **(see illustration)**.

9   Lift the panel to disengage its top edge from the door, then remove it **(see illustration)**.

10   If necessary, carefully peel the watershield from the door **(see illustration)**. Be careful not to tear it.

11   Installation is the reverse of the removal Steps. Align the trim clips with their holes **(see illustration)** and push them into position.

Base models

12   Refer to illustration 16.9 and perform Steps 1 through 3, 7, and 9 through 11 of this Section.

16.8 Pull the panel out and detach the door light socket

Rear door trim panel

Refer to illustration 16.13

13   Refer to the accompanying illustration and perform Steps 1, 3 through 5, 7, and 9 through 11 of this Section.

16.10 To gain access to the door lock mechanism and window glass, peel the watershield from the door, being careful not to tear it

16.9 Front door trim panel details (hi-series model shown, base models similar)

16.11 To install the panel, align the trim clips with their holes and push them in

16.13 Rear door trim panel details (hi-series model shown, base models similar)

11

16.15 Remove the four screws securing the door vent valve to the door inner panel and remove it

Door vent valve

Refer to illustration 16.15

14   Remove the door trim panel.

15   Remove the four screws securing the door vent valve to the door inner panel and remove the valve assembly **(see illustration)**.

16   Installation is the reverse of the removal steps.

17   Front door window glass - replacement and adjustment

Refer to illustration 17.4

Replacement

1   Remove the door trim panel and watershield (see Section 16).

2   Remove the door speakers (if equipped) (see Chapter 12).

3   Raise the window all the way.

4   Remove the inside belt weatherstrip from the door **(see illustration)**.

5   Detach the rear glass run retainer from the door and take it out.

6   Lower the window enough to provide access to the glass bracket and retention rivets. Remove the rivets.

7   Lift the glass out through the top of the door.

8   Installation is the reverse of the removal Steps, with the following additions:

   a)   *Lubricate the regulator rollers, shafts and tracks with multi-purpose grease.*

   b)   *Raise and lower the window to check its operation before installing the speakers (if equipped), watershield and door trim panel.*

Adjustment

9   Lower the glass two-to-three inches from the full-up position.

10   Loosen the three guide assembly nut and washer assemblies **(see illustration 17.3)**.

11   Push the glass toward the rear until it bottoms out within the door frame.

12   Move the window guide post toward the rear within the retention slot in the door inner panel. Tighten the three guide assembly nuts securely.

13   Raise and lower the window several times and check for proper fit.

14   Install the watershield and door trim panel.

17.4 Front door window and mechanism (four-door model shown; two-door similar)

18.6 Bend the tab down and back up carefully - if it's cracked or broken, the bracket assembly must be replaced

18 Front door window regulator - replacement

Refer to illustration 18.6

1   Remove the door trim panel and watershield (see Section 16).

2   Remove the window glass (see Section 17).

3   Remove the two nut and washer assemblies that secure the equalizer bracket **(see illustration 17.3).**

4   Carefully drill-out the rivets that secure the regulator base plate to the inner door panel.

5   Remove the regulator and glass bracket.

6   If the regulator guides must be replaced, flatten the tab in the end of the channel, then remove the arm slides from the channel **(see illustration)**. Install the new guides in the channel and bend the tab back to its original position. **Note:** *If the tab is cracked or broken during this procedure, the bracket assembly must be replaced with a new one.*

7   If a new bracket is installed, be sure the rubber bumper is installed on it in the correct position. **Warning:** *DO NOT remove the regulator counterbalance spring unless the regulator arms are secured so they can't move. The spring may unwind suddenly and cause injury.*

8   Install the regulator and glass bracket in the door. Use the base plate locator tab to position the regulator base plate.

9   Attach the regulator to the inner door panel. This can be done with rivets, or with a pair of 1/4-20 x 1-inch bolts with nuts and washers. Metric bolts, nuts and washers of the equivalent size can be substituted for the 1/4-20 fasteners. Tighten the screws securely.

10   The remainder of installation is the reverse of the removal Steps.

19 Rear door window glass - replacement

Refer to illustration 19.2

1   Remove the door trim panel and watershield (see Section 16).

2   Pull the inner and outer belt weatherstrips off the door **(see illustration).**

3   Remove the screw that secures the front retainer. Pull the retainer down and remove it through the access hole in the door.

4   Raise the window until it's four inches from the top of its travel.

5   Remove the rivets and lift the window up and out of the door.

6   Installation is the reverse of the removal Steps, with the following additions:

a) *Insert the rear edge of the window fully into the rear glass run.*

b) *Raise and lower the window several times to check operation before installing the trim panel and weathershield.*

20 Rear door window regulator - replacement

1   Remove the trim panel and watershield (see Section 16).

2   Disconnect the power window electrical connector from the regulator (if equipped).

3   Remove the door window (see Section 19).

4   Remove the nuts and washers that secure the window guide (if equipped) and lift the guide out of the door through the top.

5   If equipped with power windows, remove the motor bracket rivets. Drive out the center of each rivet with a punch, then drill out the rest of the rivet with a 1/4-inch drill. **Caution:** *Be careful not to enlarge the rivet holes with the drill.*

6   Remove the rivets and nuts that secure the regulator. Take the regulator out.

19.2 Rear door window and mechanism

11

21.2 Pry out the spring clip from the ball socket and lift the rod from the liftgate

7   Installation is the reverse of the removal Steps, with the following additions:

   a) *The regulator rivets can be replaced with 1/4-20 x 1/2-inch bolts, nuts and washers or metric equivalents.*
   b) *Raise and lower the window several times to check operation before installing the watershield and trim panel.*

21   Liftgate - removal and installation

Liftgate gas cylinder assist rod

Refer to illustration 21.2

1   Open the liftgate and prop it open. **Warning:** *The liftgate is heavy and may fall if it isn't securely supported.*
2   Use a screwdriver and pry out the spring clip from the ball socket at both ends of the assist rod **(see illustration)**.
3   Remove the liftgate assist rod.
4   Installation is the reverse of the removal Steps.

Liftgate removal and installation

Refer to illustration 21.6

5   Remove the liftgate gas cylinder assist rod as previously described in this Section. Prop the liftgate in the up position.
6   Scribe or draw lines around the liftgate hinges and bolts to ensure proper alignment on reinstallation **(see illustration)**.
7   Remove the liftgate-to-hinge nuts or screws and carefully remove the liftgate.
8   Installation is the reverse of the removal steps. Tighten the hinge nuts or screws securely.

Liftgate hinge removal and installation

9   Remove the liftgate as previously described in this Section.
10   Remove the interior upper rear trim to gain access to the hinge nuts.
11   If necessary, move the headliner away from the liftgate hinges.
12   Scribe or draw lines around the liftgate hinges and nuts to ensure proper alignment on reinstallation.

21.6 Index the hinge for proper installation before removing the two bolts securing the liftgate

22.1 Remove the screws the secure the upper part of the trim panel

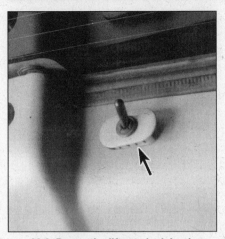

22.2 Pry up the liftgate lock knob bezel (arrow)

22.3 Remove one screw accessible through the lock knob hole

22.4 Remove the liftgate handle screws

13   Remove the nut securing the hinge to the body and remove the hinge.

14   Installation is the reverse of the removal Steps. Tighten the hinge nuts securely.

22   Liftgate panel, lock cylinder and latches - removal and installation

Liftgate panel

Refer to illustrations 22.1, 22.2, 22.3, 22.4 and 22.5

1   Remove the screws securing the panel to the liftgate assembly (see illustration).

2   Carefully pry up the liftgate lock knob bezel **(see illustration)**.

3   Remove one screw accessible through the lock knob hole **(see illustration)**.

4   Remove the liftgate inside handle screws **(see illustration)**.

5   Use a putty knife or screwdriver and pry out the plastic retainer clips securing the panel to the liftgate **(see illustration). Caution:** *Don't pull on the panel as this will rip the plastic retainer clips out of the panel.*

6   Installation is the reverse of the removal Steps.

Outside lock cylinder

Refer to illustration 22.7

7   Use a pair of pliers and slide the cylinder retainer clip away from

22.5 Details of the liftgate panel and related components

11

22.7 Details of the liftgate
latch and mechanism

the lock cylinder and liftgate **(see illustration)**.
8   Remove the lock cylinder from the liftgate.
9   Install the lock cylinder into the liftgate opening from the outside and push the retaining clip into place. Make sure it's seated completely.

Liftgate latch

Refer to illustration 22.10

10   Disconnect the actuator rods and motor rod (if equipped) from the latch **(see the accompanying illustration and illustration 22.7)**.
11   Remove the screws securing the latch to the liftgate and pull the rod and latch out as an assembly.
12   Installation is the reverse of the removal Steps.

Liftgate latch control assembly

13   Remove the outside lock cylinder as previously described in this Section.
14   Remove the latch actuator arms.
15   Remove the two bolts securing the control assembly to the liftgate **(see illustration 22.7)**.
16   Remove the latch control assembly.
17   Installation is the reverse of the removal Steps.

23   Liftgate glass and hinge - removal and installation

Refer to illustration 23.2
1   Open the liftgate window and prop it up.

22.10 The liftgate latch

23.2 Details of the liftgate window assembly

24.2a Grille installation details - Explorer models

2   Remove the retainer rings and clevis pins from both assist rods **(see illustration)**.
3   Remove the screws securing the hinges and remove the glass panel assembly.
4   If necessary, pry the assist rods from the ballstuds on the liftgate.
5   Installation is the reverse of the removal Steps.

24   Radiator grille - removal and installation

Refer to illustrations 24.2a and 24.2b
Warning: *Some models are equipped with airbags. Always disconnect the negative battery cable, then the positive battery cable and wait two minutes before working in the vicinity of the impact sensors, steering column or instrument panel to avoid the possibility of accidental deployment of the airbag, which could cause personal injury.*
1   Open the hood.
2   Remove the screws and detach the grille from the vehicle **(see illustrations)**.

25.2 Front fender mounting details

24.2b Grille installation details - Navajo models

3   Installation is the reverse of the removal procedure. Be careful not to overtighten the screws.

25   Front fender - removal and installation

Refer to illustration 25.2
Warning: *Some models are equipped with airbags. Always disconnect the negative battery cable, then the positive battery cable and wait two minutes before working in the vicinity of the impact sensors, steering column or instrument panel to avoid the possibility of accidental deployment of the airbag, which could cause personal injury.*
1   Remove the grille (see Section 24) and the headlight trim and housing.
2   Open the front door and remove the single cowl-to-fender bolt **(see illustration)**.
3   Open the hood and remove the four bolts across the top of the fender.
4   Raise the vehicle and support it securely on jackstands.
5   Remove the screws and detach the inner fender panel.
6   Remove the bolt at the lower front edge of the fender.
7   Remove the two bolts attaching the fender to the rocker panel. Carefully detach the fender from the vehicle.
8   Installation is the reverse of the removal procedure. Don't tighten any of the bolts until they are all installed.

26   Front bumper and valance - removal and installation

11

Refer to illustration 26.1
Warning: *Some models are equipped with airbags. Always disconnect the negative battery cable, then the positive battery cable and wait two minutes before working in the vicinity of the impact sensors, steering column or instrument panel to avoid the possibility of accidental deployment of the airbag, which could cause personal injury.*

26.1 Front bumper mounting details

Valance

1   Remove the screws securing the valance to the bumper **(see illustration)**.
2   Push the valance toward the rear of the vehicle and remove it.
3   Installation is the reverse of the removal Steps.

Front bumper

Note: *The bumper is heavy and somewhat awkward to remove and install - at least two people should perform this procedure.*
4   Raise the front of the vehicle, support it securely on jackstands, block the rear wheels and set the parking brake.
5   Have an assistant hold onto the bumper assembly, then remove the bolts and nuts on each side securing the bumper to the frame.
6   Installation is the reverse of the removal steps with the following additions:

a) *If you're installing a new bumper, transfer the license plate holder and any additional items to the new bumper.*
b) *The bumper can be adjusted by repositioning the fasteners in the brackets. Tighten the fastener nuts securely.*

27   Rear bumper - removal and installation

Refer to illustration 27.2
Note: *The bumper is heavy and somewhat awkward to remove and install - at least two people should perform this procedure.*
1   Remove the license plate light socket from the bumper (see Chapter 12).
2   Have an assistant hold onto the bumper assembly and remove

27.2 Rear bumper mounting details

29.2 Front bucket seat - exploded view

the nuts and retainer on each side securing the bumper to the frame (see illustration).

3   If necessary, remove the bumper brackets, stone deflector and step plate.

4   Installation is the reverse of the removal Steps with the following additions:

   a) If you're installing a new bumper, transfer the brackets, stone deflector and any additional items to the new bumper.
   b) When installing the step pad, start at the locator hole at the center of the bumper.
   c) Loosely install the bumper fasteners, then adjust the bumper position so there is a 3/4-inch horizontal gap between the bumper and body.
   d) Tighten the fasteners securely after adjustment.

28   Windshield glass - removal and installation

Replacement of the windshield and fixed glass requires the use of special fast-setting adhesive/caulk materials and some specialized tools and techniques. These operations should be left to a dealer service department or a shop specializing in automotive glass work.

29   Seats - removal and installation

Front seat

Refer to illustration 29.2

1   Remove the pin securing the insulators at the front of the seat track, then remove both seat track insulators.

2   Remove the four bolts securing the seat track to the floorpan and lift the seat from the vehicle (see illustration).

3   Installation is the reverse of the removal steps. Tighten the retaining bolts securely.

Rear seat cushion - 60/40 split seat

Refer to illustrations 29.6 and 29.7

4   Remove the rear seat latch handle.

5   Remove the outboard cushion latch cover.

6   Remove the Torx screws that secure the seat back to the cushion frame (see illustration). Separate the cushion from the seat back by pulling it forward while holding the seat back in place.

7   Remove the nuts that secure the seat cushion and frame (see illustration). Take the seat cushion and frame out.

29.6 The seat cushion frame is secured to the seat back frame with Torx screws

29.7 The seat cushion frame is secured to the floor with nuts

11

29.11 Pull the seat back away from the cushion to remove it

29.14 The latch and seat belt buckle are secured to the floor with a nut and bolt

8   Installation is the reverse of the removal Steps. Tighten the nuts and Torx screws securely.

Rear seat back - 60/40 split seat

Refer to illustrations 29.11 and 29.14

9   Remove the seat latch handle and cushion latch cover.
10   Remove the Torx screws that secure the seat back to the cushion frame.
11   Pull the seat back away from the cushion and remove it **(see illustration)**.
12   Remove the nut and bolt that secure the seat back and seat belt to the floor (on the side nearest the door).
13   Pull the seat back toward the side of the vehicle to detach it from the center pivot bracket, then lift it out.
14   If necessary, remove the nut and bolt that secure the buckle and seat back pivot bracket **(see illustration)**.
15   Installation is the reverse of the removal Steps. Tighten the nuts and Torx screws securely.

Rear seat cushion - 50/50 split seat

16   Remove the nut and detach the cushion link arm from the seat cushion.
17   Tilt the cushion forward, remove the nuts that secure it to the floor and take it out.
18   Installation is the reverse of the removal Steps. Tighten the cushion pivot and link arm nuts securely.

Rear seat back - 50/50 split seat

19   Remove the nut and detach the cushion link arm from the seat cushion.
20   Remove the nut and bolt that secure the seat back latch and seat belt to the floor (on the side nearest the door).
21   Tilt the seat back forward, pull it toward the door to disengage it from the center pivot and take it out of the vehicle.
22   If necessary, remove the link arm cover (if equipped) and link arm from the seat back.
23   If necessary, remove the pivot bracket and seat buckle from the floor.
24   Installation is the reverse of the removal steps. Tighten the retaining bolts and nuts securely.

30   Seat belt check

1   Check the seat belts, buckles, latch plates and guide loops for obvious damage and signs of wear.
2   Check that the seat belt reminder light comes on when the ignition key is turned to the Run or Start position.
3   The seat belts are designed to lock up during a sudden stop or impact, yet allow free movement during normal driving. Check that the retractors return the belt against your chest while driving and rewind the belt fully when the buckle is unlatched.
4   If any of the above checks reveal problems with the seat belt system, replace parts as necessary.

Chapter 12 Chassis electrical system

Contents

	Section
Airbag - general information	27
Brake light switch - replacement	23
Bulb replacement	17
Circuit breakers - general information	6
Connectors - general information	3
Electrical troubleshooting - general information	2
Fuses - general information	4
Fusible links - general information	5
Gauges and speedometer cable - removal and installation	22
General information	1
Headlight switch - replacement	13
Headlights - adjusting	16
Headlight bulb - replacement	15
Heated rear window and rear wiper switch - removal and installation	14

	Section
Ignition lock cylinder - replacement	9
Instrument cluster - removal and installation	21
Power door lock system - general information	26
Power window system - description and check	24
Power mirrors - removal and installation	25
Radio antenna - removal and installation	19
Radio - removal and installation	18
Speakers - removal and installation	20
Steering column switches - replacement	7
Turn signal/hazard flasher relays - replacement	8
Windshield washer reservoir and pump assembly - removal and installation	12
Windshield wiper arm - removal and installation	11
Windshield wiper motor - removal and installation	10
Wiring diagrams - general information	27

1 General information

Warning: *To prevent electrical shorts, fires and injury, always disconnect the cable from the negative terminal of the battery before checking, repairing or replacing electrical components.*

The chassis electrical system of this vehicle is a 12-volt, negative ground type. Power for the lights and all electrical accessories is supplied by a lead/acid-type battery which is charged by the alternator.

This chapter covers repair and service procedures for various chassis (non-engine related) electrical components. For information regarding the engine electrical system components (battery, alternator, distributor and starter motor), see Chapter 5.

2 Electrical troubleshooting - general information

A typical electrical circuit consists of an electrical component, any switches, relays, motors, fuses, fusible links or circuit breakers, etc. related to that component and the wiring and connectors that link the components to both the battery and the chassis. To help you pinpoint an electrical circuit problem, wiring diagrams are included at the end of this book.

Before tackling any troublesome electrical circuit, first study the appropriate wiring diagrams to get a complete understanding of what makes up that individual circuit. Trouble spots, for instance, can often be isolated by noting if other components related to that circuit are often routed through the same fuse and ground connections.

Electrical problems usually stem from simple causes such as

INSERT A FLAT BLADED
SCREWDRIVER UNDER THE
LOCKING TAB AND TWIST.
GRASP THE WIRES AND
PULL TO SEPERATE.

FLAT BLADED SCREWDRIVER

PLACE A THUMB UNDER THE LOCKING TAB AND PUSH UP. GRASP THE WIRES AND PULL TO SEPARATE.

SEE VIEW A

LOCKING TAB ONLY ON ONE SIDE

VIEW A

INSERT A FLAT BLADED SCREWDRIVER UNDER THE LOCKING TAB AND TWIST. GRASP
THE WIRES AND PULL UNTIL THE LOCKING TAB IS ON THE RAMP. TURN THE
CONNECTOR OVER AND REPEAT THE PROCEDURE ON THE OPPOSITE SIDE OF THE
CONNECTOR. THEN GRASP THE WIRES AND PULL APART.

SEE VIEW B

LOCKING TABS ARE ON BOTH SIDES OF THE CONNECTOR

VIEW B

GRASP THE WIRES WITH BOTH HANDS AND PULL THE CONNECTOR APART

3.1 Some of the various types of inline connectors used on these models

4.1a The engine compartment fuse panel is located beneath this cover

FUSE PANEL COVER

FUSE PANEL

4.1b The interior fuse panel is located above the driver's footwell - lift the handle and let the panel swing down for access

loose or corroded connectors, a blown fuse, a melted fusible link or a bad relay. Visually inspect the condition of all fuses, wires and connectors in a problem circuit before troubleshooting it.

The basic tools needed for electrical troubleshooting include a circuit tester, a high impedance (10 K-ohm) digital voltmeter, a continuity tester and a jumper wire with an inline circuit breaker for bypassing electrical components. Before attempting to locate or define a problem with electrical test instruments, use the wiring diagrams to decide where to make the necessary connections.

Voltage checks

Perform a voltage check first when a circuit is not functioning properly. Connect one lead of a circuit tester to either the negative battery terminal or a known good ground.

Connect the other lead to a connector in the circuit being tested, preferably nearest to the battery or fuse. If the bulb of the tester lights up, voltage is present, which means that the part of the circuit between the connector and the battery is problem free. Continue checking the rest of the circuit in the same fashion.

When you reach a point at which no voltage is present, the problem lies between that point and the last test point with voltage. Most of the time the problem can be traced to a loose connection. **Note:** *Keep in mind that some circuits receive voltage only when the ignition key is in the Accessory or Run position.*

Finding a short circuit

One method of finding shorts in a circuit is to remove the fuse and connect a test light or voltmeter in its place. There should be no voltage present in the circuit. Move the electrical connectors from side-to-side while watching the test light. If the bulb goes on, there is a short to ground somewhere in that area, probably where the insulation has been rubbed through. The same test can be performed on each component in a circuit, even a switch.

Ground check

Perform a ground test to check whether a component is properly grounded. Disconnect the battery and connect one lead of a self-powered test light, known as a continuity tester, to a known good ground. Connect the other lead to the wire or ground connection being tested. If the bulb goes on, the ground is good.

If the bulb does not go on, the ground is not good.

Continuity check

A continuity check determines if there are any breaks in a circuit - if it is conducting electricity properly. With the circuit off (no power in the circuit), a self-powered continuity tester can be used to check the circuit. Connect the test leads to both ends of the circuit, and if the test light comes on the circuit is passing current properly. If the light

doesn't come on, there is a break somewhere in the circuit. The same procedure can be used to test a switch, by connecting the continuity tester to the power in and power out sides of the switch. With the switch turned on, the test light should come on.

Finding an open circuit

When diagnosing for possible open circuits it is often difficult to locate them by sight because oxidation or terminal misalignment are hidden by the connectors. Merely wiggling a connector on a sensor or in the electrical connector may correct the open circuit condition. Remember this if an open circuit is indicated when troubleshooting a circuit. Intermittent problems may also be caused by oxidized or loose connections.

Electrical troubleshooting is simple if you keep in mind that all electrical circuits are basically electricity running from the battery, through the wires, switches, relays, fuses and fusible links to each electrical component (light bulb, motor, etc.) and then to ground, from which it is passed back to the battery. Any electrical problem is an interruption in the flow of electricity to and from the battery.

3 Connectors - general information

Refer to illustration 3.1

Always release the lock lever(s) before attempting to unplug inline type connectors. There are a variety of lock lever configurations **(see illustration).** Although nothing more than a finger is usually necessary to pry lock levers open, a small pocket screwdriver is effective for hard-to-release levers. Once the lock levers are released, try to pull on the connectors themselves, not the wires, when unplugging two connector halves (there are times, however, when this is not possible - use good judgment).

It is usually necessary to know which side, male or female, of the connector you're checking. Male connectors are easily distinguished from females by the shape of their internal pins.

When checking continuity or voltage with a circuit tester, insertion of the test probe into the receptacle may open the fitting to the connector and result in poor contact. Instead, insert the test probe from the wire harness side of the connector (known as "backprobing").

4 Fuses - general information

Refer to illustrations 4.1a, 4.1b, 4.3a, 4.3b, 4.3c, 4.4, 4.5, 4.6 and 4.7

The electrical circuits are protected by a combination of fuses, fusible links and circuit breakers. There are two fuse panels; one on the power distribution box in the engine compartment and one above the driver's footwell **(see illustrations).**

12

CAVITY	CIRCUIT PROTECTED
F-1	FUEL RELAY E97B-14A094-AA (30A)
F-2	HEADLAMPS E97B-14A094-BA (40A)
F-3	NOT USED
F-4	FUSE PANEL E97B-14A094-BA (40A)
F-5	POWER DOOR LOCK E97B-14A094-AA (30A)
F-6	REAR WINDOW DEF. E97B-14A094-BA (40A)
F-7	NOT USED
F-8	EEC RELAY E97B-14A094-AA (30A)
F-9	ELECTRIC SHIFT E97B-14A09-BA (40A)
F-10	IGNITION E97B-14A094-DA (60A)
F-11	UNDERHOOD LAMP, CANADIAN DRL (15A)
F-12	ALTERNATOR POWER D9ZB-14A094-DA (15A)

4.3a Engine compartment fuses - 1991 models

CAVITY	CIRCUIT PROTECTED
F-1	FUEL RELAY E97B-14A094-AA (30A)
F-2	HEADLAMPS E97B-14A094-BA (40A)
F-3	BLOWER MOTOR E97B-14A094-CA (50A)
F-4	FUSE PANEL E97B-14A094-BA (40A)
F-5	POWER DOOR LOCK E97B-14A094-AA (30A)
F-6	REAR WINDOW DEF. E97B-14A094-AA (40A)
F-7	POWER SEATS E97B-14A094-DA (60A)
F-8	EEC RELAY E97B-14A094-AA (30A)
F-9	ELECTRIC SHIFT F2AB-14A094-AA (20A)
F-10	IGNITION E97B-14A094-DA (60A)
F-11	UNDERHOOD LAMP, CANADIAN DRL (15A)
F-12	ALTERNATOR POWER D9ZB-14A094-DA (15A)

4.3b Engine compartment fuses - 1992 models

The fuse panels are equipped with miniaturized fuses because their compact dimensions and convenient blade-type terminal design allow fingertip removal and installation.

Each fuse protects one or more circuits. A fuse guide is included here (see illustrations) but consult your owner's manual - it will have the most accurate guide for your vehicle.

The cover of the footwell fuse panel contains a fuse puller tool and spare fuses (see illustration).

If an electrical component fails, always check the fuse first. A blown fuse, which is nothing more than a broken element, is easily identified through the clear plastic body or by checking it with a test light (see illustration).

To open the engine compartment fuse panel, press on the tab above the Ford emblem, then slide the cover out of its tabs and lift it off (see illustration). To open the footwell fuse panel, lift the handle and let the fuse panel swing down. Use the fuse puller tool (see illustration 4.4) to remove and insert fuses. Don't twist the fuses during removal or installation. Twisting could force the terminal open too far, resulting in a bad connection.

Be sure to replace blown fuses with the correct type and amp rating. Fuses of different ratings are physically interchangeable, but replacing a fuse with one of a higher or lower value than specified is not recommended. Each electrical circuit needs a specific amount of protection. The amperage value of each fuse is usually molded into the fuse body. Different colors are also used to denote fuses of different amperage types. The accompanying color code (see illustration) shows common amperage values and their corresponding colors. Caution: *Always turn off all electrical components and the ignition switch before replacing a fuse. Never bypass a fuse with pieces of metal or foil. Serious damage to the electrical system could result.*

If the replacement fuse immediately fails, do not replace it again until the cause of the problem is isolated and corrected. In most cases, this will be a short circuit in the wiring caused by a broken or deteriorated wire.

4.3c Passenger compartment fuses

1   Stop lamps, hazard warning lamps, speed control inhibit - 15 amp fuse
2   Horns - 20 amp
3   Lighter, flash to pass, power lumbar, multi-function switch - 20 amp circuit breaker
4   Instrument panel illumination - 10 amp fuse
5   Premium radio amplifier, trailer tow - 20 amp fuse
6   Power windows - 30 amp circuit breaker
7   Anti-lock breaks module - 20 amp fuse
8   EGO sensor heater - 10 amp fuse
9   Cluster warning lamps, electronic 4WD - 15 amp fuse
10 Speed control amplifier, radio - 15 amp fuse
11 Park/license lights - 15 amp fuse
12 Blower motor - 30 amp fuse
13 Turn signals, back-up lights, rear defroster - 15 amp fuse
14 Dome/courtesy lights/power mirror (1992 two door only) 15 amp fuse
15 Rear window washers and wipers - 15 amp fuse
16 Air conditioning switches, compressor clutch - 10 amp fuse
17 Front washers and wipers - 6 amp circuit breaker

4.4 A fuse puller and spare fuses are mounted in the cover of the interior fuse panel

4.5 To test for a blown fuse you can pull it out and inspect it for a broken element (1), or, with the circuit activated, use a test light between ground and each of the terminals (2) (if there's power to one terminal but not the other, the fuse is blown)

Fuse Value Amps	Color Code
4	Pink
5	Tan
10	Red
15	Light Blue
20	Yellow
25	Natural
30	Light Green

4.7 Each fuse amp value has a corresponding color code

5   Fusible links - general information

Refer to illustration 5.1

Some circuits are protected by fusible links. These links are used in circuits which are not ordinarily fused, such as the ignition circuit **(see illustration).**

4.6 Press down on the tab above the Ford emblem and lift the cover to gain access to the engine compartment fuses

12

WIRING ASSEMBLY — FUSE LINK
(WITH INSULATION STRIPPED BOTH ENDS)

D3AZ—14A526-H   #14 GA. WIRE — 9.00″ · 50 LENGTH
(GREEN INSULATION)

D3AZ—14A526-J   #16 GA. WIRE — 9.00″ · 50 LENGTH
(ORANGE INSULATION) AS REQ'D

D3AZ—14A526-K   #17 GA. WIRE — 9.00″ · .50 LENGTH
(YELLOW INSULATION) AS REQ'D
(SPECIAL USED WITH AIR CONDITIONING SYSTEM)

D3AZ—14A526-L   #18 GA. WIRE — 9.00″ · 50 LENGTH
(RED INSULATION) AS REQ'D

D3AZ—14A526-M   #20 GA. WIRE — 9.00″ · 50 LENGTH
(BLUE INSULATION) AS REQ'D

WIRING ASSEMBLY — FUSE LINK
(WITH EYELET TERMINAL AND ONE END STRIPPED)

D3AZ—14A526-D   #14 GA. WIRE — 9.00″ · 50 LENGTH
(GREEN INSULATION) AS REQ'D.

D3AZ—14A526-E   #16 GA. WIRE — 9.00″ · 50 LENGTH
(ORANGE INSULATION) AS REQ'D.

D3AZ—14A526-F   #18 GA. WIRE — 9.00″ · .50 LENGTH
(RED INSULATION) AS REQ'D.

D3AZ—14A526-G   #20 GA. WIRE — 9.00″ · 50 LENGTH
(BLUE INSULATION) AS REQ'D.

BUTT CONNECTOR — WIRING SPLICE

D3AZ—14488-Y   FOR #10 AND 12 GA. WIRE (LOAD CIRCUIT) AS REQ'D
D3AZ—14488-Z   FOR #14 AND 16 GA. WIRE (LOAD CIRCUIT) AS REQ'D

5.1 Fusible link service procedures

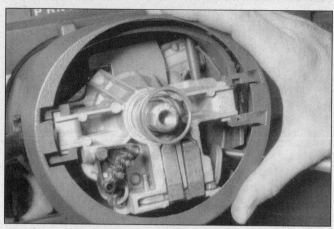

7.4 Squeeze the upper extension shroud at the top and bottom and take it off the steering column

7.5a Remove the shroud attachment screws

Although fusible links appear to be of heavier gauge that the wire they are protecting, their appearance is due to thicker insulation. All fusible links are four wire gauges smaller than the wire they are designed to protect.

Fusible links cannot be repaired, but a new link of the same size wire can be put in its place. The procedure is as follows:

a) *Disconnect the negative cable at the battery.*
b) *Disconnect the fusible link from the electrical connectors.*
c) *Cut the damaged fusible link out of the wiring just behind the connector.*
d) *Strip the insulation back approximately 1/2-inch.*
e) *Position the connector on the new fusible link and crimp it into place.*
f) *Splice and solder the new fusible link to the wires from which the old link was cut. Use rosin core solder at each end of the new link to obtain a good solder joint.*
g) *Wrap the splices completely with vinyl electrical tape around the soldered joint. No wires should be exposed.*
h) *Install the repaired wiring as before, using existing clips, if provided.*
i) *Connect the battery ground cable.*
j) *Test the circuit for proper operation.*

6   Circuit breakers - general information

Circuit breakers protect accessories such as the windshield wipers, windshield washer pump, interval wiper, low washer fluid, etc. Circuit breakers are located in the fuse box. Refer to the fuse panel guide in Section 4 and the fuse panel guide in your owner's manual for the location of the circuit breakers used in your vehicle.

Because a circuit breaker resets itself automatically, an electrical overload in a circuit breaker protected system will cause the circuit to fail momentarily, then come back on. If the circuit does not come back on, check it immediately.

a) *Remove the circuit breaker from the fuse panel* (**see illustration 4.3c**). **Note:** *The circuit breaker for the rear wiper is mounted behind the glove compartment.*
b) *Using an ohmmeter, verify that there is continuity between both terminals of the circuit breaker. If there is no continuity, replace the circuit breaker.*
c) *Install the old or new circuit breaker. If it continues to cut out, a short circuit is indicated. Troubleshoot the appropriate circuit (see the wiring diagrams at the back of this book) or have the system checked by a professional mechanic.*

7   Steering column switches - replacement

Refer to illustration 7.4, 7.5a, 7.5b, 7.6a, 7.6b, and 7.7
Warning: *Some models are equipped with airbags. Always disconnect the negative battery cable, then the positive battery cable and wait two minutes before working in the vicinity of the impact sensors, steering column or instrument panel to avoid the possibility of accidental deployment of the airbag, which could cause personal injury.*

1   Disconnect the negative cable from the battery (and if equipped with an airbag, the positive cable, too).
2   On 1994 and earlier models, remove the steering wheel (see Chapter 10).
3   Remove the screws that secure the instrument panel trim piece

7.5b Remove the lower shroud, then the upper shroud - note the position of the grommet for the horn electrical connector

7.6a Remove the lower screw . . .

7.6b . . . and the upper screw

electrical connector from the switch **(see illustration)**.

8   Remove the switch assembly.

9   Installation is the reverse of the removal steps. Be sure the horn harness grommet is positioned correctly **(see illustration 7.5b)**. Check the steering column and switch for proper operation.

8   Turn signal/hazard flasher relay - replacement

1   Disconnect the negative cable from the battery.

2   The flasher relay is located on the interior fuse panel **(see illustration 4.3c)**. Remove the flasher by pulling straight out.

3   Install the new flasher unit. Be sure to line up the metal contacts with the slots in the fuse panel. Press the flasher firmly into place.

9   Ignition lock cylinder - replacement

Refer to illustration 9.4

1   Perform Steps 1 through 5 of Section 7 to gain access to the switch. **Note:** *On 1995 and later models the steering wheel will have to be removed.*

2   Turn the ignition key lock cylinder to the first (Run) position.

3   Pry up on the tab in the ignition switch electrical connector and disconnect it.

4   Insert a small screwdriver into the ignition switch housing and release the actuator pin while pulling out on the switch **(see illustration)**.

5   Installation is the reverse of the removal steps. Install the ignition switch onto the actuator pin. It may be necessary to slightly move the switch back and forth to align the switch mounting holes.

below the steering column and take the trim piece off.

4   On models equipped with a tilt steering wheel, squeeze the upper extension shroud at the six and twelve o'clock positions and pop it free from the retaining plate **(see illustration)**.

5   Remove the two screws securing the steering column upper and lower shrouds and remove both shrouds **(see illustrations)**.

6   Remove the two screws securing the switch assembly to the steering column **(see illustrations)**.

7   Use a small screwdriver and release the tangs, then pull the

7.7 Use a small screwdriver and release the tangs to allow connector removal

9.4 Release the actuator pin while pulling out on the switch

12

10.10 Windshield wiper and arm components

10 Windshield wiper motor - removal and installation

Front wiper motor

Refer to illustration 10.10

1   Turn the windshield wiper switch On.

2   Turn the ignition switch on and keep your hand on the key. When the wiper arms move to the straight up position, turn the ignition switch Off.

3   Disconnect the battery negative cable from the battery.

4   Remove the right side wiper arm and blade assembly (see Section 11).

5   Remove the pivot nut from the right side linkage post. Allow the linkage to drop down into the cowl.

6   Remove the wiper linkage access cover. Reach through the access opening and unsnap the wiper motor clip.

7   Push the clip away from the linkage until it clears the crank pin nib, then push the clip off the linkage.

8   Remove the wiper linkage from the motor crankpin.

11.2a Lift up on the arm, pull on the slide latch and pull the arm off the spindle

9   Disconnect the electrical connector from the motor.

10   Remove the screws securing the motor and remove the motor **(see illustration)**.

11   Installation is the reverse of the removal steps. Make sure the wiper blades are in the parked position before attaching the linkage to the motor.

Rear wiper motor

12   Disconnect the negative cable from the battery.

13   Lift the wiper arm off the window. Grasp the base of the wiper arm and pull it off the motor spindle.

14   Remove the liftgate trim panel (see Chapter 11).

15   Remove the motor bracket screws and pull the motor and bracket out of the grommet.

16   Disconnect the electrical connector, detach the wiring locator pins and take the motor out.

17   Installation is the reverse of the removal steps.

11 Windshield wiper arm - removal and installation

Front wiper arm

Refer to illustrations 11.2a and 11.2b

1   **Note:** *To prevent damage to the windshield and also to make sure the wipers are operating under normal conditions, keep the windshield wet during this step. Prior to removing the wiper arm, turn the windshield wipers switch On, allow the wipers to travel through several cycles, then turn it Off. This will ensure that the wiper arm is in the parked position parallel to the base of the windshield.*

2   Swing the wiper arm and blade away from the windshield. Slide the latch away from the wiper spindle **(see illustrations)**, then pull the wiper arm assembly off the spindle.

3   Installation is the reverse of the removal steps with the following additions.

a) *Position the arm back onto the post in the parked position. Do not position the arm too low as it will hit the base of the windshield during normal wiper operation.*

b) *Make sure the latch is correctly seated in the groove in the wiper spindle.*

11.2b Be sure to pull the latch back far enough to clear the spindle

1. BEFORE THE ARM AND BLADE IS INSTALLED, THE WIPER SYSTEM MUST BE CYCLED AND PARKED.
2. LOAD DRIVE ARM ONTO PIVOT SHAFT WITH ARM HEAD IN A SERVICE POSITION.

11.5 Details of the rear wiper arm

12.1 Disconnect the electrical connector for the pump motor (arrow)

12.6 Grip the wall around the electrical terminal and pull the motor/pump assembly from the reservoir

Rear wiper arm

Refer to illustration 11.5

4   Place the rear wipers in the parked position.

5   Lift the wiper arm to its service position **(see illustration)**, then pull the arm straight off the motor spindle.

6   Installation is the reverse of the removal steps. Be sure the arm is positioned correctly on the motor spindle.

12 Windshield washer reservoir and pump assembly - removal and installation

Front washer

Refer to illustrations 12.1, 12.6 and 12.9

1   Use a small screwdriver to unlock the electrical connector tabs, then unplug the washer pump's electrical connector **(see illustration)**.

2   Remove the two screws securing the washer reservoir and pump motor assembly to the fenderwell.

3   Lift the washer reservoir up and disconnect the small hose from the base of the reservoir. Place your finger over the end of the small hose fitting on the reservoir to prevent spilling the washer fluid in the engine compartment. Remove the reservoir.

4   Drain the washer fluid from the reservoir into a clean container. If the fluid is kept clean it can be reused.

5   Use a small screwdriver and carefully pry out the retaining ring securing the pump motor in the reservoir receptacle.

6   Grasp one wall surrounding the electrical terminal with a pair of pliers, then pull the motor, seal and impeller assembly out of the

12.9 Windshield washer motor/pump installation

reservoir **(see illustration)**. **Note:** *If the impeller and seal separate from the motor they can be reassembled after removal.*

7   Flush out the reservoir with clean water to remove any residue. Inspect it for any foreign matter.

8   Inspect the reservoir pump chamber prior to installing an old motor into a new reservoir. Clean it if necessary.

9   Lubricate the outer surface of the seal with powdered graphite to make installation easier **(see illustration)**.

12

12.17 Details of the rear windshield washer reservoir and hoses

13.4 Depress the shaft release button on the switch assembly and pull the shaft out (switch removed for clarity)

10   Align the small projection on the motor end cap with the slot in the reservoir and push it in until the seal seats against the bottom of the motor receptacle in the reservoir.

11   Use a 1-inch 12-point socket and hand press the retaining ring securely against the motor and plate.

12   Connect the hose to the fitting on the base of the reservoir.

13   Install the reservoir in the engine compartment and secure with the two screws.

14   Connect the electrical connector.

15   **Caution:** *Do not operate the pump without fluid in the reservoir, as it would be damaged. Fill the reservoir with fluid, operate the pump and check for leaks.*

Rear washer

Refer to illustration 12.17

16   Remove the quarter trim panel from the driver's side of the cargo area.

17   Disconnect the filler hose from the reservoir tank **(see illustration)**.

18   Disconnect the electrical connector from the pump motor.

19   Pour the fluid into a container, then disconnect the discharge hose from the reservoir and take the reservoir out.

20   Carefully pry the pump out of the reservoir with a small screwdriver.

21   Remove the seal and filter (a one-piece assembly).

22   Installation is the reverse of the removal steps, with the following additions:

a) *Lubricate the inside of the seal with soapy water, then push the pump in and make sure it's firmly seated.*

b) *Fill the reservoir slowly so air won't be trapped in the system.* **Caution:** *Don't operate the washers without fluid in the reservoir.*

13   Headlight switch - replacement

Refer to illustrations 13.4, 13.5, 13.7 and 13.8

1   Disconnect the negative battery cable from the battery.

2   Remove the switches for the heated rear window and rear windshield wiper (see Section 14).

3   Pull the headlight switch out as far as it will go.

4   Reach up along the side of the switch (on the side nearest the driver's door) and push the knob release button **(see illustration)**. While holding the button down, pull the knob and shaft out of the switch.

5   Unscrew the switch retaining nut with your fingers **(see illustration)**. **Caution:** *The nut is plastic. Don't use tools on it.*

6   Remove two screws that secure the bottom end of the switch bracket **(see illustration 13.5)**. Pull the bracket and switch out of the instrument panel.

7   Disconnect the electrical connector from the switch **(see illustration)**. Take the switch out.

8   Installation is the reverse of the removal Steps. Align the switch tab with the notch in the instrument panel **(see illustration)**.

13.5 Unscrew the plastic retaining nut (upper arrow) with your fingers only, then remove the two screws

13.7 Lift the tangs and unplug the connector from the switch

13.8 Align the switch tab with the notch in the instrument panel

14.3 Pop the switch assembly out of the instrument panel and disconnect the electrical connectors

14.4 To replace an individual switch, squeeze the retainer tabs and push the switch out of the bracket

14 Heated rear window and rear wiper switch - removal and installation

Refer to illustrations 14.3 and 14.4

1   Disconnect the negative cable from the battery.

2   Remove the instrument cluster trim panel (see Section 21).

3   Pop the switch assembly out of the instrument panel (**see illustration**). Disconnect the electrical connectors and take the switch out.

4   To remove an individual switch, squeeze the retainer tabs and push the switch out of the bracket (**see illustration**).

5   Installation is the reverse of the removal Steps.

15 Headlight bulb - replacement

Refer to illustrations 15.3, 15.4 and 15.5

Warning: *Halogen gas filled bulbs are under pressure and may shatter if the surface is scratched or the bulb is dropped. Wear eye protection and handle the bulbs carefully, grasping only the base whenever possible. Do not touch the surface of the bulb with your fingers because the oil from your skin could cause the bulb to overheat and fail prematurely. If you do touch the bulb surface, clean it with rubbing alcohol.*

1   Open the hood.

2   Disconnect the negative battery cable from the battery.

3   Disconnect the electrical connector from the back of the headlight

(see illustration).

4   Rotate the retaining ring about 1/8-turn counterclockwise (viewed from the rear) and slide it off the base (**see illustration**).

5   Carefully pull the bulb straight out of the socket (**see illustration**). Do not rotate the bulb during removal.

6   Without touching the glass with bare fingers, insert the bulb into the socket. Position the flat on the plastic base up.

7   Align the socket locating tabs with the grooves in the forward part of the plastic base, then push the socket firmly into the base. Make sure the base mounting flange contacts the socket.

8   Slide the retaining ring on. Turn it clockwise until it hits the stop.

9   Connect the electrical connector. Test headlight operation, then close the hood.

10   Have the headlight adjustment checked and, if necessary, adjusted by a dealer service department or service station at the earliest opportunity.

16 Headlights - adjusting

Note: *The headlights must be aimed correctly. If adjusted incorrectly they could momentarily blind the driver of an oncoming vehicle and cause a serious accident or seriously reduce your ability to see the road. The headlights should be checked for proper aim every 12 months and any time a new headlight is installed or front end body work is performed. It should be emphasized that the following procedure is only an interim step which will provide temporary adjustment until the headlights can be adjusted by a properly equipped shop.*

15.3 Unplug the electrical connector from the headlight

15.4 Rotate the retaining ring about 1/8-turn counterclockwise (viewed from the rear) and slide it off the base

15.5 Pull the bulb straight out of the socket and push the new one in - don't touch the bulb glass with your bare fingers

12

17.2 Remove two screws that secure the top of the lamp housing (the screw indicated by the arrow is the headlight adjustment screw that affects the vertical position of the headlight beam)

17.3a Pull the housing straight out . . .

controlling up-and-down movement **(see illustration 17.2)** and one behind the inboard side of the headlight controlling left-and-right movement.

2   There are several methods of adjusting the headlights. The simplest method requires a blank wall 25 feet in front of the vehicle and a level floor.

3   Position masking tape vertically on the wall in reference to the vehicle centerline and the centerline of both headlights.

4   Position a horizontal line in reference to the centerline of all headlights. **Note:** *It may be easier to position the tape on the wall with the vehicle parked only a few inches away.*

5   Adjustment should be made with the vehicle sitting level, the gas tank half-full and no unusually heavy load in the vehicle.

6   Starting with the low beam adjustment, position the high intensity zone so it is two inches below the horizontal line and two inches to the right of the headlight vertical line. Adjustment is made by turning the adjusting screw closest to the fender as necessary to raise or lower the beam **(see illustration 17.2)**. The other adjusting screw should be used in the same manner to move the beam left or right.

7   With the high beams on, the high intensity zone should be vertically centered with the exact center just below the horizontal line. **Note:** *It may not be possible to position the headlight aim exactly for both high and low beams. If a compromise must be made, keep in mind that the low beams are the most used and have the greatest effect on driver safety.*

8   Have the headlights adjusted by a dealer service department or service station at the earliest opportunity.

17 Bulb replacement

Parking/turn signal/front side marker lamp

Refer to illustrations 17.2, 17.3a, 17.3b, 17.4, 17.5 and 17.6

1   Open the hood.

2   Remove the two screws that secure the top of the lamp assembly **(see illustration)**.

3   Pull the assembly straight out to expose the bulb sockets **(see illustrations)**.

4   Turn the socket in either direction to align the lugs on the socket with the notches in the housing and pull the socket out **(see illustration)**.

5   To replace the parking/turn signal bulb, remove the clip from the socket **(see illustration)**.

6   Pull the bulb straight out of the socket **(see illustration)**.

7   Installation is the reverse of the removal Steps.

Rear combination lights (stop, tail, turn and backup)

Refer to illustrations 17.8, 17.9, 17.10, 17.11 and 17.12

8   Remove the two screws securing the top of the rear combination lamp assembly **(see illustration)**.

9   Pull the housing straight out from the body **(see illustration)**.

10   Spread the connector prongs and separate the connector from the bulb socket **(see illustration)**.

11   Rotate the bulb socket to align the lugs and take the socket out of the housing **(see illustration)**.

17.3b . . . to expose the connectors

17.4 Rotate the bulb socket to align the lugs and take the socket out

17.5 Pry the retaining clip off the bulb . . .

17.6 . . . and pull the bulb out of the socket

17.8 Remove two screws that secure the top of the lamp housing

17.9 Pull the housing out of the body

17.10 Lift the retaining tabs and unplug the electrical connectors

17.11 Rotate the bulb socket and remove it from the housing

17.12 Spread the retainer prongs and pull the bulb out of the socket

12 Carefully pry apart the retaining clips and pull the bulb out of the socket **(see illustration)**.

13 Installation is the reverse of the removal Steps.

License plate bulb

Refer to illustration 17.14

14 Reach up under the bumper and grasp the socket **(see illustration)**.

15 Twist the socket counterclockwise and remove it from the housing.

16 Pull the bulb out of the socket.

17 Installation is the reverse of the removal Steps.

Cargo light

Refer to illustrations 17.18, 17.19 and 17.20

18 Carefully pry the cargo light out of the headliner **(see illustration)**. **Caution:** *Only one side of the light can be pried down. If it won't go easily, try prying the other side. Don't use excessive force.*

19 Detach the light from the connector **(see illustration)**.

17.14 Reach up under the bumper and remove the bulb socket

17.18 Carefully pry one side of the lens down - if it won't go, try the other side - don't force it

17.19 Pull the lamp down and disconnect the electrical connector

12

20   Squeeze the bulb retainer prongs together **(see illustration)**.
21   Slip the bulb off the prongs and install a new one.
22   The remainder of installation is the reverse of the removal Steps.

Dome light

Refer to illustrations 17.23a, 17.23b and 17.24

23   Use a small screwdriver and carefully pry the dome light lens away from the base **(see illustrations)**. Remove the lens.
24   Pull the bulb straight out of the socket **(see illustration)**.
25   Install a new bulb and press it in all the way, then install the dome light lens assembly.

Glove compartment light

Refer to illustrations 17.28, 17.29 and 17.30

26   Open the glove compartment and take out the contents.
27   Squeeze the sides of the glove compartment together and swing it toward you, out of the opening in the dash panel. Let the glove compartment hang down.
28   Reach into the glove compartment. Squeeze the prongs on the bulb housing together and take it out of the opening **(see illustration)**.
29   Lift the retaining tab on the electrical connector and pull the housing out of the connector **(see illustration)**.
30   Carefully pull the bulb out of the housing **(see illustration)**.
31   Installation is the reverse of the removal Steps.

Instrument cluster bulbs

Refer to illustration 17.33

32   **Note:** *The instrument cluster printed circuit board is fragile. Be careful when removing the bulb assemblies. Reach up under the instrument panel and turn the bulb/socket assembly 1/4-turn counter-clockwise.*

17.20 Squeeze the retainer prongs and remove the bulb

33   Remove the bulb from the socket and install a new bulb **(see illustration)**. **Note:** *If you cannot reach some of the bulb/sockets, remove the instrument cluster to gain access to the bulbs (see Section 21).*

High mount brake light

Refer to illustrations 17.34, 17.35, 17.36, 17.37 and 17.38

34   Remove the screws that secure the lamp assembly to the body **(see illustration)**.
35   Lift the lamp assembly off, taking care not to damage the paint **(see illustration)**.

17.23a Carefully pry the lens loose . . .

17.23b . . . and detach it from the headliner

17.24 Pull the bulb out

17.28 Squeeze the retainer tabs on the light assembly and pull it out

17.29 Disconnect the electrical connector

17.30 Pull the bulb out of the socket

17.33 Rotate the connector counterclockwise and take it out of the cluster

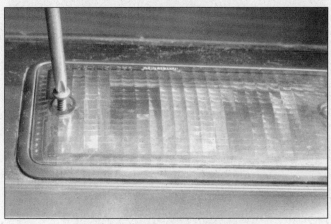

17.34 Remove the lamp body screws

37 Work the bulb socket(s) out of the lamp body **(see illustration).**
38 Pull the bulb out of the socket **(see illustration).**
39 Installation is the reverse of the removal Steps.

Vanity mirror light

Refer to illustrations 17.40 and 17.41
40 Pry the lens off the light **(see illustration).**
41 Pry the bulb out of its clips **(see illustration)** and push a new one in.
42 Push the lens back into position.

18 Radio - removal and installation

Refer to illustration 18.2
1 Remove the instrument cluster trim panel (see Section 20 of this Chapter).
2 Insert radio removal tool (Ford part No. T87P-19061-A) or equivalent into the radio face plate **(see illustration).** Push the tool in about 1-inch to release the retaining clips on each side.
3 Using the special tool, pull the radio partially out of the instrument panel, then disconnect the power, speaker and antenna wires from the radio.

17.35 Lift the lamp body off - don't damage the paint

17.36 Disconnect the electrical connector

17.37 Work the socket free of the lamp body

17.38 Pull the bulb out

17.40 Pry the lens off

17.41 Pry the bulb out of the clips and push a new one in

12

VIEW A

RADIO WIRING

ANTENNA CONNECTION

RADIO REMOVAL TOOL
T87P-19061-A

VIEW A

RADIO RETAINING SPRING

TOOL LOCKS ON SPRING HERE

TOOL INSERTION HOLES

TOOL INSERTION HOLES

18.2 Special tool used for radio removal

CAP

FRONT OF VEHICLE

SCREW

SCREW

BASE AND CABLE ASSEMBLY

COWL TOP OUTER PANEL

GROMMET

GASKET

VIEW SHOWING INSTALLATION OF ANTENNA
ON COWL TOP OUTER PANEL (RH SIDE)

19.3 Antenna mounting details

4   Pull the radio assembly out of the instrument panel.
5   Installation is the reverse of the removal steps.

19 Radio antenna - removal and installation

Refer to illustration 19.3
1   Reach under the instrument panel, pull straight out and disconnect the antenna from the rear of the radio.

FRONT OF VEHICLE

SPEAKER

WATERSHIELD

SCREW

VIEW A

STANDARD FRONT DOOR SPEAKER
INSTALLATION (2 AND 4 DOOR)

FRONT OF VEHICLE

CONNECTOR

SPEAKER

SCREW

VIEW C

FRONT DOOR SPEAKER INSTALLATION
WITH JBL SOUND (2 AND 4 DOOR)

SPEAKER

CONNECTOR

VIEW SHOWING CONNECTION OF WIRING
TO STANDARD SPEAKER
VIEW A

CONNECTOR

SPEAKER

VIEW SHOWING CONNECTION OF WIRING
TO R.P.O. SPEAKER
VIEW C

20.2 Radio speaker installation details (typical)

21.2a Push down on the ash tray retainer and pull the ash tray out

21.2b Disconnect the electrical connector from the cigarette lighter

21.3a Remove the ash tray bracket screws

2   Disconnect the antenna cable from the plastic clips along the top of the defroster nozzle.
3   Use a small screwdriver and carefully pry the antenna cap from the base and remove the cap **(see illustration)**.
4   Tie a piece of string onto the radio end of the antenna cable and the other end to the instrument panel. This will be used to pull the new antenna cable back through the same path as the old one.
5   Remove the four screws securing the antenna base to the body and slowly pull the antenna cable out through the body opening. Remove the antenna and gasket.
6   Installation is the reverse of the removal steps with the following additions.

a)   Be sure to install a new gasket.
b)   Untie the string and attach it to the new antenna cable. Slowly pull the string and antenna cable back through the body opening. Discard the string.

20 Speakers - removal and installation

Refer to illustration 20.2
Note: *The models covered by this manual come equipped from the factory with speakers in all four doors (or the doors and rear quarter trim panels on two-door models). Your particular model may vary from the following procedure due to the size and configuration of aftermarket speakers installed in some models. Speakers mounted in*

locations other than the instrument panel are removed and installed in the same manner.
1   Remove the door trim panel (see Chapter 11).
2   Remove the screws securing the speaker to the trim panel or speaker bracket **(see illustration)**.
3   Lift out the speaker and disconnect the electrical connector at the speaker. **Caution:** *Do not operate the radio with the speakers disconnected.*
4   Installation is the reverse of the removal steps.

21 Instrument cluster - removal and installation

Refer to illustrations 21.2a, 21.2b, 21.3a, 21.3b, 21.4a, 21.4b, 21.6a, 21.6b, 21.7, 21.9a, 21.9b and 21.12

Removal
1   Disconnect the negative battery cable from the battery.
2   Squeeze the ash tray retaining clip **(see illustration)** and pull the ash tray out. Disconnect the cigarette lighter electrical connector **(see illustration)** and remove the ash tray.
3   Remove the ash tray bracket screws and pull the bracket out **(see illustrations)**. Disconnect the electrical connector at the rear of the bracket and remove it.
4   Carefully pull back around the edge of the cluster trim panel **(see illustration)** and unsnap the clips that secure the trim panel to the

21.3b Pull the bracket out, disconnect the electrical connector and remove it

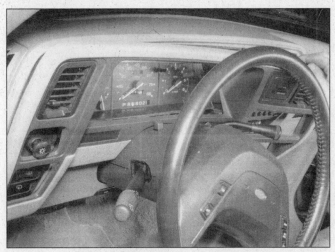

21.4a Pull the cluster trim panel out . . .

12

21.4b . . . to disengage the clips

21.6a Remove the cluster securing screws - there's a screw at each upper corner . . .

21.6b . . . and two at the bottom of the cluster

21.7 On automatic transmission models, remove the two screws and detach the gearshift indicator from the cluster

instrument panel **(see illustration)**. **Note:** *Start near the ash tray and work around the trim panel, popping the clips loose.*

5   Depress the hazard warning switch on the steering column to provide removal clearance, disconnect the 4WD electronic shift connector (if equipped) and remove the trim panel.

6   Remove the four screws securing the instrument cluster **(see illustrations)**.

21.9a Squeeze the flat on the speedometer cable (A) to disconnect it; the connectors (B) plug into sockets in the printed circuit board (instrument cluster removed for clarity)

7   On automatic transmission models, remove the screws securing the gear indicator to the instrument cluster and slide the indicator down and out of the cluster **(see illustration)**. It is not necessary to disconnect the indicator.

8   Carefully pull the instrument cluster assembly partially out from the instrument panel.

9   Reach under the instrument panel, press on the flat portion of the quick-disconnect plastic connector and detach the speedometer cable from the instrument cluster **(see illustrations)**. **Note:** *If there isn't enough slack in the speedometer cable to pull the cluster out far enough, disconnect the cable at the transmission or transfer case under the vehicle, then push it inside the vehicle while an assistant tugs on the cluster. Once there is enough slack in the cable, reach behind the cluster and disconnect it.*

10   Squeeze the locking tabs on the printed circuit electrical connectors, then disconnect them from the printed circuit board **(see illustrations 20.9a and 20.9b)**.

11   Remove the instrument cluster assembly.

Installation

12   Installation is the reverse of the removal steps, with the following additions:

a) *Apply a 3/16-inch diameter ball of silicone dielectric compound to the drive hole of the speedometer head prior to installing the cable.*

b) *There are several vibration dampers fitted over prongs on the cluster* **(see illustration)**. *These tend to fall off when the cluster is pulled out. Make sure they're all reinstalled.*

21.9b Rear view of the instrument cluster

A   Speedometer cable socket
B   Electrical connector sockets

---

22   Gauges and speedometer cable - removal and installation

Refer to illustration 22.7, 22.8, and 22.9

Speedometer cable and casing

1   Perform Steps 1 through 11 of Section 21.
2   To remove the cable only, pull out the cable core from the casing and install a new one by reversing the removal steps.
3   Remove the casing as follows:

a) *Remove the screw and clamp securing the speedometer cable to the firewall.*
b) *Working under the vehicle, remove the clamp screw and remove the cable and casing from the transmission or transfer case.*

4   Connect the speedometer casing to the head and (if removed) install the casing to the transmission using a new O-ring.
5   Install the instrument cluster (see Section 21).

Gauges

Note: *US Federal law requires that the odometer in any replacement speedometer must register the same mileage as that on the removed speedometer.*

6   Remove the instrument cluster (see Section 21).
7   Remove the lens and mask from the instrument cluster **(see**

21.12 If any of the anti-rattle insulators fall off during cluster removal, find them and reinstall them on their posts

22.7 Remove the screws and take the lens off the cluster

illustration).
8   Gently push on the back of the speedometer to loosen it from the retainer prongs in the cluster housing **(see illustration)**.
9   Lift the gauges with a gentle rocking motion to separate them from the retainer prongs in the cluster housing **(see illustration)**.
10   Installation is the reverse of the removal steps. Apply a 3/16-inch diameter ball of silicone dielectric compound to the drive hole of the speedometer head prior to installing the cable.

22.8 The instruments are removed separately

22.9 The instruments plug into prongs on the back of the cluster

12

23.1 A typical brake light switch - exploded view

25.3 Peel back the watershield

25.4 The fasteners are accessible through a hole in the door

23   Brake light switch - replacement

Refer to illustration 23.1

1   The brake light switch is located on a flange or a bracket protruding from the brake pedal support **(see illustration)**.

2   Disconnect the electrical connector from the switch.

3   Remove the hairpin retainer and spacer securing the switch to the brake pedal arm.

4   Slide the switch, pushrod, nylon washers and bushing away from the pedal, then remove the switch.

5   To install, place the switch with the U-shaped side nearest the pedal and directly over or under the pin. The bushing must be in the pushrod eyelet with the washer face on the side closes to the retaining pin.

6   Slide the switch up or down so the master cylinder pushrod and bushing are trapped, then push the switch firmly down.

7   Install the plastic washer and hairpin retainer.

8   Connect the electrical connector to the switch. Make sure the electrical connector is routed correctly and will travel the full swing of the pedal without binding.

24   Power window system - description and check

The power window system operates the electric motors mounted in the doors which lower and raise the windows. The system consists of the control switches, the motors (regulators), glass mechanisms and the associated wiring.

Diagnosis can usually be limited to simple checks of the wiring connections and motors for minor faults which can be easily repaired. These are:

a) *Inspect the power window actuating switches for broken wires and loose connections.*

b) *Check the power window fuse/and or circuit breaker.*

c) *Remove the door panel(s) and check the power window motor wires to see if they're loose or damaged. Inspect the glass mechanisms for damage which could cause binding.*

25   Power mirrors - removal and installation

Refer to illustrations 25.3 and 25.4

1   Disconnect the negative cable from the battery.

2   Remove the door trim panel (see Chapter 11).

3   Peel the watershield away from the upper front corner of the door **(see illustration)**.

4   Remove the mirror mounting fasteners **(see illustration)**.

5   Pull the mirror out, disconnect its electrical connector and remove it.

6   Installation is the reverse of the removal steps.

26   Power door lock system - general information

The power door lock system operates the door lock actuators mounted in each door. The system consists of the switches, actuators and associated electrical wiring.

Diagnosis can usually be limited to simple checks of the wiring connectors and actuators for minor faults which can be easily repaired. These include:

a) *Check the system fuse and circuit breaker.*

b) *Check the switch wiring for damage or loose connections.*

c) *Check the switch for continuity in the closed position. Also check the switches for sticking. If a switch sticks closed the actuator internal circuit breaker will trip and stay tripped until voltage is removed.*

d) *Remove the door panel(s) and check the actuator electrical connections for looseness or damage. Inspect the actuator rods and door lock linkage to make sure they are not bent, damaged or binding.*

e) *Remove the electrical connector at the actuator and with a test light or voltmeter, check for available voltage to the actuator as you cycle the switch. If voltage is present, but the actuator doesn't operate when connected, the actuator is probably defective. If no voltage is present at the connector, the switch, relay (if equipped) or wiring is probably defective.*

B	Black	P	Purple
BR	Brown	PK	Pink
DB	Dark blue	R	Red
DG	Dark green	T	Tan
GY	Gray	W	White
LB	Light blue	Y	Yellow
LG	Light green	(H)	Hash
N	Natural	(D)	Dot
O	Orange		

28.3 Wiring diagram color codes

27 Airbag - general information

Later models are equipped with a Supplemental Inflatable System (SIR), more commonly known as an airbag. This system is designed to protect the driver and front seat passenger from serious injury in the event of a head-on or frontal collision. It consists of an airbag module in the center of the steering wheel and the right side of the instrument panel, two crash sensors mounted at the front of the vehicle and a diagnostic monitor which also contains a backup power supply located in the passenger compartment.

Airbag module

Steering wheel-mounted

The airbag inflator module contains a housing incorporating the cushion (airbag) and inflator unit, mounted in the center of the steering wheel The inflator assembly is mounted on the back of the housing over a hole through which gas is expelled, inflating the bag almost instantaneously when an electrical signal is sent from the system. A coil assembly on the steering column under the module carries this signal to the module.

This coil assembly can transmit an electrical signal regardless of steering wheel position. The igniter in the airbag converts the electrical signal to heat and ignites the sodium aside/copper oxide powder, producing nitrogen gas, which inflates the bag.

Instrument panel-mounted

The airbag is mounted above the glove compartment and designated by the letters SRS (Supplemental Restraint System). It consists of an inflator containing an igniter, a bag assembly, a reaction housing and a trim cover.

This airbag is considerably larger that the steering wheel-mounted unit and is supported by the steel reaction housing. The trim cover is textured and painted to match the instrument panel and has a molded seam which splits when the bag inflates. As with the steering-wheel-mounted airbag, the igniter electrical signal converts to heat, converting sodium aside/iron oxide powder to nitrogen gas, inflating the bag.

Sensors

The system has three sensors: two forward sensors at the front of the vehicle and a safing sensor inside the electronic diagnostic monitor.

The forward and passenger compartment sensors are basically pressure sensitive switches that complete an electrical circuit during an impact of sufficient G force. The electrical signal from these sensors is sent to the electronic diagnostic monitor which then completes the circuit and inflates the airbag(s).

Electronic diagnostic monitor

The electronic diagnostic monitor supplies the current to the airbag system in the event of the collision, even if battery power is cut off. It checks this system every time the vehicle is started, causing the "AIR BAG" light to go on then off, if the system is operating properly. If there is a fault in the system, the light will go on and stay on, flash, or the dash will make a beeping sound. If this happens, the vehicle should be taken to your dealer immediately for service.

Disabling the system

Whenever working in the vicinity of the steering wheel, steering column or near other components of the airbag system, the system should be disarmed. To do this, perform the following steps:

a) Turn the ignition switch to Off.
b) Detach the cable from the negative battery terminal, then detach the positive cable. Wait two minutes for the electronic module backup power supply to be depleted.

Enabling the system

a) Turn the ignition switch to the Off position.
b) Connect the positive battery cable first, then connect the negative cable.

28 Wiring diagrams - general information

Refer to illustration 28.3

Since it isn't possible to include all wiring diagrams for every model year covered by this manual, the following diagrams are those that are typical and most commonly needed.

Prior to troubleshooting any circuit, check the fuses and circuit breakers to make sure they're in good condition. Make sure the battery is fully charged and check the cable connections (see Chapter 1). Make sure all connectors are clean, with no broken or loose terminals.

Refer to the accompanying table for the wire color codes applicable to your vehicle **(see illustration)**.

12

Headlight circuit (1992 model shown; 1991 models similar)

Exterior lighting circuit

Backup light circuit

Dome/cargo lighting circuit (part 1 of 2)

12

Dome/cargo lighting circuit (part 2 of 2)

Turn/stop/hazard lighting circuit (1991 model shown; 1992 models similar)

Instrument panel lighting circuit

Power window circuit (part 1 of 2) (1991 models)

Power window circuit (part 2 of 2) (1991 models)

Power window circuit (part 1 of 2) (1992 models)

Power window circuit (part 2 of 2)   (1992 models)

Power door lock circuit

Optional trailer adapter wiring diagram

Charging system/power distribution - 1991 models (part 1 of 4)

Charging system/power distribution - 1991 models (part 2 of 4)

Charging system/power distribution - 1991 models (part 3 of 4)

12

Charging system/power distribution - 1991 models (part 4 of 4)

Charging system circuit (1992 models)

Power distribution - 1992 models (part 1 of 10)

Power distribution - 1992 models (part 2 of 10)

12

Power distribution - 1992 models (part 3 of 10)

Power distribution - 1992 models (part 4 of 10)

Power distribution - 1992 models (part 5 of 10)

Power distribution - 1992 models (part 6 of 10)

12

Power distribution - 1992 models (part 7 of 10)

Power distribution - 1992 models (part 8 of 10)

Power distribution - 1992 models (part 9 of 10)

Power distribution - 1992 models (part 10 of 10)

12

Start/ignition system circuit (1991 models)

Starting system circuit (1992 models)

Ignition system circuit - 1992 models (part 1 of 2)

Ignition system circuit - 1992 models (part 2 of 2)

12

Electronic engine control system - 1992 models shown; 1991 models similar (part 1 of 4)

Electronic engine control system - 1992 models shown; 1991 models similar (part 2 of 4)

Electronic engine control system - 1992 models shown; 1991 models similar (part 3 of 4)

Electronic engine control system - 1992 models shown; 1991 models similar (part 4 of 4)

12

Cruise control circuit

Heater/air conditioner wiring diagram - 1992 models shown; 1991 models similar (part 1 of 2)

Heater/air conditioner wiring diagram - 1992 models shown; 1991 models similar (part 2 of 2)

Rear window defogger circuit

12

Radio and speaker wiring diagram (typical) (part 1 of 3)

Radio and speaker wiring diagram (typical) (part 2 of 3)

Radio and speaker wiring diagram (typical) (part 3 of 3)

Electronic shift control wiring diagram (1991 model shown; 1992 models similar)

12

Rear Anti-lock Brake System (RABS) (1991 model shown; 1992 model similar)

Horn and cigarette lighter wiring diagram

Front wipers and washers wiring diagram

Liftgate wipers and washers wiring diagram

12

Index

A

Air cleaner housing, removal and installation, 4-7
Air conditioning
  accumulator, removal and installation, 3-12
  compressor, removal and installation, 3-11
  condenser, removal and installation, 3-11
  system, check and maintenance, 3-10
Air filter replacement, 1-25
Airbag, general information, 12-21
Alternator, removal and installation, 5-7
Antifreeze, general information, 3-2
Anti-lock Brake System (ABS), general information, 9-2
Automatic transmission, 7B-1 through 7B-6
  diagnosis, general, 7B-1
  fluid check/change, 1-12
  general information, 7B-1
  shift cable
    adjustment, 7B-2
    removal and installation, 7B-3
  shift linkage lubrication, 1-20
  vacuum diaphragm, removal and installation, 7B-6
Automatic transmission, removal and installation, 7B-4
Axle
  arm, front, (1991 through 1994 models), removal
    and installation, 10-12
  pivot bracket (1991 through 1994 models), removal
    and installation, 10-14
  pivot bushing (1991 through 1994 models), removal
    and installation, 10-12
Axleshafts (rear), bearings and oil seals, removal
  and installation, 8-14

B

Balljoints, removal and installation, 10-7
Battery
  cables, check and replacement, 5-2
  check, maintenance and charging, 1-17
  removal and installation, 5-2
Body, 11-1 through 11-22
  repair
    major damage, 11-3
    minor damage, 11-2
Brakes, 9-1 through 9-28
  Anti-lock Brake System (ABS), general information, 9-2
  caliper, removal, overhaul and installation, 9-9
  disc, inspection, removal and installation, 9-11
  fluid level check, 1-7
  general information, 9-2
  hoses and lines, inspection and replacement, 9-19
  hydraulic system, bleeding, 9-20
  light switch, removal and installation, 9-28, 12-20
  master cylinder, removal, overhaul and installation, 9-17
  pads, replacement, 9-6
  parking brake
    adjustment, 9-20
    cables, replacement, 9-21
    shoes (rear disc brakes only), inspection and replacement, 9-26
  power booster, check, removal, installation and adjustment, 9-27
  shoes (rear), replacement, 9-12
  system check, 1-31
  wheel cylinder, removal, overhaul and installation, 9-16
Bulb replacement, 12-12
Bumper, removal and installation
  front, 11-17
  rear, 11-18

C

Caliper, brake, removal, overhaul and installation, 9-9
Camber adjustment, 10-7
Camshaft, removal, inspection and installation, 2A-15
Catalytic converter, 6-11
Charging system
  check, 5-5
  general information and precautions, 5-5
Chassis electrical system, 12-1 through 12-21
Chassis lubrication, 1-21
Check engine light, 6-2
Circuit breakers, general information, 12-6
Clutch
  components, removal, inspection and installation, 8-3
  description and check, 8-2
  fluid level check, 1-7
  hydraulic line quick-disconnect fittings, general information, 8-6
  hydraulic system, bleeding, 8-7
  master cylinder and reservoir, removal and installation, 8-6
  pedal, removal and installation, 8-7
  release bearing, removal, inspection and installation, 8-4
  release cylinder, removal and installation, 8-6
  starter interlock switch, removal and installation, 8-8
Clutch and drivetrain, 8-1 through 8-24
Coil spring (1991 through 1994 models), removal
  and installation, 10-9
Compression check, 2B-4
Connectors, electrical, general information, 12-3
Control arm (1995 and later models), removal, inspection
  and installation
  lower, 10-14
  upper, 10-15

Coolant
reservoir, removal and installation, 3-5
temperature sending unit, removal and installation, 3-5
Cooling
fan and viscous clutch, inspection, removal and installation, 3-5
system check, 1-27
system servicing (draining, flushing and refilling), 1-39
Cooling, heating and air conditioning systems, 3-1 through 3-14
Crankshaft
inspection, 2B-15
installation and main bearing oil clearance check, 2B-18
oil seals, replacement, 2A-19
pulley, front oil seal and timing chain, 2A-11
removal, 2B-11
Crankshaft and camshaft position sensors, removal and installation, 5-4
Cylinder head
cleaning and inspection, 2B-8
disassembly, 2B-7
reassembly, 2B-10
removal and installation, 2A-10
Cylinder honing, 2B-13

D

Diagnosis, 0-18
Differential lubricant level check and change, 1-23
Disc (brake), removal and installation, 9-11
Door
hinge, removal and installation, 11-7
latch striker, removal, installation and adjustment, 11-7
lock cylinder, removal and installation, 11-9
trim panel and watershield, removal and installation, 11-9
removal, installation and alignment, 11-6
window glass, replacement
front, 11-12
rear, 11-13
window regulator, replacement, 11-13
Double cardan type U-joint, overhaul, 8-10
Drag link (1991 through 1994 models), removal and installation, 10-22
Drivebelt check, adjustment and replacement, 1-15
Driveshaft
and driveaxle yoke lubrication (4WD models), 1-40
and universal joints, description and check, 8-8
removal and installation, 8-8

E

EFI
Air bypass valve, 4-9
Air Charge Temperature (ACT) sensor, 4-10
air intake throttle body, 4-8
fuel pressure regulator, 4-11
fuel rail and injectors, 4-10
Mass Air Flow (MAF) sensor, 4-10
Throttle Position Sensor (TPS), 4-9
upper intake manifold and throttle body, 4-8
Electrical troubleshooting, general information, 12-1
Electronic Engine Control (EEC-IV) system and trouble codes, 6-2
Electronic fuel injection, component removal and installation, 4-8
Emissions control systems, 6-1 through 6-12
general information, 6-1
Engine
block
cleaning, 2B-12
inspection, 2B-13

camshaft, removal, inspection and installation, 2A-15
compression check, 2B-4
coolant level check, 1-7
crankshaft
inspection, 2B-15
installation and main bearing oil clearance check, 2B-18
oil seals, replacement, 2A-19
pulley, front oil seal and timing chain, 2A-11
removal, 2B-11
cylinder head
cleaning and inspection, 2B-8
disassembly, 2B-7
reassembly, 2B-10
removal and installation, 2A-10
cylinder honing, 2B-13
initial start-up and break-in after overhaul, 2B-22
in-vehicle repairs, 2A-1 through 2A-22
main and connecting rod bearings, inspection, 2B-16
manifold, removal and installation
exhaust, 2A-9
intake, 2A-8
oil
and filter change, 1-10
level check, 1-7
pan and baffle, removal and installation, 2A-16
pump, removal and installation, 2A-18
overhaul
disassembly sequence, 2B-7
general information, 2B-3
reassembly sequence, 2B-17
piston rings, installation, 2B-17
pistons/connecting rods
inspection, 2B-14
installation and rod bearing oil clearance check, 2B-20
removal, 2B-10
rebuilding alternatives, 2B-6
removal and installation, 2B-5
removal, methods and precautions, 2B-5
repair operations possible with the engine in the vehicle, 2A-3
rocker arms and pushrods, removal, inspection and installation, 2A-6
timing chain and sprockets, inspection, removal, 2A-13
Top Dead Center (TDC) for number one piston, locating, 2A-3
valve
covers, removal and installation, 2A-4
lifters, removal, inspection and installation, 2A-15
springs, retainers and seals, replacement, 2A-7
servicing, 2B-10
Engine electrical systems, 5-1 through 5-8
Engine mounts, check and replacement, 2A-20
Exhaust manifolds, removal and installation, 2A-9
Exhaust system check, 1-28
Exhaust system service, general information, 4-12
Extension housing oil seal replacement
Automatic transmission, 7B-3
Manual transmission, 7A-4

F

Fan, engine cooling, removal and installation, 3-5
Fault finding, 0-18
Fender, front, removal and installation, 11-17
Filter replacement
air, 1-25
fuel, 1-27
oil, 1-10
Fluid level checks, 1-6
Flywheel, inspection, 8-4
Flywheel/driveplate, removal and installation, 2A-19

Front axle assembly (4WD models), removal and installation, 8-15
Front axleshaft and joint assembly, removal, component replacement and installation, 8-18
Front door window glass, replacement and adjustment, 11-12
Front door window regulator, replacement, 11-13
Front hub lock, spindle bearing and wheel bearing maintenance (1991 through 1994 4WD models), 1-34
Front wheel bearing check, repack and adjustment (2WD models), 1-33
Fuel and exhaust systems, 4-1 through 4-12
  filter replacement, 1-27
  fuel injection component removal and installation, 4-8
  lines and fittings, general information, 4-2
  pressure relief procedure, 4-1
  pump, removal and installation, 4-7
  pump/fuel pressure, check, 4-4
  system check, 1-27
  tank
    cleaning and repair, 4-6
    removal and installation, 4-5
Fuel evaporative emissions control system, 6-8
Fuses, general information, 12-3
Fusible links, general information, 12-5

G
Gauges and speedometer cable, removal and installation, 12-19
Grille, removal and installation, 11-17

H
Hazard flasher relay, replacement, 12-7
Headlight
  bulb, replacement, 12-11
  switch, replacement, 12-10
  adjusting, 12-11
Heated rear window and rear wiper switch, removal and installation, 12-11
Heater
  blower motor, replacement, 3-8
  control assembly, removal and installation, 3-7
  control cables, check and adjustment, 3-7
  core, replacement, 3-9
  general information, 3-7
Hinges and locks, maintenance, 11-3
Hood
  latch control cable, removal and installation, 11-6
  removal, installation and adjustment, 11-3
Hose check and replacement, 1-14

I
Ignition
  coil pack, removal and installation, 5-3
  module, removal and installation, 5-5
  lock cylinder, replacement, 12-7
  system
    check, 5-3
    general information, 5-3
  timing procedure, 5-5
Inlet air temperature control system, 6-10
Inner door handle and latch assembly, removal and installation, 11-8
Instrument cluster, removal and installation, 12-17
Intake manifold, removal and installation, 2A-8

L
Leaf spring (rear), removal and installation, 10-18
Liftgate
  glass and hinge, removal and installation, 11-16
  panel, lock cylinder and latches, removal and installation, 11-15
  removal and installation, 11-14
Lower control arm (1995 and later models), removal, inspection and installation, 10-14

M
Main and connecting rod bearings, inspection, 2B-16
Maintenance, 1-1
Maintenance schedule, 1-5
Manifold, removal and installation
  exhaust, 2A-9
  intake, 2A-8
Manual transmission, 7A-1 through 7A-4
  general information, 7A-2
  lubricant level check and change, 1-23
  overhaul, general information, 7A-4
  removal and installation, 7A-2
  shift lever, removal and installation, 7A-2
Master cylinder, brake, removal, overhaul and installation, 9-17

N
Neutral start switch, removal, installation and adjustment, 7B-5

O
Oil pan and baffle, removal and installation, 2A-17
Oil pump, removal and installation, 2A-18
Outer door handle, removal and installation, 11-9

P
Parking brake
  adjustment, 9-20
  cables, replacement, 9-21
  shoes (rear disc brakes only), inspection and replacement, 9-26
Pilot bearing, inspection and replacement, 8-5
Piston rings, installation, 2B-17
Pistons/connecting rods
  inspection, 2B-14
  installation and rod bearing oil clearance check, 2B-20
  removal, 2B-10
Positive Crankcase Ventilation (PCV) system, 6-8
Positive Crankcase Ventilation (PCV) valve check and replacement, 1-26
Power brake booster, check, removal, installation and adjustment, 9-27
Power door lock system, general information, 12-20
Power mirrors, removal and installation, 12-20
Power steering
  fluid level check, 1-12
  line quick disconnect fittings, 10-28
  pump, removal and installation, 10-26
  system bleeding, 10-28
Power window system, description and check, 12-20

IND

R

Radiator grille, removal and installation, 11-17
Radiator, removal and installation, 3-3
Radio antenna, removal and installation, 12-16
Radio, removal and installation, 12-15
Radius arm (1991 through 1994 models)
    removal and installation, 10-11
    replacement, 10-11
Rear axle
    assembly, removal and installation, 8-12
    description and check, 8-11
Rocker arms and pushrods, removal, inspection
    and installation, 2A-6
Rotor (brake disc), removal and installation, 9-11
Routine maintenance, 1-1
Routine maintenance schedule, 1-5

S

Safety checks, 1-10
Seat belt check, 11-20
Seats, removal and installation, 11-19
Shift lever, removal and installation, 7A-2
Shock absorbers, inspection, removal and installation
    front, 10-4
    rear, 10-17
Single cardan type U-joint, overhaul, 8-9
Spark plug and wire check and replacement, 1-18
Speakers, removal and installation, 12-17
Speedometer pinion gear and seal, removal and installation, 7A-3
Spindle, front wheel, removal and installation, 10-5
Stabilizer bar, removal and installation
    front, 10-17
    rear, 10-19
Starter
    motor and circuit, in-vehicle check, 5-7
    motor, removal and installation, 5-8
    relay, removal and installation, 5-8
Starting system, general information, 5-7
Steering
    and suspension check, 1-29
    angles and wheel alignment, general information, 10-28
    column switches, replacement, 12-6
    connecting rod (1991 through 1994 models), removal
        and installation, 10-23
    gear, removal and installation, 10-24
    pump, removal and installation, 10-26
    system bleeding, 10-28
    system, general information, 10-20
    wheel, removal and installation, 10-20
Suspension and steering systems, 10-1 through 10-28

T

Thermostat, check and replacement, 3-2
Tie-rod ends, removal and installation, 10-23
Timing chain and sprockets, inspection, removal, 2A-13
Tire and tire pressure checks, 1-9
Tire rotation, 1-14
Top Dead Center (TDC) for number one piston, locating, 2A-3
Torsion bar (1995 and later models), removal
    and installation, 10-16
Transfer case, 7C-1 through 7C-8
    electronic control module, removal and installation, 7C-4
    electronic shift controls, removal and installation, 7C-4

    front output shaft oil seal, removal and installation, 7C-4
    general information, 7C-2
    linkage adjustment, manual shift transfer case, 7C-3
    lubricant level check and change, 1-24
    rear output shaft oil seal, removal and installation, 7C-5
    removal and installation, 7C-5
    shift lever, removal and installation, 7C-3
Transmission mount, check and replacement, 7A-2, 7B-6
Transmission, automatic, 7B-1 through 7B-6
    diagnosis, general, 7B-1
    fluid check/change, 1-12
    general information, 7B-1
    removal and installation, 7B-4
    shift cable
        adjustment, 7B-2
        removal and installation, 7B-3
    shift linkage lubrication, 1-20
    vacuum diaphragm, removal and installation, 7B-6
Transmission, manual, 7A-1 through 7A-4
    general information, 7A-2
    lubricant level check and change, 1-23
    overhaul, general information, 7A-4
    removal and installation, 7A-2
    shift lever, removal and installation, 7A-2
Trouble codes, 6-2
Troubleshooting, 0-18
Tune-up and routine maintenance, 1-1 through 1-40
    introduction to, 1-6
    general information, 1-6
Turn signal/hazard flasher relay, replacement, 12-7

U

Underhood hose check and replacement, 1-14
Upholstery and carpets, maintenance, 11-2
Upper control arm (1995 and later models), removal, inspection
    and installation, 10-15

V

Valve
    covers, removal and installation, 2A-4
    lifters, removal, inspection and installation, 2A-15
    servicing, 2B-10
    springs, retainers and seals, replacement, 2A-7
Vehicle identification numbers, 0-5
Vinyl trim, maintenance, 11-2

W

Water pump, check and replacement, 3-6
Wheel alignment, general information, 10-28
Wheel cylinder, removal, overhaul and installation, 9-16
Wheels and tires, general information, 10-28
Windshield
    glass, removal and installation, 11-19
    washer
        fluid level check, 1-8
        reservoir and pump assembly, removal and installation, 12-9
    wiper
        arm, removal and installation, 12-8
        blade check and replacement, 1-38
        motor, removal and installation, 12-8
Wiring diagrams, general information, 12-21

Haynes Automotive Manuals

NOTE: New manuals are added to this list on a periodic basis. If you do not see a listing for your vehicle, consult your local Haynes dealer for the latest product information.

ACURA
*1776   **Integra** '86 thru '89 & **Legend** '86 thru '90

AMC
    Jeep CJ - *see JEEP (412)*
694   **Mid-size models,** Concord, Hornet, Gremlin & Spirit '70 thru '83
934   **(Renault) Alliance & Encore** '83 thru '87

AUDI
615   **4000** all models '80 thru '87
428   **5000** all models '77 thru '83
1117   **5000** all models '84 thru '88

AUSTIN-HEALEY
    Sprite - *see MG Midget (265)*

BMW
*2020   **3/5 Series** not including diesel or all-wheel drive models '82 thru '92
276   **320i** all 4 cyl models '75 thru '83
632   **528i & 530i** all models '75 thru '80
240   **1500 thru 2002** except Turbo '59 thru '77

BUICK
    Century (front wheel drive) - *see GM (829)*
*1627   **Buick, Oldsmobile & Pontiac Full-size (Front wheel drive)** all models '85 thru '95
    Buick Electra, LeSabre and Park Avenue; **Oldsmobile** Delta 88 Royale, Ninety Eight and Regency; **Pontiac** Bonneville
1551   **Buick Oldsmobile & Pontiac Full-size (Rear wheel drive)**
    Buick Estate '70 thru '90, Electra '70 thru '84, LeSabre '70 thru '85, Limited '74 thru '79
    Oldsmobile Custom Cruiser '70 thru '90, Delta 88 '70 thru '85, Ninety-eight '70 thru '84
    Pontiac Bonneville '70 thru '81, Catalina '70 thru '81, Grandville '70 thru '75, Parisienne '83 thru '86
627   **Mid-size Regal & Century** all rear-drive models with V6, V8 and Turbo '74 thru '87
    Regal - *see GENERAL MOTORS (1671)*
    Riviera - *see GENERAL MOTORS (38030)*
    Skyhawk - *see GENERAL MOTORS (766)*
    Skylark '80 thru '85 - *see GM (38020)*
    Skylark '86 on - *see GM (1420)*
    Somerset - *see GENERAL MOTORS (1420)*

CADILLAC
*751   **Cadillac Rear Wheel Drive** all gasoline models '70 thru '93
    Cimarron - *see GENERAL MOTORS (766)*
    Eldorado - *see GENERAL MOTORS (38030)*
    Seville '80 thru '85 - *see GM (38030)*

CHEVROLET
*1477   **Astro & GMC Safari Mini-vans** '85 thru '93
554   **Camaro V8** all models '70 thru '81
866   **Camaro** all models '82 thru '92
    Cavalier - *see GENERAL MOTORS (766)*
    Celebrity - *see GENERAL MOTORS (829)*
24017   **Camaro & Firebird** '93 thru '96
625   **Chevelle, Malibu & El Camino** all V6 & V8 models '69 thru '87
449   **Chevette & Pontiac T1000** '76 thru '87
550   **Citation** all models '80 thru '85
*1628   **Corsica/Beretta** all models '87 thru '96
274   **Corvette** all V8 models '68 thru '82
*1336   **Corvette** all models '84 thru '91
1762   **Chevrolet Engine Overhaul Manual**
704   **Full-size Sedans** Caprice, Impala, Biscayne, Bel Air & Wagons '69 thru '90
    Lumina - *see GENERAL MOTORS (1671)*
    Lumina APV - *see GENERAL MOTORS (2035)*
319   **Luv Pick-up** all 2WD & 4WD '72 thru '82
626   **Monte Carlo** all models '70 thru '88

241   **Nova** all V8 models '69 thru '79
*1642   **Nova and Geo Prizm** all front wheel drive models, '85 thru '92
420   **Pick-ups '67 thru '87** - Chevrolet & GMC, all V8 & in-line 6 cyl, 2WD & 4WD '67 thru '87; Suburbans, Blazers & Jimmys '67 thru '91
*1664   **Pick-ups '88 thru '95** - Chevrolet & GMC, all full-size pick-ups, '88 thru '95; Blazer & Jimmy '92 thru '94; Suburban '92 thru '95; Tahoe & Yukon '95
831   **S-10 & GMC S-15 Pick-ups** '82 thru '93
*24071   **S-10 & GMC S-15 Pick-ups** '94 thru '96
*1727   **Sprint & Geo Metro** '85 thru '94
*345   **Vans - Chevrolet & GMC,** V8 & in-line 6 cylinder models '68 thru '96

CHRYSLER
25025   **Chrysler Concorde, New Yorker & LHS, Dodge** Intrepid, **Eagle** Vision, '93 thru '96
2114   **Chrysler Engine Overhaul Manual**
*2058   **Full-size Front-Wheel Drive** '88 thru '93
    K-Cars - *see DODGE Aries (723)*
    Laser - *see DODGE Daytona (1140)*
*1337   **Chrysler & Plymouth Mid-size** front wheel drive '82 thru '95
    Rear-wheel Drive - *see Dodge (2098)*

DATSUN
647   **200SX** all models '80 thru '83
228   **B - 210** all models '73 thru '78
525   **210** all models '79 thru '82
206   **240Z, 260Z & 280Z** Coupe '70 thru '78
563   **280ZX** Coupe & 2+2 '79 thru '83
    300ZX - *see NISSAN (1137)*
679   **310** all models '78 thru '82
123   **510 & PL521 Pick-up** '68 thru '73
430   **510** all models '78 thru '81
372   **610** all models '72 thru '76
277   **620 Series Pick-up** all models '73 thru '79
    720 Series Pick-up - *see NISSAN (771)*
376   **810/Maxima** all gasoline models, '77 thru '84
    Pulsar - *see NISSAN (876)*
    Sentra - *see NISSAN (982)*
    Stanza - *see NISSAN (981)*

DODGE
    400 & 600 - *see CHRYSLER Mid-size (1337)*
*723   **Aries & Plymouth Reliant** '81 thru '89
1231   **Caravan & Plymouth Voyager Mini-Vans** all models '84 thru '95
699   **Challenger/Plymouth Saporro** '78 thru '83
    Challenger '67-'76 - *see DODGE Dart (234)*
610   **Colt & Plymouth Champ** (front wheel drive) all models '78 thru '87
*1668   **Dakota Pick-ups** all models '87 thru '96
234   **Dart, Challenger/Plymouth Barracuda & Valiant** 6 cyl models '67 thru '76
*1140   **Daytona & Chrysler Laser** '84 thru '89
    Intrepid - *see CHRYSLER (25025)*
*30034   **Neon** all models '94 thru '97
*545   **Omni & Plymouth Horizon** '78 thru '90
*912   **Pick-ups** all full-size models '74 thru '93
*30041   **Pick-ups** all full-size models '94 thru '96
*556   **Ram 50/D50 Pick-ups & Raider and Plymouth Arrow Pick-ups** '79 thru '93
2098   **Dodge/Plymouth/Chrysler** rear wheel drive '71 thru '89
*1726   **Shadow & Plymouth Sundance** '87 thru '94
*1779   **Spirit & Plymouth Acclaim** '89 thru '95
*349   **Vans - Dodge & Plymouth** V8 & 6 cyl models '71 thru '96

EAGLE
    Talon - *see Mitsubishi Eclipse (2097)*
    Vision - *see CHRYSLER (25025)*

FIAT
094   **124 Sport Coupe & Spider** '68 thru '78
273   **X1/9** all models '74 thru '80

FORD
10355   **Ford Automatic Trans. Overhaul**
*1476   **Aerostar Mini-vans** all models '86 thru '96

268   **Courier Pick-up** all models '72 thru '82
2105   **Crown Victoria & Mercury Grand Marquis** '88 thru '96
1763   **Ford Engine Overhaul Manual**
789   **Escort/Mercury Lynx** all models '81 thru '90
*2046   **Escort/Mercury Tracer** '91 thru '96
*2021   **Explorer & Mazda Navajo** '91 thru '95
560   **Fairmont & Mercury Zephyr** '78 thru '83
334   **Fiesta** all models '77 thru '80
754   **Ford & Mercury Full-size,** Ford LTD & Mercury Marquis ('75 thru '82); Ford Custom 500, Country Squire, Crown Victoria & Mercury Colony Park ('75 thru '87); Ford LTD Crown Victoria & Mercury Gran Marquis ('83 thru '87)
359   **Granada & Mercury Monarch** all in-line, 6 cyl & V8 models '75 thru '80
773   **Ford & Mercury Mid-size,** Ford Thunderbird & Mercury Cougar ('75 thru '82); Ford LTD & Mercury Marquis ('83 thru '86); Ford Torino, Gran Torino, Elite, Ranchero pick-up, LTD II, Mercury Montego, Comet, XR-7 & Lincoln Versailles ('75 thru '86)
231   **Mustang II** 4 cyl, V6 & V8 models '74 thru '78
357   **Mustang V8** all models '64-1/2 thru '73
*654   **Mustang & Mercury Capri** all models Mustang, '79 thru '93; Capri, '79 thru '86
*36051   **Mustang** all models '94 thru '97
788   **Pick-ups & Bronco** '73 thru '79
*880   **Pick-ups & Bronco** '80 thru '96
649   **Pinto & Mercury Bobcat** '75 thru '80
1670   **Probe** all models '89 thru '92
*1026   **Ranger/Bronco II** gasoline models '83 thru '92
*36071   **Ranger** '93 thru '96 & **Mazda Pick-ups** '94 thru '96
*1421   **Taurus & Mercury Sable** '86 thru '95
*1418   **Tempo & Mercury Topaz** all gasoline models '84 thru '94
1338   **Thunderbird/Mercury Cougar** '83 thru '88
*1725   **Thunderbird/Mercury Cougar** '89 and '96
344   **Vans** all V8 Econoline models '69 thru '91
*2119   **Vans** full size '92-'95

GENERAL MOTORS
*10360   **GM Automatic Transmission Overhaul**
*829   **Buick Century, Chevrolet Celebrity, Oldsmobile Cutlass Ciera & Pontiac 6000** all models '82 thru '96
*1671   **Buick Regal, Chevrolet Lumina, Oldsmobile Cutlass Supreme & Pontiac Grand Prix** front wheel drive models '88 thru '95
*766   **Buick Skyhawk, Cadillac Cimarron, Chevrolet Cavalier, Oldsmobile Firenza & Pontiac J-2000 & Sunbird** '82 thru '94
38020   **Buick Skylark, Chevrolet Citation, Olds Omega, Pontiac Phoenix** '80 thru '85
1420   **Buick Skylark & Somerset, Oldsmobile Achieva & Calais and Pontiac Grand Am** all models '85 thru '95
38030   **Cadillac Eldorado** '71 thru '85, **Seville** '80 thru '85, **Oldsmobile Toronado** '71 thru '85 **& Buick Riviera** '79 thru '85
*2035   **Chevrolet Lumina APV, Olds Silhouette & Pontiac Trans Sport** all models '90 thru '95
    General Motors Full-size Rear-wheel Drive - *see BUICK (1551)*

GEO
    Metro - *see CHEVROLET Sprint (1727)*
    Prizm - '85 thru '92 see CHEVY Nova (1642), '93 thru '96 see TOYOTA Corolla (1642)
*2039   **Storm** all models '90 thru '93
    Tracker - *see SUZUKI Samurai (1626)*

GMC
    Safari - *see CHEVROLET ASTRO (1477)*
    Vans & Pick-ups - *see CHEVROLET (420, 831, 345, 1664 & 24071)*

(Continued on other side)

---

* Listings shown with an asterisk (*) indicate model coverage as of this printing. These titles will be periodically updated to include later model years - consult your Haynes dealer for more information.

Haynes North America, Inc., 861 Lawrence Drive, Newbury Park, CA 91320 • (805) 498-6703

Haynes Automotive Manuals (continued)

NOTE: New manuals are added to this list on a periodic basis. If you do not see a listing for your vehicle, consult your local Haynes dealer for the latest product information.

HONDA

351	**Accord CVCC** all models '76 thru '83
1221	**Accord** all models '84 thru '89
2067	**Accord** all models '90 thru '93
42013	**Accord** all models '94 thru '95
160	**Civic 1200** all models '73 thru '79
633	**Civic 1300 & 1500 CVCC** '80 thru '83
297	**Civic 1500 CVCC** all models '75 thru '79
1227	**Civic** all models '84 thru '91
*2118	**Civic & del Sol** '92 thru '95
*601	**Prelude CVCC** all models '79 thru '89

HYUNDAI

*1552	**Excel** all models '86 thru '94

ISUZU

*1641	**Trooper & Pick-up,** all gasoline models Pick-up, '81 thru '93; Trooper, '84 thru '91
	Hombre - see CHEVROLET S-10 (24071)

JAGUAR

*242	**XJ6** all 6 cyl models '68 thru '86
*49011	**XJ6** all models '88 thru '94
*478	**XJ12 & XJS** all 12 cyl models '72 thru '85

JEEP

*1553	**Cherokee, Comanche & Wagoneer Limited** all models '84 thru '96
412	**CJ** all models '49 thru '86
50025	**Grand Cherokee** all models '93 thru '95
50029	**Grand Wagoneer & Pick-up** '72 thru '91, Grand Wagoneer '84 thru '91, Cherokee & Wagoneer '72 thru '83, Pick-up '72 thru '88
*1777	**Wrangler** all models '87 thru '95

LINCOLN

2117	**Rear Wheel Drive** all models '70 thru '96

MAZDA

648	**626** (rear wheel drive) all models '79 thru '82
*1082	**626/MX-6** (front wheel drive) '83 thru '91
370	**GLC Hatchback** (rear wheel drive) '77 thru '83
757	**GLC** (front wheel drive) '81 thru '85
*2047	**MPV** all models '89 thru '94
	Navajo - see Ford Explorer (2021)
267	**Pick-ups** '72 thru '93
	Pick-ups '94 thru '96 - see Ford Ranger (36071)
460	**RX-7** all models '79 thru '85
*1419	**RX-7** all models '86 thru '91

MERCEDES-BENZ

*1643	**190 Series** four-cyl gas models, '84 thru '88
346	**230/250/280** 6 cyl sohc models '68 thru '72
983	**280 123 Series** gasoline models '77 thru '81
698	**350 & 450** all models '71 thru '80
697	**Diesel 123 Series** '76 thru '85

MERCURY

See FORD Listing

MG

111	**MGB** Roadster & GT Coupe '62 thru '80
265	**MG Midget, Austin Healey Sprite** '58 thru '80

MITSUBISHI

*1669	**Cordia, Tredia, Galant, Precis & Mirage** '83 thru '93
*2097	**Eclipse, Eagle Talon & Plymouth Laser** '90 thru '94
*2022	**Pick-up** '83 thru '96 & **Montero** '83 thru '93

NISSAN

1137	**300ZX** all models including Turbo '84 thru '89
*72015	**Altima** all models '93 thru '97
*1341	**Maxima** all models '85 thru '91
*771	**Pick-ups** '80 thru '96 **Pathfinder** '87 thru '95
876	**Pulsar** all models '83 thru '86
*982	**Sentra** all models '82 thru '94
*981	**Stanza** all models '82 thru '90

OLDSMOBILE

	Achieva - see GENERAL MOTORS (1420)
	Bravada - see CHEVROLET S-10 (831)
	Calais - see GENERAL MOTORS (1420)
	Custom Cruiser - see BUICK RWD (1551)
*658	**Cutlass** V6 & V8 gas models '74 thru '88
	Cutlass Ciera - see GENERAL MOTORS (829)
	Cutlass Supreme - see GM (1671)
	Delta 88 - see BUICK Full-size RWD (1551)
	Delta 88 Brougham - see BUICK Full-size FWD (1551), RWD (1627)
	Delta 88 Royale - see BUICK RWD (1551)
	Firenza - see GENERAL MOTORS (766)
	Ninety-eight Regency - see BUICK Full-size RWD (1551), FWD (1627)
	Ninety-eight Regency Brougham - see BUICK Full-size RWD (1551)
	Omega - see GENERAL MOTORS (38020)
	Silhouette - see GENERAL MOTORS (2035)
	Toronado - see GENERAL MOTORS (38030)

PEUGEOT

663	**504** all diesel models '74 thru '83

PLYMOUTH

	Laser - see MITSUBISHI Eclipse (2097)
	For other PLYMOUTH titles, see DODGE.

PONTIAC

	T1000 - see CHEVROLET Chevette (449)
	J-2000 - see GENERAL MOTORS (766)
	6000 - see GENERAL MOTORS (829)
	Bonneville - see Buick FWD (1627), RWD (1551)
	Bonneville Brougham - see Buick (1551)
	Catalina - see Buick Full-size (1551)
1232	**Fiero** all models '84 thru '88
555	**Firebird** V8 except Turbo '70 thru '81
867	**Firebird** all models '82 thru '92
	Firebird '93 thru '96 - see CHEVY Camaro (24017)
	Full-size Front Wheel Drive - see BUICK, Oldsmobile, Pontiac Full-size FWD (1627)
	Full-size Rear Wheel Drive - see BUICK Oldsmobile, Pontiac Full-size RWD (1551)
	Grand Am - see GENERAL MOTORS (1420)
	Grand Prix - see GENERAL MOTORS (1671)
	Grandville - see BUICK Full-size (1551)
	Parisienne - see BUICK Full-size (1551)
	Phoenix - see GENERAL MOTORS (38020)
	Sunbird - see GENERAL MOTORS (766)
	Trans Sport - see GENERAL MOTORS (2035)

PORSCHE

*264	**911** except Turbo & Carrera 4 '65 thru '89
239	**914** all 4 cyl models '69 thru '76
397	**924** all models including Turbo '76 thru '82
*1027	**944** all models including Turbo '83 thru '89

RENAULT

141	**5 Le Car** all models '76 thru '83
	Alliance & Encore - see AMC (934)

SAAB

247	**99** all models including Turbo '69 thru '80
*980	**900** all models including Turbo '79 thru '88

SATURN

2083	**Saturn** all models '91 thru '96

SUBARU

237	**1100, 1300, 1400 & 1600** '71 thru '79
*681	**1600 & 1800** 2WD & 4WD '80 thru '89

SUZUKI

*1626	**Samurai/Sidekick &Geo Tracker** '86 thru '96

TOYOTA

1023	**Camry** all models '83 thru '91
92006	**Camry** all models '92 thru '95
935	**Celica Rear Wheel Drive** '71 thru '85
*2038	**Celica Front Wheel Drive** '86 thru '93
1139	**Celica Supra** all models '79 thru '92
361	**Corolla** all models '75 thru '79
961	**Corolla** all rear wheel drive models '80 thru '87
1025	**Corolla** all front wheel drive models '84 thru '92
*92036	**Corolla & Geo Prizm** '93 thru '96
636	**Corolla Tercel** all models '80 thru '82
360	**Corona** all models '74 thru '82
532	**Cressida** all models '78 thru '82
313	**Land Cruiser** all models '68 thru '82
*1339	**MR2** all models '85 thru '87
304	**Pick-up** all models '69 thru '78
*656	**Pick-up** all models '79 thru '95
*2048	**Previa** all models '91 thru '95
2106	**Tercel** all models '87 thru '94

TRIUMPH

113	**Spitfire** all models '62 thru '81
322	**TR7** all models '75 thru '81

VW

159	**Beetle & Karmann Ghia** '54 thru '79
238	**Dasher** all gasoline models '74 thru '81
96017	**Golf & Jetta** all models '93 thru '97
*884	**Rabbit, Jetta, Scirocco, & Pick-up** gas models '74 thru '91 & Convertible '80 thru '92
451	**Rabbit, Jetta & Pick-up** diesel '77 thru '84
082	**Transporter 1600** all models '68 thru '79
226	**Transporter 1700, 1800 & 2000** '72 thru '79
084	**Type 3 1500 & 1600** all models '63 thru '73
1029	**Vanagon** all air-cooled models '80 thru '83

VOLVO

203	**120, 130 Series & 1800 Sports** '61 thru '73
129	**140 Series** all models '66 thru '74
*270	**240 Series** all models '76 thru '93
400	**260 Series** all models '75 thru '82
*1550	**740 & 760 Series** all models '82 thru '88

TECHBOOK MANUALS

2108	**Automotive Computer Codes**
1667	**Automotive Emissions Control Manual**
482	**Fuel Injection Manual, 1978 thru 1985**
2111	**Fuel Injection Manual, 1986 thru 1996**
2069	**Holley Carburetor Manual**
2068	**Rochester Carburetor Manual**
10240	**Weber/Zenith/Stromberg/SU Carburetors**
1762	**Chevrolet Engine Overhaul Manual**
2114	**Chrysler Engine Overhaul Manual**
1763	**Ford Engine Overhaul Manual**
1736	**GM and Ford Diesel Engine Repair Manual**
1666	**Small Engine Repair Manual**
10355	**Ford Automatic Transmission Overhaul**
10360	**GM Automatic Transmission Overhaul**
1479	**Automotive Body Repair & Painting**
2112	**Automotive Brake Manual**
2113	**Automotive Detailing Manual**
1654	**Automotive Eelectrical Manual**
1480	**Automotive Heating & Air Conditioning**
2109	**Automotive Reference Manual & Dictionary**
2107	**Automotive Tools Manual**
10440	**Used Car Buying Guide**
2110	**Welding Manual**
10450	**ATV Basics**

SPANISH MANUALS

98903	**Reparación de Carrocería & Pintura**
98905	**Códigos Automotrices de la Computadora**
98910	**Frenos Automotriz**
98915	**Inyección de Combustible 1986 al 1994**
99040	**Chevrolet & GMC Camionetas** '67 al '87 Incluye Suburban, Blazer & Jimmy '67 al '91
99041	**Chevrolet & GMC Camionetas** '88 al '95 Incluye Suburban '92 al '95, Blazer & Jimmy '92 al '94, Tahoe y Yukon '95
99042	**Chevrolet & GMC Camionetas Cerradas** '68 al '95
99055	**Dodge Caravan & Plymouth Voyager** '84 al '95
99075	**Ford Camionetas y Bronco** '80 al '94
99077	**Ford Camionetas Cerradas** '69 al '91
99083	**Ford Modelos de Tamaño Pequeño** '75 al '87
99088	**Ford Modelos de Tamaño Mediano** '75 al '86
99095	**GM Modelos de Tamaño Grande** '70 al '90
99118	**Nissan Sentra** '82 al '94
99125	**Toyota Camionetas y 4-Runner** '79 al '95

* Listings shown with an asterisk (*) indicate model coverage as of this printing. These titles will be periodically updated to include later model years - consult your Haynes dealer for more information.

Over 100 Haynes motorcycle manuals also available

5-97

Haynes North America, Inc., 861 Lawrence Drive, Newbury Park, CA 91320 • (805) 498-6703